Rethinking Antifascism

Rethinking Antifascism
History, Memory and Politics, 1922 to the Present

Edited by Hugo García, Mercedes Yusta,
Xavier Tabet and Cristina Clímaco

berghahn
NEW YORK • OXFORD
www.berghahnbooks.com

Published in 2016 by

Berghahn Books

www.berghahnbooks.com

© 2016, 2018 Hugo García, Mercedes Yusta, Xavier Tabet and Cristina Clímaco

First paperback edition published in 2018

Library of Congress Cataloging-in-Publication Data

Names: García, Hugo, 1975- editor. | Yusta Rodrigo, Mercedes, editor. |
Tabet, Xavier, editor. | Clímaco, Cristina, 1965- editor.
Title: Rethinking antifascism: history, memory and political uses, 1922 to the
present / edited by Hugo García, Mercedes Yusta, Xavier Tabet and
Cristina Clímaco.
Description: New York: Berghahn Books, 2016. | Includes bibliographical
references and index.
Identifiers: LCCN 2015045874| ISBN 9781785331381 (hardback: alk. paper)|
ISBN 9781785338182 (paperback: alk. paper) |
 ISBN 9781785331398 (ebook)
Subjects: LCSH: Anti-fascist movements--History.
Classification: LCC JC481 .R4638 2016 | DDC 320.53/3--dc23 LC record
available at http://lccn.loc.gov/2015045874

British Library Cataloguing in Publication Data

A catalogue record for this book is available from the British Library

ISBN 978-1-78533-138-1 hardback
ISBN 978-1-78533-818-2 paperback
ISBN 978-1-78533-139-8 ebook

Contents

Acknowledgements

This book was conceived and written in the context of a series of international meetings on the history and memory of antifascism which took place in Geneva in 2012 ('Antifascism as a Practice and as a Discourse'), Paris in 2013 ('L'antifascisme en question, 1922–1945') and Saarbrucken in 2014 ('Anti-Fascism as a Transnational Phenomenon: New Perspectives of Research'), and has greatly benefited from the input received by participants at these meetings. We hope that this book will contribute to keeping alive this emerging and exciting line of research. We are grateful to the Institut Universitaire de France for its financial assistance, to the Laboratoire d'Etudes Romanes of the Université Paris 8, for its scientific and logistic support – especially to Fatima Zenati and the translators of this university – and to Kasper Braskén for his intelligent comments on the Introduction.

Introduction

BEYOND REVISIONISM

Rethinking Antifascism in the Twenty-First Century

Hugo García, Mercedes Yusta, Xavier Tabet and Cristina Clímaco

This book is the outcome of a collective effort by eighteen historians of seven different nationalities, and arose from historiographical questionings with evident political implications. It has its origins in the realisation, which stems from our research into three Mediterranean countries where antifascism played a leading role in the interwar period (Spain, Italy and Portugal), that the history of this movement, transnational while at the same time located within specific national contexts, has to a great extent yet to be written. In Spain, whose civil war is an inescapable reference point in the formation of a global antifascist culture in the 1930s, historians have barely broached the making of antifascism as a political culture and social movement (despite the abundant bibliography dealing with the various antifascist currents and associations), while in neighbouring Portugal, which was governed for almost half a century by a corporative and traditionalist dictatorship with fascist influences – António de Oliveira Salazar's *Estado Novo* ('New state') – work on the early opposition to the Salazar regime is very scarce and is compartmentalised into political currents.[1] In Italy, which as the cradle of fascism and antifascism has a long and rich tradition of studies on this subject, the 'crisis in the antifascist paradigm' which came into full view in the 1990s is reflected in a – in some cases, radical – re-reading of the so-called 'antifascist vulgate' and of the very origins of the current Italian Republic.[2] In these three countries, as in the rest of the world, studies on fascism and its different national varieties far outnumber those on antifascism, as Michael Seidman observes in his contribution to this volume, even though in almost all Western countries the first movement was a failure and the second a success, arguably 'the most powerful ideology of the twentieth century'.[3]

These gaps and questionings are framed within the context of a political and social crisis whose roots may be found in the ferment sparked around the world by the fall of the Berlin Wall and the break-up of the Eastern bloc. We know today that this event has not led to 'the end of history' forecast by Francis Fukuyama in 1992,[4] but it has brought about a re-examination of our view of the recent past, and in particular of the consensus on the historical role of fascism and antifascism upon which most postwar European nations were rebuilt (with the notable exceptions of Spain and Portugal).[5] Awareness of the role played by the legacy of antifascism in legitimising the Communist dictatorships in the East has contributed to a retrospective re-examination of antifascism, fed, as Stéfanie Prezioso recalls in her contribution, by the growing 'incredulity towards metanarratives' – the great narratives of the past penned by religions, science or political ideologies – which Jean-François Lyotard deemed already in 1979 as the essence of the 'postmodern condition'.[6] The 'antifascist paradigm' that dominated European historiography and politics of memory in the decades following the Second World War had much, indeed, of a metanarrative based on 'the celebration of brave partisans overthrowing fascist barbarism with the aid of the Red Army' (in the version that prevailed in the Soviet bloc, described here by José María Faraldo), or on the anonymous 'victory over *evil* and silence on the substantial levels of support for', and collaboration with, fascism and Nazism in European countries (dominant in Western democracies such as France, studied here by Gilles Vergnon).[7] This narrative was widely questioned in the 1960s by Western European student protest movements, who claimed that postwar democracies were intrinsically or potentially 'fascist' themselves; as a result of this overuse, and/or of larger social and cultural changes, the label has lost currency since then.[8] In present-day Europe the antifascist (or, in the term employed by its followers, 'Antifa') identity has been reclaimed politically mainly by a heterogeneous collective of far-left groups devoted to fighting xenophobia, classism, sexism and other forms of fascism by direct action, even though the European Antifascist Meeting held in Athens in April 2014, with delegates from eighty groups drawn from the whole continent, suggests that that the current economic and political crisis could be a conducive context for its revival.[9]

This loss of currency has contributed to the historiographical reckoning undertaken by Jacques Droz in his classic work *Histoire de l'antifascisme en Europe, 1923–1939*, published in 1985, remaining valid to a great extent thirty years later: the 'almost total absence of works of synthesis' comes in contrast to the profusion of case studies on the various national situations 'whose perusal ... would take several lifetimes'.[10]

Collective volumes and journal theme issues on the subject concentrate not so much on the political, social and cultural movement that developed between 1922 and 1945, which Bruno Groppo dubbed 'historical antifascism', but mainly on its legacy or memory since the end of the Second World War.[11] This legacy informs a large part of historiographical readings of antifascism undertaken as of 1990, and summarised by Enzo Traverso in the last chapter of this volume, beginning with the radical revisions launched in Italy by the renowned historian of fascism, Renzo De Felice, from the 1970s onwards – firstly regarding the nature of the regime, and then what he described as 'Resistance vulgate' – and followed by work published in the following decade by French authors Annie Kriegel and François Furet, and by German authors Antonia Grunberger and Dan Diner, who reduced the phenomenon to 'the new face of Stalinism' in the 1930s, the great 'myth' and the left's 'lifelong lie' in the twentieth century.[12] This view, conditioned by the use of antifascism to legitimise the 'people's democracies' of Eastern and Central Europe, the collapse of the Soviet Union, and the opening up of dictatorships in the East, has complicated the task of understanding the historicity of antifascism, stemming from the 'space of experience' and the 'horizon of expectations' of contemporaries rather than the historian[13] – which is to say, the task of seeing it not in terms of what it turned into after 1945, but as the various things that it was, and the ways in which it was perceived and lived, at the different times and places in its evolution since the 1920s.[14]

Perhaps the greatest obstacle to understanding antifascism as a historical phenomenon is the persistent tendency of historians to identify it with communism. The widespread use of a totalitarian paradigm since the 1990s – which came about by the end of the 1920s within the context of antifascism, but was alienated from the latter due to Stalinist terror, the Nazi–Soviet Pact and the Cold War – turned fascism and Nazism into a mirror-image reaction to the birth of the Soviet state, and its violence in response to that deployed by the Bolsheviks in Russia, within the context of a 'European civil war' which would wipe away the differences between political options deemed as equivalent.[15] This levelling implied linking antifascism, from its beginnings, to the crimes of communism, confirmed by the opening of archives in the East, as well as interpreting antifascist violence through the lens of those crimes, in particular the violence deployed in armed conflicts (such as the Spanish and Greek civil wars) and in the framework of different national resistance networks to Nazism or to fascist, or fascistised, dictatorships.[16] With regard to these interpretations, which underline antifascism's most sectarian and violent aspects and portray it as the bitter enemy of democracy, we think it is necessary to insist on its plural nature: for all that Communism may have been one of the main driving forces behind the great antifascist mobilisation in the years 1933–39, especially in the transnational context as Anson Rabinbach's contribution to this volume makes clear, antifascism was anything but a structured movement with a clear direction, and it was therefore translated into different and changing proposals for, and repertoires of, action.[17] In this light, the rifts need to be recalled that arose at the heart of antifascism between Communists and non-Communists, and even between different strands of Communism – revolutionaries and democrats, politicians and the apolitical, bellicists and pacifists, believers and secularists – which erupted tragically during the Spanish Civil War and resurfaced after the Hitler–Stalin Pact of 1939.[18] Putting antifascism into historical perspective, in its country-by-country variants, inevitably leads to acknowledging its many-sidedness and its link to widely varying movements and cultures, which saw in fascism a threat to their very existence: socialism, communism, anarchism, liberalism, Christianity (Catholic and Protestant), pacifism, anti-imperialism and feminism (studied in chapters 8 and 9 by Isabelle Richet and Mercedes Yusta) were perhaps the most influential, but not the only ones.

In fact, the equation between antifascism and communism has been repeatedly called into question by historians since the mid-1990s.[19] An example of this is the reflections by Alberto De Bernardi in his introduction to the collective work *Antifascismo e identità europea*, published in Italy in 2004, which is doubtless the most ambitious attempt to build an international history of the movement – and in particular of its memory and influence after the Second World War – undertaken in this period.[20] In this text, De Bernardi proposed tackling the aforementioned 'crisis in the antifascist paradigm' by reinterpreting this concept as an Italian as well as European 'political culture', born of the will to offer an alternative to the redefining of national identity brought about by fascism in Italy, based on the militarisation of society and expansionism abroad; but also of the need to define a new world order on which to build peace at a time when a clash was foreseeable between fascism, communism and liberalism. In the midst of the deep crisis experienced by liberal democracy and global capitalism after 1914, antifascism would have been the most ambitious response to the challenge to come up with new relations between liberty, equality and justice, civil rights and social rights, state and market, and political and social representation. De Bernardi interpreted it in a social-democratic tone, locating its origin 'in the cross between socialist tradition and democratic thinking'.[21] His proposal approaches those of other authors who have made important contributions to the study of antifascism in recent decades and who, in some cases, develop or extend them in this volume: according to Eric Hobsbawm, Enzo Traverso and Nigel Copsey, the various antifascist currents were ultimately united by the legacy of the Enlightenment; according to Gilles Vergnon, the antifascist movement that arose in France in 1934 was 'Jauresian' or socialist-republican in nature; Ferran Gallego has described the Spanish antifascism of the 1930s as a meeting point for republicanism, social democracy, communism and anarchism; for Andrés Bisso, 'mainstream antifascism in Argentina was predominantly liberal-socialist' and he condemned both fascism and communism as equally 'anti-nationalist'.[22] However, Tom Buchanan has rightly underlined the illiberal aspects of the concept of democracy prevailing amongst antifascists in the interwar period, which tended to lend priority to social justice over respect for pluralism.[23]

The debate over the essence of antifascism – Copsey's 'antifascist minimum', discussed by Tom Buchanan in Chapter 3– deals, in reality, with the stumbling block to its above-mentioned diversity, which is as ideological as it is social and geographical. In fact, the trend in recent historiography towards exploring the non-Communist forms that the movement adopted has been accompanied by the proliferation of comparative or transnational approaches to the phenomenon, which has been traditionally studied from a Euro- and state-centric perspective.[24] Gerd-Rainer Horn argued back in 1996 that the 'transnational consciousness' of European socialists had been one of the main forces behind their reactions to fascism in the 1930s.[25] More recently, Dan Stone has emphasised the key intellectual contribution made by Central European refugees to British antifascism and the need to 'internationalise' the history of the movement, whereas Isabelle Richet has pointed out the 'inherently transnational dimension' of women's antifascist networks in Britain in the same period.[26] Still more recently, Joseph Fronczak has made a convincing case for reinterpreting the Hands Off Ethiopia movement of 1935 as a key turning point in the emergence of a 'global left' in the twentieth century.[27] A forthcoming book by Michael Seidman will explore 'Atlantic antifascisms' in the years 1936–45, and a growing number of research projects are addressing issues such as the antifascist activities of international organisations, the circulation of antifascist exiles and ideas across nations and continents and the 'spatial politics' of antifascism.[28] The need for comparative and transnational approaches was also stressed at international conferences on the subject held in Geneva in 2012, Paris in 2013 and Saarbrücken in 2014.[29]

Indeed, antifascism appears as the ideal type of a transnational movement. Its main advocates – socialists, Communists, anarchists, liberals, Catholics, freemasons – belonged to long-standing international organisations which possessed solid communication channels and social networks. Many were part of, or closely connected to, the 'antifascist diaspora' of political refugees from countries under fascist or authoritarian rule: antifascism was, to a large extent, 'a culture of exile' built in large cities such as Paris, Moscow, Barcelona, London, New York and Buenos Aires.[30] Its activists viewed politics from a cosmopolitan perspective and felt morally obliged to engage in distant conflicts, whether in Spain or China; they shared a culture that blended concepts and symbols from all over the world and recognised one another as part of a 'common humanity'.[31] During the movement's heyday in the mid-1930s, antifascists shared slogans (*They shall not pass!*), gestures (the raised clenched fist) and an 'aesthetics of resistance' best represented by politically engaged artists such as John Heartfield and Robert Capa.[32] As some of the contributions to this volume illustrate, antifascism was not only a set of beliefs and a motivation for action for millions of people throughout the world, but also an essential part of their identity – 'less an ideology than a *mentalité*, more of a habitus than a doctrine', in the words of Anson Rabinbach.[33] Yet, it remained diverse, across nations, regions and political cultures – a meeting place for various strategies, visions and discourses rather than a unified movement.[34] These contradictory elements can only be reconciled by paying attention to the complex interplay between the individual, local, national and global dimensions of antifascism.[35]

This spatial diversity has been transferred to the scientific and social debate on the antifascist movement, where the general trends noted above merge with others belonging to various historiographical traditions and political contexts. In Italy, national and transnational, historiographical and political factors have combined to lend a particular virulence to the dispute.[36] In the 1980s what had been the dominant historiographical narrative since 1945 entered crisis, the one that presented fascism either as a moral (and temporary) sickness of the Italian people, or as a reaction by the ruling classes to the rise of Communism. A narrative which, furthermore, collectively exonerated Italians from the silence over the issue of consensus, and laid the blame for the 1940–43 war squarely on Mussolini and the Germans, in order to stress the worth of the 'second war', waged by the Resistance and the Italian Army between 1943 and 1945, as the root of Italian democracy.[37] This narrative construction was called into question in the 1990s by historians such as Renzo de Felice and popularisers like Giampaolo Pansa, who portrayed early postwar Italy as a country in the throes of murders sponsored by the Communist Party during the *resa dei conti* ('settling of accounts') in regions such as the *triangolo rosso* ('red triangle') of Emilia Romagna. Pansa denounced the 'great lie' of the 'Resistance vulgate', according to which resistants always had their hands clean and the CP's strategy was confined to fighting the Germans and the fascists, and he asserted, rather, that the Communists' strategy was defined by the USSR and aimed at taking power.[38] The revisionist movement symbolised by Pansa and his successful books is symptomatic of the 'great levelling of memories' decried by Régine Robin, which reduces the past to a great narrative of victimisation and results in the replacement of Resistance mythology by revisionist mythology.[39]

What singles out the Italian case is above all the 'political uses' of a controversy which, in principle, was historiographical. The debate slipped into the political domain due to interpretations like that of Ernesto Galli de la Loggia, who resumed the old right-wing contention that the armistice of 8 September 1943, far from representing a *riscatto*, an opportunity to redeem Italy from which the Resistance was born, in fact entailed the 'death of the country', which would never rise from the ashes of fascism.[40] During his three terms as prime minister in 1994–95, 2001–06 and 2008–11, Silvio Berlusconi's milieu appropriated the issue to try to detach antifascism from Italian national identity by demonising Communism, on the one hand, and on the other by transforming the Italian Social Movement, the successor to fascism, into a politically acceptable party. This re-examination of a vital pillar of the Republic's identity ('born of the Resistance and antifascism', according to the conventional phrase) even allowed Berlusconi to denounce the Italian Constitution, one of the most socially oriented in Europe, for its 'Soviet' features, and to play down fascist violence by describing Mussolini's regime as a benign dictatorship which 'did not murder anyone', but only sent its opponents 'on holiday'.[41]

In post-Franco Spain, the scope of revisionism has been limited by the relative political consensus inherited from the transition to democracy in the 1970s and by the fact that Spanish, unlike Italian, democracy had never been identified with antifascism, but rather with national reconciliation after the Civil War and the long Franco dictatorship. This situation notwithstanding, revisionist propositions have circulated widely since the turn of the century, precisely at the time when a sector of civil society began to reclaim the memory of antifascism in the name of the victims of Francoism.[42] The Partido Popular ('People's Party'), in government between 1996 and 2004, and since 2011, has carefully avoided any suspicion of sympathy for the dictatorship – to which it is linked by its origins as the Alianza Popular ('People's Alliance'), founded by one of Franco's ex-ministers – and even joined in a condemnation of the 1936 military rebellion issued by Parliament in 2002, although on occasions it has established a subtle link between the Republic and the Civil War.[43] Popular historians such as Pío Moa have justified the uprising as a response to prior violence by left-wing organisations – in particular, the failed revolution of October 1934, backed by the Socialist Party in the name of antifascism – and defended the dictatorship's contribution to peace and prosperity in Spain. But these propositions have had more public success than historiographical influence, as can be seen in the case of Moa, a former militant Maoist, whose work *Los mitos de la Guerra Civil* ('Myths of the Civil War', 2003) sold 150,000 copies but was condemned as 'pseudo-revisionism' and neo-Francoist by a large majority of specialists.[44] The massive biographical dictionary produced by the publicly funded Royal Academy of History also aroused near-unanimous rejection by the Spanish academic community in 2011 for including entries that did not acknowledge Franco was a dictator, or which dubbed the Second Republic's last government, led by socialist premier Juan Negrín, as 'practically totalitarian'.[45] These memory wars over the historical role of fascism and antifascism have been replayed throughout Europe, from Portugal – studied in Chapter 16 by Manuel Loff and Luciana Soutelo – to the former Eastern bloc, where the antifascist narrative has fallen into even more discredit than in the West due to its widespread identification with the traumatic experience of Communism and Soviet imperialism.[46]

As may be seen in this preliminary writing, the historiographical, memorial and political dimensions of antifascism, with the issue of revisionism as a backdrop, are closely linked and hard to untangle. We have thus opted to clarify the volume by dividing it into two parts. The chapters in the first part try to reflect, always from a transnational perspective although they broach concrete and localised cases, on the problems posed by the 'historical antifascism' that swept across Europe and other continents between 1922 and 1945. Anson Rabinbach addresses Communist antifascism in the 1930s by revisiting the international campaign to free the German Communist leader Ernst Thälmann, imprisoned by the Nazis in 1934, and showing the complex relationship between Willi Münzenberg, the legendary Comintern propagandist, and his superiors in Moscow, as well as the uneven impact of his innovative campaigns. Next, Michael Seidman challenges the traditional view of the Popular Front, which ruled France in 1936–38 as the epitome of antifascism by emphasising the contrast between its effectiveness in thwarting the domestic far right and its inability or reluctance to stop fascist and Nazi expansionism abroad. Tom Buchanan, for his part, reviews the thorough changes which British antifascist historiography has undergone since the turn of the century, discusses the problems of extending the concept of antifascism to new social and political groups, as proposed by authors like Nigel Copsey, and defends a more restricted interpretation.

Getting back to the Mediterranean area, Giulia Albanese develops some of the issues posited in this Introduction by analysing how Italian, Spanish and Portuguese historians have dealt with the crisis of liberal institutions in the 1920s and the ensuing appearance of fascist and antifascist movements, and advocating a comparative and transnational approach as the best way to understand both processes. Next, Hugo García tackles the cultural aspect of antifascism – traditionally ignored by political and social historiography – by reconstructing the appearance of a plural antifascist culture in 1930s Spain, as well as the role of external and domestic factors in its emergence and the substantial transformations that culture experienced throughout the Republican period (1931–39). Cristina Clímaco, likewise, reconstructs the origins of antifascism in Portugal, its exile after the establishment of the dictatorship in 1926, and its revival in the second half of the 1930s thanks to international events like the Spanish Civil War.

The first part of the book is closed by three contributions that recover two aspects of fascism traditionally forgotten by mainstream historiography, but which represent two important focal points for renewal in recent literature on the subject. Andrés Bisso takes the spotlight away from the European context by examining the importance, peculiarities and political actions of antifascism in Argentina, a country with many Italian immigrants but which was little affected by fascism, between the March on Rome and the rise to power of Juan Perón in 1946. Isabelle Richet and Mercedes Yusta, for their part, approach the phenomenon from a gender perspective, stressing the important yet little-known contribution by women to antifascism – the 'temple of virility' studied by Patrizia Gabrielli[47]– and the complex and changing linkage of the latter with feminism, the first author in an Italian context and the second by the path taken by two large antifascist women's organisations that arose in Europe between the mid-1930s and the beginning of the Cold War. In so doing, they illuminate both the antifascists' general attitude towards gender roles and the peculiarities of women's involvement in the movement, ranging from armed participation to 'existential antifascism'.

The contributions making up the second half contrast and complete the matters discussed in the first half, but above all they delve into the lingering memory and changing public uses to which interwar antifascism has been put since the end of the Second World War, as well as into the causes and implications of the recent revisionist trend in the literature on the topic. Robert Coale reconstructs the semantic evolution of the term in the discourse of American volunteers in the Spanish Civil War, and of the US establishment between the 1930s and the beginning of the Cold War. José María Faraldo explores the very different meanings of the concept in the Socialist bloc by demonstrating the importance which antifascism and memories of the Great Patriotic War with Nazi Germany had in the discourse that legitimised the Soviet Union from 1945 onwards – shared, to a greater or lesser extent, by the German Democratic Republic and other Soviet satellites in Central and Eastern Europe – as well as its paradoxical persistence in post-Communist Russia, reflected in its use by Vladimir Putin's government against the 2014 Ukrainian revolution. In another long term study, Gilles Vergnon examines the various forms in which the 'historical antifascism' of 1934–38 was represented in France from 1945 to the end of the twentieth century, by showing how the myth of Republican antifascism influenced not only political practice, but also historiographical discourse, and how it has been invoked in response to perceived threats to the Fifth Republic such as the war in Algeria in the 1960s and the appearance of the Front National in the 1980s.

The book ends where it started, by walking us through antifascist remembrance in Italy, Spain and Portugal. Stéfanie Prezioso and Filippo Focardi reconstruct, from different perspectives, the evolution of the historiography, public debates over and politics of memory concerning antifascism and the Resistance in Italy, by attempting to explain the links between these three topics and focusing on the recent crisis in the 'antifascist paradigm', and the appearance and peculiarities of Italian revisionism. Javier Muñoz Soro, on the one hand, and Manuel Loff and Luciana Soutelo, on the other, examine how a similar process has developed in the two Iberian countries, which were governed by dictatorships with fascist traits and sympathies until the mid-1970s: Spain, where the long-lasting Franco regime and the troubled transition to democracy have imposed to this day the identification of antifascism with the bloody Civil War of 1936–39, thereby condemning it to political irrelevance; and Portugal, where the struggle over memory revolves around trivialising the Salazar regime (the dictator was voted the greatest Portuguese in history in a poll conducted by state broadcaster RTP in 2007) and, at the same time, around the radicalisation of the 'Carnation Revolution', which began with the fall of the *Estado Novo* in 1974. Enzo Traverso closes this section of chapters, and the volume itself, by running through the book's main ideas with a general discussion of revisionism in an international context, which distinguishes 'anti-antifascist' historiography from the critical revision inherent in the field, and shows how its view of antifascism distorts the possibility of charting the movement's history and of understanding its relationship with present-day democracies.

The seventeen studies we have resumed so tightly do not seek to account for the complexity of antifascism as a historical phenomenon and a site of memory which, as we have noted, is as great as the importance it held for the lives and identities of millions of people. Neither is it our intention to offer a new 'antifascist paradigm' to replace the one under question – on occasion with good arguments – by revisionist historians. The considerable differences in standpoint between the various contributors – who for the most part have been working on the subject for years and offer us previews of ongoing research – clearly show that antifascism is still an object of historiography which is contested beginning with its very definition, and these differences are unlikely to disappear in the foreseeable future. The volume has three more modest, yet more realistic goals: first, to make known the problems – which are often similar, but at times different – set out by present-day historians of antifascism in various countries and cultures; indeed they affect many of twentieth-century history's main problems. Second, to trace the paths along which future research may be conducted, amongst them that of undertaking further comparative and transnational studies and of exploring the impact of antifascism on the non-Western world – unfortunately left out of this volume – beyond the existing literature on exiles and on the involvement of various ethnic groups in the Abyssinian and Spanish conflicts.[48] Last, but not least, the book aims to underline the implications the historiographical treatment of the phenomenon has for our identity as citizens of democracies which, to a greater or lesser extent, were born of the 'great antifascist crusade' of the years 1933–45, so apparently remote from our post-totalitarian world.[49]

Translated by Martin Roberts

Notes

1. Chapter 5 in this work deals with Spanish historiography; more details in Hugo García, 'El antifascismo en España (1933–1939): una historia pendiente', in *Claves del mundo contemporáneo*, eds Teresa María Ortega and Miguel Ángel del Arco, Granada, 2013. Regarding Portugal, see António Costa Pinto, *Salazar's Dictatorship and European Fascism. Problems of Interpretation*, New York, 1995; Irene Pimentel, *Historia da oposição à ditadura*

em Portugal, Porto, 2014; and Cristina Clímaco's chapter in the present volume.

2. A recent analysis of this issue is in Gregorio Sorgonà, 'Storiografia del fascismo e dibattito sull'antifascismo', *Studi storici* 1 (2014), 213–26.

3. See Chapter 2 in this volume by Michael Seidman.

4. Francis Fukuyama, *The End of History and the Last Man,* New York, 1992.

5. See, for instance, *The Politics of Memory in Postwar Europe,* eds Richard Ned Lebow, Wulf Kansteiner and Claudio Fogu, Durham, 2006; *L'Europa e le sue memorie : politiche e culture del ricordo dopo il 1989,* eds Filippo Foccardi and Bruno Groppo, Rome, 2013; and Anson Rabinbach, 'Introduction: Legacies of Antifascism', *New German Critique* 67 (Winter 1996), 3–17.

6. Jean-François Lyotard, *The Postmodern Condition: A Report on Knowledge,* Manchester, 1984, xxiv (translation of *La condition postmoderne : rapport sur le savoir,* Paris, 1979).

7. Dan Stone, *Goodbye to All That? The Story of Europe since 1945,* Oxford, 2014, 60.

8. Ben Mercer, 'Specters of Fascism: The Rhetoric of Historical Analogy in 1968', *The Journal of Modern History,* 88 (March 2016): 96–219.

9. Some of the most active groups are Antifaschistische Aktion in Germany, Anti-fascist Network in Britain, Action antifasciste Paris-Banlieue in the Paris region, Antifascismo Militante in Italy and Antifa in Spain. See Valerio Gentili, *Antifa: storia contemporanea dell'antifascismo militante europeo,* Rome, 2013; Bettina Blank, *Deutschland, einig Antifa?: Antifaschismus als Agitationsfeld von Linksextremisten,* Baden-Baden, 2014; Dave Hahn, *Physical Resistance: A Hundred Years of Anti-Fascism,* Winchester, 2014; and Gilles Vergnon, *L'antifascisme en France de Mussolini à Le Pen,* Rennes, 2009, 163–210. Javier Muñoz Soro deals with the Spanish case in Chapter 15.

10. Jacques Droz, *Histoire de l'antifascisme en Europe, 1923–1939,* Paris, 1985, 7.

11. Bruno Groppo, 'Fascismes, antifascismes et communismes', in *Le siècle des communismes,* eds Michel Dreyfus et al., Paris, 2000, 502. See, for instance, *Antifascismo e identità europea,* eds Alberto De Bernardi and Paolo Ferrari, Rome, 2004; the dossier 'Legacies of Antifascism', edited by Rabinbach; or the dossier 'L'Antifascisme revisité. Histoire – Idéologie – Mémoire', coordinated by Carola Hähnel-Mesnard for the magazine *Témoigner. Entre Histoire et Mémoire* 104 (2009). The exception is Larry Ceplair, *Under the Shadow of War: Fascism, Anti-Fascism and Marxists, 1918–1939,* New York, 1987.

12. Renzo De Felice, *Fascism: An Informal Introduction to Its Theory and Practice (An Interview with Michael A. Ledeen).* New Brunswick, NJ, 1976; and De Felice, *Rosso e Nero,* Milan, 1995, especially 12–25; Annie Kriegel, 'Le mythe stalinien par excellence: l'antifascisme', in *Il Mito dell'Urss: la cultura occidentale e l'Unione Sovietica,* eds Marcello Flores and Francesca Gori, Milan, 1990, 217–23; François Furet, *The Passing of an Illusion: The Idea of Communism in the Twentieth Century,* Chicago, 1999, 216 (*Le passé d'une illusion. Essai sur l'idée communiste au XXe siècle,* Paris, 1995); Antonia Grunenberg, *Antifaschismus – Ein deutscher Mythos,* Reinbeck, 1993; Dan Diner, 'On the Ideology of Antifascism', in *New German Critique* 67, 123–32.

Another instance of this view is *Der missbrauchte Antifaschismus. DDR-Staatsdoktrin und Lebenslüge der deutschen Linken*, eds Manfred Agethen, Eckhard Jesse and Ehrhart Neubert, Freiburg, 2000.

13. Reinhart Koselleck, *Futures Past: On the Semantics of Historical Time*, New York, 1985. On state antifascism in the Soviet bloc, see also Josie McLellan, *Antifascism and Memory in East Germany: Remembering the International Brigades 1945–1989*, Oxford, 2004.

14. The proposal made with regard to Italy by Leonardo Rapone in his introduction to *Antifascismo e società italiana*, Turin, 1999, 7–9.

15. Anson Rabinbach, 'Public Intellectuals and Totalitarianism: A Century's Debate', in *Intellectuals and their Publics: Perspectives from the Social Sciences*, eds Christian Fleck et al., Ashgate, 2012, 107–40. See also Antonia Grunberger, 'Antitotalitarianism versus Antifascism: Two Legacies of the Past in Germany', *German Politics and Society* 15(2) (1997), 76–90; and Stéfanie Prézioso, 'Antifascism and Anti-Totalitarianism: The Italian Debate', *Journal of Contemporary History* 43(4) (2008), 555–72. 'European Civil War', in Ernst Nolte, *Der europaische Bürgerkrieg, 1917–1945: Nationalsozialismus und Bolshevismus*, Berlin, 1987.

16. Italian and Spanish historiographies have particularly stood out in this respect. See, for example, Giampaolo Pansa, *Il sangue dei vinti. Quello che accadde in Italia dopo il 25 aprile*, Milan, 2003; and César Vidal, *Paracuellos-Katyn: un ensayo sobre el genocidio de la izquierda*, Madrid, 2005.

17. Droz, *Histoire de l'antifascisme*, 7–8; Ceplair, *Under the Shadow of War*, 2–5; Rabinbach, 'Introduction: Legacies of Antifascism', 16; Groppo, 'Fascismes, antifascismes et communismes', 502–6. On communist antifascism, see also Stanley G. Payne, 'Soviet Anti-Fascism: Theory and Practice, 1921–45', *Totalitarian Movements and Political Religions* 4(2) (Autumn 2003), 1–62; and Bernhard H. Bayerlein, 'Abschied von einem Mythos. Die UdSSR, die Komintern und der Antifaschismus 1930–1941', *Osteuropa* 59 (7/8) (2009), 125–48.

18. For a detailed account of these conflicts in 1930s Spain, see Ferrán Gallego, *La crisis del antifascismo. Barcelona, mayo de 1937*, Barcelona, 2007; on the impact of the German–Soviet Pact on international antifascism, see Bernhard Bayerlein, *Der Verräter, Stalin, bist Du!' Vom Ende der internationalen Solidarität. Komintern und kommunistische Parteien im Zweiten Weltkrieg 1939–1941*, Berlin, 2008.

19. See H. García, 'Presente y futuro de una ilusión: la historiografía sobre el antifascismo desde Furet, 1996–2015', *Ayer*, 100 (2015), 233–247.

20. Alberto De Bernardi, 'Introduzione. L'antifascismo: una questione storica aperta', in *Antifascismo e identità europea*, XI–XXXII.

21. Ibid., XXII.

22. Eric Hobsbawm, *Age of Extremes: The Short Twentieth Century, 1914–1991*, London, 1994, 147–50; Enzo Traverso, *À feu et à sang : De la guerre civile européenne, 1914–1945*, Paris, 2007, 305–18, and Chapter 17; Nigel Copsey, 'Preface: Towards a New Anti-Fascist "Minimum"?', in *Varieties of Anti-Fascism: Britain in the Inter-War Period*, eds Nigel Copsey and Andrzej Olechnowicz, Basingstoke, 2010, xviii; Vergnon, *L'antifascisme en France*,

61–63, and Chapter 12; Gallego, *La crisis del antifascismo*, 318; Andrés Bisso, 'La recepción de la tradición liberal por parte del antifascismo argentino', *Estudios Interdisciplinarios de América Latina y el Caribe* 12(2) (Jul–Dec 2001), 85–113, and Chapter 7. The same pluralist approach may be found in the recent work by Christopher Vials, *Haunted by Hitler: Liberals, the Left and the Fight against Fascism in the United States*, Amherst, 2014.

23. Tom Buchanan, 'Anti-fascism and Democracy in the 1930s', *European History Quarterly* 32(1) (2002), 39–57, and Chapter 3.

24. Glenda Sluga, 'Fascism and Anti-Fascism', in *The Palgrave Dictionary of Transnational History*, ed. Akira Iriye, Basingstoke, 2009, 381–82.

25. Gerd-Rainer Horn, *European Socialists Respond to Fascism*, Cambridge, 1996, 117–36.

26. Dan Stone, 'Anti-Fascist Europe Comes to Britain: Theorising Fascism as a Contribution to Defeating it', in *Varieties of Anti-Fascism*, 183–84; Isabelle Richet, 'Marion Cave Roselli and the Transnational Women's Anti-fascist Networks', *Journal of Women's History* 24(3) (2012), 117–39.

27. Joseph Fronczack, 'Local People's Global Politics: A Transnational History of the Hands Off Ethiopia Movement of 1935', *Diplomatic History*, 2014, online.

28. David Featherstone, 'Black Internationalism, Subaltern Cosmopolitanism, and the Spatial Politics of Antifascism', *Annals of the Association of American Geographers* 103(6), 2013, 1406–20. Some of the most attractive projects that may be found online as of October 2014 are: Kasper Braskén, 'The Origins of "Anti-Fascism": Transnational Movements against Nazism, Fascism and the "White Terror" in Europe, 1923–1939'; Andrea Acle-Kreysing, 'Anti-fascist Exile in Mexico City and Buenos Aires: The Construction of a Transatlantic Political Culture (1930s–1940s)'; Jens Spath, 'Antifaschismus in Westeuropa. Politik und Erinnerung deutscher, französischer und italienischer Sozialisten 1945-um 1960'; and Adrian Zimmermann, 'The International Labour movement's struggle against fascism. Some starting points for a research project in transnational labour history'.

29. 'Antifascism as a Practice and as a Discourse', Geneva, May–June 2012; 'L'Antifascisme en question, 1922–1945', Paris, June 2013; and 'Anti-fascism as a Transnational Phenomenon: New Perspectives of Research', Saarbrücken, October 2014.

30. Enzo Traverso, 'Intellectuals and Anti-Fascism: For a Critical Historization', *New Politics* IX: 4, 2004, online; Anson Rabinbach, 'Paris, Capital of Anti-fascism', in *The Modernist Imagination: Intellectual History and Critical Theory*, eds Warren Breckman et al., New York, 2009, 183–209; Stone, 'Anti-Fascist Europe Comes to Britain'; Fronczak, 'Local People's Global Politics'.

31. Stéfanie Prezioso, '*Aujourd'hui en Espagne, demain en Italie*: l'exil antifasciste italien et la prise d'armes révolutionnaire', *Vingtième siècle. Revue d'histoire* 93 (2007), 79–92; Tom Buchanan, 'Shanghai–Madrid Axis'? Comparing British Responses to the Conflicts in Spain and China, 1936–39', *Contemporary European History* 21(4) (November 2012), 533–52; Featherstone, 'Black Internationalism', 1406–20; and Rabinbach, 'Introduction: Legacies of Antifascism', 7.

32. Gilles Vergnon, 'Le *poing levé*, du rite soldatique au rite de masse', *Le Mouvement social* 212 (July–September 2005), 77–91; Cristina Cuevas Wolf, 'Montage as Weapon: The Tactical Alliance between Willi Münzenberg and John Heartfield', *New German Critique* 107 (2009), 197–203.
33. Rabinbach, 'Paris, Capital of Anti-fascism', 184. See especially the chapters in this volume by Robert Coale, Isabelle Richet and Hugo García.
34. See, for instance, Copsey, 'Preface: Towards a New Anti-Fascist "Minimum"?', xiv–xxi.
35. Fronczak, 'Local People's Global Politics'; Tim Kirk and Anthony McElligott, 'Introduction. Community, Authority and Resistance to Fascism', in *Opposing Fascism: Community, Authority and Resistance in Europe*, eds Tim Kirk and Anthony McElligot, Cambridge, 1999, 1–11.
36. See the chapters by Stéfanie Prezioso and Filippo Focardi in this volume.
37. On the crisis in the antifascist paradigm, see Sergio Luzzato, *La crisi dell'antifascismo*, Turin, 2004; Enzo Collotti (ed.), *Fascismo e antifascismo. Rimozioni, revisioni, negazioni*, Bari, 2000; and Angelo Del Boca (ed.), *La storia negata. Il revisionismo e il suo uso politico*, Vicenza, 2009. Also in 2009, Giampaolo Pansa published his biography, entitled, cursorily, *Il Revisionista* (Milan, 2009).
38. Pansa, *Il sangue dei vinti*.
39. Régine Robin, *La mémoire saturée*, Paris, 2003.
40. Ernesto Galli della Loggia, *La morte della patria. La crisi dell'idea di nazione tra Resistenza, antifascismo e Repubblica*, Rome and Bari, 1996.
41. 'Berlusconi: La Costituzione è di ispirazione sovietica', *La Reppublica*, 12 April 2003; 'Mussolini non hai ammazzato nessuno', *Corriere della Sera*, 11 September 2003. See Giovanni De Luna, 'Revisionismo e Resistenza', in *La storia negata*, ed. A. Del Boca, 293–328.
42. Carolyn Boyd, 'The Politics of History and Memory in Democratic Spain', *Annals of the American Academy of Political and Social Science* 617 (2008), 133–48. See the detailed discussion of the Spanish case by Javier Muñoz Soro in this volume.
43. On 28 August 2013, Rafael Hernando, PP spokesman in the Spanish Parliament, stated, 'The Republic's consequences led to a million dead'. *El País*, 28 August 2013.
44. Enrique Moradiellos, 'Critical Historical Revision and Political Revisionism: The Case of Spain', International *Journal of Iberian Studies* 21(3) (2008), 219–29; Javier Rodrigo, *Cruzada, paz, memoria. La Guerra Civil en sus relatos*, Granada, 2013, 128–42. Cf. Enzo Traverso's observations in the last chapter of this volume on the 'anti-antifascist' historiography that has arisen in recent years.
45. José Luis Ledesma, 'El Diccionario Biográfico Español, el pasado y los historiadores', *Ayer* 88(4) (2012), 247–65.
46. Stone, *Goodbye to all that?*, 265–90; see also Giorgios Antoniou, 'The Lost Atlantis of Objectivity: The Revisionist Struggles between the Academic and Public Spheres', *History and Theory*, theme issue 46 (December 2007), 92–112; and Michal Kopeček (ed.), *Past in the Making: Historical Revisionism in Central Europe after 1989*, Budapest and New York, 2008.

47. Patrizia Gabrielli, *Tempio di virilità: l'antifascismo, il genere, la storia*, Milan, 2008.
48. See, besides the already mentioned articles by Joseph Fronczak and David Featherstone, V. G. Venturini, *Never Give In: Three Italian Antifascist Exiles in Australia, 1924–1956*, Sydney, 2007; M. Framke, *Delhi – Rom – Berlin. Die indische Wahrnehmung von Faschismus und Nationalsozialismus 1922–1939*, Darmstadt, 2013.
49. Arthur Koestler, *The Invisible Writing*, London, 2005 [1954], 229. Antifascism's contributions to postwar European democracies are described in Geoff Eley, 'Legacies of Antifascism: Constructing Democracy in Postwar Europe', *New German Critique* 67 (Winter 1996), 73–100, and, more extensively, in De Bernardi and Ferrari, *Antifascismo e identità europea*, 197–355.

References

Agethen, M., E. Jesse and E. Neubert (eds). *Der missbrauchte Antifaschismus: DDR-Staatsdoktrin und Lebenslüge der deutschen Linken*. Freiburg, 2000.

Antoniou, G. 'The Lost Atlantis of Objectivity: The Revisionist Struggles between the Academic and Public Spheres'. *History and Theory*, theme issue 46 (Dec 2007), 92–112.

Bayerlein, B.H. *Der Verräter, Stalin, bist Du!' Vom Ende der internationalen Solidarität. Komintern und kommunistische Parteien im Zweiten Weltkrieg 1939–1941*. Berlin, 2008.

———. 'Abschied von einem Mythos. Die UdSSR, die Komintern und der Antifaschismus 1930–1941'. *Osteuropa* 59 (7/8) (2009), 125–48.

Bisso, A. 'La recepción de la tradición liberal por parte del antifascismo argentino'. *Estudios Interdisciplinarios de América Latina y el Caribe* 12(2) (Jul–Dec 2001), 85–113.

Blank, B. *Deutschland, einig Antifa?: Antifaschismus als Agitationsfeld von Linksextremisten*. Baden-Baden, 2014.

Boyd, C. 'The Politics of History and Memory in Democratic Spain'. *Annals of the American Academy of Political and Social Science* 617 (2008), 133–48.

Buchanan, T. 'Anti-fascism and Democracy in the 1930s'. *European History Quarterly* 32(1) (2002), 39–57.

———. 'Shanghai–Madrid Axis'? Comparing British Responses to the Conflicts in Spain and China, 1936–39'. *Contemporary European History* 21(4) (Nov 2012), 533–52.

Ceplair, L. *Under the Shadow of War: Fascism, Anti-Fascism and Marxists, 1918–1939*. New York, 1987.

Collotti, E. (ed.). *Fascismo e antifascismo. Rimozioni, revisioni, negazioni*. Bari, 2000.

Copsey, N., and A. Olechnowicz (eds). *Varieties of Anti-Fascism: Britain in the Inter-War Period*. Basingstoke, 2010.

Cuevas Wolf, C. 'Montage as Weapon: The Tactical Alliance between Willi Münzenberg and John Heartfield'. *New German Critique* 107 (2009), 197–203.

De Bernardi, A., and P. Ferrari (eds). *Antifascismo e identità europea*. Rome, 2004.

De Felice, R. *Fascism: An Informal Introduction to Its Theory and Practice (An Interview with Michael A. Ledeen)*. New Brunswick, NJ, 1976.
———. *Rosso e Nero*. Milan, 1995.
De Luna, G. 'Revisionismo e Resistenza', in A. Del Boca (ed.), *La storia negata. Il revisionismo e il suo uso político*. Vicenza, 2010, 293–328.
Del Boca, A. (ed.). *La storia negata. Il revisionismo e il suo uso político*. Vicenza, 2009.
Diner, D. 'On the Ideology of Antifascism'. *New German Critique 67, Legacies of Antifascism* (Winter 1996), 123–32.
Droz, J. *Histoire de l'antifascisme en Europe, 1923–1939*. Paris, 1985.
Eley, G. 'Legacies of Antifascism: Constructing Democracy in Postwar Europe'. *New German Critique* 67 (Winter 1996), 73–100.
Featherstone, D. 'Black Internationalism, Subaltern Cosmopolitanism, and the Spatial Politics of Antifascism'. *Annals of the Association of American Geographers* 103(6) (2013), 1406–20.
Focardi, F., and B. Groppo (eds). *L'Europa e le sue memorie : politiche e culture del ricordo dopo il 1989*. Rome, 2013.
Framke, M. *Delhi – Rom – Berlin. Die indische Wahrnehmung von Faschismus und Nationalsozialismus 1922–1939*. Darmstadt, 2013.
Fronczak, J. 'Local People's Global Politics: A Transnational History of the Hands Off Ethiopia Movement of 1935'. *Diplomatic History*, (2015) 39 (2): 245–274 first published online February 13, 2014.
Fukuyama, F. *The End of History and the Last Man*. New York, 1992.
Furet, F. *The Passing of an Illusion: The Idea of Communism in the Twentieth Century*. Chicago, 1999 (translation of *Le passé d'une illusion. Essai sur l'idée communiste au XXe siècle*. Paris, 1995).
Gabrielli, P. *Tempio di virilità: l'antifascismo, il genere, la storia*. Milan, 2008.
Gallego, F. *La crisis del antifascismo. Barcelona, mayo de 1937*. Barcelona, 2007.
Galli della Loggia, E. *La morte della patria. La crisi dell'idea di nazione tra Resistenza, antifascismo e Repubblica*. Rome and Bari, 1996.
García, H. 'El antifascismo en España (1933–1939): una historia pendiente', in T.M. Ortega and M. Ángel del Arco (eds), *Claves del mundo contemporáneo*. Granada, 2013.
———. 'Presente y futuro de una ilusión: la historiografía sobre el antifascismo desde Furet, 1996–2015', *Ayer*, 100 (2015), 233–247.
Gentili, V. *Antifa: storia contemporanea dell'antifascismo militante europeo*. Rome, 2013.
Groppo, B. 'Fascismes, antifascismes et communismes', in M. Dreyfus et al. (eds), *Le siècle des communismes*. Paris, 2000.
Grunenberg, A. 'Antitotalitarianism versus Antifascism: Two Legacies of the Past in Germany'. *German Politics and Society* 15(2) (1997), 76–90.
———. *Antifaschismus – Ein deutscher Mythos*. Reinbeck, 1993.
Hahn, D. *Physical Resistance: A Hundred Years of Anti-Fascism*. Winchester, 2014.
Hähnel-Mesnard, C. (ed.). 'L'Antifascisme revisité. Histoire – Idéologie – Mémoire'. Special issue of *Témoigner. Entre Histoire et Mémoire* 104 (2009).
Hobsbawm, E. *Age of Extremes: The Short Twentieth Century, 1914–1991*. London, 1994.
Horn, G.-R. *European Socialists Respond to Fascism*. Cambridge, 1996.

Kirk, T., and A. McElligot (eds). *Opposing Fascism: Community, Authority and Resistance in Europe*. Cambridge, 1999.

Koestler, A. *The Invisible Writing*. London, 2005 [original edn 1954].

Kopeček, M. (ed.). *Past in the Making: Historical Revisionism in Central Europe after 1989*. Budapest and New York, 2008.

Koselleck, R. *Futures Past: On the Semantics of Historical Time*. New York, 1985.

Kriegel, A. 'Le mythe stalinien par excellence: l'antifascisme', in M. Flores and F. Gori (eds), *Il Mito dell'Urss: la cultura occidentale e l'Unione Sovietica*. Milan, 1990.

Lebow, R.N., W. Kansteiner and C. Fogu (eds). *The Politics of Memory in Postwar Europe*. Durham, 2006.

Ledesma, J.L. 'El Diccionario Biográfico Español, el pasado y los historiadores'. *Ayer* 88(4) (2012), 247–65.

Luzzato, S. *La crisi dell'antifascismo*. Turin, 2004.

Lyotard, J.-F. *The Postmodern Condition: A Report on Knowledge*. Manchester, 1984 (translation of *La condition postmoderne : rapport sur le savoir*, Paris, 1979).

McLellan, J. *Antifascism and Memory in East Germany: Remembering the International Brigades 1945–1989*. Oxford, 2004.

Mercer, B. 'Specters of Fascism: The Rhetoric of Historical Analogy in 1968', *The Journal of Modern History*, 88 (March 2016), 96–219

Moradiellos, E. 'Critical Historical Revision and Political Revisionism: The Case of Spain'. *International Journal of Iberian Studies* 21(3) (2008), 219–29.

Nolte, E. *Der europaische Bürgerkrieg, 1917–1945: Nationalsozialismus und Bolshevismus*. Berlin, 1987.

Pansa, G. *Il sangue dei vinti. Quello che accadde in Italia dopo il 25 aprile*. Milan, 2003.

———. *Il Revisionista*. Milan, 2009.

Payne, S.G. 'Soviet Anti-Fascism: Theory and Practice, 1921–45'. *Totalitarian Movements and Political Religions* 4(2) (Autumn 2003), 1–62.

Pimentel, I. *História da oposição á ditadura em Portugal*. Porto, 2014.

Pinto, A. Costa. *Salazar's Dictatorship and European Fascism: Problems of Interpretation*. New York, 1995.

Prezioso, S. 'Antifascism and Anti-Totalitarianism: The Italian Debate'. *Journal of Contemporary History* 43(4) (2008), 555–72.

———. '*Aujourd'hui en Espagne, demain en Italie*: l'exil antifasciste italien et la prise d'armes révolutionnaire'. *Vingtième siècle. Revue d'histoire* 93 (2007), 79–92.

Rabinbach, A. (ed.), 'Legacies of Antifascism'. *New German Critique* 67 (Winter 1996).

———. 'Paris, Capital of Anti-fascism', in W. Breckman et al. (eds), *The Modernist Imagination: Intellectual History and Critical Theory*. New York, 2009.

———. 'Public Intellectuals and Totalitarianism: A Century's Debate', in C. Fleck et al. (eds), *Intellectuals and their Publics: Perspectives from the Social Sciences*. Ashgate, 2012, 107–40.

Rapone, L. *Antifascismo e società italiana*. Turin, 1999.

Richet, I. 'Marion Cave Roselli and the Transnational Women's Anti-fascist Networks'. *Journal of Women's History* 24(3) (2012), 117–39.

Robin, R. *La mémoire saturée*. Paris, 2003.

Rodrigo, J. *Cruzada, paz, memoria. La Guerra Civil en sus relatos*. Granada, 2013.

Sluga, G. 'Fascism and Anti-Fascism', in A. Iriye (ed.), *The Palgrave Dictionary of Transnational History*. Basingstoke, 2009, 381–82.

Sorgonà, G. 'Storiografia del fascismo e dibattito sull'antifascismo'. *Studi storici* 1 (2014), 213–26.

Stone, D. 'Anti-Fascist Europe Comes to Britain: Theorising Fascism as a Contribution to Defeating it', in N. Copsey and A. Olechnowicz (eds), *Varieties of Anti-Fascism: Britain in the Inter-War Period*. Basingstoke, 2010, 183–201.

———. *Goodbye to All That? The Story of Europe since 1945*. Oxford, 2014.

Traverso, E., 'Intellectuals and Anti-Fascism: For a Critical Historization'. *New Politics* IX: 4, 2004, online.

———. *À feu et à sang : De la guerre civile européenne, 1914–1945*. Paris, 2007 (translated to English as *Fire and Blood: The European Civil War 1914–1945*, London and New York, 2016).

Venturini, V.G. *Never Give In: Three Italian Antifascist Exiles in Australia, 1924–1956*. Sydney, 2007.

Vergnon, G. 'Le *poing levé*, du rite soldatique au rite de masse'. *Le Mouvement social* 212 (Jul–Sep 2005), 77–91.

———. *L'antifascisme en France de Mussolini à Le Pen*. Rennes, 2009.

Vials, C. *Haunted by Hitler: Liberals, the Left and the Fight against Fascism in the United States*. Amherst, 2014.

Vidal, C. *Paracuellos-Katyn: un ensayo sobre el genocidio de la izquierda*. Madrid, 2005.

PART ONE

HISTORICAL ANTIFASCISM, 1922–45

New Perspectives, New Research Topics

1

FREEDOM FOR THÄLMANN!

The Comintern and the Orchestration of the Campaign to Free
Ernst Thälmann, 1933–39

Anson Rabinbach

In 1925, an astrologer named A.M. Grimm published the horoscope
of Ernst Johannes Fritz Thälmann, born in Hamburg on 16 April 1886:
'Thälmann', he declared, 'is an enthusiastic, energetic and stubborn pi-
oneer of his cause with tough willpower and patience; a man that does
not allow himself to be subverted'. His chances of success, Grimm predicted, 'were better than those of Hitler'.[1] Astrology, obviously, is not an
exact science. The head of the German Communist Party was famously
murdered in Buchenwald on 18 August 1944, less than a year before
the demise of Hitler and his Reich. A note scribbled by Himmler four
days earlier records that Hitler personally ordered his death.[2] Before
that, he spent eleven years in German prisons – Moabit, Hannover and
Bautzen – though he was never in a concentration camp for any length
of time. During his eleven-year ordeal, Thälmann's 'bald pate' or his
Hamburg sailor's cap (*Mütze*) adorned banners and pamphlets from
Brussels to Barcelona, from Montmartre to Montevideo. The sustained
campaign to win his release mobilised the entire *communisant* left in
the early 1930s and ultimately gave his name to the famous 'Thälmann
Battalion' of German volunteers in Spain.

The Thälmann campaign was in many respects typical of the
Comintern's (Communist International) mobilisation of public opinion in the West during the early 1930s. It overlapped with the successful campaign, also organised by the Comintern's propaganda expert
Willi Münzenberg, to free the four Communist defendants accused
of conspiracy to set fire to the Reichstag in February 1933 and, as in
the Reichstag campaign, demonstrated the efficacy and degree of independence from obsolete Communist Party tactics developed by

Münzenberg during his Paris exile. Moreover, the Thälmann campaign was characteristic of how Münzenberg's style of 'propaganda as
a weapon' virtually invented a popular antifascism that enlisted the
participation of prominent West European politicians and intellectuals as well.[3] Although the Comintern remained an instrument of Soviet
foreign policy, Münzenberg's political style – the production of mass
spectacles and the orchestration of public opinion by manipulation of
the press – was, at least for a time, beyond the grip of the Comintern's
Executive (ECCI).[4]

Encouraged by the unexpected acquittal of the four Reichstag
fire defendants handed down by Leipzig Supreme Court president
Wilhelm Bünger at 10 AM on 23 December 1933, Münzenberg planned
a new offensive on behalf of the most important Communist prisoner
in Germany. Ernst Thälmann, the fiery orator and leader of Europe's
largest Communist Party had been held in Berlin's Moabit Prison just
north of the Spree River since 3 March, when he was arrested in a gar-
den plot on the outskirts of the city. Although the Münzenberg campaign hailed the Reichstag trial verdict as a resounding victory, the
prospects for Thälmann were by no means rosy. Despite the acquittal,
Dimitrov and his three Communist co-defendants were not freed, and
rumours circulated that a treason trial for Thälmann was in the offing.[5]
After the verdict, Göring made no bones about claiming that Dimitrov
still 'deserved the gallows, if only for his criminal and seditious activities in Germany before the Reichstag fire'.[6] Göring also boasted that
the accused Communist Reichstag deputy Ernst Torgler 'did not have
it so bad in jail, and had long since broken with Communism', while
Thälmann still had not changed, because 'he was too dumb and has
no clue what Communism is'.[7] In January the defence committee released its first post-trial statement under the heading 'Acquitted, but
not Released', a warning that the defendants 'are still threatened with
murder', as had been openly announced by Göring.[8]

In some respects, the two antifascist campaigns were twins. Both
were orchestrated by Münzenberg, the Comintern's 'supraparty' impresario. Both created a profusion of committees, declarations, pe-
titions, conclaves of jurists, and a multitude of letter-writing and
postcard actions. But in many respects they were opposites. Whereas
the Reichstag fire campaign had high visibility, a courtroom drama, a
courageous hero (Dimitrov), stock company villains (Göring), a perfect
'fool' (Marinus van der Lubbe) and a thrilling unexpected outcome, the
Thälmann campaign revolved around a largely invisible, long-suffer-
ing figure who lacked any of the political or oratorical gifts of Dimitrov,
apart from his stubborn tenacity. Unlike the Reichstag fire campaign,

the absence of a public trial indicated that the acquittal in Leipzig had taught the Nazis a valuable lesson about jurisprudence, public opinion and the international press. Although the Reichstag fire was the occasion for the elimination of civil liberties and parliamentary rule by the Enabling Act of 23 March 1933, the trial remained within the Weimar system of jurisprudence, with some restrictions. Hearing of the acquittal, Goebbels was beside himself, writing in his diary: 'This is what happens to a revolution when you put it in the hands of jurists. This court must disappear. Bring on a court for the protection of the German people'.[9] In November 1935 he noted that Hitler had decided to delay judicial proceedings to 'put an end to the publicity as soon as possible'.[10] In conformity with Goebbel's diatribe, Thälmann's status was changed from a defendant awaiting trial to a prisoner indefinitely placed under 'protective custody'.

Like the Reichstag fire campaign, the case of Thälmann served to alert the French – and beyond France, the international public – to the brutality, arbitrariness and injustice of the Nazi regime. If the Reichstag fire trial promoted unity among the opponents of Hitler throughout the world, the Thälmann case was divisive. For those outside the Communist orbit, Thälmann was regarded as a corrupt and servile lackey of Stalin. In 1928 he was implicated in a financial scandal, the 'Wittorf affair' – a cover up of embezzled KPD funds – and was reinstated as party chairman only by the direct intervention of Stalin.[11] During the early 1930s, he repeatedly quoted Stalin's axiom that fascism and social democracy were 'twin brothers'.[12] Above all, for the SPD and the non-Communist anti-Nazi left, Thälmann was anathema for his role in the April 1932 presidential run off election when he ran against Hitler and Hindenburg. The SPD supported Hindenburg in order to block Hitler, and saw Thälmann's candidacy as *the* obstacle to a democratic–republican solution to the crisis of the Weimar Republic.

In March, just after his arrest, the Executive Committee of the Communist International (ECCI) issued a proclamation calling upon all Communists to work for the imprisoned leader's freedom.[13] The Dimitrov campaign occupied the full energies of the Münzenberg organisation in the autumn and winter of 1933, and the Thälmann case was put on hold until the verdict. In November 1933, Münzenberg announced the creation of a committee for the liberation of Dimitrov, Thälmann, Popov, Tanev and all imprisoned antifascists – notable was the absence of Torgler, whose fate was obviously deemed insignificant – financed by his International Red Aid (IAH) and placed under the umbrella of his World Committee for the Victims of German Fascism in Paris.[14] Once the three 'Bulgarian' defendants were repatriated to the Soviet Union on 27 February 1934, the campaign turned its energy to the jailed KPD leader, with the assumption that a Thälmann trial was in the offing and that a carefully prepared indictment would directly follow the Reichstag trial.

As Münzenberg wrote in a secret communiqué to the newly installed 'foreign bureau' of the exiled German KPD, reconstituted in Paris under the leadership of Franz Dahlem, Wilhelm Pieck and Wilhelm Florin in the summer of 1934: 'To compensate for their defeat in the Reichstag trial the Hitler people are preparing a trial against Thälmann which is also meant to be a trial against the KPD ... We too are forced to ratchet up our efforts against the Hitler–government' and 'will have to gain broad proletarian support for the campaign'.[15] In other words, a public defence of Thälmann would have to appeal to a different audience than the Reichstag fire campaign. While intellectuals and sympathetic middle-class supporters of the left could be counted on to rally to Dimitrov and the others accused of conspiracy in the name of an obvious injustice, Thälmann's role as KPD leader 'naturally created certain difficulties' when it came to their participation. Left unsaid was Thälmann's reputation as a thick-headed and slavish Stalinist whose incessant assaults on the integrity of the Social Democrats were notorious.

Unlike the Reichstag fire campaign, the international efforts on behalf of Thälmann tended to be conducted by both the official Communist parties and by the supraparty Thälmann Committee. To be sure, Münzenberg had always been a loyal and disciplined Communist, a member of the KPD's Central Committee, a member of its Reichstag fraction, and an unwavering defender of the party during its political gyrations during the Weimar era. At the same time, his successes in creating impressive international organisations and campaigns featuring high profile literary, scientific and political celebrities, required that he maintain a credible distance from Moscow, which of course made him all the more indispensable, and suspect.[16] Münzenberg's genius was to orchestrate events that went far beyond the narrow radius of the Comintern, creating temporary alliances and often producing spectacular results while at the same time clandestinely consulting with Moscow and arranging Soviet financial support for his vast enterprises.[17]

Before his exile in Paris, Münzenberg's great triumph as the impresario of international antifascism was the orchestration of the August 1932 World Congress against Imperialist War. On the eve of the congress, Münzenberg travelled to Moscow to review the details and finances with his Comintern patrons. Under the banner of what Trotsky dismissively called 'the malady of the love of peace', the congress featured testimonials and speeches by such luminaries as George Bernard Shaw, Maxim Gorki, Mrs Sun Yat Sen, Albert Einstein, Heinrich Mann, Upton Sinclair, Theodore Dreiser and John Dos Passos. Avoiding the spotlight as always, Münzenberg relied on his French emissary in chief, the communist writer Henri Barbusse, who persuaded Romain Rolland to headline the congress.[18] Despite efforts by several governments to prevent it from taking place, and despite threats by socialist parties to expel those members who attended, some three hundred Social Democrats participated. In line with its nebulous paeans to peace, its main focus was not the Nazis, but 'French militarism'.

Just a few weeks later, it was no longer possible to divert attention from Nazi Germany or from the Comintern's disastrous policy of accusing the Social Democrats of 'social fascism' – despite the absence of any signal from Moscow. Just five days before the Reichstag fire, the KPD representative in the Comintern Executive (ECCI), Fritz Heckert, proposed a European Antifascist Workers Congress modelled on the Amsterdam anti-war congress.

For the Comintern, the suggestion that antifascist unity could not be accomplished without the support of the leaders of the Second International bordered on betrayal.[19] The Comintern leaders (Béla Kun, Osip Piatnitsky and Dmitry Manuilsky) feared that initiatives such as Amsterdam Pleyel would permit 'counter-revolutionary' elements to gain a foothold in its supraparty organisations. During his visit to Moscow in the summer of 1933, perhaps for the first time, Münzenberg found himself on very shaky ground: Comintern head, Béla Kun reprimanded him for trying to 'assume the leadership of the whole [antifascist] movement' and for operating with a 'free hand', to which Münzenberg replied that he had no intention of doing so, and had always acted in strict compliance with the ECCI's instructions.[20] A few weeks later, Kun drafted a memorandum on the 'tasks of the Party-press in the struggle against Social Democracy, Fascism, and the danger of war', declaring that there could be no talk of unity between Socialists and Communists.[21]

The Comintern's watchful eye revealed a degree of paranoia and suspicion that can best be explained by what the poet Aleksander Wat called the Stalinist principle of 'the Third'.[22] From this perspective the party acts not as a directing force but as a mediator and permanent presence in all undertakings involving two or more persons, organisations or constituencies, since all such combinations, especially those including Social Democrats, were ipso facto suspect. Münzenberg's talent was to maintain the appearance of independence while remaining fully subordinate to the Comintern, though not entirely subordinate to the European Communist parties.

On 5 January 1934 the Thälmann Committee was established with Barbusse as its 'Honorary President', with Romain Rolland, Professor Paul Langevin and André Gide as 'Honorary Chairmen', and with André Malraux as 'President and Chairman'. In fact, there were two committees with the same name, address, phone number and presidents, both under Münzenberg's control: the 'International Committee for the Liberation of Dimitrov, Thälmann, and all imprisoned antifascists' and a French 'Committee for the Liberation of Thälmann and all imprisoned antifascists'.[23] Directives were simultaneously issued from Moscow, from the International Committee in Paris, from the KPD in exile in Prague and even from Amsterdam, a situation that one Comintern official (Heinrich) called 'untenable'.[24] In a confidential memorandum, Münzenberg admitted that the 'International Committee' existed in 'name only', while the five famous 'presidents' and 'honorary chairmen' were in fact only representative figures.[25]

After the repatriation of Dimitrov, Tanev and Popov to Moscow on 27 February 1934, the fate of Thälmann became the sole focus of Münzenberg's efforts.[26] Thälmann's legal situation was murky. For four years, he would remain in a kind of legal limbo between his Gestapo captors and the German judiciary. Goebbels was wary of creating a spectacle, welcoming each postponement of the trial. The leading Nazi jurists, echoing his sentiments, withheld release of the indictment, contemplating a 'juridical' or 'administrative' procedure rather than a high-profile treason trial.[27] Although Thälmann relished the prospect of a public trial, his comrades in Moscow and in the newly constituted exile Communist leadership were of a different opinion – that he was of considerably more use as an imprisoned rather than a free party leader.[28]

On Thälmann's birthday, the 16th of April, mass rallies on behalf of the jailed KPD leader were held throughout the world. In October, some two thousand people crowded London's Kingsway Hall to condemn the absence of any legal process and to demand his release. The words 'Release Thälmann' were painted on the stern of a German freighter harboured in the Surrey Docks, and in a particular stroke of ingenuity, the Walt Disney cartoon film, 'Peculiar Penguins', was interrupted by pro-Thälmann slogans that were projected onto the screen at the London Pavilion Cinema.[29] In Paris there were more than forty Thälmann events, including a petition campaign and a delegation sent to the German embassy. Henri Barbusse produced a brochure entitled

'Do you Know Thälmann?', taking time out from his biography of Stalin to extol his proletarian provenance and his working man's physique: 'A powerful figure, a healthy and solid frame, a strong voice, the fine plain expressive face of a worker conscious of the power of his class, strengthened by his revolutionary theory, unshakably confident of victory'.[30] Left unmentioned in this catalogue of virtues were his less attractive qualities, his ready submissiveness to party doctrine, his narrow-mindedness, his rigidity, and above all, his lack of intellectual gifts, observed by Margarethe Buber-Neumann, who recalled that when she first heard him, she was 'shocked by the … mixture of primitive drivel and poorly understood Marxist jargon'.[31]

An internal Comintern assessment in March 1934 reveals a crisis-ridden organisation. Münzenberg's coffers were exhausted, and he was unable to attract as broad a following as the Reichstag fire campaign.[32] On 24 April the German legal code was revised to create 'People's Courts' (*Volksgerichte*) composed of five judges, three to be appointed directly by the chancellor, to conduct treason trials.[33] These summary courts were denounced by the KPD in exile as a death sentence for 'our Comrade Thälmann'; whether they were in fact created 'only because of Thälmann', as the anti-Nazi press claimed, is uncertain.[34] The *Manchester Guardian* warned that 'Thälmann's life is in danger', referring to Goebbels inflammatory comment that the Reichstag fire trial had shown that 'a trial conducted in the old manner … would be detrimental to the interests of the German state'.[35] The Paris Committee was energised by the chance to portray the new Nazi courts as 'illegal contrivances' created to avoid a public judicial trial for Thälmann.[36]

As a shift towards a potential alliance between the Socialist and Communist parties gained ground in Moscow during the summer of 1934, the 'supraparty' organisations gradually lost their raison d'être. What use were they in recruiting Socialists and independents to the Communist cause if Socialists and Communists could officially join forces?

Thälmann's birthday on 16 April 1935 was the occasion for an international display on his behalf. He was sent thousands of greetings and congratulatory telegrams.[37] Telephone calls flooded the switchboards of German embassies throughout the world. Donations, floral displays and countless resolutions swamped the prison authorities. Thälmann received encomiums from famous writers such as Thomas and Heinrich Mann, Lion Feuchtwanger, Romain Rolland, Stefan Zweig and Maxim Gorki.[38] Yet, despite all efforts, the Thälmann campaign was clearly not an unmitigated success. As the committee admitted, 'up to now it has not resulted in a broad mass movement in any country'. The name Ernst Thälmann is 'still completely inadequately popularised', an internal memorandum admitted in June 1935.[39]

By the summer of 1936, the Thälmann campaign ground to a standstill. The committee reported that the period between August and December 1936 saw the 'deepest slump' and a general shift in attention to the international solidarity campaign in favour of manifestations on behalf of the Spanish Republic. The simple truth was that the Comintern and the KPD had abandoned any interest in Thälmann's release.[40] Thälmann was far more useful as a symbol, for example, in coupling the phrase Thälmann 'has not been forgotten' with initiatives connected to the Spanish Civil War.

As the prospect of a trial evaporated in the course of 1934 and early 1935, the campaign shifted to Thälmann's situation in prison. In the absence of a public trial, the campaign had little choice but to make use of challenges to the strict prohibition on visits to him (apart from his wife Rosa, their daughter Irma, and his lawyers) to keep Thälmann's name in the press. Stirring up publicity around the visits of prominent foreigners was already a familiar tactic since the much publicised trip of André Malraux and André Gide to Berlin on behalf of Dimitrov and Thälmann on 3–4 January 1934. The two famous writers demanded a meeting with Minister Goebbels and with Hitler. When told that Goebbels was in Munich and that Hitler had refused, they met a representative of the former and gave him a letter on behalf of Dimitrov.[41] It is evident that the Thälmann Committee knew that the chances of an actual meeting with Goebbels or Hitler was unlikely, and that the trip had more propaganda value for French public opinion than for its impact on German leaders.[42]

In light of the lack of any newsworthy developments in the case, the committee seized on the tactic of producing streams of visitors who were dispatched to Berlin in the hope of stirring up publicity around almost universally abortive efforts to visit Thälmann. Münzenberg funded delegations of physicians, lawyers and workers from France, Belgium and Switzerland. For example, in March 1934 a Doctor Cord was received by Gestapo *Kriminalrat* Reinhold Heller, as well as Rudolf Diels, chief of the Gestapo, but was unable to gain any information about the health of Thälmann.[43] Just a few days later, a delegation of workers from several Paris enterprises arrived in Berlin and were taken to the Moabit prison. Typically, the visitors enquired about Thälmann's health, or demanded proof of life. Of course, the organisers knew that they were not permitted to see him but that was not their purpose. First and foremost, the visitations called attention to the fact that outside of

Germany the treatment of Thälmann and other prisoners was a matter of public concern.

In May 1934 a new possibility for attracting attention to Thälmann's plight centred on a plan to send a three-man workers' delegation from the Saar to attempt another visit – which of course, as Münzenberg remarked, 'our comrades had helped to organise'.[44] This time, however, the chances of success were augmented by the upcoming 13 January 1935 plebiscite of the Saar region, a coal-rich swatch of German-speaking territory between France and Germany that had been under the trusteeship of the League of Nations since 1919 and was now permitted to choose between either belonging to Germany or remaining under the League. The Saar plebiscite was the focus of an intense National Socialist campaign (*'Heim ins Reich'*) – as well as a Communist-led counter-campaign to maintain the status quo. A number of the Münzenberg men cut their political teeth on this unhappy campaign, including the writer Gustav Regler (who was born in the Saar) and the famous Soviet journalist Ilya Ehrenburg, who reported on the futile campaign for *Izvestia*. Unlike previous petitioners, who were routinely rejected, turning away a three-man workers' delegation from the Saar (composed of SPD members) would hardly demonstrate German government goodwill towards the labourers of the Saar basin, whose votes the Nazis were courting. In the end, the visit turned out to be a minor publicity sensation.[45]

Arriving at the Berlin-Alexanderplatz railway station on 17 May, the delegation went directly to the Reich Justice Ministry where a civil servant assured them that 'Thälmann was doing well and looked just fine'. Though they replied that they 'could hardly doubt the honesty of a German civil servant', one of the delegates countered that their comrades back home would not believe such assurances, and would ask: 'If that is so, why didn't they let you see him and speak to him?' Apparently insulted, the official responded that since so many delegations had been turned away, 'I don't want to be responsible for setting a precedent'. The delegates then asked to see Minister Goebbels, but upon arriving at the Propaganda Ministry they were told to see the man in charge of the Saar Question (*Saar Referent*), a certain Herr [Karl] Kuhlmann, who was currently in Hamburg. At that moment, an SA man appeared and led them out of the building and straight to Gestapo headquarters, where they were forced to wait with a group of women whose husbands had been summoned there and had not returned. The women, told that no information was available about their men, were made to take leave, which they did while tearfully bidding the Gestapo a final (mandatory) 'Heil Hitler'. 'Here we saw', noted the Saar delegates, 'a particularly dramatic example of the constraints under which the German people have to live. The women even had to say 'Heil Hitler' to the tormentors who had robbed them of their men'. So ended the first day. The following morning the delegation went to Moabit prison, where a similar scene transpired – 'Thälmann is OK', and so on. To the surprise of the delegation, however, they were brought face to face with Kuhlmann, who asked them if they had not been afraid at Gestapo headquarters the previous day. '*Jawohl*', they answered in unison and recounted the story of the women, to which he reacted uncomfortably, but soon recovered, and invited them to remain over the holidays (*Pfingsten*) at his expense, offering them some anti-Communist literature. He even suggested without irony that that they might make propaganda for the Third Reich when they returned home. A few hours later, they were brought before yet another ministry official, named Kaufmann,[46] to whom they persisted in emphasising that 'it would be of the greatest importance for the German Reich if we could go home, now, before the plebiscite, and say Ernst Thälmann has not been mistreated. On the following day, they returned to Gestapo headquarters and waited while Kaufmann consulted with Himmler. To their great surprise, Kaufmann reported that Himmler had tentatively approved a visit to Thälmann, and then took them all to lunch (with cigarettes and beer) at the nearby Thomaskeller. In the afternoon, after discussing the political situation in the Saar with Kaufmann and promising to produce a report at the end of their journey, they returned to their hotel. The following morning at 10 AM, after being granted permission at the Gestapo headquarters, the delegation was brought back to Moabit and told that only one of them could see Thälmann. Asked what they would say to him, Kurt Thomas, a member of the Social Democratic Party since 1920 (the man who had been so designated), said: 'I would first and foremost ask him if he had been mistreated or tortured'. That question was of course rejected out of hand. Only the following questions were permitted and were to be put by the accompanying prison official:

1. Do you have enough to eat?
2. Do you receive mail?
3. Are you allowed to write?
4. How often and for how long can you go for a walk?
5. Are you allowed to smoke?
6. Is it possible to buy additional foodstuffs?

'And then the great moment came; we saw Ernst Thälmann, the leader of the German proletariat'. Thälmann told them straight away that the food was insufficient and that without packages from his family he would not survive. He received mail only from his wife, his parents, and from an unnamed plasterer in Saxony. But when Thomas asked spontaneously, 'How are you doing generally in prison?', Thälmann answered that he was being mistreated. As Thomas was ushered out of the room, Thälmann gave the balled-fist salute and shouted: 'I have been, and continue to be, mistreated. Give the Saar workers my greetings'. The interview ended abruptly. The delegation was ushered out of the prison and taken straight back to Kuhlmann at the Propaganda Ministry, where they expected the worst. What transpired next was bizarre. Instead of being arrested, the three were treated to lunch and beer, on 'Joseph' (Goebbels) as their jovial companion from the Propaganda Ministry joked, and they were then escorted on a tour of the Oranienburg concentration camp. Shown the confiscated weapons, badges, and Marxist books ('mostly from Russia'), they were led to a barracks where they spoke to a group of inmates – Communists and Social Democrats – who were forced to sleep stacked three to a bunk in a damp room. The tour continued with a trip to see the dirigibles (Zeppelins) at Tempelhof airfield, at the conclusion of which they were asked to write a brief report on the situation in the Saar. Shocked by the pro-Communist political nature of the resulting text, Herr Kaufmann warned them: 'If I read about any of this in the Saarland press, there will be the devil to pay!' On the following day they returned to Saarbrücken.

The episode was recounted (minus the beer and tours) in the international press and the final words of Thälmann, the balled fist and the abrupt conclusion of the interview widely disseminated. The *Pariser Zeitung*, for example, featured the incident in a story entitled 'With Thälmann in prison'.[47] Once again, the Propaganda Ministry was trumped by the Münzenberg operation. Perhaps the ministry saw the potential for a small victory among Saar workers – most of whom did vote for annexation. The dramatic scene was not to be repeated – no other visitors were ever permitted to speak with Thälmann, and his contact with the outside world was severely restricted. However, the tactic of political visitations carefully organised in Paris continued unabated, 'almost daily' according to the pro-Nazi *Hamburger Anzeiger*.[48] A youth group that attempted to visit him on 15 August 1934 reported on their failed effort to a crowd of twelve hundred (according to the police) on 4 September.[49] In August 1935, an international criminal law congress convened in Berlin.[50] The anti-Nazi and democratic jurists who attended the congress from a variety of countries, including Austria, Rumania, France, Belgium and Great Britain, were told that 'Thälmann did not like visitors'. After protests from the French, Belgian and Spanish delegations, a compromise was reached: delegations could see the prisoner from outside his window and visit Thälmann's cell in his absence.[51] Some fifty jurists were taken to Moabit prison where they were permitted to observe Thälmann for a moment while walking in the prison yard from the window of a gallery on the second floor. Among them was the French attorney Pierre Kaldor, who was also a member of the International Thälmann Committee in Paris. According to the visitors, Thälmann appeared 'sickly'.[52]

Visiting Thälmann or, more accurately, attempting to visit him, had become a political tactic that emerged in the course of 1934 and continued until he was moved to a less accessible prison in Hanover in August 1937. Given the apparent decision not to try Thälmann in November 1935, the planned visit of delegations (and their almost certain refusal) to Berlin was accelerated.[53] In 1936 alone, some twenty delegations from all over Europe travelled to Berlin and other German cities in support of Thälmann and other imprisoned antifascists, though only a fraction were able to reach their destinations. Nazi authorities, so the committee reported, simply 'sat them in a chair near the door'. Only rarely 'did the delegations succeed in attracting the attention or support of the foreign press representatives in Germany'.[54] In August, 1934, for example, a delegation of ten antifascist youths from England, Spain and France was briefly detained in Berlin.[55] But such publicity-generating incidents were in the main avoided by the German authorities, who plainly understood the purpose of such visits and kept the delegations far from Thälmann.

The absent Thälmann, rendered voiceless by his Nazi captors and virtually invisible to his visitors, was made into a pastiche of iconography – writing desk, glasses, pipe – by his Communist saviours, and subsequently symbolically conjoined with the German volunteers in Spain: 'Their heroism was to stand beside the mutual heroism of Thälmann'.[56] A carefully cultivated image of 'Teddy' (his popular nickname) Thälmann as the most prominent Communist prisoner of the Nazis began to take shape. His proletarian visage, Hamburg sailor cap and ubiquitous pipe appeared on countless brochures and in the exile press. Revered as a true son of the working class, the most popular Weimar party leader, adored by workers and schoolchildren, Thälmann emerged as the 'symbol of the antifascist struggle in Germany and in the entire world', a public image that was elaborated, recirculated and refurbished during its half century as a state cult in the GDR.[57] Through radio broadcasts, interviews and newspaper articles, and through Popular Front organisations, the Thälmann campaign was increasingly tied to, if not overwhelmed by, publicity on behalf of the volunteers in Spain. Funds collected on his behalf were in large part funnelled to support for the Spanish Republicans.[58]

In October 1936, Wilhelm Pieck sent a brief note to Dimitrov, general secretary of the Comintern, informing him that Thälmann's health was labile (*Schwankend*), and he was suffering from nose and anal bleeding, but that his mood was generally good and that he received regular visits from his wife. However, Pieck added, 'There is a heightened sense that there will be no trial', adding, apparently on the basis of inaccurate information, that he had been moved from Berlin.[59]

Of greater consequence was the 1994 publication of Thälmann's secret (smuggled out by his wife and daughter) prison letters to Stalin, and his notes from 1939 to 1941, which reveal that, despite his very real suffering in the 'darkest prison of Germany's fascist hell', his 'friend' Stalin gave little thought to the possibility of securing the freedom of his most loyal German comrade – even when the pact with Hitler posed just such an opportunity. In August 1939 the Hitler–Stalin pact seemed, at least for the first year, to portend a new opportunity for his release. These letters (in reality a mixture of congratulatory epistles, personal notations, and in the later stages, newspaper summaries) attest to Thälmann's growing despair and the crushing of his hopes. Stalin, one can only hypothesise, was not interested in having two incorruptible Communist heroes in Moscow (Dimitrov had already assumed the role) and Thälmann could be counted on to remain a mute symbol – as he proved to be – only if he remained in prison. Thälmann's reactions to news of the Molotov–Ribbentrop pact of 23 August 1939, which he believed would lead to his release, are a poignant reminder of the cruelty of the Soviet leader and the abject loyalty of his minions. Of course, Thälmann tried to make sense of the consequences of the pact, not merely for global political realities, but for his own situation. 'The hour of my liberation is now hopefully soon to come. I am completely convinced, that in the negotiations in Moscow between Stalin and Molotov on the one hand, and Ribbentrop and Graf (Count) von der Schulenburg on the other, that the case of Thälmann has been raised.'[60]

The 'real' Thälmann, or at least the Thälmann evident in these letters, displays – as one can imagine many German communists must have felt – a combination of abject loyalty, confusion and despair at the news of the pact. Given his personal situation, his need to accept, indeed even to proclaim Stalin's decision as something he had 'wished and hoped for', is understandable.[61] On his 55th birthday and ninth year of imprisonment he acknowledged that, after 1939, his fate was apparently no longer of great concern to Stalin who did not especially want such an important a figure in Moscow – a feeling no doubt shared by Wilhelm Pieck, Walter Ulbricht and Franz Dahlem, the new 'foreign' party leadership elected after the Seventh Congress. Besides Thälmann's realisation that Stalin would do nothing on his behalf, there is one other dimension to these letters that cannot be left uncommented: Thälmann's anti-Semitism. Though it is not entirely clear why, his first reaction included the previously uncharacteristic line: 'The international campaign of the Jews (*Judentum*) against Germany has had an impact on the German people, that has until now not registered the importance of the Jews in the world in all its magnitude'.[62] A sop to his jailers? An appeal to Stalin's baser instincts, especially in the new circumstance of an alliance with National Socialism? Thälmann's own anti-Semitism bubbling to the surface? No ready answer is at hand.

The campaign to free Thälmann was in many ways the mirror opposite of the Reichstag fire campaign. It revealed many of the weaknesses of Comintern-inspired antifascism in the 1930s. Mass mobilisation was difficult to sustain in the case of a German Communist leader, especially when the Comintern's denunciation of the non-Communist and Social Democratic left was relentless. Despite Münzenberg's creative deployment of the 'visit' to call attention to Thälmann's plight, his captors were sometimes able to manipulate visitors to their own advantage. More importantly, the National Socialist regime became adept at preventing the kind of propaganda debacle they suffered in the Reichstag fire trial. Despite the well-organised efforts of the committee in Paris, one observer noted: '[I]nternational protests, which we support with all our energy, are of little help. Those who terrorise are entirely insensitive to protests – they only bend before power! Dimitrov was only saved when Göring understood that the Soviet Union – which had a monopoly on foreign trade and a Red Army – would become involved'.[63] The Comintern was also virtually destroyed in Stalin's terror. At Stalin's orders, 133 out of 492 Comintern staff members became victims of the 'Great Purge', and several hundred German Communists and antifascists who had either fled from Nazi Germany or were convinced to relocate in the Soviet Union were murdered. Once antifascism became the official policy of the Soviet Union, all non-Communist antifascists were suspect and supraparty organisations, most notably Münzenberg's, came under intense scrutiny. In November 1937, Münzenberg was accused of being a 'Trotskyite', which, as Münzenberg well knew, carried a death sentence, and his organisation was rapidly shut down and its funds confiscated.[64] Ironically, in the era of the popular fronts what was left of the Comintern was reduced to a weapon to assert Soviet authority beyond its borders. Many of Thälmann's closest associates were victims of Stalin's murderous 1937 purge.[65] As a potential threat to Stalin and a rival to the KPD exile leadership of Wilhelm Pieck and Walter Ulbricht in Moscow, the Molotov–Ribbentrop pact definitively ended Communist efforts on Thälmann's behalf. He remained in prison, rarely acknowledged, until he was brought to Buchenwald to be murdered, eight years later.

Notes

1. A.M. Grimm, *Hindenburg: Sein Horoskop und diejenigen von Marx, Hellpach, Ludendorff, Thälmann, Jarres, Held, Hitler*, Selbstverlag A.M. Grimm, 1925.
2. Heinrich Himmler, Reichsführer SS, note on a conversation with Adolf Hitler at the Wolfsschanze, 14 August 1944. Buchenwald Concentration Camp Museum, exhibition vitrine 4/31.
3. W. Münzenberg, *Propaganda als Waffe*, Paris, 1934.
4. For a comprehensive survey of Thälmann's career and subsequent mythologisation after 1945, see R. Lemmons, *Hitler's Rival: Ernst Thälmann in Myth and Memory*, Lexington, KY, 2013. A more polemical account is T. Gabelmann, *Thälmann ist niemals gefallen: Eine Legende Stirbt*, Berlin, 1996. An overview of Comintern policies in the 1930s is in J. Agnew and K. McDermott (eds), *The Comintern: History of International Communism from Lenin to Stalin*, London, 1996. On the role of Willi Münzenberg in orchestrating the Comintern campaigns in the 1930s, see S. McMeekin, *The Red Millionaire: A Political Biography of Willy Münzenberg, Moscow's Secret Propaganda Tsar in the West, 1917–1940*, New Haven, CT, 2004. The Reichstag Fire campaign is discussed in A. Rabinbach, 'Staging Antifascism: The Brown Book of the Hitler Terror', *New German Critique* 103, 35(1) (Spring 2008): 97–126. On popular front antifascism in France, see A. Rabinbach, 'Paris, Capital of Antifascism', in W. Breckman et al. (eds), *The Modernist Imagination: Intellectual History and Critical Theory Essays in Honor of Martin Jay*, New York and Oxford, 2009, 183–210.
5. 'Trotz Freispruchs weiter in Haft', *Pariser Tageblatt* 1(13) (24 December 1933), 1.
6. 'Deutsche Nachrichtenbüro', *Internationale Pressekorrespondenz*, 4 March 1934, 404.
7. 'Das blutdürstige Schwein: Göring über Torgler, Thälmann und F. Seger', *Neuer Vorwärts* 46, 29 April 1934, 2. For the background, see N. Podewin and L. Heuer, *Ernst Torgler: ein Leben im Schatten des Reichstagsbrandes: 25.04.1893 Berlin – 19.01.1963 Hannover*, Berlin, 2006, 133.
8. 'Acquitted, but not Released!', *Internationale Pressekorrespondenz*, 5 January 1934, 10.
9. 'Die Tagebücher von Joseph Goebbels', in Elke Fröhlich (ed.), *Auftrag des Instituts für Zeitgeschichte und mit Unterstützung des Staatlichen Archivdienstes Russlands* (III, October 1932 – March 1934). Munich and New York, 1998–2005, 343.
10. R.G. Reuth, *Joseph Goebbels, Tagebücher*, Munich, 1992, vol. 2, 905.

11. On the Wittorf affair, see Gabelmann, *Thälmann ist niemals gefallen*, 38–47.
12. E. Thälmann, *Im Kampf gegen die fascistische Diktatur (1932)*, 16–17, cited in D. Pike, *Lukács and Brecht*, Chapel Hill, NC, 1985, 79, n. 21.
13. Lemmons, *Hitler's Rival*, 73.
14. 'Compte-rendu sur l'activité du Comité d'aide français aux victimes du fascisme hitlérien', in G. Badia et al. (eds), *Les bannis de Hitler. Accueil et luttes des exilés en France 1933–1939*, Vincennes, 1984, 202.
15. Rossiiskii gosudarstvennyi arkhiv sotsial'no-politicheskoi istorii (Russian State Archive of Socio-Political History, RGASPI), and Agency Federal'noe arkhivnoe agentstvo Rossii (Ros. 1917–1940). Cited as RGASPI, 495.60.246, 10 February 1934.
16. H. Gruber, 'Willi Münzenberg's German Communist Propaganda Empire 1921–1933', *The Journal of Modern History* 38(3) (September 1966), 278–97.
17. McMeekin, *Red Millionaire*.
18. D.J. Fischer, *Romain Rolland and the Politics of Intellectual Engagement*, Berkeley, 1988, 147–77.
19. RGASPI, F495. op.60. d.246., Berlin, 12 April 1933; 'An das Amsterdamer Komitee in Prag zu Händen der Architekt Kreutzer'.
20. Ibid.
21. P. Broué, *Histoire de l'Internationale communiste, 1919–1943*, Paris, 1997, 548–49.
22. A. Wat, *My Century: The Odyssey of a Polish Intellectual*, trans. R. Lourie, New York, 1988, 145–46.
23. Badia, *Les bannis de Hitler*, 202.
24. Bundesarchiv Berlin-Lichterfelde (BArch) NY 4003/56, 'Rechtsanwälte für Thälmann', 13 November 1935.
25. BArch, NY 4003/56, 'Die Thälmann-Kampagne von Juli 1936 bis Juni 1937', 17.
26. The December 1933 exchange of telegrams published in A. Dallin and F.I. Firsov (eds), *Dimitrov and Stalin, 1934–1943: Letters from the Soviet Archives*, New Haven, CT, 2000, and the correspondence between Göring's ministry and the Soviet ambassador in Berlin in the Comintern Archives offer no support whatsoever for the canard that a deal had been struck between Stalin and Hitler to free the Bulgarian communist defendants even before the trial began. For the most egregious example of this legend, see S. Koch, *Double Lives: Spies and Writers in the Secret Soviet War of Ideas Against the West*, New York, 1993. After the not guilty verdict was read, KPD chairman Wilhelm Pieck sent a telegram to Osip Piatnitsky, a member of the political secretariat of the ECCI and the senior Soviet official responsible for the Reichstag fire campaign, suggesting that '[i]t would be politically expedient if the Sov[iet] gov[ernment] is prepared to offer Com[rade] Dimitrov and the other Bulgarian com[rades] the right of asylum in the USSR'. The message was forwarded to Stalin on 29 December 1933. Bulgaria in the meantime had deprived the defendants of citizenship. On 16 February 1934 the Soviet embassy in Berlin sent a note informing the German foreign office that the three Bulgarians had been granted Soviet citizenship and requesting their prompt release to the Soviet Union (Dallin and Firsov, *Dimitrov and Stalin*,

5–6). See also Firsov, 'Stalin und die Komintern', *Voprosy istorii* 9 (1989), 11. On 26 February 1934, the day before the Bulgarians were flown to Moscow, Göring, in whose name the prisoners were to be released, registered his outrage at a 'premature suspension of the imprisonment imposed on Dimitrov, Popov and Tanev'. The presumption that Dimitrov's demeanor in the court could only be explained by his having a priori knowledge of an arrangement to free him is belied by his diaries. See B.H. Bayerlein (ed.), *Georgi Dimitroff, Tagebücher 1933–1945*, Berlin, 2001, 72, 89. In short, there was no pretrial deal. The origin of this myth is R. Fischer, *Stalin under deutsche Kommunismus*, Bd. 2., *Die Bolschewisierung des deutschen Kommunismus ab 1925*, Berlin, 1991, 337–38. See also R. Diels, *Lucifer ante Portas: Zwischen Severing und Heydrich*, Zurich, 1949, 268–70.

27. E. Czichon et al. (eds), *Thälmann: ein Report*, Berlin, 2010, 746.

28. A. Fuhrer, *Ernst Thälmann: Soldat des Proletariats*, Munich, 2011, 307; R. Sassning, *Zur NS-Haftzeit Ernst Thälmanns*, Berlin, 1997, 38.

29. '"Release Thälmann" Again', *Manchester Guardian Weekly* (22 October 1934), 1.

30. H. Barbusse, *Do You Know Thälmann?*, New York, 1934, 1.

31. Cited in A. Leo, '"Deutschlands unsterblicher Sohn…" der Held des Widerstands Ernst Thälmann', in R. Gries and S. Satjukow (eds), *Sozialistische Helden. Eine Kulturgeschichte von Propagandafiguren in Osteuropa und der DDR*, Berlin, 2002, 106.

32. BArch, NY 4003/56, 'Die Finanzlage des Internationalen Thälmann-Komitees', n.d.

33. 'Französischer Juristenprotest gegen Thälmann-Prozess', *Pariser Tageblatt* 2(158), 19 May 1934, 2.

34. W. Pieck, 'The "People's Court" of the Hitler Dictatorship', *Internationale Pressekorrespondenz*, 1 May 1934, 757.

35. 'Thälmann's Trial', *Manchester Guardian*, 16 October 1934, 1.

36. New York Public Library (*C+p.v.3184), mimeographed document, International Committee for the liberation of THAELMANN and all the imprisoned antifascists, Paris, 1935, 3.

37. Lemmons, *Hitler's Rival*, 65.

38. BArch, NY 4003/56, 'Die Thälmann-Kampagne von Juli 1936 bis Juni 1937', 3.

39. Ibid., 'Die Einschätzung der Gesamt-Entwicklung der Thälmann and Antiterror-Kampagne', 25 June 1937 (signed by Belfort). The claim that of all antifascist organisations created in France the Thälmann Committee was 'the most effective' (*le plus efficace*) is patently false. See Badia, *Les bannis de Hitler*, 199.

40. Lemmons, *Hitler's Rival*, 96.

41. Malraux's 1972 recollection that the two actually met Goebbels has long since been disproved. J. Lacouture, *Malraux: une vie dans le siècle* [new edn], Paris, 1976; H. Godard and J.-L. Jeannelle (eds), *Modernite du Miroir des limbes: un autre Malraux*, Paris, 2011; C. Malraux, *Le bruit de nos pas*, Paris, 1992; R.S. Thornberry, *André Malraux et l'Espagne*, Geneva, 1977, 20, 237–38.

42. For the claim that Malraux and Gide were 'duped', see Koch, *Double Lives*, 123–24. The entire affair is discussed in detail in G. Schmigalle, 'Malraux

et Münzenberg: sur un livre de fausses révélations', http://www.andremal-raux.com/malraux/articles/Schmigalle.pdf (visited on 18 November 2005). Also see O. Todd, *Malraux: A Life*, trans. J. West, New York, 2005, 103.
43. Badia, *Les bannis de Hitler*, 219.
44. RGASPI, 495.60.246, 'Deutsche Kampagne – Kampf um Thälmann', 8 June 1934.
45. 'Report of the Saar Delegation for Ernst Thälmann', RGASPI, 495.60.246, 'Deutsche Kampagne – Kampf um Thälmann', 8 June 1934.
46. Possibly Karl Kaufmann, Gauleiter of Hamburg.
47. 'Bei Thälmann im Gefängnis: Erster Besuch von Arbeiter-Delegierten in Berlin', *Pariser Tageblatt* 2(163), 24 May 1934, 2.
48. 'Sie wollen Thälmann Besuchen', *Hamburger Anzeiger*, 26 April 1934, 2.
49. Cited in Badia, *Les bannis de Hitler*, 223.
50. Lemmons, *Hitler's Rival*, 65.
51. 'Göbbelstheater in einer Moabiter Zelle: Thälmann liebt keine Besuche', *Pariser Tageblatt* 3(621), 28 August 1935, 2.
52. 'Mittelalterlicher oder zivilsierter Strafvollzug?', *Pariser Tageblatt* 3(620), 24 August 1935, 2.
53. BArch, NY 4003/56, 'Budget', 17 March 1936.
54. Ibid., 'Bemerkungen zu Thälmannkampagne', n.d.
55. 'Arrestation d'une delegation de la jeunesse antifasciste Internationale', *Le Temps*, 30 August 1934.
56. BArch, NY 4003/56, 'Die Thälmann-Kampagne von Juli 1936 bis Juni 1937', 11.
57. See Lemmons, *Hitler's Rival*; and René Börrnet, *Ernst Thälmann als Leitfigur der kommunistischen Erziehung in der DDR*, Braunschweig, 2003.
58. BArch, NY 4003/56, 'Die Thälmann-Kampagne von Juli 1936 bis Juni 1937', 12.
59. Ibid., Wilhelm Pieck to Georgii Dimitroff, 21 October 1936.
60. E. Thälmann, *An Stalin: Briefe aus dem Zuchthaus 1939 bis 1941*, eds W. Adolphi and J. Schütrumpf, Berlin, 1994, 35.
61. Ibid., 14.
62. Ibid., 19.
63. E.H. Carr, *Twilight of the Comintern 1930–35*, New York, 1983, 120.
64. R. Müller, 'Bericht des Komintern-Emissärs Bohumir Šmeral über seinen Pariser Aufenthalt 1937' (Document), in *Exil und Remigration. Exilforschung: Ein Internationales Jahrbuch* 9 (1991), 236–61.
65. Broué, *Histoire de l'Internationale communiste*, 724–25.

References

Agnew, J., and K. McDermott (eds). *The Comintern: History of International Communism from Lenin to Stalin*. London, 1996.
Badia, G., et al. (eds). *Les bannis de Hitler. Accueil et luttes des exilés en France 1933–1939*. Vincennes, 1984.
Barbusse, H. *Do You Know Thälmann?* New York, 1934.

Bayerlein, B.H. (ed.). *Georgi Dimitroff, Tagebücher 1933–1945.* Berlin, 2001.
Börrnet, R. *Ernst Thälmann als Leitfigur der kommunistischen Erziehung in der DDR.* Braunschweig, 2003.
Broué, P. *Histoire de l'Internationale communiste, 1919–1943.* Paris, 1997.
Carr, E.H. *Twilight of the Comintern 1930–35.* New York, 1983.
Czichon, E., et al. (eds). *Thälmann: ein Report.* Berlin, 2010.
Dallin, A., and F.I. Firsov (eds). *Dimitrov and Stalin, 1934–1943: Letters from the Soviet Archives.* New Haven, CT, 2000.
'Die Tagebücher von Joseph Goebbels', in E. Fröhlich (ed.), *Auftrag des Instituts für Zeitgeschichte und mit Unterstützung des Staatlichen Archivdienstes Russlands.* Munich and New York, 1998–2005.
Diels, R. *Lucifer ante Portas: Zwischen Severing und Heydrich.* Zurich, 1949.
Firsov, F.I. 'Stalin und die Komintern', *Voprosy istorii* 9 (1989), 3–19.
Fischer, D.J. *Romain Rolland and the Politics of Intellectual Engagement.* Berkeley, 1988.
Fischer, R. *Stalin under deutsche Kommunismus, Bd. 2., Die Bolschewisierung des deutschen Kommunismus ab 1925.* Berlin, 1991.
Fuhrer, A. *Ernst Thälmann: Soldat des Proletariats.* Munich, 2011.
Gabelmann, T. *Thälmann ist niemals gefallen: Eine Legende Stirbt.* Berlin, 1996.
Godard, H., and J.-L. Jeannelle (eds). *Modernité du Miroir des limbes: un autre Malraux.* Paris, 2011.
Grimm, A.M. *Hindenburg: Sein Horoskop und diejenigen von Marx, Hellpach, Ludendorff, Thälmann, Jarres, Held, Hitler.* Selbstverlag A.M. Grimm, 1925.
Gruber, H. 'Willi Münzenberg's German Communist Propaganda Empire 1921–1933', *The Journal of Modern History* 38(3) (September 1966), 278–97.
Koch, S. *Double Lives: Spies and Writers in the Secret Soviet War of Ideas Against the West.* New York, 1993.
Lacouture, J. *Malraux: une vie dans le siècle.* Paris, 1976.
Lemmons, R. *Hitler's Rival: Ernst Thälmann in Myth and Memory.* Lexington, KY, 2013.
Leo, A. '"Deutschlands unsterblicher Sohn…" der Held des Widerstands Ernst Thälmann', in R. Gries and S. Satjukow (eds), *Sozialistische Helden. Eine Kulturgeschichte von Propagandafiguren in Osteuropa und der DDR.* Berlin, 2002.
Malraux, C. *Le Bruit de nos pas.* Paris, 1992.
McMeekin, S. *The Red Millionaire: A Political Biography of Willy Münzenberg, Moscow's Secret Propaganda Tsar in the West, 1917–1940.* New Haven, CT, 2004.
Müller, R. 'Bericht des Komintern-Emissärs Bohumir Šmeral über seinen Pariser Aufenthalt 1937' (Document), in *Exil und Remigration. Exilforschung: Ein Internationales Jahrbuch* 9. Munich, 1991.
Münzenberg, W. *Propaganda als Waffe.* Paris, 1934.
Pike, D. *Lukács and Brecht.* Chapel Hill, NC, 1985.
Podewin, N., and L. Heuer. *Ernst Torgler: ein Leben im Schatten des Reichstagsbrandes: 25.04.1893 Berlin – 19.01.1963 Hannover.* Berlin, 2006.
Rabinbach, A. 'Paris, Capital of Antifascism', in W. Breckman et al. (eds), *The Modernist Imagination: Intellectual History and Critical Theory Essays in Honor of Martin Jay.* New York and Oxford, 2009, 183–210.

———. 'Staging Antifascism: The Brown Book of the Hitler Terror'. *New German Critique* 103, 35(1) (Spring 2008), 97–126.

Reuth, R.G. *Joseph Goebbels, Tagebücher*. Munich, 1992, vol. 2.

Sassning, R. *Zur NS-Haftzeit Ernst Thälmanns*. Berlin, 1997.

Thälmann, E. *An Stalin: Briefe aus dem Zuchthaus 1939 bis 1941*, eds Wolfram Adolphi and Jörn Schütrumpf. Berlin, 1994.

Thornberry, R.S. *André Malraux et l'Espagne*. Geneva, 1977.

Todd, O. *Malraux: A Life*, trans. Joseph West. New York, 2005.

Wat, A. *My Century: The Odyssey of a Polish Intellectual*, trans. Richard Lourie. New York, 1988.

Anson Rabinbach is Philip and Beulah Rollins Professor of History at Princeton University and was director of the Program in European Cultural Studies from 1998 to 2009. He has been awarded fellowships at the American Academy, Berlin (2005) and by the Guggenheim Foundation. As a Fulbright Senior Scholar he was visiting professor at Smolny College, St Petersburg (2004), at the Institute for Twentieth-Century History Jena (2009), the Simon-Dubnow Institut (Leipzig, 2014), and was a fellow at the École des Hautes Etudes en Sciences Sociales, Paris. His research focuses on the cultural and intellectual history of modern Europe. Among his books are: *The Crisis of Austrian Socialism: From Red Vienna to Civil War 1927–1934* (1981), *The Human Motor: Energy, Fatigue, and the Origins of Modernity* (1991), and *In the Shadow of Catastrophe: German Intellectuals between Apocalypse and Enlightenment* (1996). He has recently completed a documentary history of Nazi Germany, *The Third Reich Sourcebook*, co-edited with Sander Gilman (2013). His current research is a conceptual history of the twentieth century, entitled 'Concepts that Came in from the Cold: Total War, Totalitarianism, Genocide'.

2

WAS THE FRENCH POPULAR FRONT ANTIFASCIST?

Michael Seidman

Compared with its enemy, antifascism has received little attention. Publications about fascism far outnumber those on antifascism. A WorldCat keyword search for fascism revealed 57,000 titles, whereas another for antifascism found only 1,300. Yet in almost all Western countries – except, of course, Italy, Germany and Spain – fascism was a failure, and antifascism a success. It became perhaps the most powerful ideology of the twentieth century. Surprisingly, no historian or social scientist has attempted to define the nature, types and history of antifascisms.

During the interwar period, the more antifascism encompassed a broad range of opinion, the more successful it became. It sought consensus, not synthesis. Historians and social scientists have ignored the inclusiveness and diversity of antifascism – ideological, religious and racial – and many have identified antifascism as an ecumenical movement which was primarily, if not exclusively, a movement of the left or, at least, 'democratic'.

My own definition differs, and proposes a tripartite minimum. First, antifascism made working or fighting against fascism the top priority, which meant a rejection of uncompromising anti-Communism and anti-capitalism. Antifascists recognised the need to collaborate with Communists and capitalists, even though conservative antifascists completely opposed the Soviet model, and revolutionary antifascists the liberal one. Antifascists chose to fight a multi-front war against the Axis, not the Soviet Union or the Western Allies. The anti-appeasers knew that you could remain particular about your friends, but not about your allies. Second, antifascism refused conspiratorial theories that charged that plotting by both plutocrats and Jews was responsible for negative social, economic and political developments, especially preparations for an antifascist war.[1] Antifascists rejected this form of anti-Semitism, even if they shared other varieties. In direct contrast to the German National Socialists, most of them did not regard the Jewish issue as central. Third, antifascists refused pacifism and believed that state power was necessary to stop both domestic fascisms and the Axis war machine. They risked their empires to fight a long and global war to stop the spread of fascism. Antifascism meant concrete sacrifice, not merely hostile attitudes, to defeat fascism.[2]

Like fascism, antifascism adopted distinct forms in different periods. Two basic types of antifascism emerged from 1936 to 1945. The first was the revolutionary antifascism promoted by most Republican parties and unions during the Spanish Civil War (1936–39) and often dominant in countries, like Spain, with a weak bourgeoisie. Revolutionary antifascism engaged in terror, collectivisation of private property, and violent anti-clericalism. It identified capitalism with fascism, and was uninterested in the considerable differences between Italian and German fascisms or between fascist and authoritarian regimes. The revolutionary antifascism of the Spanish conflict encouraged the end of pacifism among sectors of the left, but because of the Spanish Republic's disrespect for private property and its violent anti-clericalism it did not prefigure – as many have argued – the antifascist alliance of the Second World War. Revolutionary antifascism re-emerged in Eastern Europe with the Hitler–Stalin pact (August 1939 – June 1941), when it influenced the behaviour of the American, British and French Communist parties, which condemned the war as 'imperialist'. Like the appeasers in the 1930s, Communists in this period preferred pacifism to antifascism. Revolutionary antifascism also revived at the end of the Second World War when it became the official ideology of the Soviet bloc and helped to lend it legitimacy against a new adversary – the 'fascist' West. As in the Republican zone during the Spanish Civil War, revolutionary antifascism in the new 'popular democracies' labelled as 'fascist' any opposition – including workers' strikes and revolts – against Communist-supported governments.

The second type of antifascism was non-revolutionary and even counter-revolutionary. The lack of reflection on this variety of antifascism mirrors the general historiographical neglect of counter-revolutions (another WorldCat keyword search shows revolution with 1,200,000 entries and counter-revolution with 5,000). The most important study has neglected to examine conservative antifascism as a variety of counter-revolution. It describes a variety of counter-revolutions but associates all of them with 'monopolistic control of state and government by a new political elite', a definition that certainly does not describe the Atlantic counter-revolutions at the end of the Second World War.[3] The lack of discussion concerning the character of antifascism stands in sharp contrast to the constant debate over fascism's revolutionary or counter-revolutionary nature. The conflation of the two forms of antifascism has muddled many analyses.[4]

Counter-revolutionary antifascism defended – although not always by democratic means – the old regimes of liberal democracy. Of course, the 'counter-revolutionary' label is no more popular than 'fascist'. For example, the American government called its attempt to turn back Communist revolution in Vietnam and elsewhere 'counter-insurgency', not counter-revolution. In a similar way, counter-revolutionary antifascism never claimed to be restoring the old order but rather instituting a new and more hopeful period of history for which it – like other counter-revolutions – was willing to fight.[5]

The French Popular Front fostered a hesitant counter-revolutionary anti-fascism. Neither fascism nor the extreme right ever came into power during the Popular Front period beginning in June 1936 when its government took power and ending in November 1938 when the forty-hour week was terminated. French antifascism rallied the left against the exaggerated threat of domestic 'fascism' rather than combating its more lethal foreign strand.[6] Although the leftist coalition was successful in opposing the domestic extreme right, the Popular Front was unable and unwilling to stop fascist expansionism abroad. French antifascists were more willing to fight Colonel de la Rocque than Adolf Hitler: 'The 6 February 1934 hides the 30 January 1933'.[7]

The Popular Front originated from the struggle against what was perceived to be internal fascism – the alleged coup de force by the right-wing leagues of 6 February 1934. Using physical and verbal violence, the *ligueurs* attempted to assault the Palais Bourbon, the symbol of parliamentary power in France.[8] Various scandals involving major political figures had partially discredited the Third Republic (1870–1940) and encouraged the extreme right to attack and to attempt to overthrow it. However, the police proved loyal to the regime and prevented the demonstrators from reaching the National Assembly. During the confrontations, fifteen died, fourteen of whom were members of the right-wing leagues, and nearly fifteen hundred were injured.[9] Street pressure led to the formation of a government of 'national union' which included right-wing parliamentarians and, for the first time, Marshal Philippe Pétain. The left believed that the extreme right had tried unsuccessfully to imitate Benito Mussolini's March on Rome, and it equated the right – including the conservative government of 'national union' – with what Léon Blum called 'la réaction fasciste'.[10] Socialists – including intellectuals like Blum – used the 'fascist' label almost as indiscriminately as Communists.

The fear of domestic fascism inspired the leftist unity of the Popular Front. The major organisations of the left became committed to the defence of the democratic and capitalist parliamentary Republic. Activists began to invigorate a movement 'against war and fascism', one year after Hitler had taken power. On 12 February 1934 the CGT (Confédération générale du travail) called for a general strike to defend the Republic.[11] As in the other democracies, trade unionists opposed fascism as a form of union busting. When the unions' defence against fascism was connected to work stoppages, the results were impressive: 45 per cent of workers in Paris and the provinces followed the general strike, and the Parisian demonstration assembled three hundred thousand.[12] Antifascism easily outmatched its enemy in the streets.

The antifascism of the French Popular Front became a non-revolutionary ideology. With their Socialist and Radical coalition partners, Communists mobilised and temporarily defended the French Republic, a position that allowed them, perhaps for the first time, to become integrated into the nation.[13] This new orientation reflected the progressive, although uneven, 'nationalisation' of the PCF (Parti communiste français).[14] Negotiations between the major labour federations, the Communist CGTU (Confédération générale du travail unitaire) and the non-Communist CGT began and eventually culminated in reunification of the CGT in March 1936. Thus, Communist trade unionists joined centrist and rightist Socialists who wanted to combat fascism by bolstering democratic and parliamentary traditions.

The enlightened middle classes who wished to protect Republican liberties were also supportive of the antifascist coalition. The Radicals were the swing party of the Third Republic and represented a large portion of the French middle classes. Even though many of their constituents were sceptical of the Popular Front's economic programme – especially its limitation of the working week to forty hours – the Radicals joined the alliance and confirmed its parliamentary prospective. In many districts Radical deputies often depended upon the votes of Communists and Socialists to win elections. Freemasons, whose members included prominent Radicals, were particularly active, and founded numerous Popular Front committees throughout France.[15]

The Popular Front won the May 1936 general elections, and in June Blum became the first Socialist and first Jew to become prime minister in France. In contrast to Spain, where full-scale revolution erupted in the Republican zone after the civil war broke out, the stability of the French state and society precluded large-scale political and anti-clerical violence and spontaneous collectivisation of private property. Nevertheless, wage earners took advantage of the Socialist Blum's stated reluctance to use force against them by launching a great strike wave when he took office in June. Workers occupied factories, thereby exceeding the programme of the Popular Front, which called for a shorter working week, higher wages, paid vacations, and nationalisation of defence industries. The work stoppages of June were followed by many months of resistance to work – absenteeism, lateness, fake illnesses, low productivity, slowdowns, indiscipline, indifference, and even sabotage. These actions and attitudes generally harmed output and decreased productivity. Indiscipline that challenged industrial hierarchy was hardly compatible with the greater commodity consumption that the Popular Front had promised. More than any other aspect of the Popular Front programme, the work stoppages and the subsequent refusal to work in large factories alienated conservative and centrist members of the Radical party who believed that nefarious Communist manoeuvres encouraged workplace indiscipline which was damaging the French economy. Despite the tireless efforts of an active extreme left, the work stoppages did not become revolutionary. Workers wanted higher pay and less work, not an anarchist, councilist or Soviet revolution.

The Popular Front prefigured the Vichy regime by fighting more against the internal than the external enemy. When it began to govern in June 1936, it banned the right-wing leagues that had participated in the riot of 6 February – the Croix de Feu, Jeunesses Patriotes, Solidarité française and Francisme. These prohibitions obtained broad support from influential centrist French politicians, such as Laurent Bonnevay, deputy from the Rhône since 1902. Bonnevay considered himself a 'moderate Republican' but not 'moderately republican'. In other words, he was fully committed to the conservative Third Republic and supported the disarmament of the extreme-right leagues.

Also, like Vichy, the Popular Front sought to reconcile workers with the middle classes. Yet the forty-hour week divided the two classes. Wage earners certainly considered it the most significant antifascist reform. They correctly identified fascism with a long and tiring work routine for low wages. However, for many peasants, small business owners and the elderly, the strict application of the short working week was legislated laziness, as workers in other major European nations, especially Germany, were labouring many more hours. The goal of the forty-hour week was to stimulate the economy, but the limited number of available skilled workers created a production bottleneck. Higher wages produced an inflationary situation where more money was available to purchase the same or diminishing number of commodities. In France in 1937, when the forty-hour week was in effect in many industrial branches, production was 25 per cent inferior to that of 1929, whereas Great Britain and Germany had significantly exceeded their 1929 levels.[16]

The briefer working week showed the ambivalent nature of Socialist and even Communist antifascism, since the PCF and its followers in the CGT fought hard to preserve a working week that hindered French arms production. In metallurgical factories, the forty-hour week obligated employers to hire relatively unskilled workers who were less productive than their more experienced counterparts.[17] The inability of the limited numbers of skilled workers to work more than forty hours, when prior to the Popular Front legislation they had laboured 52 to 60 hours, resulted in a significant loss of production.[18] In addition, the unions increased their power on the shop floor and encouraged an atmosphere of resistance to wage labour. The spread of permissiveness may have pleased workers after the long working weeks and harsh discipline of the early 1930s, but worker gains alienated employers and their supervisory personnel. A good number of both became more sympathetic to fascism, which they identified with tighter workplace discipline and higher output.[19]

The inability to fight foreign fascism was an analytical as well as political failure. Antifascists of all sorts were stuck in nineteenth-century concepts. For most of the French left, fascism became synonymous with the eternal counter-revolutionary who had combated the French Revolution and reinvented himself during the Boulanger and Dreyfus affairs. In other words, fascism was merely another way to designate the reactionaries of big business and the Church.[20] Marxists equated Bonapartism with fascism and believed that the latter represented the final crisis of capitalism. Leftist revolutionaries viewed fascism as the new mask of the counter-revolution, which could only be prevented by workers' revolution.

The Socialist leader, Léon Blum, saw fascism as a replay of the monarchist nationalism of the fin de siècle.[21] For Blum, Hitler was a new Boulanger or Déroulède. Trapped in the framework of the previous century, he underestimated Nazism's aggressive violence and genocidal racism. Indeed, Blum thought that the strength of Nazism had peaked in 1930 and continued to underestimate its popular support, a common error of the left and the right, both of which continued to see the Nazi regime as a mask behind which the traditional German elites pulled the strings.[22] His analysis ignored the mass radicalisation which was the base of fascism.[23] Even as late as 1934, Blum continued to believe that Mussolini was more dangerous than Hitler.[24] Unlike his Socialist colleague, Jean Zyromski, who advocated a Franco-Russian alliance that could block German aggression, Blum expressed scepticism during 1934 that the proposed Franco-Russian treaty and French rearmament would bolster French security.[25]

Versailles guilt was shared by many in all walks of life, demonstrating that it was not only the French military but also public opinion that based strategy on the last war. The supposed injustices inflicted on Germany and Italy became the problem, not the aggression of fascism. Thus, the left often concluded that vengeful right-wing French nationalists – not Nazis – were responsible for German fascism. Before the Popular Front, the Communists had blamed French 'imperialism' for provoking German chauvinism.[26] Guilt over Versailles was one of the foundations of Socialist (and, for that matter, bourgeois) pacifism. Paul Faure, number two in the Socialist Party, and, less consistently, Blum himself championed Versailles culpability. The Socialists and even their Communist partners accepted with resignation and even pacifist pride the remilitarisation of the Rhineland in March 1936, which violated not only the Versailles Treaty but also the Locarno Agreement. Indeed, when Blum became prime minister in June 1936, he pursued disarmament negotiations with Germany and – like much of the French public until the end of 1938 – was willing to make colonial concessions to the Third Reich.[27]

Fearing deep divisions within his own country and his own party, Blum's Popular Front government refused overt aid to the Spanish Republic, demonstrating that its pacifism and fear of a wider European conflict trumped its antifascism. Blum's Spanish policy of non-intervention has been seen as 'the central foreign policy issue of Blum's premiership', 'a bankrupt policy which helped seal the fate of the Spanish Republic'.[28] Some have speculated that intervention would have sparked a civil war in France. National unity and Socialist party cohesion took precedence over antifascism. The social democratic Blum would not risk civil or general war to take decisive steps to aid revolutionary Spain. The Spanish Revolution aroused anti-Communism and encouraged the French right to view Stalin, not Hitler, as their main enemy. Soviet support for the Spanish Republic, the latter's own revolutionary record, and the corresponding rise of a fellow (although non-revolutionary) Popular Front in France bolstered pro-fascist sentiment. To many on the right, fascism – the alliance of Nazis, Fascists, and Spanish Nationalists – seemed to be an effective way to block Communist influence.

Furthermore, French intervention in the Spanish conflict might have diverted French resources to a peripheral Iberian theatre when they should have been directed to confront the most powerful enemy – Nazi

Germany. In fact, in 1937 Hitler expressed the desire for the Spanish war to continue as long as possible – even to the end of 1940 – in order to divide his potential enemies.[29] In other words, Franco may have won the war too quickly from the Nazi perspective, rather than too slowly as many of his critics and even supporters have argued. Blum's and the left's inability to correctly analyse Nazism proved more consequential than French failure to intervene on the side of the Spanish Republic. It is significant that the largest demonstration during the French Popular Front did not concern the Spanish war, *Anschluss,* or the Munich agreement, but instead protested the violent intervention of Italian Fascism in France itself. On 9 June 1937 Mussolini's agents assassinated Carlo and Nello Rosselli, leaders of the antifascist organisation Giustizia e Libertà ('Justice and Freedom'), at Bagnoles-de-l'Orne. Two hundred thousand people accompanied the bodies to the Père-Lachaise cemetery in Paris.[30]

In 1936 and 1937 Blum proved reluctant to reinforce cooperation with the Soviet Union which the Popular Front coalition – with the significant exception of the Communists – still regarded with suspicion, despite the USSR's attempt to form alliances with the Western democracies.[31] At the end of 1937 when the Popular Front foreign minister, Yvon Delbos, went to visit France's Eastern allies – Poland, Romania, Yugoslavia and Czechoslovakia – he pointedly omitted a trip to the Soviet Union, and pressed the Czechs to make concessions to their German minority. Unlike Faure, Blum may not have been an advocate of 'unconditional pacifism', but he was enough of a pacifist politician to concede German domination of the Sudetenland.[32] Furthermore, French soldiers, diplomats and politicians – again with the exception of the Communists – generally underestimated the Red Army and feared that the Soviet Union wanted to provoke a war which would weaken France and strengthen its Communist partner.

Fighting German aggression in the Sudetenland would have entailed a split with the powerful pacifist wing in the SFIO (Section française de l'Internationale ouvrière). Blum favoured pacifism over antifascism, and in any case preferred party unity.[33] To prevent domestic fascists from taking state power and destroying his cherished SFIO was one of the major reasons behind his support for the Popular Front.[34] Until December 1938, the Socialist leader 'had pushed his friends very far to conciliate Hitler'.[35] Blum's brief second government in March 1938 did little to revive a Russian alliance.[36] Blum came to believe that the Sudetenland could be separated from Czechoslovakia if the latter received guarantees that it would be preserved.[37] In the Socialist newspaper, *Le Populaire*, he preached conciliation and whole-heartedly approved of the meeting between Chamberlain and Hitler at Berchtesgaden on 15 September.[38] Thus, unlike his British counterpart – Labour Party leader and anti-appeaser Clement Attlee – Blum welcomed the Munich agreement as an opportunity to 'return to work and get some sleep. We can enjoy the beauty of the autumn sun'.[39] His attitude towards Chamberlain's concessions to Hitler was more ambivalent: 'War has probably been avoided, but under such conditions that even though I have always fought for peace, I cannot be joyful and am torn between cowardly relief and shame'.[40] Thus, Munich was hardly – as one recent history has claimed – a refutation of the 'values of the Popular Front'.[41] Blum and the Popular Front proved incapable of 'Defending Democracy'.[42] The Popular Front was considerably less antifascist than its historians have indicated.

The French and British left's reluctance to rearm contributed to the significant, if not decisive, lead in weapons production by Germany, which had begun serious rearmament in 1934–35.[43] Thus, the French Popular Front and the left in general showed an incapacity to fight foreign fascism. Like his pacifist colleagues, Blum consistently opposed preventive war against Nazism and believed that the arms race – not hyper-nationalism – caused conflict.[44] Nevertheless, Blum's Popular Front government initiated the first significant French rearmament programme, but the post-Popular Front government of Radical Edouard Daladier during late 1938 and 1939 embarked upon a much more intensified effort. French rearmament took the form of selective doses of limited spending on the air force (1934–35), army (1936–37), and air force again (1938–40).[45] Historians agree that the results of French rearmament efforts were negligible before 1939.[46] French military expenditures increased from 6 per cent of national income in 1936 to 8 per cent in 1938. The great change came in 1939 when military expenditures reached 28 per cent of national income.[47] Likewise, in Great Britain, military expenditures jumped from 8 percent of national income in 1938 to 22 percent in 1939. In contrast, German rearmament already consumed 13 percent of GNP in 1936, 17 percent in 1938, and jumped to 23 percent in 1939. In other words, the French and British efforts – although substantial if added together – were far outclassed by Germany before 1939. The initial German head start was partially responsible for the fall of France in 1940.[48] Although the Socialist Blum and the Conservative Chamberlain obviously had strong ideological differences, their governments made generally similar efforts to prepare for the coming conflict.

It has been pointed out that the modest rearmament in Britain and France was not an alternative to appeasement but rather a different aspect of it.[49] Arms were not for fighting but rather for negotiating a European détente, based upon a renunciation of Versailles and the re-establishment of the traditional balance among the great powers. Both the French and British used their rearmaments as bargaining chips to deter the fascist powers rather than attempt to mobilise the nation for the coming war. British opinion remained ambivalent about a military pact with France since it would have meant an admission of failure to reconcile Germany and Italy.[50] After the war, Blum admitted that he had failed to break with powerful pacifist currents in his party over the Munich agreement.[51] He also regretted not responding militarily to Hitler's re-militarisation of the Rhineland.[52] Furthermore, as a Socialist and a disciple of Jean Jaurès, he opposed the offensive and mobile strategy proposed by Charles de Gaulle and supported the defensive and static one adopted by the French military establishment.[53]

The right was as or more appeasement-oriented than the left, but the right united in opposing the most important piece social legislation of the Popular Front, the forty-hour week, which it termed an obstacle for French production and national defence. The right and even the centre throughout 1938 pushed the agenda of putting France back to work by demanding an end to the forty-hour week and an intensification of productivity. Therefore it was not 'the problem of foreign policy' that destroyed the Popular Front in 1938,[54] but rather the forty-hour week, which involved both foreign and domestic concerns. Counter-revolutionary antifascists, such as Paul Reynaud and a post-Munich Daladier, tied increased production to resistance against Nazism. At the end of 1937, German war preparations impressed Reynaud, although he was a member of the appeasement-oriented and pro-Franco Alliance démocratique. Reynaud wrote of the necessity to prepare for the coming conflict by boosting defence production and maintaining the Soviet alliance.[55] Reynaud was one of the leaders of the anti-Munich minority faction in Daladier's cabinet.

From April to August 1938, Daladier accomplished politically what Blum could not. In March 1938 the Radical leader formed a government with support from both left and right, even if the left was increasingly distrustful and the right more enthusiastic.[56] Daladier's determination to break strikes and, most importantly, to end the forty-hour week meant an eventual rupture with his left partners. On 25 August 1938, Blum wrote 'the divine-right and reactionary bosses have been attacking the forty-hour week legislation for a year. During the last few weeks, the attack has been more violent and determined than ever. The struggle is political and social, not economic. This is proven because the great majority of industrial firms are working fewer than forty hours'.

Like many in and out of the government, Blum was misinformed, since in the autumn of 1938 at least 80 per cent were labouring forty hours.[57] Blum's hostility to ending the short working week was repeated in November when he called Reynaud's plan to end five days of eight hours a 'violent declaration of war' against the weekend and, more generally, against the social reforms of the Popular Front.[58] Blum argued that only by maintaining the existing social gains of the Popular Front could the 'devoir patriotique' be accomplished.[59] Reynaud proved instrumental in busting strikes at the end of November 1938 and ending the forty-hour week.[60] The Daladier–Reynaud government proved to be more antifascist than the Popular Front itself. Like most of the right, after Munich it refused to give Germany total carte blanche in the East.

Blum's defence of the forty-hour week was backed by a united Socialist Party which opposed without dissension Reynaud's imposition of a six-day working week, piecework and overtime.[61] Even the so-called antifascist faction of the SFIO, which remained close to the PCF line, called Reynaud's productivist measures the domestic equivalent to the Munich agreement. According to Zyromski's *Bataille Socialiste*, 'Munich was the capitulation of democracy to external fascism. Reynaud's decree-laws are the capitulation of democracy to the domestic fascism of banks and trusts'.[62] Faure's pacifist faction also opposed the decree-laws. The pacifist position had a consistent anti-war logic and was particularly influential in the countryside where almost half of French people still dwelled. The *paulfauristes* believed that Stalin was trying to provoke a war between the Western democracies and Germany, and sometimes hinted that Jews were involved in this endeavour.[63] Despite his anti-Communism, Faure, like many Marxists, regarded fascism as inseparable from capitalism; thus he saw no point in joining Anglo-American (and even less Soviet) imperialism to fight German imperialism.[64] Faure was therefore willing to ally with the right to stop war.[65]

The supposed antifascist defence of the forty-hour week ignored the multiple fascist aggressions and the large German lead in weapons production. The left believed – somewhat magically – that France could compete with a demographically superior Nazi Germany, where workers were labouring fifty to sixty hours per week. Supporters of the Spanish Republic – including the CGT leader, Léon Jouhaux – also rejected the abolition of the forty-hour week. Jouhaux nonetheless demanded a firm stance against German expansionism, which in his eyes was responsible for the threat of war.[66] During the Popular Front the PCF maintained that democracy needed to be defended since fascism totally eliminated the possibility of working-class betterment, let alone revolution. Like the entire left, the Communists also defended a working week 'of two Sundays', which they realised was the most significant and popular proletarian achievement of the Popular Front.

The application of the forty-hour week contributed to the weakness of French aviation and therefore encouraged concessions at Munich.[67] In nationalised aviation firms, senior administrators condemned '*la vague générale de paresse*' and planned to use overtime and 'especially to strengthen the authority of the factories' management'.[68] In 1938, the employers' organisation, Constructeurs de cellules, appealed to the minister of aviation for 'the development of piecework'.[69] An investigation claimed that workers' refusal of overtime had 'nearly paralysed overall production'.[70] The inquiry calculated that, on average, aviation workers performed only three hours of overtime per year and had the right to recover these hours. Wage earners' insistence on this right made overtime 'nothing more than a costly shift of the schedule'.[71]

In public, Popular Front organisations continued to insist that unions were willing to make the workers labour overtime for national defence. The workers, they stated, were willing to contribute to the antifascist cause, donating to the Spanish Republic an extra hour without pay. In private, though, the CGT leader, Ambroise Croizat, admitted that the forty-hour week hindered aircraft production and that overtime was necessary, but he considered that 'the working masses' were 'insufficiently informed of industrial necessities'.[72] Looking back during the Second World War, a clandestine issue of *Le Populaire* reproached workers for failing to labour overtime during the Popular Front.[73] Even after Munich, in October 1938, the Socialists refused to grant the Daladier government full powers unless it promised not to tamper with the abbreviated working week.[74] Socialists, Communists, and their trade union supporters failed to recognise what their counterparts in Spain and elsewhere had learned – that effective preparation for war and war itself demanded severe sacrifice.

Many rank-and-file workers knew that 'fascism' meant extended labour under strict discipline. 'Antifascism' therefore signified less work and more personal freedom in the workplace. The workers' priorities obviously conflicted with national defence, but the left generally refused to face the dilemma.[75] This was also true for revolutionary antifascists, who often shared with more moderate leftists the same analysis of fascism as a purely reactionary and bourgeois phenomenon. Revolutionary antifascists – anarchists, Socialists (Marceau Pivert and Daniel Guérin), Trotskyites and dissident Communists – held that antifascism always had to be revolutionary, not merely a defence of the bourgeois Republic.[76] Members of the Trotskyite Fourth International

– who shared the pre-Popular Front Communist analysis – believed that the confrontations between the fascist and democratic powers were a result of equally condemnable 'imperialisms'.[77] After the *Anschluss*, Pivert alleged that the Daladier cabinet was the first step towards a 'dictature fasciste'.[78] He refused to fight for the Czechs since the Socialist party permitted the suppression of the Spanish Revolution. His extreme-left faction was expelled from the SFIO in April 1938.

For pacifists, Czechoslovakia was a bastard creation of Versailles.[79] Simone Weil – full of Versailles and other varieties of guilt – believed that Czechoslovakia was an unviable state that oppressed the Sudeten Germans, an analysis shared by some Christian democrats and the extreme right and left.[80] Although she had fought with revolutionaries in 1936 in Spain, in 1938 Weil had little if any objection to German domination of Czechoslovakia. She wrote in May 1938 that the hegemony of the Reich 'might, in the end, be acceptable for Europe'.[81] Other revolutionaries – Maurice Chambelland and Pierre Monatte of *La Révolution prolétarienne* – chose pacifism over antifascism, whether revolutionary or not. Like the Socialist reformists around the journal *Syndicats*, these revolutionaries supported Munich.[82] Leon Trotsky himself argued that antifascism was merely a cover for counter-revolutionary manipulation. Unlike in Spain, where revolutionary antifascism dominated its Popular Front, in France revolutionary antifascism played only a marginal part.

In conclusion, the French Popular Front failed to combat Nazism, the most radical form of fascism and the most dangerous to the French Republic. The French Popular Front's foreign policy differed little from that of its appeasing British ally. Its social legislation restrained its own relatively modest rearmament campaign. Only after counter-revolutionary antifascists, led by the Radical, Prime Minister Daladier, destroyed the Popular Front by terminating the forty-hour week and limiting the power of union delegates, did France escalate its war preparations and attempt to catch up with Germany's lead in armaments production. Despite their willingness to break with the left, the overwhelming majority of counter-revolutionary antifascists nevertheless succumbed to the Nazi challenge in June 1940. At that time, most feared revolution and anarchy more than fascism.

After the fall of France, de Gaulle reached the same analysis as his sponsor, Prime Minister Winston Churchill, who saw the war as a global struggle in which the Anglo-Saxon powers would victoriously employ their immeasurable resources. The general began to rebuild an antifascist coalition in London, the capital of counter-revolutionary antifascism. Following the invasion of the USSR in June 1941, French antifascists constructed an even broader antifascist alliance than that of the Popular Front. With the indispensable help of the Western Allies, they reconquered France in 1944–45. Unlike the revolutionary antifascism of the Spanish Civil War and of Eastern Europe in the final months of the Second World War, the Allied presence and the Gaullist Resistance restrained revolutionary antifascist currents. Thus, Spanish Republican exiles in France contributed to the victory of the expansive antifascist alliance of the Second World War, in contrast to the defeat of their own more radical and less inclusive coalition during the Spanish Civil War. The French counter-revolutionary antifascist coalition restored equal rights and free elections. Likewise, it protected religion and most private property. Its nationalisations looked back to the Jacobin confiscations of 'traitors' during the French Revolution as well as to the legal expropriations of the Popular Front. Yet in contrast to the Popular Front, the patriotic atmosphere of the Liberation encouraged leftist parties and unions to promote heightened productivity in the workplace. The new Republic continued the traditions of the old.

Notes

1. J. Palacios and S. Payne, *Franco: A Personal and Political Biography*, Madison, WI, 2014, which shows that the refusal of Franco's regime to break with the Axis was based in part upon its evaluation that Jews controlled the Allies.
2. Cf. N. Copsey, 'Towards a New Anti-Fascist "Minimum"', in N. Copsey and A. Olechnowicz (eds), *Varieties of Anti-Fascism: Britain in the Inter-War Period*, Basingstoke, 2010; and N. Copsey, *Anti-Fascism in Britain*, Basingstoke, 2000, which makes a distinction between 'active' and 'passive' antifascism. The former involves 'actions' that oppose fascism; the latter a 'hostile attitude'. This definition may be appropriate for an analysis of British antifascism but is less useful for understanding international antifascism. Supporters of Franco and Pétain, including high-ranking Catholic clerics, often held hostile attitudes towards fascists who played important roles in these regimes. Depending on the period, even Franco and Pétain themselves made statements and gestures hostile to fascism – and so did a good number of upper class Germans who went into 'internal exile', but never lifted a finger to oppose Nazism until its defeat was certain.
3. A.J. Mayer, *Dynamics of Counterrevolution in Europe, 1870–1956: An Analytic Framework*, New York, 1971, 115.
4. Cf. J. Jackson, *The Popular Front in France: Defending Democracy, 1934–38*, Cambridge, 1988, 189, 202–3.
5. D. Hucker, *Public Opinion and the End of Appeasement in Britain and France*, Farnham, Surrey, 2011, 15, 30.
6. J. Plumyène and R. Lasierra, *Les fascismes français, 1923–63*, Paris, 1963, 7, 10; S. Payne, *Civil War in Europe, 1905–1949*, New York, 2011, 110.

7. Y. Lacaze, *L'opinion publique française et la crise de Munich*, Berne, 1991, 606.
8. J. Vigreux, *Le front populaire, 1934–1938*, Paris, 2011, 12; S. Berstein, *Léon Blum*, Paris, 2006, 388.
9. Berstein, *Blum*, 389.
10. Ibid., 391, 407.
11. X. Vigna, *Histoire des ouvriers en France au XXe siècle*, Paris, 2012, 121.
12. Berstein, *Blum*, 400.
13. Vigreux, *Le front populaire*, 35–36.
14. G. Vergnon, *L'antifascisme en France de Mussolini à Le Pen*, Rennes, 2009, 75.
15. Vigreux, *Le front populaire*, 31; André Combes, *La franc-maçonnerie sous l'Occupation: Persécution et résistance (1939–1945)*, Monaco, 2001, 289.
16. Berstein, *Blum*, 549.
17. R. Aron, 'Réflexions sur les problèmes économiques français', *Revue de Métaphysique et de Morale* 44(4) (October 1937), 803.
18. R. Frankenstein, *Le prix du réarmement français, 1935–39*, Paris, 1982, 235. However, the author concludes that the forty-hour week was ultimately a minor obstacle to heightened production, and blames shortfalls on the capitalists.
19. M. Seidman, *Workers against Work: Labor in Barcelona and Paris during the Popular Fronts*, Berkeley, CA, 1991, 302; Vigna, *Histoire*, 139–40.
20. Vergnon, *L'antifascisme*, 63, 83.
21. J. Droz, *Histoire de l'antifascisme en Europe, 1923–1939*, Paris, 1985, 100.
22. Lacaze, *L'opinion*, 123, 384.
23. M. Dreyfus, 'Les socialistes européens et les Fronts populaires: un internationalisme déclinant', in S. Wolikow and A. Bleton-Ruget (eds), *Antifascisme et nation: les gauches européennes au temps du Front populaire*, Dijon, 1998, 24.
24. Lacaze, *L'opinion*, 384; R. Gombin, *Les socialistes et la guerre: La S.F.I.O. et la politique étrangère française entre les deux guerres mondiales*, Paris, 1970, 178.
25. Gombin, *Les socialistes*, 191, 193, 201.
26. Lacaze, *L'opinion*, 408.
27. Ibid., 385, 583.
28. Jackson, *Popular Front*, 202, 209.
29. Z. Steiner, *The Triumph of the Dark: European International History 1933–1939*, Oxford, 2011, 242.
30. Droz, *Histoire de l'antifascisme*, 61.
31. Jackson, *Popular Front*, 195–98.
32. Ibid., 191; Annie Lacroix-Riz, *Le choix de la défaite: Les élites françaises dans les années 1930*, Paris, 2010, 388.
33. Lacaze, *L'opinion*, 388, 397, 399, 596.
34. Berstein, *Blum*, 420, 439.
35. Gombin, *Les socialistes*, 180. See also Lacroix-Riz, *Le choix*, 417–18.
36. A. Adamthwaite, *France and the Coming of the Second World War, 1936–1939*, London, 1977, 89.
37. Gombin, *Les socialistes*, 234.
38. Adamthwaite, *France*, 211; Cf. Frankenstein, *Le prix*, 186.
39. Gombin, *Les socialistes*, 234.
40. Cited in Lacaze, *L'opinion*, 394.
41. Vigreux, *Le front populaire*, 94.

42. Cf. Jackson, *Popular Front*, and Adamthwaite, *France*, 354.
43. J.-L. Crémieux-Brilhac, *Les français de l'an 40*, 2 vols, Paris, 1990, vol. 2, 195; P. Jackson, *France and the Nazi Menace: Intelligence and Policy Making, 1933–1939*, Oxford, 2000, 67.
44. Gombin, *Les socialistes*, 178–79, 189, 207.
45. A. Adamthwaite, *Grandeur and Misery: France's Bid for Power in Europe, 1914–1940*, London, 1995, 144.
46. Berstein, *Blum*, 482; Frankenstein, *Le prix*, 22, 31–32.
47. Adamthwaite, *France*, 164; Jackson, *Nazi Menace*, 324. Cf. Vigreux, *Le front populaire*, 70 and Lacroix-Riz, *Le choix*, 478. Figures differ somewhat in Frankenstein, *Le prix*, 35.
48. Crémieux-Brilhac, *Les français*, 2: 229; Jackson, *Nazi Menace*, 83, 241, 390. K.-H. Frieser and J.T. Greenwood, *The Blitzkrieg Legend: The 1940 Campaign in the West*, Annapolis, MD, 2005, 21–48. This illuminating treatment attributes the German victory in the West not to Allied material inferiority but rather to the innovations of certain German generals; nonetheless, it demonstrates Allied operational inferiority at critical moments during the battle of France. Likewise, J. Jackson, *The Fall of France: The Nazi Invasion of 1940*, Oxford, 2003, 164–79.
49. Adamthwaite, *France*, 243.
50. Ibid., 51.
51. Lacaze, *L'opinion*, 383.
52. Gombin, *Les socialistes*, 206.
53. É. Roussel, *Charles de Gaulle*, Paris, 2002, 67, 70; Frieser and Greenwood, *Blitzkrieg*, 328.
54. Jackson, *Popular Front*, 212.
55. Lacaze, *L'opinion*, 325.
56. Berstein, *Blum*, 585.
57. Adamthwaite, *Grandeur*, 143.
58. Cited in Berstein, *Blum*, 594.
59. Lacaze, *L'opinion*, 393.
60. Adamthwaite, *France*, 289; Robert Frank, 'La gauche sait-elle gérer la France? (1936–1937 / 1981–1984)', *Vingtième siècle* 6 (1985), 15.
61. M. Sadoun, *Les socialistes sous l'Occupation: Résistance et collaboration*, Paris, 1982, 16.
62. Cited in ibid., 16.
63. Ibid., 50; Lacaze, *L'opinion*, 398.
64. Sadoun, *Les socialistes*, 48–50, 82.
65. Lacroix-Riz, *Le choix*, 538.
66. Lacaze, *L'opinion*, 455, 457; D.W. Pike, *Les Français et la guerre d'Espagne*, Paris, 1975, 88.
67. Jackson, *Nazi Menace*, 275, 279.
68. Société nationale de constructions aéronautiques du nord, 19 October 1938, Société nationale aérospatiale.
69. Conseil d'administration, chambre syndicale de constructeurs, 17 March 1938, Archives nationales, Paris, 91 AQ 80; Frankenstein, *Le prix*, 278.

70. 'Les causes', 13 September 1938, in 'Les insuffisances actuelles de la production aéronautique', Service historique de l'armée de l'air, Vincennes, Z11606.
71. Roos, 'La situation de l'industrie aéronautique', 1937, Service historique de l'armée de l'air, Vincennes, Z11606.
72. Croizat quoted by E. du Réau, 'L'aménagement de la loi instituant la semaine de quarante heures', R. Rémond and J. Bourdin (eds), *Edouard Daladier: Chef du gouvernement*, Paris, 1977, 136.
73. R. Jacomet, *L'armement de la France (1936–1939)*, Paris, 1945, 260.
74. Adamthwaite, *France*, 129.
75. This is also the historiographic case. Cf. Lacroix-Riz, *Le choix*, 556–66.
76. D. Guérin, *Fascisme et Grand Capital*, cited in Vergnon, *L'antifascisme*, 86–87.
77. Lacaze, *L'opinion*, 441, 450.
78. Ibid., 387.
79. N. Ingram, *The Politics of Dissent: Pacifism in France, 1919–1939*, Oxford, 1991, 230.
80. Lacaze, *L'opinion*, 555, 558.
81. Ibid., 444.
82. Jackson, *Popular Front*, 247.

References

Adamthwaite, A. *France and the Coming of the Second World War, 1936–1939*. London, 1977.
———. *Grandeur and Misery: France's Bid for Power in Europe, 1914–1940*. London, 1995.
Aron, R. 'Réflexions sur les problèmes économiques français'. *Revue de Métaphysique et de Morale* 44(4) (October 1937), 803.
Berstein, S. *Léon Blum*. Paris, 2006.
Combes, A. *La franc-maçonnerie sous l'Occupation: Persécution et résistance (1939–1945)*. Monaco, 2001.
Copsey, N. *Anti-Fascism in Britain*. Basingstoke, 2000.
———. 'Towards a New Anti-Fascist "Minimum"', in N. Copsey and A. Olechnowicz (eds), *Varieties of Anti-Fascism: Britain in the Inter-War Period*. Basingstoke, 2010.
Crémieux-Brilhac, J.-L. *Les français de l'an 40*. 2 vols. Paris, 1990.
Dreyfus, M. 'Les socialistes européens et les Fronts populaires: un internationalisme déclinant', in S. Wolikow and A. Bleton-Ruget (eds), *Antifascisme et nation: les gauches européennes au temps du Front populaire*. Dijon, 1998.
Droz, J. *Histoire de l'antifascisme en Europe, 1923–1939*. Paris, 1985.
Frank, R. 'La gauche sait-elle gérer la France? (1936–1937 / 1981–1984)', *Vingtième siècle* 6 (1985), 3–21.
Frankenstein, R. *Le prix du réarmement français, 1935–39*. Paris, 1982.
Frieser, K.-H., and J.T. Greenwood. *The Blitzkrieg Legend: The 1940 Campaign in the West*. Annapolis, MD, 2005.

Gombin, R., *Les socialistes et la guerre: La S.F.I.O. et la politique étrangère française entre les deux guerres mondiales*. Paris, 1970.

Hucker, D. *Public Opinion and the End of Appeasement in Britain and France*. Farnham, Surrey, 2011.

Ingram, N. *The Politics of Dissent: Pacifism in France, 1919–1939*. Oxford, 1991.

Jackson, J. *The Popular Front in France: Defending Democracy, 1934–38*. Cambridge, 1988.

———. *The Fall of France: The Nazi Invasion of 1940*. Oxford, 2003.

Jackson, P. *France and the Nazi Menace: Intelligence and Policy Making, 1933–1939*. Oxford, 2000.

Jacomet, R. *L'armement de la France (1936–1939)*. Paris, 1945.

Lacaze, Y. *L'opinion publique française et la crise de Munich*. Berne, 1991.

Lacroix-Riz, A. *Le choix de la défaite: Les élites françaises dans les années 1930*. Paris, 2010.

Mayer, A.J. *Dynamics of Counterrevolution in Europe, 1870–1956: An Analytic Framework*. New York, 1971.

Palacios, J., and S. Payne. *Franco: A Personal and Political Biography*. Madison, WI, 2014.

Payne, S. *Civil War in Europe, 1905–1949*. New York, 2011.

Pike, D.W. *Les Français et la guerre d'Espagne*. Paris, 1975.

Plumyène, J., and R. Lasierra. *Les fascismes français, 1923–63*. Paris, 1963.

Réau, E. du. 'L'aménagement de la loi instituant la semaine de quarante heures', in R. Rémond and J. Bourdin (eds), *Edouard Daladier: Chef du gouvernement*. Paris, 1977, 129–49.

Roussel, É. *Charles de Gaulle*. Paris, 2002.

Sadoun, M. *Les socialistes sous l'Occupation: Résistance et collaboration*. Paris, 1982.

Seidman, M. *Workers against Work: Labor in Barcelona and Paris during the Popular Fronts*. Berkeley, CA, 1991.

Steiner, Z. *The Triumph of the Dark: European International History 1933–1939*. Oxford, 2011.

Vergnon, G. *L'antifascisme en France de Mussolini à Le Pen*. Rennes, 2009.

Vigna, X. *Histoire des ouvriers en France au XXe siècle*. Paris, 2012.

Vigreux, J. *Le front populaire, 1934–1938*. Paris, 2011.

Michael Seidman is professor of history at the University of North Carolina Wilmington. His first book – *Workers against Work: Labor in Barcelona and Paris during the Popular Fronts, 1936–38* (1991) – has been translated into six languages. He has also written *Republic of Egos: A Social History of the Spanish Civil War* (2002; Spanish translation, 2003); *The Imaginary Revolution: Parisian Students and Workers in 1968* (2004); and *The Victorious Counterrevolution: The Nationalist Effort in the Spanish Civil War* (2011; Spanish translation, 2012). He is completing a new book, *Atlantic Antifascisms, 1936–1945*.

3

'BEYOND CABLE STREET'

New Approaches to the Historiography of Antifascism in
Britain in the 1930s

Tom Buchanan

The literature on antifascism in Britain during the 1930s has developed
rapidly in recent years, allowing a far more complex, nuanced and
scholarly picture to emerge. Historians have increasingly sought to go
beyond the physical, often violent, resistance to fascism on the streets,
and asked, instead, how democratic values were promoted and safe-
guarded by a diverse range of actors. This new complexity is welcome,
but it also poses fresh questions: how helpful is the concept of antifascism once it has been broadened out in this fashion, has something essential been lost in the process, and what held together the 'mosaic' (as
one leading authority has described it)[1] of antifascism? This chapter
will provide both a review and a critique of the new literature.

Antifascism in Britain can be traced back to the 1920s, when small
fascist organisations – imitative of Italian fascism – gained some sali-
ence during the 1926 General Strike. However, it only became central
to British politics during the 1930s, when the Great Depression, the
rise of political violence associated with Sir Oswald Mosley's British
Union of Fascists (BUF), and the proliferation of aggressive fascist
and authoritarian regimes in Europe created a sense of acute political
and societal crisis. The decision by the 7th Congress of the Communist
International (July–August 1935) to abandon sectarianism and adopt
instead the 'People's Front against Fascism and War' confirmed the
new importance (already evident on the ground in some instances)
that Communist parties now gave to antifascism. In the British case,
antifascism has typically been treated by historians as referring to two
distinct but interrelated phenomena. The first was the active resistance to Mosley's 'Blackshirts', which reached a crescendo with the

street battles in the East End of London (primarily between antifascist protestors and the police) in October 1936. The second was the movements which, especially in the later 1930s, opposed the rise of fascist regimes in Europe and, hence, challenged the British government's policy of 'appeasement'. The various responses to the Spanish Civil War (1936–39) – where the death of more than five hundred Britons invested the antifascist cause with a sombre grandeur – form a significant subset of the latter category. However, as we shall see, there may well have been other, largely forgotten or ignored, forms of 'antifascism'.

For many years the historiography focused on the left, and above all on divisions within the left over how to respond to fascism. The Communist Party of Great Britain (CPGB) took centre stage in these accounts, whether in mobilising resistance to the BUF, organising the International Brigades in Spain, or inspiring a range of antifascist cultural movements such as the Left Book Club, Unity Theatre and *Left Review*. Conversely, the role of the Labour Party and the trade unions tended to be belittled: they were often seen as cravenly hostile to taking action, and (to some extent accurately) motivated more by anti-Communism than antifascism. According to this view, the triumphs of antifascism were won in spite of the official leaders of the labour movement, while its failures were their responsibility.[2] This narrative of Communist leadership began to be challenged in the 1970s. Hence, the Communist militant Joe Jacobs noted in his memoirs that the Communist Party only took the lead against Mosley's intended march through the East End of London on 4 October 1936 (later immortalised as 'The Battle of Cable Street') in response to rank-and-file pressure from within the CPGB and radical Jewish antifascist groups.[3] Up until the last minute – as the hastily amended leaflets reveal[4] – the party line had been that Communists should attend a planned rally for Spain in Trafalgar Square and only then join the anti-Mosley demonstration. Jacobs was highly critical of local Communist Party leaders such as Phil Piratin, for whom 'Cable Street' offered an unexpected – and perhaps unwarranted – career boost.[5] (Piratin would fight and win the 1945 general election in Mile End as 'a fighter against fascism'.[6]) Despite these dissident voices, the Communist Party continued to influence the historical narrative well into the 1980s, when the party's favoured publisher Lawrence & Wishart produced a stream of books on aspects of British antifascism, the Spanish Civil War and the crisis of the 1930s, all of which re-emphasised the centrality of the party's role.[7] While scholarly, these books also tended to have a contemporary political agenda. They were informed by a putative similarity between the politics of the 1930s and that of the 1980s, and the need to build broad, Popular Front-style alliances against Thatcherism.[8]

Since the 1980s, much has changed. First, a great deal of new archival evidence has become available. The opening of the CPGB and Moscow Comintern archives, followed by the ongoing release of MI5/Special Branch surveillance files of British 'subversives', has enabled a thorough reassessment of the politics of the left (albeit one that must remain provisional for as long as many MI5 files remain closed). Secondly, the history of British fascism has been substantially rewritten. In addition to Martin Pugh's provocative synthesis *Hurrah for the Blackshirts!*,[9] there has been much pioneering research including Thomas Linehan's detailed social history of the BUF in the East End, Julie Gottlieb's work on the attraction that fascism held for women, Philip Coupland's study of BUF ideology, and Matthew Worley's book on Mosley's New Party.[10] The most significant characteristic of this literature is the shift in emphasis away from the tight focus on Sir Oswald Mosley, the brilliant opportunist: instead, we see the outlines of a genuine fascist 'movement', with original ideas and a mass membership. Nigel Copsey has noted the irony in the relative historical neglect of antifascism compared to the burgeoning literature on British fascism, given that the BUF's followers only numbered in their thousands while hundreds of thousands took part in antifascist activities.[11]

Copsey is the central figure in the new literature on British antifascism. In 2000 he published a detailed political history which places the activism of the 1930s within a far broader chronology, as well as raising a number of conceptual issues which have informed subsequent debate. In particular, he posed the question of whether antifascism could take both 'active' and 'passive' forms. The concept of 'passive' antifascism opened the possibility that not only the Labour Party (and other political organisations that were not on the left) but also the state and the media could all conceivably be thought of as 'antifascist'. Copsey has also been involved in a number of edited volumes, of which the most valuable is *Varieties of Anti-fascism*.[12] This book casts the net very wide indeed, to include liberal, middle-class, feminist and religious opinion, as well as previously neglected intellectuals such as Aurel Kolnai. In one of the most thought-provoking contributions, Philip Williamson argues that the Conservatives should be seen as the leading 'non-fascist' party (contrary to Martin Pugh's argument that many party members were quasi-fascists) and that the Tory-dominated National Government of the 1930s was 'central to understanding' British antifascism, given its commitment to upholding liberal democratic values.[13] In a similar vein, Richard Thurlow argued that Britain's security services were successfully pragmatic in their handling of the BUF, and that the British state only made errors of judgement at moments of political panic. Hence, he sees the Public Order Act of 1936 (which gave the state new powers, including a ban on the public wearing of political uniforms) as a massive over-reaction after the ugly scenes at Cable Street.[14] In Copsey's own contribution to the volume he makes the case that the Labour movement – by refusing to endorse violent antifascism and by upholding parliamentary democracy – played a vital role in denying political space to the BUF.[15] According to this approach, therefore, the Communist Party's 'active' antifascism and Labour's 'passive' antifascism were simply two halves of the same walnut.

There have also been significant developments in two related fields. First, there has been renewed scholarly interest in the Jewish response to the rise of the BUF. In particular, an excellent collection of essays edited by Tony Kushner and Nadia Valman places the events of Cable Street firmly in the context of ethnic relations in the East End of London.[16] Kushner's own chapter provides a fascinating account of how the Communist Party's 'powerful narrative' of Cable Street intersected over time with the changing lives, memories and political perceptions of the local Jewish community. Secondly, there has been a flurry of recent publications on the National Council for Civil Liberties (NCCL), notably Janet Clark's book *At Liberty to Protest* (2012). The NCCL was established in 1934 in response to police violence and the use of *agents provocateurs* against unemployed 'hunger marchers'. While not strictly speaking an 'antifascist' organisation, by the later 1930s it was deeply involved in combating the BUF, while also seeking to prevent the British state from slipping into illiberalism in its response to political extremism. Clark, on the basis of significant new archival sources, argues compellingly that the NCCL had far greater influence on the police and Home Office than has previously been acknowledged. However, her book is unconvincing on the central (and essential) question of the NCCL's relationship with the Communist Party. Clark argues that, with regard to the question of whether the NCCL 'was under the covert control of the Communist Party ... the balance of the evidence suggests not'.[17] However, given the current state of the evidence – above all the incomplete and ongoing release of MI5/Special Branch papers – such a judgement is surely premature.

As one might expect, the revisionists have not had it all their own way. There has been a vigorous restatement of the orthodox Marxist position by the historian David Renton. In particular, Renton has turned the discussion back to the question of social class. He strongly disputes Linehan's argument that the BUF had a substantial working class following, while also reasserting the degree of working-class unity that underpinned antifascism. Renton's numerous contributions have undoubtedly helped to keep debate alive.[18] However, at least amongst academic historians, he has been fighting something of a rearguard action.

One obvious criticism of the recent work on antifascism is that by making everyone who was not a fascist, in effect, an antifascist, the term is in danger of losing all meaning. This need not be the case if one focuses on the deliberate creation of what D.L. LeMahieu called 'a culture for democracy' in the interwar years,[19] and Copsey appears broadly to be advocating this view. It is one that deserves serious consideration and is supported by research in related fields. For instance, Helen McCarthy's recent work has emphasised the role of mass membership, non-party, interwar organisations such as the League of Nations Union in promoting a sense of citizenship and democratic participation.[20] The contribution of the official Labour movement in this regard has long been unfairly neglected. To take one example, the Trades Union Congress (TUC) seized on the centenary of the 'Tolpuddle Martyrs' in 1934 not only as an excuse for ancestor worship, but also as an opportunity to assert the value of the institutions that previous generations had established in an increasingly inhospitable contemporary climate. As the Chairman of the TUC noted in a memorial volume, 'Organised labour is called upon, in our time, to defend the right to combine. In some countries the institutions of free citizenship have been shattered, and dictatorships have been erected on the ruins'.[21] In August 1934 the TUC received a poignant telegram from trade unionists in the Saarland, a territory that would soon return to Germany following a referendum: 'Fighting to preserve last stronghold German liberty and trade unionism Saar miners union sends fraternal greetings memory Tolpuddle'.[22]

At the same time, there is a danger that the measured verdict of history can be confused with the emotions and perceptions of the time. For instance, Williamson is surely correct to say that the National Government – which believed that domestic stability would repel external instability – played a major role in minimising the threat of extremism in Britain in the 1930s. However, it is clear that the left was wholly unconvinced by the democratic credentials of the National Government, and, indeed, saw it as a fascist threat in its own right. In 1935 Georgi Dimitrov (General Secretary of the Comintern) told the CPGB that 'at the present stage, fighting the fascist danger in Britain means primarily fighting the National Government and its reactionary measures',[23] and there are many examples of domestic politicians taking a similar view. For instance, Aneurin Bevan described the police reforms of 1933 as an 'entirely fascist development';[24] Hugh Dalton wrote in his diary that Stafford Cripps 'sees fascism peeping out everywhere in this country', while the Independent Labour Party described the Public Order Act as a 'fascist bill to stop fascism'.[25] Others saw 'fascism' as already present in a Britain characterised by mass unemployment and (since the defeat of the 1926 General Strike) aggressive employers. In a speech given in May 1936 the Communist leader of the South Wales coal miners, Arthur Horner, called on his members to fight against 'scab unionism, which is Fascism in embryo'. He went on to say that in Taff Merthyr, the heart of the Welsh coalfield, '[t]here is every characteristic of Fascism ... No free trade unions, victimisation, harder work for lower wages, imprisonment and ruthless brutality'.[26] Such views may, with hindsight, appear exaggerated, but they were genuinely held at the time. They were reinforced by the fact that the Public Order Act was first used not against British fascists but against the striking coal miners in Harworth, Nottinghamshire.[27] It hardly needs to be said that the left was even more suspicious of the National Government's foreign policy, and almost always depicted Neville Chamberlain as – if not actually in league with – at the very least desperate to please Hitler, Mussolini and Franco.

While one should welcome the way in which the net has been spread wider, it is also clear that there are still many unexplored questions closer to home. For instance, the nature of the Communist Party's own 'antifascism' surely needs to be investigated further. After all, whatever the rank and file may have understood by antifascism, if one reads the *Daily Worker* in the late 1930s it is clear that the struggle against 'Trotskyism' in the Soviet Union (or, indeed, Spain) was seen as a central component. Coverage of the Soviet show trials of 1936–38 repeatedly emphasised that the defendants were acting as 'agents of fascism'. A *Daily Worker* editorial in March 1938 made clear that this danger was not confined to the Soviet Union: 'We are in a world where every non-Fascist country is being menaced by intervention from without and conspiracy from within. All praise to the Soviet Union which has exterminated the pro-Fascist conspiracy within its borders'.[28] Such thinking persisted well beyond the 1930s. Bob Cooney, who fought with the International Brigades in Spain, described in 1944 how membership of the CPGB 'fitted me for the struggle against the Trotskyists who do the work of Fascism within the working class movement'. He compared support for strikes during the Second World War to the activities of the 'Spanish Trotskyists who were so anti-Republican that they opened the front to Fascism'.[29] Years later, in her official history of the CPGB, Noreen Branson sought to explain British Communist responses to the Moscow Trials on the grounds that 'the notion that Trotskyists could be allied with fascists, or used as tools of the latter, seemed plausible after the experience of the POUM in Spain'.[30] Whether British Communists thought that the hapless POUM (Partido Obrero de Unificación Marxista – the Spanish Workers' Party of Marxist Unification) really were 'fascists' is a moot point. Far more important is to acknowledge that the defence of the Soviet Union remained at the centre of their conception of antifascism.

One could also argue that the net could be spread even wider geographically. In all the recent literature there is no mention of foreign fascist movements further away than Europe, and, as I have recently argued, the impact of the Sino-Japanese war on British opinion has been remarkably neglected. Indeed, in the autumn of 1937, when Chinese cities were being devastated by aerial bombardment, China briefly eclipsed Spain in the antifascist imagination.[31] Yet, in the literature under discussion here there is only one reference to the war in China, when Copsey notes that at the Bermondsey anti-Mosley demonstration in October 1937 a CPGB leaflet referred to a Chinese baby 'deliberately murdered with thousands of kiddies and mothers by Japanese fascists'.[32] While academics have long debated whether Japan in the later 1930s was formally 'fascist' or not, activists at the time were in no doubt that it was. Cartoons routinely showed the Japanese militarists alongside Hitler and Mussolini; and in a drawing entitled 'The Shadow', published in *Left Review*, it is the danger from the East that threatens to sow death over England.[33] There is, therefore, every reason to 'globalise' British antifascism, and this is particularly true of the later 1930s when the threat posed by the BUF appeared greatly reduced. However, in the process one immediately encounters the problem of British imperialism. As George Orwell wrote in July 1939, British left-wing politics were 'always partly humbug': 'One threat to the Suez Canal, and "anti-fascism" and "defence of British interests" are discovered to be identical'.[34] It can certainly be argued that one of the consequences of the rise of antifascism was that the British left in the later 1930s soft pedalled its formerly strident anti-imperialism. Violent denunciation of Japan's imperial ambitions in China, for instance, took the place of criticism of Britain's own long-established role in the region.[35] When the Archbishop of Canterbury spoke out against the bombing of Chinese cities, supporters of Japan's actions lost no time in drawing to his attention pamphlets from a decade earlier criticising British behaviour in all too similar terms.[36]

Copsey rightly accepts that the broader approach taken in *Varieties of Anti-fascism* may be attacked on the grounds of conceptual over-stretch.[37] The problem is that, once the definition is broadened in this manner, one has to ask what is left to bind antifascism (and antifascists) together. For instance, were Catholics who opposed Nazism 'antifascists', even when they might also strongly support Franco's (Nazi-backed) Nationalist rebels? This was a very real dilemma, as Cardinal Hinsley, the leader of the Church in England and Wales, famously had a signed photograph of Franco on his desk, while also being regarded as an enemy by the Nazis during the Second World War.[38] Likewise, where do we place George Orwell? He fought as an antifascist with the POUM militia in Spain, but after experiencing political persecution by the Republican authorities he returned to Britain deeply disillusioned. In 1937 he would argue that antifascism was itself a form of fascism. In an unpublished response to the questionnaire published as *Authors take sides on the Spanish War* he wrote that 'on the Government side ... Fascism is being riveted on the Spanish workers under the pretext of resisting fascism'.[39] In Orwell's novel *Coming up for Air* (1939) there is a memorable scene in which George Bowling visits a Left Book Club meeting and witnesses a speaker rousing the audience to violent frenzy against the fascists[40] – a chilling forerunner of the 'two minutes hate' in *Nineteen Eighty-Four*. Even so, few could doubt that Orwell was an antifascist – and when finally war came in September 1939 he duly did what he could for the war effort (and was disappointed not to be allowed to fight).

Copsey's solution to this problem is to call for a 'new anti-fascist "minimum"':[41] 'What all antifascists shared in interwar Britain, at a minimum, was political and moral opposition to fascism rooted in the *democratic* values of the Enlightenment tradition. This was true right across the spectrum, including the Communist Party regardless of the totalitarian potential of Leninism–Stalinism'. He adds that there were three very different democratic traditions: liberal democracy, social democracy and people's or workers' democracy, the common denominator being the ideal of 'rule by the people' and commitment to Enlightenment values of humanism, rationalism, progressivism and universalism. That is all very well, but did antifascist propaganda really promote humanism and rationalism? In fact, it was often aimed at dehumanising the fascists so that they could be physically attacked, or (as with the BUF in 1940) jailed without trial. Orwell's haunting image of the Left Book Club speaker using a spanner to smash human faces to pulp is not that far wide of the mark. It is worth noting that it was Phil Piratin, the much maligned leader of the CPGB in the East End, who understood that a policy of 'beat the fascists whenever you see them' could be counterproductive. The local fascists might well be ordinary workers – many of them trade unionists – who must be reached by example and persuasion rather than violence.[42]

It might also be asked whether, in swinging the pendulum towards more liberal, 'passive' forms of antifascism, there is a danger of losing sight of a significant truth – that for 'active' antifascists, both in the 1930s and since, violence has always been an essential component of their political identity.[43] Antifascist activism – whether disrupting BUF meetings, engaging in running street battles, erecting barricades or rolling marbles under the hooves of police horses – was hazardous, but it was also exciting and politically affirming. The writer Philip Toynbee recalled how, as a schoolboy, he and Esmond Romilly prepared to confront the BUF rally at Olympia Hall in 1934: 'In the afternoon we bought knuckle-dusters at a Drury Lane ironmongers, and I well remember the exaltation of trying them on'.[44] Tony Gilbert, who later fought in Spain, admitted: 'I was excited [by the antifascist mobilisations]. I was exhilarated by it … I was seeing the power of people being able to stop something that was hateful to them'.[45] There was also some fulfilment to be gained from inflicting injury on fascist opponents. One Scottish activist recalled being wrongly accused of having kicked a fascist in the eye: 'His eye was split right across, so I just said at the time, "I wish tae Christ it had been me". I'd at least [have] felt some satisfaction'.[46] Antifascism thereby gave new licence to violent behaviour that was increasingly regarded as aberrant. As Jon Lawrence has convincingly argued, rowdiness and political violence had rapidly become unacceptable within mainstream politics in the years after 1918.[47] Nigel Copsey has recently warned against seeing violence as 'the single most important feature defining the Communist antifascist experience in interwar Britain',[48] and rightly notes that the Communist Party leadership consistently advocated restraint.[49] However, this simply raises another question: if violence was not the most important feature, then what was? The question of violence within antifascism is surely one that historians will wish to return to.

The other major problem with Copsey's 'antifascist minimum' is that the different versions of 'democracy' were so different that they barely recognised each other's democratic credentials. As I have argued elsewhere,[50] although there was a conception of democracy in the antifascism of the Popular Front era, one should not be blind to the fact that the Stalinist version was highly instrumental and tailored towards Communist political activism. As Harry Pollitt told the CPGB congress in March 1938: 'Democracy does not mean the abandonment of the class struggle, but freedom to carry the struggle forward ... democracy is not abstract, it means that the people have definite rights – the right to organise, the right to strike, the right to vote, the right to free speech. These rights are weapons'.[51] A cartoon from the Labour Party's *Daily Herald* in October 1937 symbolises the yawning gulf that separated Communist democracy from the other forms. While British voters can do nothing to alleviate the devastation caused by fascism in Spain and China, the cartoon claims, at least they can defend democracy by voting for Labour in the municipal elections.[52] In other words, antifascism may well have brought liberal democracy and social democracy closer together, but did little, in practical terms, to reconcile them with Communist notions of democracy. Accordingly, the quest for an 'antifascist minimum' may well be a quixotic one.

The flow of new archival sources, combined with a relaxation of once rigid conceptual boundaries, makes this an interesting time to be working on British antifascism. It is no longer just a story of Communist militants 'beating the fascists'; the antifascist credentials of many other groups are now being belatedly recognised. However, there is still a great deal to be done to integrate what we already know. For instance, far more needs to be done to link the British involvement in the Spanish Civil War into the wider story of British antifascism. After all, from the summer of 1936 onwards, British antifascism was increasingly displaced to Spain. As one Scottish volunteer put it: 'if we were going to be *antifascist in the real sense of the word* it was our job to try and help' the Spanish Republic by joining the International Brigades.[53] Likewise, there are also substantial areas of scholarly endeavour, such as the torrent of work on the literature and politicised literary culture of the 1930s, that could be more fully encompassed.[54] Finally, as the area of study widens ever further, historians will inevitably be tempted to impose new frameworks and models. This is not necessarily wise or fruitful; far better to map out the very real differences between these various antifascist groups than to erect a normative 'minimum'.

Notes

1. N. Copsey, *Anti-Fascism in Britain*, Basingstoke, 2000, 2–4.
2. See, for instance, CPGB, *Report of the Central Committee to the 14th National Congress* (1937), 7–8.
3. J. Jacobs, *Out of the Ghetto: My Youth in the East End, Communism and Fascism, 1913–1939* [1978], London, 1991.

4. Reproduced in Jacobs, *Out of the Ghetto*, 244.
5. For a more sympathetic account of Piratin's role, see Kevin Marsh and Robert Griffiths, *Granite and Honey: The Story of Phil Piratin, Communist MP*, Croydon, 2012.
6. T. Kushner and N. Valman, *Remembering Cable Street: Fascism and Anti-Fascism in British Society*, London, 2000, 138.
7. See J. Fyrth (ed.), *Britain, Fascism and the Popular Front*, London, 1985; H. Francis, *Miners against Fascism: Wales and the Spanish Civil War*, London, 1984; J. Fyrth, *The Signal was Spain: The Aid Spain Movement in Britain, 1936–39*, London, 1986; B. Alexander, *British Volunteers for Liberty: Spain, 1936–39*, London, 1982; N. Branson, *History of the Communist Party of Great Britain*, London, 1985, vol. 3 (1927–1941).
8. This case is most explicitly stated in Jim Fyrth's introduction to *Britain, Fascism and the Popular Front*, 24–28.
9. M. Pugh, *Hurrah for the Blackshirts! Fascists and Fascism in Britain between the Wars*, London, 2005.
10. T. Linehan, *East London for Mosley: The British Union of Fascists in East London and South-West Essex, 1933–40*, London, 1996; J. Gottlieb, *Feminine Fascism: Women in Britain's Fascist Movement, 1923–1945*, London, 2000; P.M. Coupland, 'The Blackshirted Utopians', *Journal of Contemporary History* 33(2) (April 1998), 255–72; M. Worley, *Oswald Mosley and the New Party*, Basingstoke, 2010.
11. Copsey, *Anti-fascism in Britain*, 2.
12. N. Copsey and A. Olechnowicz (eds), *Varieties of Anti-fascism: Britain in the Inter-war Period*, Basingstoke, 2010.
13. P. Williamson, 'The Conservative Party, Fascism and Anti-fascism, 1918–1939', in *Varieties of Anti-fascism*, 73, 86.
14. R. Thurlow, 'Passive and Active Anti-fascism: The State and National Security, 1923–1945', in *Varieties of Anti-fascism*, 162–80.
15. N. Copsey, '"Every time they made a Communist, they made a Fascist": The Labour Party and Popular Anti-fascism in the 1930s', in *Varieties of Anti-fascism*, 52–72.
16. Kushner and Valman, *Remembering Cable Street*. See also, Henry Felix Srebrnik, *London Jews and British Communism, 1935–1945*, Ilford, 1995.
17. J. Clark, *At Liberty to Protest: The NCCL and the Policing of Interwar Politics*, Manchester, 2012, 184. See also J. Clark, 'Sincere and Reasonable Men? The Origins of the National Council for Civil Liberties', *Twentieth Century British History* 20(4) (2009).
18. See, especially, Renton's collection of essays on antifascism, *This Rough Game: Fascism and Anti-fascism*, Stroud, 2001.
19. D.L. LeMahieu, *A Culture for Democracy*, Oxford, 1988.
20. H. McCarthy, *The British People and the League of Nations: Democracy, Citizenship and Internationalism, c.1918–1945*, Manchester, 2011; H. McCarthy, 'Parties, Voluntary Associations and Democratic Politics in Interwar Britain', *The Historical Journal* 50(4) (Dec. 2007).
21. A. Conley, 'Foreword' to Trades Union Congress General Council's *The Book of the Martyrs of Tolpuddle, 1834–1934*, London, 1934, xi–xii.

22. Cited in Clare Griffiths, 'Remembering Tolpuddle: Rural History and Commemoration in the Inter-War Labour Movement', *History Workshop Journal* 44 (1997), 159–60.
23. K. Hodgson, *Fighting Fascism: The British Left and the Rise of Fascism, 1919–39*, Manchester, 2010, 115.
24. Clark, *At Liberty to Protest*, 21.
25. Hodgson, *Fighting Fascism*, 110, 113.
26. Francis, *Miners against Fascism*, 82.
27. Clark, *At Liberty to Protest*, 130.
28. *Daily Worker*, 15 March 1938.
29. Marx Memorial Library, London, International Brigade Memorial Archive, Box A-15/3, Bob Cooney typescript, 'Proud Journey', 1944, 1–2.
30. Branson, *History of the CPGB*, 248.
31. T. Buchanan, *East Wind: China and the British Left, 1925–1976*, Oxford, 2012. See also, T. Buchanan, 'Shanghai–Madrid Axis? Comparing British Responses to the Conflicts in Spain and China, 1936–39', *Contemporary European History* 21(4) (Nov. 2012).
32. *Varieties of Anti-fascism*, 66.
33. *Left Review* (Jan. 1938), 732–33.
34. He did go on to concede, however, that '[i]t would be very shallow as well as unfair to suggest that there is *nothing* in what is now called "anti-Fascism" except a concern for British dividends'. S. Orwell and I. Angus (eds), *The Collected Essays, Journals and Letters of George Orwell*, Harmondsworth, 1970, vol. 1, 434.
35. See N. Redfern, *Class or Nation: Communists, Imperialism and Two World Wars*, London, 2005, 94–95.
36. Lambeth Palace archives, Lang 6, fols. 25–27, Viscount H. Kano to Lang, 30 Sept. 1937, citing the ILP pamphlet *What is Happening in China?* (1926), which alleged that British shelling had killed thousands of civilians at Wanhsien.
37. N. Copsey, 'Preface: Towards a New Anti-fascist Minimum', in *Varieties of Anti-fascism*, xiv–xxi, here xiv.
38. T. Moloney, *Westminster, Whitehall and the Vatican: The Role of Cardinal Hinsley, 1935–1943*, London, 1985, 71.
39. P. Davidson (ed.), *Orwell in Spain*, London, 2001, 249.
40. G. Orwell, *Coming up for Air* [1939], Harmondsworth, 1980, 143–52.
41. Copsey, 'Preface', in *Varieties of Anti-fascism*, xiv–xxi.
42. P. Piratin, *Our Flag Stays Red*. London, 1948, 17, 18.
43. This point was recently stated by the 'street-fighting antifascist' Dave Hann, whose posthumously published book drew on interviews with fellow activists. D. Hann, *Physical Resistance: Or a Hundred Years of Anti-fascism*, Alresford, Hants, 2013; introduction by L. Purbrick.
44. P. Toynbee, *Friends Apart: A Memoir of Esmond Romilly and Jasper Ridley in the Thirties*, London, 1954, 21.
45. R. Baxell, *Unlikely Warriors: The British in the Spanish Civil War and the Struggle against Fascism*, London, 2013, 38.

46. I. MacDougall, *Voices from the Spanish Civil War: Personal Recollections of Scottish Volunteers in Republican Spain, 1936–39*, Edinburgh, 1986, interview with George Watters, 33–34.

47. J. Lawrence, 'Forging a Peaceable Kingdom: War, Violence and Brutalisation in post-First World War Britain', *Journal of Modern History* 3 (2003), 557–89; J. Lawrence, 'The Transformation of British Public Politics after the First World War', *Past and Present* 190 (2006), 185–216; J. Lawrence, 'Fascist Violence and the Politics of Order in Inter-war Britain: The Olympia Debate Revisited', *Historical Research*, lxxvi (2003); see also M. Petrie, 'Public Politics and Traditions of Popular Protest: Demonstrations of the Unemployed in Dundee and Edinburgh, c.1921–1939', *Contemporary British History*, 2013.

48. N. Copsey, 'Communists and the Inter-war Anti-fascist Struggle in the United States and Britain', *Labour History Review* 76(3) (Dec. 2011), 184–206, here 199.

49. See the debate in *Discussion*, May, June and July 1936.

50. T. Buchanan, 'Anti-fascism and Democracy in the 1930s', *European History Quarterly* 32(1) (Jan. 2002), 39–57.

51. CPGB, *For Peace and Plenty: Report of the Fifteenth Congress of the CPGB* (1938), 59–64.

52. *Daily Herald*, 20 October 1937.

53. MacDougall, *Voices from the Spanish Civil War*, 171, citing John Londragan. Emphasis added.

54. The following list is far from exhaustive: Valentine Cunningham, *British Writers of the Thirties*, Oxford, 1988; J. Montefiore, *Men and Women Writers of the 1930s: The Dangerous Flood of History*, London, 1996; M. Joannou, *Women Writers of the 1930s: Gender, Politics and History*, Edinburgh, 1999; P. Bounds, *British Communism and the Politics of Literature, 1928–1939*, Pontypool, 2012.

References

Alexander, B. *British Volunteers for Liberty: Spain, 1936–39*. London, 1982.

Baxell, R. *Unlikely Warriors: The British in the Spanish Civil War and the Struggle against Fascism*. London, 2013.

Bounds, P. *British Communism and the Politics of Literature, 1928–1939*. Pontypool, 2012.

Branson, N. *History of the Communist Party of Great Britain*. London, 1985, vol. 3 (1927–1941).

Buchanan, T. 'Anti-fascism and Democracy in the 1930s'. *European History Quarterly* 32(1) (Jan. 2002), 39–57.

———. 'Shanghai–Madrid Axis? Comparing British Responses to the Conflicts in Spain and China, 1936–39'. *Contemporary European History* 21(4) (Nov. 2012).

———. *East Wind: China and the British Left, 1925–1976*. Oxford, 2012.

Clark, J. 'Sincere and Reasonable Men? The Origins of the National Council for Civil Liberties'. *Twentieth Century British History* 20(4) (2009).

————. *At Liberty to Protest: The NCCL and the Policing of Interwar Politics.* Manchester, 2012.

Copsey, N. *Anti-fascism in Britain.* Basingstoke, 2000.

————. 'Communists and the Inter-war Anti-fascist Struggle in the United States and Britain'. *Labour History Review* 76(3) (Dec. 2011), 184–206.

Copsey, N., and A. Olechnowicz (eds). *Varieties of Anti-fascism: Britain in the Inter-war Period.* Basingstoke, 2010.

Coupland, P.M. 'The Blackshirted Utopians'. *Journal of Contemporary History* 33(2) (April 1998), 255–72.

Cunningham, V. *British Writers of the Thirties.* Oxford, 1988.

Davidson, P. (ed.). *Orwell in Spain.* London, 2001.

Francis, H. *Miners against Fascism: Wales and the Spanish Civil War.* London, 1984.

Fyrth, J. (ed.). *Britain, Fascism and the Popular Front.* London, 1985.

————. *The Signal was Spain: The Aid Spain Movement in Britain, 1936–39.* London, 1986.

Gottlieb, J. *Feminine Fascism: Women in Britain's Fascist movement, 1923–1945.* London, 2000.

Griffiths, C. 'Remembering Tolpuddle: Rural History and Commemoration in the Inter-war Labour Movement'. *History Workshop Journal* 44 (1997), 159–60.

Hann, D. *Physical Resistance: Or a Hundred Years of Anti-fascism.* Alresford, Hants, 2013; introduction by Louise Purbrick.

Hodgson, K. *Fighting Fascism: The British Left and the Rise of Fascism, 1919–39.* Manchester, 2010.

Jacobs, J. *Out of the Ghetto: My Youth in the East End, Communism and Fascism, 1913–1939.* London, 1991.

Joannou, M. *Women Writers of the 1930s: Gender, Politics and History.* Edinburgh, 1999.

Kushner, T., and N. Valman. *Remembering Cable Street: Fascism and Anti-Fascism in British Society.* London, 2000.

Lawrence, J. 'Fascist Violence and the Politics of Order in Inter-war Britain: The Olympia Debate Revisited'. *Historical Research* lxxvi (2003), 238–67.

————.'Forging a Peaceable Kingdom: War, Violence and Brutalisation in post-First World War Britain'. *Journal of Modern History* 3 (2003), 557–89.

————. 'The Transformation of British Public Politics after the First World War'. *Past and Present* 190 (2006), 185–216.

LeMahieu, D.L. *A Culture for Democracy.* Oxford, 1988.

Linehan, T. *East London for Mosley: The British Union of Fascists in East London and South-West Essex, 1933–40.* London, 1996.

MacDougall, I. *Voices from the Spanish Civil War: Personal Recollections of Scottish Volunteers in Republican Spain, 1936–39.* Edinburgh, 1986.

Marsh, K., and R. Griffiths. *Granite and Honey: The Story of Phil Piratin, Communist MP.* Croydon, 2012.

McCarthy, H. 'Parties, Voluntary Associations and Democratic Politics in Interwar Britain'. *The Historical Journal* 50(4) (Dec. 2007).

————. *The British People and the League of Nations: Democracy, Citizenship and Internationalism, c.1918–1945.* Manchester, 2011.

Moloney, T. *Westminster, Whitehall and the Vatican: The Role of Cardinal Hinsley, 1935–1943*. London, 1985.

Montefiore, J. *Men and Women Writers of the 1930s: The Dangerous Flood of History*. London, 1996.

Orwell, G. *Coming up for Air*. Harmondsworth, 1980.

Orwell, S., and I. Angus (eds). *The Collected Essays, Journals and Letters of George Orwell*. Harmondsworth, 1970, vol. 1.

Petrie, M. 'Public Politics and Traditions of Popular Protest: Demonstrations of the Unemployed in Dundee and Edinburgh, c.1921–1939'. *Contemporary British History*, 2013.

Piratin, P. *Our Flag Stays Red*. London, 1948.

Pugh, M. *Hurrah for the Blackshirts! Fascists and Fascism in Britain between the Wars*. London, 2005.

Redfern, N. *Class or Nation: Communists, Imperialism and Two World Wars*. London, 2005.

Renton, D. *This Rough Game: Fascism and Anti-fascism*. Stroud, 2001.

Srebrnik, H.F. *London Jews and British Communism, 1935–1945*. Ilford, 1995.

Toynbee, P. *Friends Apart: A Memoir of Esmond Romilly and Jasper Ridley in the Thirties*. London, 1954.

Trades Union Congress General Council. *The Book of the Martyrs of Tolpuddle, 1834–1934*. London, 1934.

Worley, M. *Oswald Mosley and the New Party*. Basingstoke, 2010.

Tom Buchanan is Professor of Modern British and European History at OUDCE, University of Oxford, and a fellow of Kellogg College. He has written three books and numerous articles on British involvement in the Spanish Civil War. His most recent book is *East Wind: China and the British Left, 1925–1976* (2012). He is currently writing a book on Amnesty International and human rights activism in postwar Britain.

♪ 4

Searching for Antifascism

Historiography, the Crisis of the Liberal State and the Birth of Fascism and Antifascism in Italy, Spain and Portugal

Giulia Albanese

In the course of the 1920s, Italy, Spain and Portugal witnessed the crisis of their liberal regimes and the rise of dictatorial ones. While the context in which these crises occurred and the nature of these dictatorships were different, the reasons for the weaknesses of these liberal states were partly similar. Moreover, significant attempts were made to imitate the Italian fascist movement by Spanish and Portuguese conservative and right-wing groups.

The Italian example had much to teach not only the radical right, but also left-wing movements, including the radical left, for which the issue of fascism and the organisation of an antifascist front was destined to become a priority over the next decades. Nonetheless, in contrast to the amount of attention that has been paid to the later development of fascism, the first strategies and attempts to oppose fascism in the 1920s have largely been overlooked by historians. The aim of this chapter is to launch a reflection on the way in which the historiographies of Italy, Spain and Portugal have analysed the crisis of the liberal state and the rise of conservative and fascist movements, as well as of organised antifascist movements.

The Value of a Comparative Approach

From a historical perspective, Italy, Spain and Portugal present certain similarities, particularly in the social, economic and cultural spheres, as well as some notable differences – including macroscopic ones – when it comes to their historical and political trajectories.[1] The institutions of these three states were all relatively recent – although the Portuguese

Republic (1910) was much younger than the Kingdom of Italy (1861) and the restored Spanish monarchy (1875) – and included a liberal constitution, which only in Portugal, however, acquired a Republican form. Despite the prominence of the Catholic religion in all three countries, only in Spain had the relations with ecclesiastical institutions been smooth; and this raised problems of legitimacy for both the Republic of Portugal and the Kingdom of Italy. These elements have been invoked to justify comparative research on liberal institutions in the late nineteenth and early twentieth century, as well as on the economic history of these countries.

Italy, Spain and Portugal subsequently faced and overcame the challenge of the First World War in very different ways. Italy joined the conflict after a short period of neutrality with almost 6 million soldiers (out of 35 million inhabitants) and part of its territory turned into a battlefield. Following a crushing defeat at Caporetto in 1917, it succeeded in winning the war, if only from a strictly military perspective. Portugal lingered in its neutrality up until 1916, when it chose to enter the conflict with 105,000 men (out of 6 million inhabitants). These soldiers fought far away from home, on the Western Front or in the colonies; for the most part they experienced defeat – a very bitter one on the Western Front – even though the country ultimately won the war as a member of the Entente. Spain, instead, opted for neutrality. Notwithstanding the huge differences in their experience of war, these countries were deeply affected by the conflict, from a socio-economic as well as from a political point of view.[2] Furthermore, in both Italy and Portugal, albeit with different foundations and assumptions, the myth of a mutilated victory emerged, particularly in connection with the diplomatic outcomes of the war and the costs-to-benefits ratio of a conflict that caused deep divisions and political discord.

Historiography and the social sciences have considered the reasons for the development of this crisis and the birth of authoritarian and fascist regimes that followed, enlightening different elements. In these countries, the period between the end of the war and the early 1920s was one of social tensions and of transformations of the political framework, including party politics. These years witnessed a huge rise in political violence and new developments in the political thought of social, political, economic and religious elites. Generally speaking, it is only by comparing these countries in these years that is possible to uncover the reasons for the crisis of liberal institutions. The drive towards the democratisation of politics and society – which shaped liberal thought and institutions, and which all three countries were trying to promote during the last years of these institutions – was far from being extensively accepted by the local ruling classes. Although in all three states there had been some degree of acceptance of the principles of liberalism and the political forms they inspired, these were enacted with some peculiarities, as demonstrated for example by the electoral methods and the ways in which electoral majorities were built (see the development of *transformismo* in Italy, compared to *caciquismo* in the Iberian countries). Nonetheless, the majority of the ruling classes and the social elites were not at all willing to accept the transformation of society and its institutions that such principles entailed. This contrast between the form and content of liberal politics was only made stronger by the Russian Revolution and the revolutionary aspirations of Socialist, Communist and anarchist groups. In the last period of the liberal institutions in the three countries, governments were ruling mostly with a Parliament unable to legislate due to its divisions, and lasted only a few months, while the rift between the establishment and society was perceived as continuously growing.

The crisis of liberal institutions stemmed from these contradictions in all three cases, although the contexts, the experiences of the war and the ways in which institutions, political groups and society reacted to this conflict determined different historical trajectories. Nonetheless, it is also important to recognise their common roots. The attention devoted to the Italian experience by Spanish and Portuguese politicians and observers is an important element, because it reveals to what extent certain problems were perceived in a similar way in the three contexts. A comparative perspective may thus help to raise new questions, shed light on common issues and uncover national histories that partly diverge from those handed down to us by the historiographical traditions of these countries.

In Italy, the rise to power of fascism and the relative smoothness with which the fascist regime developed until its fall in 1945 have ensured a greater and more constant focus on the crisis of the liberal state and the origins of fascism ever since the aftermath of the Second World War, and the subject has become a classic theme in Italian national historiography. Things have been very different in Spain and Portugal. In Spain, the limited experience of the dictatorship of Miguel Primo de Rivera (1923–30) and the impact of the Spanish Civil War (1936–39) led to a greater focus on the crisis of the Republican experience (1931–36), on the Civil War and on the Francoist regime (1939–75), rather than on the crisis of the constitutional monarchy or of Primo de Rivera's dictatorship. Moreover, the endurance of Franco's dictatorship limited the development of a free national historiography until the coming of democracy.[3] In Portugal, António de Oliveira Salazar rose to power after seven years of coups d'état and political developments, which ultimately led to the creation of the *Estado Novo* in 1933. This, together with the fact that Salazar remained in power until 1968 and his regime lasted until 1974, explains the late emergence of a national historiography and the limited interest – until recent years – in the crisis of the First Republic.

The moments and ways in which the collapse of each of these three constitutional and liberal regimes occurred, then, had significant repercussions on the historiography of the three countries, which long envisaged their national experiences as being cut off from the wider European context. Moreover, the different ways in which the dictatorial experience shaped their historical trajectories, especially during and after the Second World War, determined great differences in the development of the historiography of the three cases.

The Role of the Great War and of Violence in the Crisis of the Liberal State

Over the past twenty-five years, the impact of the First World War on socio-political conflict and its role in triggering political and paramilitary violence has been at the centre of a meaningful historiographical renewal. George Mosse's questions regarding the brutalisation of politics during the war, as well as the attention paid – by Mosse and other scholars – to the vast field of cultural transformations and their socio-political repercussions, which came to affect and forever alter Europe over the course of the conflict, have posed, and continue to pose, new challenges to European historiography.[4] In some ways these issues have affected the ways in which national historiographies have looked at their own past, by revealing common and transnational processes throughout Europe.

Although Spain, Portugal and (to a lesser extent) Italy are rarely considered in wide comparative studies of postwar Europe, the comparative investigation of these three countries in the light of the European context may be regarded as paradigmatic. It shows that despite the very different ways in which they experienced the war, the processes of mobilisation triggered by the conflict and the transformation of the relation between violence and politics in those years must be seen as crucial elements. This holds true not just for those countries directly engaged in the conflict, but also for those that experienced it indirectly, without the mobilisation of their army, as in the case of Spain, where the crushing defeat suffered by the Spanish Army in 1921 at the hands of the Berber rebels at Annual in north-eastern Morocco contributed to the national crisis. Moreover, the failure of liberal institutions can be seen as involving not only those countries that lost the war, but even the victors, as in the case of Italy and Portugal.[5] There is a further issue that we should consider, and which has been completely overlooked so far: the importance of the processes of mobilisation that these countries experienced, even before actually joining the conflict. This mobilisation reveals a tendency towards the radicalisation of political conflict in the three countries prior to their participation in the war, through which it is possible to question the notion that the postwar brutalisation of politics was rooted in the conflict itself (a notion partly disproved by the degree of political brutalisation found in the neutral Spain of the 1910s and 1920s).[6]

This anticipation focuses our attention on the processes of transformation of political cultures and societies that were already underway before the First World War, but which only became mass phenomena – especially in Italy – with the mass mobilisation entailed by the conflict.

It is interesting to note that all this has only led to a limited redefinition of the first postwar phase and the crisis of the liberal state in Spain in Portugal, whereas in Italy – for understandable reasons, related to the points outlined above – a further reflection on the early postwar period has long been underway. In Italy, Mosse's thesis ushered in a new stage in the study of the origins of fascism, which emphasised the issue of violence by approaching it as a key to interpret the development of the fascist movement and their coming to power.[7]

This perspective can hardly be said to have had the same impact in Spain and Portugal. Still, it is worth noting that Spanish historians have come to raise similar questions with regard to violence via different routes, and particularly in relation to the Civil War: a subject that has led them to investigate – in an exemplary, in-depth manner – the practice, culture, roots and aims of political violence. Since the 1990s, scholars of contemporary Italy have learned much from this research.[8] For reasons I have yet to fully investigate, the issue of violence in Portugal is still not regarded as central to the reflection on the political, social and economic crisis in the immediate aftermath of the war, even though the impact of violence, and its importance as a language and tool for political struggle, can hardly be disputed, even in relation to the 1910s and 1920s. It is nonetheless true that in Spain and Portugal the processes leading to the transformation of society into a 'mass' society, while at work in cities and in the more developed rural areas, failed to provide the same drive for change that was ensured in Italy by the war and the new relations between state and society – although, at least to some extent, similar phenomena are also observed in these two countries.[9]

It seems to me, however, that only in the case of Italy, and to a lesser degree Spain, have these historiographical developments fostered an analysis not just of the relation between the brutalisation of politics and the origins of fascism – or Primo de Rivera's dictatorship – but also of the wider transformation of social and political struggle in the postwar period, before the rise of authoritarian and fascist regimes. It is not simply a matter, then, of taking into account the studies conducted on the various political institutions at work in the social and parliamentary sphere in the three countries: the transformation of the courses of action and political practices of the various political factions must also be examined.[10] This constitutes a crucial starting point for any attempt to understand the origins of fascism, as well as those of antifascism, along with the political cultures and forms of mobilisation the latter could deploy in the face of the rise of fascist or pro-fascist parties and movements in the 1920s. Thus certain studies on the *Biennio Rosso* ('two red years'; 1919–20), as well as on early reactions to fascism in Italy, have drawn attention to the issue of the organisation and political praxis of the Italian left in the aftermath of war, but also – albeit not explicitly enough – on the topic of the use of political violence within this context.[11] The field of enquiry, however, is still wide open in Italy: much more in-depth research on the relation between ideology and mobilisation, and politics and violence, is required in order to examine the transformation, interrelation and interpenetration of different political cultures in the immediate aftermath of the conflict. In Spain, by contrast, these topics would appear to have been revisited in relation to the period under consideration almost exclusively through Eduardo Gonzalez Calleja's studies on the use of violence and its expressions, given the little interest shown for the period itself on account of the greater focus on the 1930s – the Civil War and its consequences.[12]

There has been one phase of studies – a distant one not to be idealised, and spanning different periods, given the radically different histories of Italy, Spain and Portugal in the latter half of the twentieth century – in which the central questions raised by Marxist historiography provided some common frameworks for historians in the three countries. This historiography explored the relations between society, politics and the economy, with an emphasis on the formation of Socialist and Communist trade unions and parties, by investigating social movements, strikes and demonstrations. While such topics are no longer on most historians' agenda, the studies from that period still provide a crucial starting point for any attempt to address certain historical questions in parallel, and draw possible comparisons. To this day, they constitute the most relevant historiography for anyone wishing to examine the origins of the antifascist movement in Spain and Portugal.[13]

The Crisis of Liberal Institutions and the Birth of Fascism

As regards the crisis of liberal institutions, in recent years the centenary of the establishment of the First Portuguese Republic has led to the publication of numerous studies on the topic.[14] In Italy, the 150th anniversary of Italian unification has not really fostered any original reflection on the limits of liberalism, a central topic in the 1960s – for the focus has been more on the origins of the unified state than on its crisis.

With respect to Portugal, a rather clear distinction has been observed up until this day between two strongly opposed interpretations of the Republic. On the one hand there are those historians who point to the limits of the Republic to explain its crisis and the failure to bring about a lasting revolution – for instance, by stressing the ambiguous role of the army or the limits of liberalism, or by arguing that the monarchy or, to a lesser degree, Salazar's regime had a greater potential for reform and integration. On the other hand, there are those who have focused on the profound transformations and moves towards democratisation achieved by the Republic by comparison with the monarchical state. This debate is in many ways similar to that which has long characterised the analysis of liberal Italy and the origins of fascism. In the case of Spain, scholars have first concentrated – as in the case of Portugal – on the significance of the country's military tradition and coups, as well as on the tension between the army and liberal institutions – and, later, on the impact of the military crisis of Annual. Only in recent years has attention shifted to the European-wide crisis of liberal institutions, of which the Spanish case is but one example, within a context profoundly shaped by the First World War.[15] A more in-depth investigation of these topics from a comparative perspective might bring out the significance and limits of the political, institutional and socio-economic modernisation that was launched in the nineteenth century and which (at least apparently) constituted one of the aims pursued through the establishment of liberal institutions. This issue is to be carefully examined if we are to make sense of the authoritarian reaction that occurred in the three countries in the 1920s through coups d'état and dictatorships (as well as of the kind of modernisation promoted by these regimes).

Over the years, several studies – including comparative ones – have illustrated the ways in which these experiences led to more or less significant changes, depending on the context, related to the transformation of existing institutions, access to voting, literacy rates, industrialisation, the socio-economic framework and urbanisation levels, as well as the extension of social and political rights, and bribery rates related to these institutional and electoral transformations.[16] The combination of these elements accounts for the nature and significance of the transformation of pre-existing institutions into liberal ones through a drive towards the modernisation and democratisation of society, albeit it with many limitations and contrasts.

In this context those studies focusing on the Church, and particularly on the pontificate of Pius XI (1922–39), have provided a considerable contribution to our understanding of fascism. It seems to me that a more interesting topic is the circulation of ideas and political or religious projects in this domain, which also provides a common ground for the historiographies of each of the three countries. The latter share not just the experience of a concordat – signed, in all three cases, albeit at different moments, under a dictatorship – but also, in the case of Italy and Portugal, a similar process of rapprochement between public and religious institutions, which crucially contributed to lending greater legitimacy to the state.[17]

The analysis of fascism and fascist movements in the interwar period has opened up new prospects for cross-exchanges between historians working on the subject. In a collected volume on European fascism published back in 1968, Stuart Woolf was the first to discuss the Iberian peninsula as part of a genuinely scholarly rather than an ideologically informed analysis of the development and spread of a European-wide political ideology and praxis that was seen to have taken various different forms, all falling within the category of fascism.[18] Over the years, the transformation of historiographical paradigms, combined with the development of a range of different working hypotheses aimed at providing a definition of fascism and fascist movements that might take account of all the various dictatorial, right-wing and/or reactionary regimes in interwar Europe, has contributed to increasing the focus on Spain and Portugal. Still, there is a tendency to marginalise these cases by viewing them within the category of authoritarianism, thereby emphasising the traditional elements of these regimes while overlooking their modernising aspects.[19] Moreover, when it comes to the 1920s, some of the most interesting studies explicitly focused on the Iberian peninsula were published in the 1980s and 1990s (let us think, in particular, of Ben-Ami's works on Spain in the 1980s and Costa Pinto's on

Portugal in the early 1990s).[20] Despite the fact that much research – particularly on Spain – has contributed to elucidating the limits and strong points of this comparative approach on these issues, it seems that much work remains to be done on the impact of the rise of Italian fascism in the 1920s. This problem does not merely concern the historiography of Spain and Portugal: while Italy has witnessed a broader engagement with these topics, much progress still remains to be made in order to fully transcend the polemics and strings attached to the debate within the country itself, so as to more fully and explicitly address the issue of cross-national ties and of the impact of a crisis that extended well beyond the Italian peninsula. In this regard, the kind of analysis in question might provide a substantial contribution to the historiography of antifascism.

Conclusion: Rethinking Antifascism in the Light of Fascism

While increasingly attentive to the limits of liberalism and its possibility to serve as a cradle for fascist and authoritarian movements, historiography has been less interested in the question of the groups that actively confronted the growth of fascism in Southern Europe, or in how the transnational links among these movements actually worked.

In all three countries, the phase of studies on the developments of working-class movements and their activities, which we considered above, has led to an analysis of the various left-wing movements, including in relation to fascism, the Third International and the establishment of international networks of opposition and resistance to the dictatorships of the 1920s.[21] Many of these, however, are rather conventional and outdated studies that hardly add anything new to what has emerged in recent years with regard to the rise of right-wing, fascist or fascistic movements. Such works do not really help us to understand the social, political or ideological complexity of those years of transition – and, most of all, they do not answer the questions that contemporary historians might wish to raise with regard to these experiences. Still, the little that may be gleaned from these studies shows that both right-wing and left-wing movements in Spain and Portugal had a considerable grasp of the political processes underway in Italy. This, in turn, points to the existence of international relations – beyond the Third International – and to a capacity to analyse the international scenario certainly greater than the capacity and opportunity these movements had to develop effective political strategies and plans of action in their own countries. It is now time to ask ourselves up to which point the failure of left-wing parties and unions to resist fascism in Italy and Primo de Rivera in Spain was meaningful for the opposition to the dictatorship in other countries in the 1920s; what political and intellectual resources these movement could mobilise in order to understand, confront and react to the explosion of a reactionary right that was experimenting with new political languages and practices; and, finally, to what extent the transnational dialogue between different working-class organisations and left-wing movements had an impact on national experiences.

Translated from the Italian by Sergio Knipe

Postscript

This chapter is part of a comparative study that the author is conducting on the crisis of liberal institutions and the rise of dictatorships in Italy, Spain and Portugal in the 1920s. Since the research is still ongoing, the results presented here should be considered as provisional and open to reassessment in the light of future reflections.

Notes

1. For a preliminary historical overview of these developments based on a comparative approach, I shall refer to A. Costa Pinto, 'Political Violence and Institutional Crisis: Italy, Spain and Portugal', in A. Costa Pinto (ed.), *The Nature of Fascism*, Basingstoke and New York, 2010, 186–96.
2. Among the most recent overviews of the history of each of these countries during the conflict, see M. Isnenghi and G. Rochat, *La Grande Guerra 1914–1918*, Milan, 2004 (1st edn, 2000); A. Gibelli, *La grande guerra degli italiani 1915–1918*, Milan, 1998; F. Ribeiro de Meneses, *União sagrada e sidonismo. Portugal em guerra (1916–18)*, pref. by N. Severiano Teixeira, Lisbon, 2000; A. Afonso and C. de Matos Gomes (eds), *Portugal e a Grande Guerra: 1914–1918*, Matosinhos, 2010; F.J. Romero Salvadó, *Spain 1914–1918: Between War and Revolution*, London and New York, 1999.
3. For recent historiographical accounts of Primo de Rivera's dictatorship, see P. Montes, 'La dictadura de Primo de Rivera y la historiografía. Una confrontación metodológica', *Historia Social* 74 (2012), 167–84; and C. González Martínez, 'La Dictadura de Primo de Rivera: una propuesta de análisis', *Anales de Historia Contemporánea* 16 (2000), 337–408.
4. The literature on these topics is so vast that I will only refer here to some of the main works, inspired by the following two studies: G. Mosse, *Fallen Soldiers: Reshaping the Memory of the World Wars*, Oxford, 1990; and A. Becker

and S. Audoin-Rouzeau, *14–18 Retrouver la guerre*, Paris, 2000. Recent comparative pictures often focus exclusively on the case of Italy, overlooking – understandably so, at times – not just Spain but also Portugal: see S. Audoin-Rouzeau and C. Prochasson (eds), *Sortir de la Grande Guerre. Le monde et l'après-1918*, Paris, 2008; R. Gerwarth and J. Horne (eds), *War in Peace: Paramilitary Violence in Europe after the Great War*, Oxford, 2012 (the English edition of this volume does not even mention the case of Italy, which in the Italian edition is discussed by Emilio Gentile – a leading expert on the subject but not a member of the team responsible for the publication of the volume); J. Winter and A. Prost, *The Great War in History: Debates and Controversies, 1914 to the Present*, Cambridge, 2005 (1st edn, 2004).

5. See F.J. Romero Salvadó, *Spain 1914–1918*; and *The Foundations of Civil War: Revolution, Social Conflict and Reaction in Liberal Spain 1916–1923*, Abingdon and New York, 2008; F. Ribeiro de Meneses, *Portugal 1914–1926: From the First World War to Military Dictatorship*, Bristol, 2004; E. González Calleja, *El Máuser y el sufragio. Orden público, subversión y violencia política en la crisis de la Restauración (1917–1931)*, Madrid, 1999.

6. See M. Fuentes Codera, 'Los intelectuales españoles y la Gran Guerra: ¿un caso excepcional?', *Storica* 46 (2010), 49–78; A. Ventrone, *La seduzione totalitaria. Guerra, modernità e violenza politica (1914–1918)*, Rome, 2003; 'Le trasformazioni della politica: i giovani e l'interventismo nell'Italia del 1915', in F. Rasera and C. Zadra (eds), *Volontari italiani nella Grande Guerra*, Rovereto, 2008, 73–80. See also the *Ayer* special issue edited by Fuentes Codera, with detailed discussions of the cases of Italy, Spain and France; cf. Fuentes Codera, 'La Gran Guerra de los intelectuales: España en Europa', *Ayer* 91 (2013).

7. M. Franzinelli, *Squadristi. Protagonisti e tecniche della violenza fascista 1919–1922*, Milan, 2003; E. Gentile, *Storia del Partito fascista 1919–1922. Movimento e milizia*, Rome and Bari, 1989; S. Reichardt, *Camicie nere, camicie brune. Milizie fasciste in Italia e in Germania*, Bologna, 2009 (1st edn, 2002); G. Albanese, *Alle origini del fascismo. La violenza politica a Venezia 1919–1922*, Padua, 2001.

8. In this respect, a crucial bridge between Italy and Spain has been found in the journal *Spagna contemporanea*, first published in Italy in 1992, and in some of Gabriele Ranzato's books, which have especially contributed to extending the debate beyond the sphere of research specifically focusing on Spanish history. In particular, see G. Ranzato, *Guerre fratricide. Le guerre civili in età contemporanea*, Turin, 1994; and *Il linciaggio di Carretta – Roma, 1944. Violenza politica e ordinaria violenza*, Milan, 1997 – where, in my opinion, the analysis of Italian events is deeply indebted to Spanish historiography.

9. See, among the recent studies, Ribeiro de Meneses, *Portugal 1914–1926*; and A. Quiroga, *Making Spaniards: Primo de Rivera and the Nationalisation of the Masses, 1923–30*, Basingstoke and New York, 2007.

10. An important comparative study of these aspects with a focus on Italy and Spain (as well as on Romania) is provided by D. Riley, *The Civic Foundations of Fascism in Europe, 1870–1945*, Baltimore, 2010; and 'Civic Association and Authoritarian Regimes in Interwar Europe: Italy and Spain in Comparative

perspective', *American Sociological Review* 70 (2005), 288–310, although I do not completely agree with Riley's analysis.

11. After the classic research produced in the 1960s and 1970s, and Roberto Vivarelli's analysis, several studies on the *Bienno Rosso* have been published in Italy in recent years. See especially R. Bianchi, *Pace, pane, terra. Il 1919 in Italia*, Rome, 2006; AA.VV., *I due bienni rossi del Novecento 1919– 1920 e 1968–1969*, Rome, 2006; F. Fabbri, *Le origini della guerra civile. L'Italia dalla Grande Guerra al fascismo, 1918–1921*, Turin, 2009. Roberto Bianchi has also measured the weight of these phenomena at an international level: R. Bianchi, 'Les mouvements contre la vie chère en Europe au lendemain de la Grande Guerre', in *Le XXe siècle des guerres*, Paris, 2004, 237–45. On Spain, where social tensions reached their peak in a three-year period known as the 'Bolshevik' years, see A. Delgado Larios, '¿Problema agrario andaluz o cuestión nacional? El mito del Trienio Bolchevique en Andalucia (1918–1920)', *Cuadernos de Historia Contemporanea* 3 (1991), 97–124. This work is particularly helpful for contextualising the historical debate and public rhetoric on the subject. In Portugal the topic would not appear to have been thematised to the same degree as in other European countries, even though the economic crisis and social tensions made themselves felt in similar ways in this country as well; see A.J. Telo, *Decadência e queda da I Republica Portuguesa*, Lisbon, 1980.

12. See in particular E. González Calleja and F. del Rey Reguillo, *La defensa armada contra la revolución. Una historia de las guardias cívicas en la España del siglo XX*, Madrid, 1995; E. González Calleja, *La razón de la fuerza. Orden público, subversión y violencia política en la España de la Restauración (1875–1917)*, Madrid, 1998; and González Calleja, *El Máuser y el sufragio*.

13. For Spain the bibliography on the *trienio bolchevique* is particularly relevant (a critical analysis of this literature may be found in Delgado Larios, quoted above), although the last years have witnessed a renewal of research on this topic, according to Hugo Garcia, 'El antifascismo en España (1933– 39): una historia pendiente', in *Claves del mundo contemporáneo*, eds. Teresa María Ortega and Miguel Ángel del Arco, Granada, 2013. For Portugal, see in particular Telo, *Decadência e queda da I República Portugues*, which is still one of the most complete histories of the period, but also César Oliveira, *O Operariado e a Primeira República (1910–1924)*, Lisbon, 1990.

14. Among the most noteworthy studies are: F. Rosas and M.F. Rollo, *História da Primeira República Portuguesa*, Lisbon, 2009; A. Costa Pinto and P.J. Fernandes (eds), *A Primeira République Portuguesa*, Lisbon, 2010; A.C. Pinto, *A Primeira República e os conflitos da modernidade (1919–1926)*, Lisbon, 2011; F. Ribeiro de Meneses (ed.), *A primeira République Portuguesa: diplomacia, guerra e império*, Lisbon, 2011; V. Pulido Valente, *A 'República velha' (1910– 1927)*, Lisbon, 1997.

15. F.J. Romero Salvadó and A. Smith (eds), *The Agony of Spanish Liberalism: From Revolution to Dictatorship 1913–23*, Basingstoke and New York, 2010; González Martínez, 'La dictadura de Primo de Rivera', 340–42.

16. Among the most relevant studies, see S. Casmirri and M. Suárez Cortina (eds), *La Europa del Sur en la época liberal. España, Italia y Portugal. Una perspectiva comparada*, Cassino, 1998; G. Tortella, *El desarrollo de la España*

contemporánea. Historia económica de los siglos XIX y XX, Madrid, 1994; and Javier Tusell's theme issue *El sufragio universal*, in *Ayer* 3 (1991).

17. See L. Salgado de Matos, *A Separação do Estato e da Igreja. Concórdia e conflito entre a Primeira República e o Catolicismo*, Alfragide, 2010; and V. Neto's overview *A questão religiosa: Estado, Igreja e conflitualidade sócio-religiosa*, in F. Rosas and M.F. Rollo (eds), *História da Primeira República Portuguesa*, Lisbon, 2009. On Spain, see C. Adagio, *Chiesa e Nazione in Spagna. La dittatura di Primo de Rivera*, Milan, 2004. On Italy, see R. Pertici, *Chiesa e Stato in Italia: dalla Grande Guerra ai nuovo Concordato (1914–1984)*, Bologna, 2009; A. Guasco, *Cattolici e fascisti. La Santa Sede e la politica italiana all'alba del regime (1919–1925)*, Bologna, 2013; and L. Ceci, *L'interesse superiore. Il Vaticano e l'Italia di Mussolini*, Rome and Bari, 2013. In addition to the standard studies on the subject, some important new ones have been published in recent years, among which I wish to refer to D. Menozzi and R. Moro (eds), *Cattolicesimo e totalitarismo. Chiese e culture religiose tra le due guerre mondiali (Italia, Spagna, Francia)*, Brescia, 2004; and A. Botti, F. Montero and A. Quiroga (eds), *Católicos y patriotas. Religión y nación en la Europa de entreguerras*, Madrid, 2013.

18. S. Woolf, *European Fascism*, London, 1968. On this topic, see Costa Pinto, *The Nature of Fascism* (also providing original considerations on the subject).

19. G. Albanese, 'Comparare i fascismi. Una riflessione storiografica', *Storica* 43–45 (2009), 313–44.

20. S. Ben-Ami, *Fascism from Above: The Dictatorship of Primo de Rivera in Spain, 1923–1930*, Oxford, 1983; and A. Costa Pinto, *The Blue Shirts: Portuguese Fascists and the New State*, New York, 2000 (1st edn, 1994). See also A. Costa Pinto, *Salazar's Dictatorship and European Fascism: Problems of Interpretation*, New York, 1995.

21. See, for example, N. Poulantzas, *Fascismo e dittatura. La terza internazionale di fronte al* fascismo, Milan, 1971; A. Agosti, *La terza internazionale: storia documentata*, Rome, 1974; J. Droz, *Histoire de l'antifascisme en Europe (1923–1939)*, Paris, 2001. The literature on left-wing movements in these years is quite large, and comprehends the history of the different parties, among them Socialist, Communist and anarchist movements, and of single events of resistance or mobilisation. See, for example, E. Francescangeli, *Arditi del popolo – Argo Secondari e la prima organizzazione antifascista (1917–1922)*, Rome, 2000; L. Branciforte, *El Socorro Rojo Internacional en España (1923–1939)*, Madrid, 2011; L.H. Afonso Manta, *A Frente Popular Antifascista: o primeiro esboço de unidade antifascista*, Lisbon, 1976; and J. Neves, *Comunismo e Nacionalismo em Portugal – Política, Cultura e História no Século XX*, Lisbon, 2008.

References

AA.VV. *I due bienni rossi del Novecento 1919–1920 e 1968–1969*. Rome, 2006.

Adagio, C. *Chiesa e Nazione in Spagna. La dittatura di Primo de Rivera*. Milan, 2004.

Afonso, A., and C. de Matos Gomes (eds). *Portugal e a Grande Guerra: 1914–1918.* Matosinhos, 2010.

Afonso Manta, L.H. *A Frente Popular Antifascista: o primeiro esboço de unidade antifascista.* Lisbon, 1976.

Agosti, A. *La terza internazionale: storia documentata.* Rome, 1974.

Albanese, G. *Alle origini del fascismo. La violenza politica a Venezia 1919–1922.* Padua, 2001.

———. 'Comparare i fascismi. Una riflessione storiografica'. *Storica* 43–45 (2009), 313–44.

Audoin-Rouzeau, S., and C. Prochasson (eds). *Sortir de la Grande Guerre. Le monde et l'après-1918.* Paris, 2008.

Becker, A., and S. Audoin-Rouzeau. *14–18 Retrouver la guerre.* Paris, 2000.

Ben-Ami, S. *Fascism from Above: The Dictatorship of Primo de Rivera in Spain, 1923–1930.* Oxford, 1983.

Bianchi, R. 'Les mouvements contre la vie chère en Europe au lendemain de la Grande Guerre', in *Le XXe siècle des guerres.* Paris, 2004, 237–45.

———. *Pace, pane, terra. Il 1919 in Italia.* Rome, 2006.

Botti, A., F. Montero and A. Quiroga (eds). *Católicos y patriotas. Religión y nación en la Europa de entreguerras.* Madrid, 2013.

Branciforte, L. *El Socorro Rojo Internacional en España (1923–1939).* Madrid, 2011.

Casmirri, S., and M. Suárez Cortina (eds). *La Europa del Sur en la época liberal. España, Italia y Portugal. Una perspectiva comparada.* Cassino, 1998.

Ceci, L. *L'interesse superiore. Il Vaticano e l'Italia di Mussolini.* Rome and Bari, 2013.

Costa Pinto, A. *Salazar's Dictatorship and European Fascism: Problems of Interpretation.* New York, 1995.

———. *The Blue Shirts: Portuguese Fascists and the New State.* 2nd edn. New York, 2000.

———. 'Political Violence and Institutional Crisis: Italy, Spain and Portugal', in A. Costa Pinto (ed.), *The Nature of Fascism.* Basingstoke and New York, 2010, 186–96.

Costa Pinto, A., and P.J. Fernandes (eds). *A Primeira República Portuguesa.* Lisbon, 2010.

Delgado Larios, A. '¿Problema agrario andaluz o cuestión nacional? El mito del Trienio Bolchevique en Andalucia (1918–1920)'. *Cuadernos de Historia Contemporanea* 3 (1991), 97–124.

Droz, J. *Histoire de l'antifascisme en Europe (1923–1939).* Paris, 2001.

Fabbri, F. *Le origini della guerra civile. L'Italia dalla Grande Guerra al fascismo, 1918–1921.* Turin, 2009.

Francescangeli, E. *Arditi del popolo – Argo Secondari e la prima organizzazione antifascista (1917–1922).* Rome, 2000.

Franzinelli, M. *Squadristi. Protagonisti e tecniche della violenza fascista 1919–1922.* Milan, 2003.

Fuentes Codera, M. 'Los intelectuales españoles y la Gran Guerra: ¿un caso excepcional?'. *Storica* 46 (2010), 49–78.

———. 'La Gran Guerra de los intelectuales: España en Europa', theme issue, *Ayer* 91 (2013).

Garcia, H. 'El antifascismo en España (1933–39): una historia pendiente', in *Claves del mundo contemporáneo*, eds. Teresa María Ortega and Miguel Ángel del Arco. Granada, 2013.

Gentile, E. *Storia del Partito fascista 1919–1922. Movimento e milizia*. Rome and Bari, 1989.

Gerwarth, R., and J. Horne (eds). *War in Peace: Paramilitary Violence in Europe after the Great War*. Oxford, 2012.

Gibelli, A. *La grande guerra degli italiani 1915–1918*. Milan, 1998.

González Calleja, E. *La razón de la fuerza. Orden público, subversión y violencia política en la España de la Restauración (1875–1917)*. Madrid, 1998.

———. *El Máuser y el sufragio. Orden público, subversión y violencia política en la crisis de la Restauración (1917–1931)*. Madrid, 1999.

González Calleja, E., and F. del Rey Reguillo. *La defensa armada contra la revolución. Una historia de las guardias cívicas en la España del siglo XX*. Madrid, 1995.

González Martínez, C. 'La Dictadura de Primo de Rivera: una propuesta de análisis'. *Anales de Historia Contemporánea* 16 (2000), 337–408.

Guasco, A. *Cattolici e fascisti. La Santa Sede e la politica italiana all'alba del regime (1919–1925)*. Bologna, 2013.

Isnenghi, M., and G. Rochat. *La Grande Guerra 1914–1918*. 2nd edn. Milan, 2004.

Menozzi, D., and R. Moro (eds). *Cattolicesimo e totalitarismo. Chiese e culture religiose tra le due guerre mondiali (Italia, Spagna, Francia)*. Brescia, 2004.

Montes, P. 'La dictadura de Primo de Rivera y la historiografía. Una confrontación metodológica'. *Historia Social* 74 (2012), 167–84.

Mosse, G. *Fallen Soldiers: Reshaping the Memory of the World Wars*. Oxford, 1990.

Neto, V. *A questão religiosa: Estado, Igreja e conflitualidade socio-religiosa*, in F. Rosas and M.F. Rollo (eds), *História da Primeira República Portuguesa*, Lisbon, 2009.

Neves, J. *Comunismo e Nacionalismo em Portugal – Política, Cultura e História no Século XX*. Lisbon, 2008.

Oliveira, C. *O Operariado e a Primeira República (1910–1924)*. Lisbon, 1990

Pertici, R. *Chiesa e Stato in Italia: dalla Grande Guerra ai nuovo Concordato (1914–1984)*. Bologna, 2009.

Pinto, A.C. *A Primeira República e os conflitos da modernidade (1919–1926)*. Lisbon, 2011.

Poulantzas, N. *Fascismo e dittatura. La terza internazionale di fronte al fascism*. Milan, 1971.

Pulido Valente, V. *A 'República velha' (1910–1927)*. Lisbon, 1997.

Quiroga, A. *Making Spaniards: Primo de Rivera and the Nationalisation of the Masses, 1923–30*. Basingstoke and New York, 2007.

Ranzato, G. (ed.). *Guerre fratricide. Le guerre civili in età contemporánea*. Turin, 1994.

———. *Il linciaggio di Carretta – Roma, 1944. Violenza politica e ordinaria violenza*. Milan, 1997.

Reichardt, S. *Camicie nere, camicie brune. Milizie fasciste in Italia e in Germania*. 2nd edn. Bologna, 2009.

Ribeiro de Meneses, F. *União sagrada e sidonismo. Portugal em guerra (1916–18)*. Lisbon, 2000.

———. *Portugal 1914–1926: From the First World War to Military Dictatorship.* Bristol, 2004.

———. (ed.). *A primeira Républica Portuguesa: diplomacia, guerra e imperio.* Lisbon, 2011.

Riley, D. 'Civic Association and Authoritarian Regimes in Interwar Europe: Italy and Spain in Comparative perspective'. *American Sociological Review* 70 (2005), 288–310.

———. *The Civic Foundations of Fascism in Europe, 1870–1945.* Baltimore, 2010.

Romero Salvadó, F.J. *Spain 1914–1918: Between War and Revolution.* London and New York, 1999.

———. *The Foundations of Civil War: Revolution, Social Conflict and Reaction in Liberal Spain 1916–1923.* Abingdon and New York, 2008.

Romero Salvadó, F., and A. Smith (eds). *The Agony of Spanish Liberalism: From Revolution to Dictatorship 1913–23.* Basingstoke and New York, 2010.

Rosas, F., and M.F. Rollo (eds). *História da Primeira República Portuguesa.* Lisbon, 2009.

Salgado de Matos, L. *A Separação do Estado e da Igreja. Concórdia e conflito entre a Primeira República e o Catolicismo.* Alfragide, 2010.

Telo, A.J. *Decadência e queda da I República Portuguesa.* Lisbon, 1980.

Tortella, G. *El desarrollo de la España contemporánea. Historia económica de los siglos XIX y XX.* Madrid, 1994.

Ventrone, A. *La seduzione totalitaria. Guerra, modernità e violenza politica (1914–1918).* Rome, 2003.

———. 'Le trasformazioni della politica: i giovani e l'interventismo nell'Italia del 1915', in F. Rasera and C. Zadra (eds), *Volontari italiani nella Grande Guerra.* Rovereto, 2008, 73–80.

Winter, J., and A. Prost. *The Great War in History: Debates and Controversies, 1914 to the Present.* 2nd edn. Cambridge, 2005.

Woolf, S. *European Fascism.* London, 1968.

Giulia Albanese is associate professor of Modern History at the University of Padua. She is particularly interested in the crisis of liberal institutions in the 1920s, postwar political violence and fascism. She has published widely on the origins of fascism (*La Marcia su Roma*, 2006; *Alle origini del fascismo. La violenza politica a Venezia 1919–1922*, 2001) and on fascism in Italy (*In the Society of Fascists: Acclamation, Acquiescence and Agency in Mussolini's Italy*, ed. with Roberta Pergher, 2012; and *Il ventennio fascista 1919–1945*, ed. with Mario Isnenghi, 2008). Her new book – *Dittature mediterranee. Sovversioni fasciste e colpi di stato in Italia, Spagna e Portogallo* – on the crisis of liberal institutions and the beginning of dictatorships in Southern Europe in the 1920s will be published in 2016.

⸎ 5

Was there an Antifascist Culture in Spain during the 1930s?

Hugo García

The Loyalists' tenacious but vain resistance to the Nationalist rebels and their Italian and German allies during the Spanish Civil War (1936–39) remains an unparalleled symbol of the mobilising power – and the flaws – of antifascism.[1] The lack of a comprehensive history of this movement in Spain – only partially remedied by Ferran Gallego's inspiring study of the Barcelona May Days of 1937 – is therefore a surprising gap in the vast bibliography on the conflict.[2] For reasons that it would be interesting to explore (the influence of class and political categories; a persistent belief in Spain's difference; a retrospective projection of the Republic's defeat), most historians continue to see the interwar Spanish left as a 'fissiparous coalition that achieved only the unity of despair', only accidentally connected to larger trends in world history.[3] This chapter argues, instead, that their experience cannot be understood without taking into account the transnational spread of an antifascist culture – the emergence of an 'informal global left', actively opposed to an expanding and increasingly aggressive far right – that took place during these years.[4] Thanks to its unique civil conflict, Spain is an ideal laboratory to analyse the issues that preoccupy current historians of antifascism. This chapter discusses three of these issues, derived from the general problem posed in its title: Was there an antifascist culture in Spain during the 1930s? If there was, what was it like, and to what extent was it shared by ordinary Spaniards?

Antifascism without Fascism?

The question is in itself problematic, as fascism *sensu stricto* remained a marginal force in Spain until the Civil War – François Furet even claimed that 'Spain in 1936 was one of the least appropriate European countries for an analysis in terms of fascism/antifascism'.[5] The Spanish left was certainly familiar with Italian fascism, even if few could match the expertise of Andrés Nin, the Catalan Communist leader who wrote a lengthy report on 'international fascism' for the Red International of Labour Unions (Profintern) in July 1923, shortly before General Miguel Primo de Rivera ended a half century of parliamentary rule in Spain through a bloodless coup d'état.[6] Since 1925, critics of Primo de Rivera's dictatorship started to point out its 'mimicry' with that of Mussolini.[7] In February of that year, Federico García Lorca denounced the Lateran Treaty between Mussolini and Pope Pius XI in his poem 'Cry to Rome', written 'from the tower of the Chrysler Building' in New York, while advancing a sort of Popular Front *avant la lettre* made of a 'crowd with hammer, violin or cloud'.[8] Francisco Largo Caballero, Socialist minister of labour in the first Republican government, had predicted, days before the change of regime in April 1931: 'If we overthrow the monarchy [of Alfonso XIII, 1902–31], fascism will also die in Europe'.[9]

Nevertheless, antifascism did not play a significant role in the movement that proclaimed the Second Republic. Miguel de Unamuno, a leading opponent of the Spanish dictatorship, described it to Henri Barbusse in 1929 as a 'praetorian tyranny' but not as fascist, as its single party Unión Patriótica (Patriotic Union) had no doctrine apart from sustaining the monarchy.[10] A European-wide report prepared by the Socialist International in the same year pointed out that the Primo de Rivera regime could only be described as fascism 'with certain reservations', and that unlike that of Mussolini in Italy it had not led to 'a complete oppression of the working class'.[11] Apart from the Communists and the anarchists, who attacked the new Republic as 'a Republican fascism, disguised in a Phrygian bonnet', most left-wing Spaniards believed that fascism could not triumph in a traditional and backward country such as Spain.[12] Even when self-proclaimed fascist groups – including José Antonio Primo de Rivera, the son of the former dictator – launched a propaganda campaign in Madrid in March 1933, Luis de Tapia, a Republican sympathiser, jokingly wrote that 'the daring fascists we see in my nation / smell of sacristans of the Sacred Heart!'[13] Henceforth, however, an increasingly active and massive antifascism emerged in Spain, growing faster than in any other country. In December 1933, Socialists, Communists and anarchists founded in Catalonia a 'Workers' Alliance against Fascism', the first agreement ever in an entire region among the three main branches of the workers' movement.[14] The narrow victory of the even broader Frente Popular ('Popular Front') in the parliamentary election of February 1936 likewise preceded that of the French Front Populaire – which, ironically, had inspired the creation of the Spanish coalition.

In the absence of a Spanish equivalent of the French riots of 6 February 1934, this sudden outburst of antifascism can only be explained by taking cultural transfers into consideration. A wide range of sources reflect the 'transnational consciousness' of the Spanish left and its concern over the rise of the far right in Europe even before 1931.[15] At least a dozen books on this topic appeared in Spain in the late 1920s and early 1930s, including translations of works by foreign critics of fascism such as Italian Luigi Sturzo and German Hermann Heller – who died in November 1933 in Madrid after being forced to leave Germany by the new Nazi government – and studies by local politicians such as Ángel Ossorio, Marcelino Domingo and the above-mentioned Andrés Nin.[16] The left-wing press regularly published articles on and by antifascist refugees such as Aurelio Natoli, an Italian freemason who wrote for the bestselling *Heraldo de Madrid*, and Ludwig Stautz, a German anarchist who launched the bilingual periodical *Der Antifaschist/El antifascista* in Barcelona in June 1933.[17] Illustrated magazines such as *Orto*, *Octubre* and *Nueva Cultura* published anti-Nazi photomontages by John Heartfield and similar works by talented Spanish graphic artists such as Josep Renau.[18] The ideas, values and imagery of antifascism entered Spain through established institutions – the Workers' Internationals, the League for the Rights of Man, and freemasonry were probably the most important – and also, as we will see, through new associations founded for that purpose.[19] But informal social channels were also crucial: those Spanish activists who had lived in Paris and Berlin and frequented the European 'antifascist Bohemia' in the 1920s, such as Nin, Unamuno, Francesc Macià, Julio Álvarez del Vayo, Julián Gorkin and Valeriano Orobón would later play active roles in the antifascist movement under the Republic.[20]

Foreign influences, combined with the radicalisation of the Spanish right after the change of regime, account for the left's increasing concern about fascism since the summer of 1932, when the Nazis' great gains in the German federal election of 31 July were followed by a failed monarchist coup in Seville on 10 August. Hitler's rise to power in January 1933 was, in Spain as elsewhere, a 'transformative event' for both the left and the right, that started to consider fascism as an international phenomenon and no longer as an Italian peculiarity.[21] Observers of various affiliations such as Manuel Chaves Nogales (liberal), Antonio Ramos Oliveira (Socialist) and Cipriano Rivas Cherif (the brother-in-law of the left Republican leader Manuel Azaña) travelled to Germany and described the climate of terror that prevailed in the new Reich.[22] Luis Araquistáin, veteran socialist leader and Spanish ambassador to Germany, resigned and started to campaign for the PSOE to seize power and thus avoid the fate of the SPD.[23] It was at this critical juncture that Henri Barbusse, Lord Marley and Ellen Wilkinson visited Madrid, in early July, in order to promote the foundation of a Spanish Relief Committee for the Victims of German Fascism, the spearhead of Comintern antifascism in Spain.[24] The banning of Austrian social democracy and the subsequent establishment of a 'Christian corporate State' by Chancellor Dollfuss in February 1934 increased the alarm in the country, where many saw Dollfuss as the model of José María Gil Robles, the leader of the Catholic CEDA.[25] The PSOE's decision to promote an armed insurrection in early October 1934 rather than allowing the CEDA to enter government, under the slogan 'Better Vienna than Berlin', and its support by a variety of other groups, suggests that fear of foreign and domestic fascism greatly influenced leftist perceptions and strategy throughout these years.[26]

There was, without doubt, an element of paranoia and/or political calculation in these warnings against the fascist peril: many in the left probably used the word as a 'bogeyman' and a 'joker', as Unamuno observed in mid-1933 and many historians have pointed out since.[27] However, it can also be argued that both the CEDA and other right-wing groups were experiencing varying degrees of fascistisation – as Gil Robles' decision to attend the Nazi rally at Nüremberg in September 1933 suggests – and hence posed plausible threats to the Republic as it had been conceived.[28] Leaving this important question open, as of 1933 many Spaniards were labelling as fascist not only self-proclaimed followers of Mussolini and Hitler, but also suspected enemies of the Republic and 'the people', including the entire political right (ranging from Falange, the party of the young Primo de Rivera, to the CEDA, often described as 'Vaticanist' or 'clerical fascism') and even rival groups within the left, as well as the aristocracy, the employers, the army and the Catholic Church.[29] In fact, this semantic field grew as antifascism became a mass movement: as early as September 1933, the anarchist journal *Orto* called on the left to unite in 'a single combat front' against a new enemy that 'summarise[d] all the enemies of the past'.[30] Many Spaniards in the 1930s probably understood fascism as a synonym for 'reaction' – as was common in France at the time, according to Gilles Vergnon – even if lucid observers such as Nin and his fellow dissident communist Joaquín Maurín pointed out the very substantial differences between Italian and German fascism and the CEDA.[31] However, these nuances would not prevent Maurín and Nin's POUM from joining Republicans, Socialists, the Stalinist PCE and Ángel Pestaña's tiny Syndicalist Party in the Frente Popular in January 1936.[32]

Antifascism, or Antifascisms?

The debate on the chances of fascism in Spain was conditioned from the start by the profound disagreements and bitter rivalries that fragmented the Spanish left in the 1930s, famously described by George Orwell as 'a plague of initials'.[33] The antifascist movement was, as Ferran Gallego has pointed out, a meeting point for republicanism, social democracy, communism and anarchism – the four hegemonic left-wing cultures between the wars.[34] Both these and the rest of the groups that remained loyal to the Republic after 1936 – notably moderate Basque nationalists and liberal Catholics – had different and, at some points, irreconcilable political views, even regarding fascism.[35] For liberal republicans such as Unamuno, Chaves Nogales and José Ortega y Gassset, this was a brutal, anti-democratic and primitive ideology, but so was Bolshevism.[36] Christian democrats such as Ossorio, José Bergamín and Alfredo Mendizábal likewise believed that both doctrines were equally 'anti-Christian', 'pantheist' and 'totalitarian'.[37] Marxists, in Spain as elsewhere, saw fascism primarily as a tool of capitalism against the working class.[38] Orthodox Communists such as Santiago Montero Díaz, Communist dissenters such as Nin, and revolutionary Socialists such as Araquistáin agreed that fascism was the last stage of capitalism and Hitler its 'new Messiah', as Renau depicted him in a Heartfield-esque photomontage published in *Orto* in August 1932.[39]

In practice, however, discourses on fascism were not so easy to differentiate, even within a single organization. Inside the PSOE the orthodox Marxist views of Araquistáin and Largo Caballero coexisted with those of Julián Besteiro, leader of the party's right wing, who, in a controversial speech given in April 1935, compared 'fascist anti-Marxism' with 'revolutionary Marxism' – and condemned both.[40] The anarcho-syndicalist CNT-FAI was even more plural, including syndicalists such as Pestaña, who agreed with Marxists that fascism was 'the natural product of the capitalist crisis', and libertarian Communists such as Juan García Oliver, who in April 1932 described fascism, in typically liberal terms, as 'the idea of government that destroys the personality of the individual and all the achievements of the French Revolution'.[41] The prevailing view within the movement was, however, that of Federica Montseny and Camillo Berneri, who labelled as fascist anyone who put bounds to individual freedom – including Spanish Republicans, Soviet

Communists, British Labourites and American New Dealers – even if Pestaña, Valeriano Orobón and others were advocating a 'workers' antifascist front' from 1933 onwards.[42]

Disagreements over fascism were complicated further by different conceptions and practices of antifascism. Republican and moderate socialist intellectuals remained true to the Dreyfusard tradition symbolised by the Spanish Grand Orient and the *Ateneo de Madrid* ('Athenæum of Madrid'), and denounced fascism in enlightened and humane declarations such as the manifesto 'against Hitlerism' that Unamuno, Luis Jiménez de Asúa, Gregorio Marañón and Luis Recasens signed in mid June 1933 – shortly before founding the above-mentioned Relief Committee for the Victims of German Fascism – or the manifesto against the Italian invasion of Abyssinia signed by Jiménez de Asúa, Ossorio, García Lorca, Antonio Machado and other progressives in November 1935.[43] Young members of Esquerra Republicana de Catalunya (Catalan Republican Left), often accused by their opponents of representing a sort of 'Catalan fascism' because of their ultra-nationalist youth militia, responded to the mass rally that the Juventud de Acción Popular (the radicalised CEDA juvenile organisation) held in El Escorial on 22 April by promoting an 'antifascist' demonstration attended by some two hundred thousand people in Barcelona on 29 April.[44] Trade unionists preferred a direct-action antifascism, and promoted strikes against 'fascist employers', and political work stoppages against, for instance, the above-mentioned rally at El Escorial.[45] In the spring and summer of 1934 many young Socialists, Communists, anarchists and even independent Radical-Socialists proved their antifascism by setting fire to churches and fighting – 'by words, by fists, by stone or by the gun' – members of right-wing organisations, thus triggering a conflict spiral that set the stage for the October revolt and gave the movement its first martyrs.[46]

Spanish antifascism was, in short, as plural as its broad political and social basis; this is why the road towards political unity of the left proved so slow and conflictive. Many early antifascists, most notably Unamuno, distanced themselves from the movement due to their abhorrence of revolutionary ideas and methods, and the bulk of the CNT-FAI did not join the Popular Front until the Civil War.[47] Even during the war, disagreements and conflicts continued to arise inside the self-proclaimed 'España antifascista', with some one thousand Loyalists killed in inner quarrels.[48] Even if all political groups claimed to be antifascist, the formula obviously meant different things to each of them. For the Republican, Socialist and Communist majority, it meant simply unity in front of the rebellion, the need to prioritise victory and consensus over divisive social and economic goals – hence the oft-repeated slogan 'antifascist unity', often abridged to '¡*antifascismo!*'[49] Many anarchists, left-wing Socialists and POUM members argued, instead, that the war was a new stage of social revolution; according to the editor of the anarcho-syndicalist daily, *CNT*, José García Pradas, 'being antifascist means being revolutionary' and had nothing to do with the 'democratic Republic' or 'the interests of the petty bourgeoisie'.[50]

Yet, as Ferran Gallego has observed, these contradictions may be interpreted as the disagreements that inevitably arise within a culture 'under construction'.[51] The groups that claimed to be antifascist over these years did share certain values, both negative and positive, which provided the common ground on which the unitary movement could grow.[52] They were, above all, morally and intellectually opposed to the monarchical and clerical recent past. However much political leaders and intellectuals theorised on the nature of fascism, the rank and file probably understood it as a return to authoritarianism and oppression, an end to the civil liberties and economic advantages brought by the Republic, such as the agrarian reform and shorter working hours.[53] Antifascists also agreed that *fascists* should be excluded from politics: as the PCE's general secretary José Díaz stated at a meeting on 1 June 1936, democracy was fine 'for us, for the workers, for the people; but not for the enemies of the workers and the people'.[54] Even Republicans did not fully trust in a parliamentary and pluralist regime; rather, they shared Manuel Azaña's 1930 call for a 'republican Republic' that inevitably excluded large sections of Spanish society from political participation.[55] Even if they did not agree with large sections of the workers' movement that this goal should be reached either by legal means or by force, some probably applauded the new premier Santiago Casares Quiroga, a trusted man of Azaña, when he proclaimed on 19 May 1936 that his government was 'belligerent against fascism', and would play a minor yet significant role in the massacres of Catholic priests that occurred in Loyalist Spain during the first months of Civil War.[56] And it is no small irony that an anarchist, Juan García Oliver, was responsible as minister of justice for establishing labour camps in Republican Spain in May 1937, aimed at solving the problem of 'politicofascist delinquency'.[57]

Spanish antifascists also shared positive values, a similar political culture based on common experiences and cultural influences.[58] Their populist and exclusivist conception of democracy was linked to their vision of the new regime as the first step towards a revolution that would achieve social justice, suppress privileges and give the workers land and freedom, such as those that had taken place in France, Russia and Mexico. They also had a deep faith in education and culture as tools to awaken the Spanish people from their secular apathy; their profound hostility to the Catholic Church derived from their belief that clericalism had been the main obstacle to progress and enlightenment throughout Spanish history. Finally, they understood history as a series of struggles between progress and reaction that would inevitably lead to the victory of progress, freedom and justice; the 'Antifascist calendar', printed by the CNT-FAI in Spring 1937 in the midst of Civil War, reflected this by commemorating the execution of anarchist Francisco Ferrer in 1909 (the Spanish equivalent of the Dreyfus affair), the proclamation of the Republic in 1931 and the electoral victory of the Frente Popular in 1936 together with the seizure of the Bastille, the Paris Commune, the Chicago general strike, the February 1917 revolution in Russia and the murder of Giacomo Matteotti by fascist *squadristi* in 1924.[59]

In short, Spanish antifascism inherited – or superimposed itself on – the radical culture that middle-class Republicans and revolutionary workers had shared since the 'democratic revolution' of 1868 and the short-lived First Republic of 1873.[60] In fact, many of the symbols of the Second Republic came from the nineteenth century, including the tricolour federal flag, the *Himno de Riego* ('Riego's hymn', written in 1820) and visual icons of the nation such as the matron and the lion. Obviously, this tradition was closely bound to the common culture of the European left; in Furet's words, the rhetoric of Spanish Republicans during the Civil War reflects 'European revolutionary romanticism in a wide range of forms –those of Bakunin and Marx, Sorel and Lenin', and many others.[61] Indeed, their views on fascism and democracy were not so different from those that prevailed among the Italian, the French and even the British left, even if revolutionary and anti-clerical ideas were much more widespread in Spain.[62] A deeper exploration of their ideas about religion, national identity, gender relations or war would probably reveal further analogies pointing to the existence of a global left culture in the 1930s, and thus help to explain the profound impact of the Spanish Civil War in Europe and beyond.

A Culture or a Propaganda Campaign?

But was antifascism really a culture, a set of widely shared ideas, values and symbols, or merely a successful propaganda campaign? The evidence suggests that the movement for left-wing unity that developed in Spain between 1933 and 1936 was driven at least as much by political manoeuvres as by grass-root pressures – an 'antifascist demand' similar to the one that spread in France after the events of February

1934.[63] The Popular Front, according to Ricard Vinyes and Manuel Tuñón de Lara, was merely the tip of the iceberg formed by a broad and interclass social movement that challenged deep-rooted organizational rivalries in the name of popular self-defence against political and economic fascism.[64] Significantly, coalitions among Republicans, Socialists, Communists and anarchists were formed much earlier in regions and provinces (Catalonia, Asturias, Málaga), where control by party elites was weaker, than at national level. Members of the FUE, the largest federation of university students, played a crucial role in the antifascist movement, as they had in the downfall of the monarchy in 1931.[65] Spontaneous protests before German and Italian consulates and 'Death to Hitler' graffiti in the mountains near Madrid accompanied the antifascist declarations of left-wing parties and trade unions in the spring of 1933.[66] Political elites undoubtedly boosted the movement as they attempted to control it through front organizations such as the Comintern-sponsored International Red Aid and the broader National Committee to Aid Victims of the October revolt; these seem to have been especially successful in creating a large space of socialisation and debate beyond party structures.[67] However, these organizations had their own dynamic, as studies on the local committees of the Popular Front in Asturias and the Women's Committee against War and Fascism suggest.[68] Unsurprisingly, this 'mobilised mass base of the Popular Front' would head resistance to the military rebels in the early stages of the Civil War, leaving their local imprint on Spanish antifascist culture.[69]

On another level, the spread of antifascism in Spain brought not only new tactics and a new political discourse, but also symbolic transformations that reflected an accelerated process of politicisation similar to that triggered by previous social revolutions in France, Russia and Mexico.[70] The traditional symbols of the left were replaced by, or combined with, new symbols forged in the struggles against domestic and, more often, foreign fascism. Changes in everyday language were especially significant. The form of address *camarada* (comrade), linked to the Russian *tovarisch* and used mainly by Communists during the 1920s, was gradually adopted by other workers' organisations, replacing more traditional terms such as *ciudadanos* (citizens), *hermanos* (brothers) and *compañeros* (companions, mates).[71] The term *antifascistas* was used even more frequently by all political groups, especially during the Civil War, although Manuel Azaña and Juan Negrín, the highest representatives of the Republic, preferred the neutral *Españoles*. The nineteenth-century republican greeting *Salud y República* ('Cheers and Republic') evolved after 1934 into *Salud, Salud, camaradas*, or *Salud y antifascismo*.[72] The slogan Unión de Hermanos Proletarios (U.H.P., 'Union of Proletarian Brothers'), born during the Asturias revolt of October 1934, became a commonplace appeal to unity during the war, when it was used by government troops during the bitter internal conflicts of May 1937 in Barcelona.[73]

A new body language accompanied changes in discourse. The raised clenched fist, first adopted by German Communists in the mid-1920s, spread quickly from the spring of 1934 – shortly after it arrived in France, according to Gilles Vergnon – and became the main salute and sign of identity among antifascist activists.[74] It is true that moderate Republicans initially disliked its classist and violent overtones: Diego Martínez Barrio, leader of Unión Republicana and Grand Master of the Spanish Grand Orient, politely declined to use it in response to his working-class audience during a meeting held in Seville days after the victory of the Popular Front.[75] After 18 July 1936, however, the raised fist became the ubiquitous symbol of Republican resistance to fascism, as Soviet journalist Mikhail Koltsov remarked with surprise on a tour of Loyalist Spain in August 1936.[76]

However, the intransigence of Spanish antifascist culture did not only stem from Communist sources. It may also be found in *A las barricadas* ('To the barricades'), a translation of the German version of the Polish revolutionary song *Warszawianka* (1905), which was introduced into Spain by German anarchists in mid-1933, and became the most popular hymn of the CNT-FAI during the Civil War.[77] Likewise, the slogan ¡*No pasarán!* ('They shall not pass!'), which spread at roughly the same time and also became famous during the war, was an echo of French anti-German propaganda during the battle of Verdun in 1916. Casares Quiroga, later prime minister under Azaña, used it during a meeting in Barcelona in early 1934 – that is, one month before Léon Blum did the same in the French Chamber against the far right *ligues* – to call Republicans and Socialists to rise 'against those people who want to establish fascism in Spain and tell them, "You shall not pass"'.[78] Belligerent and virile images reflecting both the 'friend–enemy logic' of antifascism and the symbolic masculinisation of social revolutions in the twentieth century are also widespread in Loyalist war posters.[79]

In other realms, antifascist culture was built mainly through the aggregation of old symbols. Historic hymns such as the *Marseillaise*, the *Himno de Riego*, The Internationale, the Catalan *Els Segadors* ('The harvesters') or the Basque *Euzko Gudariak* ('Basque soldiers') symbolised, often simultaneously, the identity of large groups of activists, together with antifascist tunes such as Rafael Alberti's *Song to Thälmann* or the Spanish version of Brecht and Eisler's *United Front Song*.[80] Nor was there a single flag of antifascism, as León Felipe regretted in his

Whitmanesque poem *La insignia* ('The badge', 1937), which called on 'Spanish revolutionaries' to unite under a 'single red star' made of blood.[81] The tricolour flag of the Republic likewise coexisted with the regional flags of Catalonia, the Basque Country, Valencia and Andalusia, the red and black of the CNT-FAI and the red of the Communist Party, as well as with that of the Catalan Front d'Esquerres ('Left Front'), modelled on those of the German SPD and the French Popular Front.[82] The Republican wartime calendar was also highly eclectic, celebrating the symbols of all the families of the Spanish left – the First of May; the popular uprising in Madrid against the French Army on 2 May 1808; the victory of the Popular Front on 16 February 1936; the Catalan revolution on 19 July 1936; the suppression of Catalan autonomy by Philip V on 11 September 1714; Columbus's discovery of America on 12 October 1492; the resistance of Madrid on 7 November 1936 (and the Bolshevik revolution nineteen years earlier) – and even Christmas, solemnly celebrated by Negrín in 1938 as part of his policy of 'religious normalisation'.[83]

The syncretic character of this emerging antifascism reflects the need to emphasise the values that united its supporters and concealed their differences, but also its remarkable social spread between 1933 and 1939. Antifascism probably succeeded in Spain thanks to its conceptual vagueness, its ability to explain the 1930s in terms familiar to very different people, as well as to its obvious political advantages within a recent and poorly institutionalised party system and under an electoral law that favoured majorities.[84] After the victory of the Popular Front in February 1936, and especially after the military coup of 18 July, which persuaded all political actors including the CNT-FAI to join the institutions of the beleaguered Republic, it also enjoyed the wholehearted support of the state. Loyalist war propaganda proved a powerful tool of nationalisation at all levels of society, from the Popular Army to the school, especially as it was simultaneously promoted by the state, the Catalan and Basque regional governments, political parties, trade unions and a myriad of supraparty organisations such as the 'Alliance of Antifascist Intellectuals' and the 'Antifascist Youth Alliance'.[85] It probably counteracted to some extent the decrease in militancy and the rise of opportunist attitudes caused by the sufferings and shortages brought by the war, although the evidence for this is fragmentary.[86] The texts presented to the 'antifascist short story competition' organised by the PCE in Gijón in May 1937, and some of the drawings made by children at school during the war, suggest at least the emergence of an antifascist collective identity in Republican Spain.[87] The values expressed in primary school textbooks such as the 'Antifascist school primer' may be behind the decision of some Spaniards to join the anti-Franco *maquis* (guerrilla) after the Civil War, or to engage in the French *Résistance*.[88] Milton Wolff, the last commander of the American Lincoln Battalion in the International Brigades, may have exaggerated when he recalled having met 'a people who lived, slept, and ate antifascism', but apparently he was not so far of the mark.[89]

Conclusion: A Culture in the Making

The complex elaboration of its symbols reflects another feature of antifascism – in Spain and elsewhere – that needs to be emphasized before concluding: its historicity. Far from being a rigid doctrine, antifascism was a mass political and social movement that changed greatly throughout its very brief life. The proletarian, combative version of 1933–34 differs significantly from the humanist and democratic culture that surrounded the making of the Popular Front, best represented by the People's Olympics that the Catalan Left Front organised in Barcelona in July 1936 in order to compete with the Berlin Games, but were thwarted by the military rebellion.[90] Both are, in turn, markedly different from the culture that dominated Loyalist Spain during the Civil War, a state antifascism able to reconcile – imperfectly but effectively until near the end – Republicans and Communists, Catholics and anarchists, Spanish, Catalan and Basque nationalists; and also a war culture that could justify or silence the massacre of more than fifty thousand alleged fascists, including antifascist traitors such as Andrés Nin and Camillo Berneri.[91] In short, antifascism may be better understood as a constantly evolving reality – as was its enemy, according to Robert Paxton[92] – than as an essence; its dynamism accounts for the aggregate and contradictory nature of its ideas, values and symbols. Be that as it may, an antifascist culture, the offspring of native radicalism combined with the global culture of the left in the 1930s, was certainly in the making in Spain before it was brutally suppressed – as in a self-fulfilling prophesy – by the Nationalists and their fascist allies, and turned into a nostalgic minority strand in exile and in national collective memory.[93]

English version revised by Jane Wintle Taylor

Notes

1. J. Droz, *Histoire de l'antifascisme en Europe, 1923–1939*, Paris, 1985, 236–52; E. Hobsbawm, *Age of Extremes: The Short Twentieth Century, 1914–1991*, London, 1994, 156–61.

2. F. Gallego, *Barcelona, mayo de 1937: la crisis del antifascismo en Cataluña*, Barcelona, 2007.
3. R. Carr, 'A Revolution Betrayed', *The Observer*, 6 February 1972. I am grateful to Paul Preston for tracking down this reference.
4. J. Fronczak, 'Local People's Global Politics: A Transnational History of the Hands Off Ethiopia Movement of 1935', *Diplomatic History*, 2014, online version accessed June 2014.
5. F. Furet, *The Passing of an Illusion: The Idea of Communism in the Twentieth Century*, Chicago, 1999, 248.
6. A. Nin, *Struggle of the Trade Unions against Fascism*, Chicago, 1923.
7. Luis de Zulueta, 'Del habeas corpus al frasco de ricino', *La Libertad*, 18 January 1925, in M. Peloille, *Fascismo en ciernes: España, 1922–1930, textos recuperados*, Toulouse, 2005, 121–23.
8. F. García Lorca, 'Cry to Rome', *Selected Poems*, translated by Martin Sorrell, Oxford, 2007, 139.
9. Largo Caballero, in S. Ben-Ami, *The Origins of the Second Republic in Spain*, Oxford, 1978, 231.
10. Miguel de Unamuno, letter to Henri Barbusse, 4 March 1929, in M. Urrutia León, *Miguel de Unamuno desconocido*, Salamanca, 2007, 215.
11. J. Deutsch (ed.), *Le fascisme en Europe. Rapport présenté à la Commission internationale de défense contre le fascisme*, Brussels, 1930, 215. Instead, the fourth congress of the Profintern, held in April 1928, labelled Primo de Rivera's Spain as 'fascist', together with Italy, Portugal, Poland, Lithuania and Bulgaria. S.G. Payne, 'Soviet Anti-Fascism: Theory and Practice, 1921–45', *Totalitarian Movements and Political Religions* 4(2) (Autumn 2003), 13.
12. 'Manifiesto de los treinta' (written by the dissident faction of the anarchist Confederación Nacional del Trabajo, CNT), in *L'Opinió*, Barcelona, 30 August 1931 and *La Tierra*, Madrid, 1 September 1931. The Communist MP José Antonio Balbontín used very similar terms to attack the Republican–Socialist government of Manuel Azaña in Parliament in December 1932: see *Diario de Sesiones de las Cortes*, 13 December 1932, 10124.
13. L. de Tapia, '¿Fascistas?', *La Libertad*, 18 March 1933.
14. G.-R. Horn, *European Socialists Respond to Fascism*, Cambridge, 1996, 58.
15. Horn, *European Socialists*, 117–34; S. Souto, *Y Madrid, ¿qué hace Madrid? Movimiento revolucionario y acción colectiva (1933–1936)*, Madrid, 2004, 45–47. Cristina Clímaco describes in the next chapter the close relations between Spanish and Portuguese antifascists in these years.
16. See L. Sturzo, *Italia y el fascismo*, Madrid, 1930; G. Salvemini, *El terror fascista: 1922–1926*, Barcelona, 1931; F. Nitti, *Fugados del infierno fascista*, Madrid, 1931; A. Kurella, *Mussolini desenmascarado*, Madrid, 1931; P. Nenni, *Seis años de guerra civil en Italia*, Barcelona, 1931; H. Heller, *Europa y el fascismo*, Madrid, 1931; K. Radek, *El porqué del fascismo*, Madrid, 1933; J. Strachey, *La amenaza del fascismo*, Madrid, 1934; Á. Ossorio, *Un libro del abate Sturzo*, Madrid, 1928; M. Domingo, *Una dictadura en la Europa del siglo XX*, Madrid, 1929; and A. Nin, *Las dictaduras de nuestro tiempo*, Madrid, 1929.
17. S. Castro, *Egidio Reale, tra Svizzera e Europa*, Milan, 2011, 129–33; C. García and H. Piotrowski, 'Emigración alemana en Barcelona a principios del siglo

XX', in Dieter Nelles et al., *Antifascistas alemanes en Barcelona (1933–1939)*, Barcelona, 2010, 51–56.

18. C. Cuevas Wolf, 'Montage as Weapon: The Tactical Alliance between Willi Münzenberg and John Heartfield', *New German Critique* 107 (2009), 197–203.

19. J.A. Ayala, 'Fascismo y masonería en la II República', in *La masonería y su impacto internacional*, Madrid, 1989, 119–53.

20. J. Gorkin, 'Bohemia antifascista', *Luz*, 2 August 1933; E. González Calleja, 'Más allá de La Rotonde: los exiliados antiprimorriveristas en París (1923–1930)', in F. Martínez López et al. (eds), *París, ciudad de acogida: el exilio español durante los siglos XIX y XX*, Madrid, 2010, 183–234.

21. D. McAdam and W.H. Sewell, Jr. 'It's About Time: Temporality in the Study of Social Movements and Revolutions', in R. Aminzade (ed.), *Silence and Voice in the Study of Contentious Politics*, Cambridge, 2001, 101–12.

22. M. Semolinos, *Hitler y la prensa de la II República española*, Madrid, 1985, 167–274; F. Santos, *Españoles en la Alemania nazi. Testimonios de visitantes del Tercer Reich entre 1933 y 1945*, Madrid, 2012, 219–77.

23. J.F. Fuentes, 'Luis Araquistáin, embajador de la II República en Berlín (1932–1933)', *Spagna contemporanea* 8 (1995), 19–30. PSOE stands for Partido Socialista Obrero Español (Spanish Socialist Workers' Party).

24. *El Sol, Heraldo de Madrid* and *La Voz*, 11 July 1933.

25. G. Martínez de Espronceda, *El canciller de bolsillo: Dollfuss en la prensa de la II República española*, Zaragoza, 1989, 127–37. CEDA was the acronym of the Confederación Española de Derechas Autónomas (Spanish Confederation of Autonomous Right-wing Groups), founded in March 1933.

26. Horn, *European Socialists*, 128. Cf. Payne, 'Soviet Anti-Fascism', 27.

27. Unamuno, 'La revolución de dentro', *Ahora*, 1 August 1933; Santos Juliá, *La izquierda del PSOE (1935–1936)*, Madrid, 1977, 265–75; Fernando del Rey, 'La República de los socialistas', in F. del Rey (ed.), *Palabras como puños. La intransigencia política en la Segunda República española*, Madrid, 2010, 199–200.

28. This is the view of P. Preston, *The Coming of the Spanish Civil War: Reform, Reaction and Revolution in the Spanish Second Republic*, London, 2003, 128–30; E. González Calleja, *Contrarrevolucionarios. Radicalización violenta de las derechas durante la Segunda República*, Madrid, 2011, 127–72; and F. Gallego, *El evangelio fascista: la formación de la cultura política del franquismo (1930–1950)*, Barcelona, 2014, 155–76. Cf. the revisionist view of M. Álvarez Tardío, 'The CEDA: Threat or Opportunity?', in M. Álvarez Tardío and F. del Rey (eds), *The Spanish Second Republic Revisited: From Democratic Hopes to Civil War (1931–1936)*, Brighton, 2011, 60–67.

29. J.F. García Santos, *Léxico y política en la Segunda República*, Salamanca, 1980, 291–300; F. del Rey (ed.), *Palabras como puños, passim*. Similarly loose interpretations of fascism prevailed in Britain, France, Portugal and Argentina, as Tom Buchanan, Gilles Vergnon, Cristina Clímaco and Andrés Bisso show in their contributions to this volume.

30. 'Por un frente único contra el fascismo internacional', *Orto* 16 (September 1933), in J. Paniagua (ed.), *Orto (1932–1934). Revista de documentación social*, Valencia, 2001, vol. II, 1017–20.

31. G. Vergnon, *L'antifascisme en France de Mussolini à Le Pen*, Rennes, 2009, 88; A. Nin, 'Las posibilidades de un fascismo español', *Comunismo* [April 1933], in *La revolución española, 1930–1937*, Barcelona, 1978, 143–48; J. Maurín, *Revolución y contrarrevolución en España*, Paris, 1966 [1935], 217.

32. POUM stands for Partido Obrero de Unificación Marxista (Workers' Party of Marxist Unification), a dissident Communist party founded by Maurín and Nin in September 1935.

33. G. Orwell, *Homage to Catalonia* [1938], in *Orwell in Spain*, London, 2001, 169.

34. Gallego, *Barcelona, mayo de 1937*, 318.

35. J. Jiménez Campo, *El fascismo en la crisis de la II República*, Madrid, 1979, 55–58.

36. Unamuno, 'La I.O.N.S.', *Ahora*, 1 November 1933; M. Chaves Nogales, 'Lecture in Seville, 23 June 1933', in *Bajo el signo de la esvástica*, Córdoba, 2012, 141–48; J. Ortega y Gasset, *The Revolt of the Masses* [1930], New York and London, 1994, 92–94.

37. Ossorio, *Un libro del abate Sturzo*, 69–78; Bergamín, '¡Adelante con los faroles! o los aficionados al fascismo', *Luz*, 31 October 1933; Mendizábal, 'Una mitología política (Los principios anticristianos del racismo)', *Cruz y Raya*, 5 August 1933, 77–112.

38. A.J. Gregor, *The Faces of Janus: Marxism and Fascism in the Twentieth Century*, New Haven, CT, 2000, 19–44; Payne, 'Soviet Anti-Fascism', 4–21.

39. S. Montero Díaz, 'Fascismo', in *Cuadernos de Cultura* 53, Valencia, 1932, online; L. Araquistáin, 'Condotieros y fascistas', *Leviatán* 2 (June 1934), 42–51; Nin, 'Las posibilidades de un fascismo español', 143–48; Renau, in *Orto* 6 (August 1932), in Paniagua, *Orto (1932–1934)*, vol. I, 341.

40. J. Besteiro, 'Marxismo y antimarxismo', in *Obras completas*, Madrid, 1983, vol. III, 227–334.

41. A. Pestaña, '¿Puede venir el fascismo a España?', *Sindicalismo*, 15 September 1933, in *Trayectoria sindicalista*, Barcelona, 1974, 644–47; García Oliver, 'El fascismo y las dictaduras', *Tierra y Libertad*, 1 April 1932, in *El eco de los pasos*, Paris, 1978, 140. CNT stands for Confederación Nacional del Trabajo (National Confederation of Labour); FAI for Federación Anarquista Ibérica (Iberian Anarchist Federation).

42. F. Montseny, 'Fascismos', *La Revista Blanca*, 1 May 1933, 708–10; C. Berneri, 'Moscú y Berlín', *Orto* 15 (August 1933), in *Orto (1932–1934)*, vol. II, 989–93; Gallego, *Barcelona, mayo de 1937*, 189–96.

43. 'Los intelectuales, contra el hitlerismo', *El Sol*, 10 June 1933; 'Un generoso manifiesto de los intelectuales españoles', *La Libertad*, 26 December 1935.

44. *Heraldo de Madrid* and *Luz*, 30 April 1934. On the debate on 'Catalan fascism', see A. González i Vilalta, *Cataluña bajo vigilancia. El consulado italiano y el fascio de Barcelona (1930–1943)*, Barcelona, 2013, 122–40.

45. S. Juliá, *Madrid, 1931–1934: de la fiesta popular a la lucha de clases*, Madrid, 1984, 327–38; S. Lowe, *Catholicism, War and the Foundation of Francoism: The Juventud de Acción Popular in Spain, 1931–1939*, Brighton, Sussex, 2010, 20–27.

46. *Heraldo de Madrid*, 23 April 1934; *Luz*, 26 April 1934; *El Sol*, 15 May 1934; Souto, *¿Y Madrid, qué hace Madrid?*, 86–164; B.D. Bunk, *Ghosts of Passion: Martyrdom, Gender and the Origins of the Spanish Civil War*, Durham, NC,

2007, 61–87. The quotation comes from the song 'The Ghosts of Cable Street' (1987), by the British folk punk group The Men They Couldn't Hang.

47. On the ambivalent relationship between both groups, see J. Getman-Eraso, '"Cease Fire, Comrades!" Anarcho-syndicalist Revolutionary Prophesy, Anti-Fascism and the Origins of the Spanish Civil War', *Totalitarian Movements and Political Religions*, Vol. 9 (1), March 2008, 93–114.

48. M. Aguilera, *Compañeros y camaradas. Las luchas entre antifascistas en la Guerra Civil española*, Madrid, 2012, 359–69.

49. See, for instance, the parliamentary debate on 'antifascist unity' in *Diario de sesiones de las Cortes*, 2 October 1937, 13–18.

50. J. García Pradas, *Antifascismo proletario*, Barcelona [1938], 27.

51. Gallego, *Barcelona, mayo de 1937*, 143.

52. N. Copsey, 'Preface: Towards a New Anti-Fascist "Minimum"?', in N. Copsey and A. Olechnowicz (eds), *Varieties of Anti-Fascism: Britain in the Inter-War Period*, London, 2010, xiv–xxi.

53. M. Seidman, *Workers against Work: Labor in Paris and Barcelona during the Popular Fronts (1936–38)*, Berkeley, CA, 1991, 29, 167.

54. J. Díaz, *Tres años de lucha*, Bucarest, 1974, 189.

55. M. Azaña, "Llamada al combate. Alocución en el banquete republicano de 11 de febrero de 1930", in *Obras completas. Vol. II. Junio de 1920-abril de 1931*, edited by Santos Juliá, Madrid, 2008, 937–40.

56. Casares Quiroga, quoted in S.G. Payne, *Spain's First Democracy: The Second Republic, 1931–1936*, Madison, WI, 327; M. Thomas, *The Faith and the Fury: Popular Anticlerical Violence and Iconoclasm in Spain, 1931–1936*, Eastbourne, 2013, 88.

57. García Oliver, Speech in Valencia, 31 December 1936, in J. Ruiz, '"Work and don't lose hope!" Republican Forced Labour Camps during the Spanish Civil War', *Contemporary European History* 18(4) (2009), 424.

58. I have developed this argument in 'La República de las pequeñas diferencias: cultura(s) de izquierda y antifascismo(s) en España, 1931–1939', in M. Pérez Ledesma and R. Cruz (eds), *Historia de las culturas políticas en España y América Latina*, vol. 4, Madrid, 2015, 207–37.

59. *Almanaque antifascista*, Barcelona, 1937.

60. Á. Duarte, 'La esperanza republicana', in M. Pérez Ledesma and R. Cruz (eds), *Cultura y movilización en la España contemporánea*, Madrid, 1997, 199.

61. Furet, *The Passing of an Illusion*, 259.

62. C. Natoli, 'La formacione della cultura política dell'antifascismo italiano', in A. di Bernardi and P. Ferrari (eds), *Antifascismo e identità europea*, Rome, 2004, 70–71; Vergnon, *L'antifascisme en France*, 61–63; T. Buchanan, 'Antifascism and Democracy in the 1930s', *European History Quarterly*, 32 (2002), 51–52, and his chapter in this volume.

63. Vergnon, *L'antifascisme en France*, 50.

64. R. Vinyes, *La Catalunya populista. El frontpopulisme en l'exemple catalá*, Barcelona, 1983, 336; Tuñón de Lara, *Tres claves de la Segunda República*, Madrid, 1985, 326.

65. E. González Calleja, *Rebelión en las aulas: movilización y protesta estudiantil en la España contemporánea, 1865–2008*, Madrid, 2009, 139–209.

66. *Luz*, 20 March 1933; *La Voz*, 24 March 1933; *Luz*, 5 June 1933.

67. L. Branciforte, *El Socorro Rojo Internacional (1923–1939): relatos de la solidaridad antifascista*, Madrid, 2011, 137–85.
68. H. Graham, 'Spain 1936. Resistance and Revolution: The Flaws in the Front', in T. Kirk and A. McElligott (eds), *Opposing Fascism*, Cambridge, 1999, 63–79; M. Yusta, 'La construcción de una cultura política femenina desde el antifascismo (1934–1950)', in A. Aguado and T.M. Ortega López (eds), *Feminismos y antifeminismos. Culturas políticas e identidades de género en la España del siglo XX*, Valencia, 2011, 253.
69. Graham, 'The Flaws in the Front', 64; P. Radcliff, 'The Culture of Empowerment in Gijón, 1936–37', in M. Richards and C. Ealham (eds), *The Splintering of Spain: Cultural History and the Spanish Civil War*, Cambridge, 2005, 133–58.
70. S. Holguín, *Creating Spaniards: Culture and National Identity in Republican Spain*, Madison, WI, 2002, 52–55.
71. C. Serrano, 'Le paradigme perdu. *Camarada, compañero, ciudadano...* (contribution à l'étude du vocabulaire politique espagnol)', *Bulletin Hispanique* 101(2) (1999), 557–71.
72. On these linguistic uses, see also Robert S. Coale's chapter in this volume.
73. Gallego, *Barcelona, mayo de 1937*, 583.
74. G. Vergnon, 'Le poing levé, du rite soldatique au rite de masse', *Le Mouvement social* 212 (2005), 83–85.
75. *ABC*, Madrid, 15 February 1936.
76. M. Koltsov, *Diario de la guerra de España*, Madrid, 1978, 23, 57.
77. J.L. Gutiérrez Molina, *Valeriano Orobón Fernández. Anarcosindicalismo y revolución en Europa*, Valladolid, 2002, 63.
78. *La Voz*, 7 January 1934; Vergnon, *L'antifascisme en France*, 43–44.
79. A. Rabinbach, 'Paris, Capital of Antifascism', in W. Breckmann et al. (eds), *The Modernist Imagination: Intellectual History and Critical Theory*, 2013, 204; E. Hobsbawm, 'Man and Woman: Images on the Left', in *Workers: Worlds of Labor*, New York, 1984, 83–102.
80. M. Bertrand de Muñoz, *Si me quieres escribir: canciones políticas y de combate de la guerra de España*, Madrid, 2009; Jürgen Schebera (ed.), *España en el corazón: canciones de la Guerra Civil española* (box set with 7 CDs; textbook in Spanish, English and German), Berlin, 2014.
81. León Felipe, 'La insignia', *Poesías completas*, Madrid, 2004, 191–211.
82. E. Ucelay-da Cal, *La Catalunya populista: imatge, cultura i política en l'etapa republicana, 1931–1939*, Barcelona, 1982, 235.
83. For details and references, see García, 'La República de las pequeñas diferencias'.
84. S. Juliá, 'El sistema de partidos de la Segunda República', in Santos Juliá (ed.), *Política en la Segunda República*, *Ayer* 20 (1995), 111–39.
85. M. Aznar Soler, *República literaria y revolución (1920–1939)*, Sevilla, 2010, vol. 2, 423–531; Sandra Souto, *Paso a la juventud: movilización democrática, estalinismo y revolución en la República española*, Valencia, 2013, 273–412. The organisations were called Alianza de Intelectuales Antifascistas and Alianza Juvenil Antifascista, respectively.
86. Cf. M. Seidman, *Republic of Egos: A Social History of the Spanish Civil War*, Madison, WI, 2002, 63–74.

87. L. Arias-González and Francisco de Luis Martín, 'Mentalidad popular y subliteratura política durante la guerra civil: el concurso de cuentos anti-fascistas de Gijón (1937)', *Bulletin Hispanique* 93 (1991), 403–21; Anthony L. Geist and Peter N. Carroll (eds), *They Still Draw Pictures: Children's Art in Wartime, from the Spanish Civil War to Kosovo*, Urbana, 2002, 34, 58.
88. *Cartilla Escolar antifascista*, 1937; J. Marco, *Guerrilleros y vecinos en armas*, Granada, 2012, 13–14.
89. M. Wolff, 'Spanish Lesson', in A. Bessie (ed.), *The Heart of Spain*, New York, 1952, 452, quoted in A. Rabinbach, 'Introduction: Legacies of Antifascism', *New German Critique* 67 (1996), 8.
90. C. Santacana and X. Pujadas, 'The Popular Olympic Games, Barcelona 1936: Olympians and Antifascists', *International Review for the Sociology of Sport* 27(2) (1992), 139–48.
91. J.L. Ledesma, 'Una retaguardia al rojo: las violencias en la zona republi-cana', in F. Espinosa (ed.), *Violencia roja y azul. España: 1936–1950*, Barcelona, 2009, 159–92.
92. R.O. Paxton, *The Anatomy of Fascism*. New York, 2005, 14–15.
93. See Ángel Duarte, *El otoño de un ideal. El republicanismo histórico español y su declive en el exilio de 1939*, Madrid, 2009, and Javier Muñoz Soro's chapter in this volume.

References

Aguilera, M. *Compañeros y camaradas. Las luchas entre antifascistas en la Guerra Civil española*. Madrid, 2012.
Álvarez Tardío, M. 'The CEDA: Threat or Opportunity?', in M. Álvarez Tardío and F. del Rey (eds), *The Spanish Second Republic Revisited: From Democratic Hopes to Civil War (1931–1936)*. Brighton, 2011, 58–79.
Araquistáin, L. 'Condotieros y fascistas', *Leviatán* 2 (June 1934), 42–51.
Arias-González, L., and M.F. de Luis. 'Mentalidad popular y subliteratura política durante la guerra civil: el concurso de cuentos antifascistas de Gijón (1937)'. *Bulletin Hispanique* 93 (1991), 403–21.
Ayala, J.A. 'Fascismo y masonería en la II República', in *La masonería y su impacto internacional*. Madrid, 1989, 119–53.
Aznar Soler, M. *República literaria y revolución (1920–1939)*. Sevilla, 2010, vol. 2.
Ben-Ami, S. *The Origins of the Second Republic in Spain*. Oxford, 1978.
Bertrand de Muñoz, M. *Si me quieres escribir: canciones políticas y de combate de la guerra de España*. Madrid, 2009.
Besteiro, J. 'Marxismo y antimarxismo', in *Obras completas*. Madrid, 1983, vol. III, 227–334.
Branciforte, L. *El Socorro Rojo Internacional (1923–1939): relatos de la solidaridad antifascista*. Madrid, 2011.
Buchanan, T. 'Anti-fascism and Democracy in the 1930s'. *European History Quarterly* 32 (2002), 39–57.
Bunk, B.D. *Ghosts of Passion: Martyrdom, Gender and the Origins of the Spanish Civil War*. Durham, NC, 2007.

Castro, S. *Egidio Reale, tra Svizzera e Europa*. Milan, 2011.

Chaves Nogales, M. *Bajo el signo de la esvástica*. Córdoba, 2012.

Copsey, N., 'Preface: Towards a New Anti-Fascist "Minimum"?', in N. Copsey and Andrzej Olechnowicz (eds), *Varieties of Anti-Fascism: Britain in the Inter-War Period*. London, 2010, xiv–xxi.

Cuevas Wolf, C. 'Montage as Weapon: The Tactical Alliance between Willi Münzenberg and John Heartfield'. *New German Critique* 107 (2009), 197–203.

Deutsch, J. (ed.). *Le fascisme en Europe. Rapport présenté à la Commission internationale de défense contre le fascisme*. Brussels, 1930.

Díaz, J. *Tres años de lucha*. Bucarest, 1974.

Díaz, S.M. 'Fascismo'. *Cuadernos de Cultura* 53, Valencia, 1932, online.

Domingo, M. *Una dictadura en la Europa del siglo XX*. Madrid, 1929.

Droz, J. *Histoire de l'antifascisme en Europe, 1923–1939*. Paris, 1985.

Duarte, Á. 'La esperanza republicana', in M. Pérez Ledesma and R. Cruz (eds), *Cultura y movilización en la España contemporánea*. Madrid, 1997, 169–99.

———. *El otoño de un ideal. El republicanismo histórico español y su declive en el exilio de 1939*. Madrid. 2009.

Felipe, L. *Poesías completas*. Madrid, 2004.

Fronczack, J. 'Local People's Global Politics: A Transnational History of the Hands Off Ethiopia Movement of 1935'. *Diplomatic History, 2014, online*.

Fuentes, J.F. 'Luis Araquistáin, embajador de la II República en Berlín (1932–1933)'. *Spagna contemporánea* 8 (1995), 19–30.

Furet, F. *The Passing of an Illusion: The Idea of Communism in the Twentieth Century*. Chicago, 1999.

Gallego, F. *Barcelona, mayo de 1937: la crisis del antifascismo en Cataluña*. Barcelona, 2007.

———. *El evangelio fascista: la formación de la cultura política del franquismo (1930–1950)*. Barcelona, 2014.

García Lorca, F. *Selected Poems*. Translated by M. Sorrell. Oxford, 2007.

García Oliver, J. *El eco de los pasos*. Paris, 1978.

García Pradas, J. *Antifascismo proletario*. Barcelona, [1938].

García Santos, J.F. *Léxico y política en la Segunda República*. Salamanca, 1980.

García, C., and H. Piotrowski. 'Emigración alemana en Barcelona a principios del siglo XX', in D. Nelles et al., *Antifascistas alemanes en Barcelona (1933–1939)*. Barcelona, 2010, 15–28.

Garcia, H. 'La República de las pequeñas diferencias: cultura(s) de izquierda y antifascismo(s) en España, 1931–1939', in M. Pérez Ledesma and R. Cruz (eds), *Historia de las culturas políticas en España y América Latina*, vol. 4. Madrid, 2015, 207–37.

Geist, A.L., and P.N. Carroll (eds). *They Still Draw Pictures: Children's Art in Wartime, from the Spanish Civil War to Kosovo*. Urbana, 2002.

Getman-Eraso, J. '"Cease Fire, Comrades!" Anarcho-syndicalist Revolutionary Prophesy, Anti-Fascism and the Origins of the Spanish Civil War', *Totalitarian Movements and Political Religions*, Vol. 9 (1), March 2008, 93–114.

González Calleja, E. *Rebelión en las aulas: movilización y protesta estudiantil en la España contemporánea, 1865–2008*. Madrid, 2009.

———. 'Más allá de La Rotonde: los exiliados antiprimorriveristas en París (1923–1930)', in F. Martínez López et al. (eds), *París, ciudad de acogida: el exilio español durante los siglos XIX y XX*. Madrid, 2010, 183–234.

———. *Contrarrevolucionarios. Radicalización violenta de las derechas durante la Segunda República*. Madrid, 2011.

González i Vilalta, A. *Cataluña bajo vigilancia. El consulado italiano y el fascio de Barcelona (1930–1943)*. Barcelona, 2013.

Graham, H. 'Spain 1936. Resistance and Revolution: The Flaws in the Front', in T. Kirk and A. McElligott (eds), *Opposing Fascism*. Cambridge, 1999, 63–79.

Gregor A.J. *The Faces of Janus: Marxism and Fascism in the Twentieth Century*. New Haven, CT, 2000.

Gutiérrez Molina, J.L. *Valeriano Orobón Fernández. Anarcosindicalismo y revolución en Europa*. Valladolid, 2002.

Heller, H. *Europa y el fascismo*. Madrid, 1931.

Hobsbawm, E. 'Man and Woman: Images on the Left', in *Workers: Worlds of Labor*. New York, 1984, 83–102.

———. *Age of Extremes: The Short Twentieth Century, 1914–1991*. London, 1994.

Holguín, S. *Creating Spaniards: Culture and National Identity in Republican Spain*. Madison, WI, 2002.

Horn, G.-R. *European Socialists Respond to Fascism*. Cambridge, 1996.

Jiménez Campo, J. *El fascismo en la crisis de la II República*. Madrid, 1979.

Juliá, S. *La izquierda del PSOE (1935–1936)*. Madrid, 1977.

———. *Madrid, 1931–1934: de la fiesta popular a la lucha de clases*. Madrid, 1984.

———. 'El sistema de partidos de la Segunda República', in Santos Juliá (ed.), *Política en la Segunda República, Ayer* 20 (1995), 111–39.

Koltsov, M. *Diario de la guerra de España*. Madrid, 1978.

Kurella, A. *Mussolini desenmascarado*. Madrid, 1931.

Ledesma, J.L. 'Una retaguardia al rojo: las violencias en la zona republicana', in F. Espinosa (ed.), *Violencia roja y azul. España: 1936–1950*, Barcelona, 2009, 152–250.

Lowe, S. *Catholicism, War and the Foundation of Francoism: The Juventud de Acción Popular in Spain, 1931–1939*. Brighton, Sussex, 2010.

Marco, J. *Guerrilleros y vecinos en armas*. Granada, 2012 (translated as *Guerrilleros and Neighbours in Arms. Identities and Cultures of Anti-fascist Resistance in Spain*, Chicago, 2016).

Martínez de Espronceda, G. *El canciller de bolsillo: Dollfuss en la prensa de la II República española*. Zaragoza, 1989.

Maurín, J. *Revolución y contrarrevolución en España*. Paris, 1966 [1935].

McAdam, D. and W.H. Sewell Jr. 'It's About Time: Temporality in the Study of Social Movements and Revolutions', in R. Aminzade (ed.), *Silence and Voice in the Study of Contentious Politics*. Cambridge, 2001, 89–125.

Natoli, C. 'La formacione della cultura política dell'antifascismo italiano', in A. di Bernardi and P. Ferrari (eds), *Antifascismo e identità europea*. Rome, 2004.

Nenni, P. *Seis años de guerra civil en Italia*. Barcelona, 1931.

Nin, A. *Struggle of the Trade Unions against Fascism*. Chicago, 1923.

———. *Las dictaduras de nuestro tiempo*. Madrid, 1929.

———. *La revolución española, 1930–1937*. Barcelona, 1978.

Nitti, F. *Fugados del infierno fascista*. Madrid, 1931.

Ortega y Gasset, J. *The Revolt of the Masses*, New York and London, 1994 [1930].

Orwell, G. *Homage to Catalonia* [1938], in *Orwell in Spain*. London, 2001.

Ossorio, Á. *Un libro del abate Sturzo*. Madrid, 1928.

Paniagua, J. (ed.). *Orto (1932–1934). Revista de documentación social*. Valencia, 2001.

Paxton, R.O. *The Anatomy of Fascism*. New York, 2005.

Payne, S.G. *Spain's First Democracy: The Second Republic, 1931–1936*, Madison, WI, 1993.

———. 'Soviet Anti-Fascism: Theory and Practice, 1921–45'. *Totalitarian Movements and Political Religions* 4(2) (Autumn 2003), 1–62.

Peloille, M. *Fascismo en ciernes: España, 1922–1930, textos recuperados*. Toulouse, 2005.

Pestaña, A. *Trayectoria sindicalista*, Barcelona, 1974.

Preston, P. *The Coming of the Spanish Civil War: Reform, Reaction and Revolution in the Spanish Second Republic*. London, 2003.

Rabinbach, A. 'Introduction: Legacies of Antifascism'. *New German Critique* 67 (1996), 3–17.

———. 'Paris, Capital of Antifascism', in W. Breckmann et al. (eds), *The Modernist Imagination: Intellectual History and Critical Theory*. New York, 2013.

Radcliff, P. 'The Culture of Empowerment in Gijón, 1936–37', in M. Richards and C. Ealham (eds), *The Splintering of Spain: Cultural History and the Spanish Civil War*. Cambridge, 2005, 183–209.

Radek, K. *El porqué del fascismo*. Madrid, 1933.

Rey, F. del. 'La República de los socialistas', in F. del Rey (ed.), *Palabras como puños. La intransigencia política en la Segunda República española*. Madrid, 2010, 158–225.

Ruiz, J. '"Work and don't lose hope!" Republican Forced Labour Camps during the Spanish Civil War', *Contemporary European History* 18(4) (2009), 419–41.

Salvemini, G. *El terror fascista: 1922–1926*. Barcelona, 1931.

Santacana, C., and X. Pujadas. 'The Popular Olympic Games, Barcelona 1936: Olympians and Antifascists', *International Review for the Sociology of Sport* 27(2) (1992), 139–48.

Santos, F. *Españoles en la Alemania nazi. Testimonios de visitantes del Tercer Reich entre 1933 y 1945*. Madrid, 2012.

Schebera, J. (ed.). *España en el corazón: canciones de la Guerra Civil española* (box set with 7 CDs; textbook in Spanish, English and German). Berlin, 2014.

Seidman, M. *Workers against Work: Labor in Paris and Barcelona during the Popular Fronts (1936–38)*. Berkeley, CA, 1991.

———. *Republic of Egos: A Social History of the Spanish Civil War*. Madison, WI, 2002.

Semolinos, M. *Hitler y la prensa de la II República española*. Madrid, 1985.

Serrano, C. 'Le paradigme perdu. *Camarada, compañero, ciudadano...* (contribution à l'étude du vocabulaire politique espagnol)'. *Bulletin Hispanique* 101(2) (1999), 557–71.

Souto, S. *Y Madrid, ¿qué hace Madrid? Movimiento revolucionario y acción colectiva (1933–1936)*. Madrid, 2004.

———. *Paso a la juventud: movilización democrática, estalinismo y revolución en la República española*. Valencia, 2013.

Strachey, J. *La amenaza del fascismo*. Madrid, 1934.

Sturzo, L. *Italia y el fascismo*. Madrid, 1930.

Thomas, M. *The Faith and the Fury: Popular Anticlerical Violence and Iconoclasm in Spain, 1931–1936*. Eastbourne, 2013.

Tuñón de Lara, M. *Tres claves de la Segunda República*. Madrid, 1985.

Ucelay-da Cal, E. *La Catalunya populista: imatge, cultura i política en l'etapa republicana, 1931–1939*. Barcelona, 1982.

Urrutia León, M. *Miguel de Unamuno desconocido*. Salamanca, 2007.

Vergnon, G. 'Le poing levé, du rite soldatique au rite de masse'. *Le Mouvement social* 212 (2005), 77–91.

———. *L'antifascisme en France de Mussolini à Le Pen*. Rennes, 2009.

Vinyes, R. *La Catalunya populista. El frontpopulisme en l'exemple catalá*. Barcelona, 1983.

Wolff, M. 'Spanish Lesson', in A. Bessie (ed.), *The Heart of Spain*. New York, 1952, 451–53.

Yusta, M. 'La construcción de una cultura política femenina desde el antifascismo (1934–1950)', in A. Aguado and T.M. Ortega López (eds), *Feminismos y antifeminismos. Culturas políticas e identidades de género en la España del siglo XX*. Valencia, 2011, 253–81.

Hugo García is associate professor of Modern History at the Universidad Autónoma de Madrid (Spain). He has published *The Truth about Spain! Mobilizing British Public Opinion, 1936–1939* (Sussex Academic Press, 2010), as well as numerous articles on propaganda, public opinion, political cultures, social movements and literature in interwar Spain and Europe. He is editing a forthcoming special issue of *Contemporary European History* on 'Transnational Anti-fascism'.

6

PORTUGAL WITHIN THE EUROPEAN ANTIFASCIST MOVEMENT, 1922–39

Cristina Clímaco

The word 'antifascism' was widely used in Portugal after the Carnation Revolution of 25 April 1974 by the political movements that appeared on the revolutionary and post-revolutionary scene, and it was eventually monopolised by the Portuguese Communist Party (PCP). Once the revolutionary momentum was lost, the word gradually started fading out of everyday language; as democracy grew stronger and became a routine, normal part of national life, antifascism was sent back to its historical past. To recall it would bring back both memories and worries. In the collective memory of the nation, the history of antifascism refers to the final period of the *Estado Novo* ('New State', 1933–74). A significant part of its own history is therefore missing: the 1930s, repressed in the history of opposition that struggled to be told for the interwar period.

The word is absent from the two reference dictionaries regarding the history of Portugal in the twentieth century: the *Dicionário de História do Estado Novo*[1] and the supplement of the *Dicionário de História de Portugal.*[2] Rather, the first dictionary proposes 'antifascist unity' and 'Republican opposition', while the *Suplemento* focuses on the opposition – especially after the Second World War – and the various forms it took: Catholic, democratic and right-wing opposition to Marcelo Caetano. The preference given to the adjective 'antifascist' over the noun 'antifascism' reflects the influence of memory along with a desire to highlight the plurality of the components of antifascism, but also illustrates how difficult it is to conceptualise.[3] In the 1930s, for instance, Portugal's antifascist opposition was composed of the entire Republican, anarchist and Communist opposition parties. It also combined the anarcho-syndicalist, Socialist and Communist labour movements and the members of the military who were hostile to the dictatorship. Given this political configuration, it is clear that the Communists were not predominant in the Portuguese antifascist movement, even though they would set the rhythm of its construction after 1935. However, the Portuguese historiography of antifascism still focuses too closely on its Communist aspect. For instance, Fernando Rosas defined 'antifascist unity' as:

> the phrase used to describe the coalition of various organizations, currents and personalities that opposed the *Estado Novo*. As the main focus of the Portuguese Communist Party's tactics, it was designed to make the regime fall – especially after the Seventh Congress of the Communist International (CI) in 1935, when the course of action for the establishment of the unitary popular fronts against fascism was defined.[4]

As Bruno Groppo noted,[5] the conceptions and the sensibilities of antifascism did not only apply to Communists. In Portugal, the movement was inspired by Republicans, even though the creation of a Popular Front would be attributed to the Communists. As early as 1927, Republicans were looking to unify their actions. Fernando Rosas pointed out that they proposed a united front, but only in the context of preparing the *revolução* – a military movement that would put an end to the dictatorship established in May 1926 to reinstate a parliamentary regime. In this 'united front' ahead of its time, revolts and attempted revolts[6] were based on the alliance of parties and Republican political currents with the military, considering the fact that participation of the labour movement in these revolts was not popular even amongst conspirators. Dissension over this issue conditioned on-site action and roughly followed the right–left division. However, the level of military staff had been steadily decreasing, as military failures accumulated, and it took men to lead the *revolução* – soldiers first, and then armed civilians. Anarchists, anarcho-syndicalists and Communists therefore joined these military movements against the regime, either in the context of an agreement in principle (anarchist current), or in their own names (as was the case with the Communists, although they had received orders to the contrary from the PCP's and the CI's central committees).

Although Fernando Rosas considers Republican revolts to be one of the first expressions of unity against the dictatorship, the joint action would only be like a copy of the original agreement made on 5 October 1910, whose victory was assured by popular support. Therefore, there is no reason to see them as the early shaping of the Popular Fronts. Since the review *Seara Nova* ('New Harvest') was founded in October 1921, its contributors had been reflecting upon the fascist danger and they promoted initiatives even before the Republic fell, making it possible to date the origins of antifascism back to before the Seventh

Congress of the Communist International, and even before the tactical agreements of the Republican revolts, the first of which was made in 1927. Although the convergence of interests was made possible only after the Republic fell,[7] especially with anarcho-syndicalists, and even if the presence of Communist militants seemed hard to eradicate through Communist hierarchy, it nevertheless implied that the ground had been prepared beforehand.

The Beginnings of Antifascism in Portugal (1922–1926)

Mussolini's rise to power in Italy in October 1922 raised awareness and concerns among the Portuguese left wing. The Republican newspaper *A Capital* ('The capital') closely covered the days following the March on Rome. It considered the vast postwar European crisis to be the context that allowed Mussolini's seizure of power, and presented the Italian case as an example to learn from.[8] The newspaper identified similarities with the situation in Portugal (partitocracy, urban protests, political instability and corruption) and called on the Portuguese to remain vigilant.[9] At first, the autistic Partido Democrático ('Democratic Party'), which had always had communication problems with others, and was resolutely in place since 1919, would drift towards 'Italian style' authoritarianism. The fascist model, however, became a general reference for the extreme right[10] and would find followers in Portugal – among those people who came from a radical right-wing background, and more precisely from the Integralismo Lusitano ('Lusitanian Integralism' movement, founded in 1914). The first attempt at creating a fascist party was made in 1923.[11] Its scope remained rather limited since it competed for political space with a myriad of other political movements, currents and sensibilities, ranging from the Integralismo Lusitano to the various parts of the conservative Republican, Catholic and anti-liberal right-wing spectrum.

According to the Republican left, fascism corresponded with the doctrines of the Portuguese radical right, regardless of the existence of ideological or organisational links with the movement that radiated from Italy. The word 'fascism' simultaneously juxtaposed several realities in some sort of concentric circles that opened or closed depending on the object to define. Its plasticity allowed the Portuguese left to restrict it to the Italian case, but also to assimilate it to national incarnations of fascist ideology and, even more frequently, to consider any dictatorship-like form based on repression and on the restriction of freedom as fascist. Fascism then began to be perceived as a danger, and was denounced as such by *Seara Nova*. In the same way, *O Comunista*, the young PCP's newspaper, dedicated a series of articles to fascism in 1923,[12] while fascism was denounced as early as 1924 by the anarcho-syndicalist General Labour Confederation's (Confederação Geral do Trabalho, CGT) newspaper *A Batalha* ('The Battle').[13]

The role played by *Seara Nova* and its intellectuals in the 1920s and 1930s merits our attention. The journal defined itself as 'radical and non-Jacobin'.[14] As an intellectual movement of political reflection, it was on the left of the Republican spectrum,[15] and aimed at both working towards the nation's rebirth and giving the Republic a sense of morality. The journal sharply criticised what had been accomplished since 1910, and the shortcuts that the regime had taken. It denounced the dangers threatening the renovation of the Republican idea, embodied by the Integralismo Lusitano and the Cruzada Nuno Álvares ('Nuno Álvares Crusade')[16] (a civic movement born in 1918), which became its favourite targets. The journal accused the two social and political projects of being capable of destroying the Republic and democracy.

Primo de Rivera's rise to power in Spain in 1923 invigorated the currents that believed that such a dictatorship would solve the crisis of the regime. Rumours that had been circulating of a new *pronunciamiento* during the first months of 1926 gradually became louder. The entire Republican political forces that stood against the Partido Democrático positioned themselves to overthrow António Maria da Silva, president of the council, who was no longer able to retain power, despite his party's victory in the late 1925 elections.

At that time, the Cruzada Nuno Álvares decided to accelerate its revolutionary dynamics.[17] *Seara Nova* chose the same time to denounce the fascist threat and promote an expanded form of antifascism.[18] The Portuguese antifascist struggle was composed of three inseparable elements: the threat of the establishment of a dictatorship in Portugal, the fight against the national channels of fascism, and the struggle for international solidarity. The left's call for unity went beyond the Republican camp.

Seara Nova's antifascist call resounded in the left-wing Republican press, and especially in *A Capital* and *A Choldra* (the latter was the press outlet for the Esquerda Democrática ('Democratic Left'), a party founded in 1925 when the left wing of the Partido Democrático split up). The campaign started with Raul Proença's article 'Fascism and its Impact in Portugal',[19] published by *Seara Nova* on 6 March 1926.[20] It continued with the organisation of an 'antifascist week' in Lisbon from 14 to 24 March. For Raul Proença and the tribunes of the antifascist week, the origins of fascism were rooted in the First World War: '[F]ascism is nothing but a serious moral and spiritual illness caused by the war. In no way is it a normal evolution of society'.[21] Contrary to an influenza confined to the borders of a country, the fight against fascism had to rely on the organisation of large antifascist movements everywhere in Europe, for 'imperialism would sprout up from the national fascisms we would have allowed to develop. Exacerbated and megalomaniac, they would most certainly collide and cause a war the likes of which have never been seen before'. The call remained unanswered in Europe until the rise of Nazism a few years later, when the warning issued in 1926 by Portuguese antifascists was heard at the European level.

In early 1926, it became urgent to take action, as Raul Proença realised. Such action was embodied by the 'antifascist week' and resulted in a series of conferences on fascism in Lisbon. The places where the conferences were held show an opening on the labour movement, and the attempt to create a common antifascist propaganda. Most conferences took place at the trade unions' headquarters (army arsenal, naval arsenal, metalworkers, building workers, dockers, railway workers, assistants and stone carvers), or in prestigious institutions of popular education (Universidade Livre, 'Free University') or Republicanism (Grémio Escolar Republicano, or 'Republican student union', Centro Republicano José Domingues dos Santos). Although most speakers belonged to the core of *Seara Nova* (Jaime Cortesão, Câmara Reys, David Ferreira, Rodrigues Miguéis), the presence of members from various political horizons, such as Emílio Costa (libertarian), Ladislau Batalha (Socialist), Manuel da Silva Campos (Communist) and Pina de Morais (Esquerda Democrática), indicated a desire to unite the left. The closing meeting was held on 24 March, in the gymnasium of Camões secondary school. It brought all the speakers together and gave rise to a great celebration of antifascism.

The 'antifascist week' emphasised two main ideas: the role of the labour movement in strengthening the antifascist struggle and the need to rethink its alliance with the Republic. All discourses leaned in favour of a union of the left against the fascist threat, but this union was not equally understood by each current. The Republican left knew about the existence of a fascist movement in Portugal but it did not consider it a threat to the Republic, but rather a 'temporary illness'.[22] Although the fascist threat was not immediate, it was still in the background; there was a dormant feeling of fascism originating from Italy and spreading across Europe that only a great union could stop:

> Mussolini is a pretentious madman willing to extend this regime to the whole of Europe. But it is impossible, for every single liberal of Europe

is determined to prevent that from happening ... We must fight for those poor enslaved Italians, to save them from the terrible claws of that human beast, in the name of freedom, the most beautiful manifestation of human civilisation.[23]

So far, the plan for action was twofold: domestic vigilance and international solidarity. In fact, in March 1926, the danger came from the conservative sectors who claimed that only a dictatorship could restore order to the country. Republicans believed that the Republic had created the conditions for the onset of fascism[24] by distancing itself from the popular classes, an idea that the anarcho-syndicalists also bought into.[25] This brings us back to what the movement of 5 October intended to carry out when it was deflected by the oligarchies to which the Republic had submitted itself in order to build a strong democracy –the only means of fighting against dictatorships.[26] The left Republican discourse stated that the people were the repository of freedom and progress, and that they would step in every time those values were threatened – as they did in 1919, against the monarchists.[27] Emílio Costa, an anarchist intellectual, shared the idea of the people as the repository of freedom. He saw fascism as an imported movement with a multifarious face that grew only because of the collapse of the working class after the crisis of indifference, lethargy and disorientation caused by the war. To resist this fascism, Costa believed that the working classes should merge into one powerful organisation: '[A] dictatorship is easy and deadly if the people remain indifferent. But if they react, it becomes unworkable'.[28] For the non-Republican left, the fascist threat was not as introspective. If *A Batalha* called for action[29] against an imminent new military movement in early 1926, re-establishing a democracy would have been enough to stop fascism.[30] For the Communists, the threat was not fascism, but *Riverism* (a military dictatorship such as that of Miguel Primo de Rivera) in the Spanish style. However, they believed that the proletariat could stand up to it.[31]

The antifascist momentum had been launched and was self-sustaining – or at least it seemed to come from the conferences held at the headquarters of the Lisbon Trade Union Federation, the capital of anarcho-syndicalism,[32] and at the Caixa Económica Portuguesa (Portuguese Savings Bank) by the PCP,[33] after the closing of the 'antifascist week'. But as *Seara Nova* had foretold,[34] the only thing that remained of these antifascist meetings after the military movement of 28 May 1926 was the camaraderie of a shared experience. During a congress held on 29 and 30 May, the PCP suggested a united front against the *putsch* to the General Confederation of Labour (CGT), *Seara Nova* and Esquerda Democrática, but the proposal had no impact.

Antifascism 'On Hold' (1926–1933)

The new government gradually started repressing the actions of the leftist forces. The first Republicans were arrested towards the end of June, the PCP's headquarters was taken over by the police, and members of the Central Committee were arrested in August. However, the repression only properly started after the revolt in February 1927. Republicans were then split between the prospect of leading a domestic underground opposition or of going into exile. Anarchists and anarcho-syndicalists, for their part, were punished for taking part in the revolt by the banning of the CGT and the closing down of the *A Batalha* headquarters by the police.[35] After that, it was all downhill for the PCP until 1929, when the party only had forty-nine militants and approximately five hundred sympathisers.[36] After 1931, the PCP became part of intellectual and student circles, which would ensure its renewal.

As for the Republican parties, with the exception of the Partido Democrático, they were young and still trying their hand at the political game. From 1911, and more particularly after December 1918 and the end of Sidónio Pais' dictatorship, their endless restructuring (on either side of the Partido Democrático) weakened these parties – they became ephemeral, constantly looking to establish themselves solidly, mainly amongst urban electors, and angled to attempt *putsches* in order to gain access to power. They had few members, no party structure and no bureaucratic apparatus that would cover the entire national territory[37] to help them to win the elections. They organised around political sensibilities that gravitated towards charismatic personalities[38] rather than ordered and structured political parties. Once the dictatorship was in place, the different Republican parties survived by forming into small groups, as did the Partido Democrático.[39] However, they retained their ability to mobilise their circles of influence, which informally extended to the working class through their electoral base of urban petty bourgeoisie, salesmen and public servants. Their advantage lay in successfully establishing themselves in the armed forces, especially amongst middle-ranking officers – the background of a number of Republican leaders, something the regime would be unable to erase completely despite the purges it promoted after each revolt. Furthermore, once underground, clientelistic relationships, personal properties and family networks provided these Republican groups with a significant logistic and fallback base. Going underground and adopting a military-like resistance forced the old Republican parties to change and to develop a military structure

– either by means of influence amongst active officers or by organising combat groups with the members of the military who had survived the purges. This tendency strengthened with time; a group's survival and its place within the Republican opposition depended on its military abilities. Therefore, the *Budas* (a group ideologically placed in the wake of *Seara Nova* and heir to the antifascism of March 1926 through Jaime Cortesão) put forth their military power when vying for a place in the opposition's political game. The year 1927 saw the start of a revolutionary dynamic that would continue until 1938, when the regime foiled the last revolt of the opposition and de-structured the PCP, even though the Republican movement would decline after 1931. The PCP would have to deal with these kinds of groups when seeking to set up the Portuguese Popular Front (FPP), which had a long history of attempts at unity and ideological compromises.

The period starting in 1927 was one of immediate action when revolutionary training intensified.[40] In Paris, the *seareiros* helped to establish a government programme aimed at regenerating the Republic, reforming the institutions and setting up a new economic and social policy that would lay the foundations for the rally of the Republican opposition. The task was hard and the path risky. However, the *Liga*'s programme would not succeed in gathering all Republican parties. In order to achieve a consensus, Republicans put their antifascist agenda on hold. The government programme was therefore cut shorter at each revolutionary failure, until it became a mere set of principles. Debates over ideological beliefs and doctrinal principles and the spreading of Republican ideas were postponed. One of the revolutionary leaders once exclaimed he needed weapons, not paper.

Due to exile and hiding, the Republicans' discourse focused once more on domestic issues. Two major concerns stand out: the unity of the Republican family and criticising the wrongdoings of the dictatorship, especially in the financial and colonial fields. Former president of the Republic, Bernardino Machado, was the only consensual figure of the Republican opposition. While in exile, he reflected on the nature of the Portuguese, Italian and Spanish dictatorships and agreed with the theory developed during the 'antifascist week', according to which the Italian and Spanish regimes represented the last stage of the crisis of the liberal monarchy's constitutional parties – a crisis Portugal had already overcome with the establishment of the Republic. The Portuguese dictatorship was of another nature. It arose from the breach of a 1910 contract between the people and the constitutional Republican parties – a breach caused by hard-line propaganda, the economic interests of the main newspaper owners, and clericalism. It was not fascist, but militarist,[41] and would become both militarist and clerical with Salazar's accession to the Ministry of Finance in 1928.[42] Republicans would use this taxonomy until the late 1930s, even though Radicals started using the term 'fascist' at the beginning of the Spanish Civil War – but not systematically, unlike Communists and anarchists. Depending on the political environment, Portugal was not immediately classified as a fascist country. Only after the events of February 1934 in France did Angelo Tasca, an Italian Socialist in charge of the foreign politics section of the newspaper *Le Populaire*, add Portugal to the list of fascisms.[43]

What became of the participants of the 'antifascist week' after they went into exile? From Paris, Raul Proença continued to reflect upon the dangers threatening democracy and the role of intellectuals in society before illness unexpectedly stopped him in 1931; Jaime Cortesão followed a path that would lead him to revolutionary action. Their relationship with other exiles (particularly Spanish and Italian ones), their contact with organisations such as the League for the Rights of Man or the 'Action Internationale Démocratique pour la Paix' ('International Democratic Action for Peace'), and their relations with leftist writers and intellectuals helped Portuguese exiles enter French antifascist circles. Let us consider, for example, the friendship between the *seareiro* António Sérgio and Paul Langevin, member of the League and co-founder of the *Comité de vigilance des intellectuels antifascistes* ('Vigilance Committee of Antifascist Intellectuals') in 1934. The Portuguese opponents, escaped from the African colonies, were authorized to live in France thanks to the efforts of the League at the Paris Préfecture de Police, efforts that were renewed when the exiles' stay was threatened by the tightening of immigration laws in the second half of the 1930s. The exile was also rooted in the anti-colonial movement in the late 1920s, for reasons explained by *Le Cri des Peuples* ('The Cry of Peoples'), a newspaper founded by Bernard Lecache for the defence of national minorities and oppressed peoples. According to this newspaper, deportees and natives shared a common battleground resulting from the subversive action of the former in the colonies and the discontent of the latter, whose nature was fully in agreement with the fight against democracies and dictatorships.[44] The leftist press gave visibility to the participation of the exiles in pacifist initiatives in Paris, and especially to those involving Afonso Costa, a figurehead of the Portuguese Republic, former prime minister and leader of the Portuguese opposition between 1926 and 1937.[45] Costa's social network in exile also included the Radical Party and Freemasonry (French and Belgian). Moreover, exiles of different nationalities met in the *salon* of Ms. Ménard-Dorian, secretary of the League for the Rights of Man, including Bernardino Machado, the president of the Republic in office during the putsch of May 1926, Italians Francesco Nitti and Filippo Turati, and Spaniards Miguel de Unamuno and Eduardo Ortega y Gasset.[46]

The advent of the Second Spanish Republic made the French left lose interest in the Portuguese opposition. The political leaders and military executives of the resistance movement moved to Spain, the new rear base of the armed struggle against the Portuguese dictatorship. After April 1931, Portuguese Republicans were welcome in Spain – a first demonstration of antifascist solidarity. The leftist press (*El Sol, El Imparcial, Claridad, Heraldo de Madrid, El Liberal*) waged an intense campaign against the Portuguese dictatorship, while leftist governmental circles provided both logistical and material help to the *revolução*. The *Ateneo* played a major role in the dialogues between the different left parties: during a meeting in honour of the Portuguese exiles, Ortega y Gasset argued that in order to strengthen the Spanish Republic, the Portuguese dictatorship had to disappear.[47] In early 1936, a 'Friends of Portugal' group was founded to denounce the repression of Salazar's dictatorship. Their most visible action was to send Salazar an open letter signed by about twenty political and trade union organisations, and by political and intellectual figures.

The Portuguese Republican left was so close to the Spanish Socialists that these offered them, in the summer of 1934, the weapons stored and hidden in Spain for the Portuguese revolution, which had been acquired some time before with the complicity of the Spanish government.[48] When the Portuguese involvement in the arms trafficking was discovered, the Republican leaders took refuge in France, and their relations with the French antifascist movement became tighter. The stay in France of prestigious historian Jaime Cortesão allows us to sound out the dynamics of Portuguese antifascism; in June 1935 he represented the Portuguese intellectuals in the First Congress of Antifascist Writers in Paris,[49] and was later invited to participate in the general assembly of the International Association of Writers held in London in June 1936.[50] Cortesão remained committed to the intellectual antifascist movement, and represented Portugal again, together with Gonzalo de Reparaz, in the Second Congress of Antifascist Writers held in mid-1937 in Republican Spain and Paris.[51]

The Republican left's steps towards exile resulted in breaks in perception and identification. Until the end of the 1930s, their rallying calls were made in the name of 'liberals', showing their growing awareness that Europe was becoming bipolar and oscillating between democracy and dictatorship. In Republican political culture, the former was the fruit of liberal governments produced by law, while the latter emanated from authoritarian governments, imposed by force. But the concept of 'dictatorship of the proletariat' acted as a disruptive factor. Bernardino Machado and Raul Proença both immediately rejected the idea in the name of freedom: 'fascisms and bolshevisms, also anti-human'.[52] Jaime Cortesão and the *Budas* showed that they were more open to compromise, and ignored a few aspects of Communist authoritarianism – a recurring question among European left-wing parties. The *Budas* slid towards socialism, and kept a close political and personal relationship with Spanish Socialist leaders Indalecio Prieto and, particularly, Francisco Largo Caballero.

From May 1926, the unions remained active in semi-legal conditions; they were engaged in more immediate struggles than antifascism, such as the eight-hour working day and the protection of workers in cases of occupational injury.[53] These issues led to the creation of the Lisbon Inter-Trade Union Commission in favour of shorter working hours in March 1930, turned after the anarcho-syndicalists' departure into an alternative central union body to the CGT and the Federation of Labour Associations (Socialist trade unions), adopting the acronym CIS. The decrees that established national trade unions in September 1933 were a death warrant for free trade unionism; however, they did create favourable conditions within the labour movement for a joint response, incidentally combined with the Republican opposition.

The Portuguese Popular Front (1934–1938)

Portugal had few developed cities and was industrially and economically backward: this is why the traditionally anarcho-syndicalist movement did not reach the same strength in Portugal as it did in other European countries. The number of unionised workers is still hard to determine because the organisations tended to inflate the figures. In 1932,[54] there were not 15,000 members as the CIS had claimed but only 2,000.[55] The Communists were not the only ones to inflate figures; during its golden age, the CGT had claimed some 120,000 to 150,000 members, although its members did not exceed 35,000.[56] In these conditions, the labour movement paled in comparison to the Communists within the Popular Front when it was first created, and it was not until the Republican opposition's participation that the gathering would gain in consistency, as noted by the CI.

The response to the trade unions's 'fascistisation', embodied by the general revolutionary strike of 18 January 1934, which brought together the CGT, the CIS, the FAO and the Sindicatos Autónomos (Autonomous

Unions), was an attempt to unify the front *avant la lettre*. The gathering was larger than the labour movement itself since the strike was to blend with a new Republican revolt. The PCP blamed the anarchists for the failure, reviving ancient rivalries between both currents,[57] and thus ruining any possibility of a future united front.

The PCP went through a phase of hesitation and tactical indefinition.[58] After the failure of 18 January, it went back to the 'class against class' strategy until the CI's policy evolved. In April 1934, a draft letter from the Latin secretariat addressed to the Portuguese section ordered the strategy to be orientated towards a united antifascist front against the dictatorship.[59] In September, and then in November, the CI reaffirmed its directives, advising the PCP to propose a 'common action against fascism' to the Republicans, and to set up a 'united front' in preparation for the National Assembly in December. It also advised the anarchists to propose common actions in order to fight for the liberation of prisoners and political deportees and against the 'fascistisation' of trade unions, to continue the struggle in favour of freedom of association, economic and social reforms, production and distribution of propaganda, and to organise demonstrations and strikes against the repression.[60] Favouring a 'class against class' strategy, the PCP did not fully understand this particular approach. In March 1935, *Avante* ('Forward') once more accused Republicans and anarchists of being at the vanguard of fascism and capitalism.[61]

At the end of 1934, Bento Gonçalves hinted at a slight shift towards a 'united front' strategy[62] in an article published in *Correspondance Internationale*, but it was based on the principle of a 'front united from below', which, according to him, better suited to the pre-insurrectionary situation Portugal was going through.[63] It was not until April 1935 that *Avante* called for 'all anarchist and anarcho-syndicalist militants or Republican groups' to set up a united platform of action, but without letting go of the idea of a 'front united from below'. The PCP only redefined its strategy and implemented initiatives at a higher level after the Seventh Congress of the CI. When delegates returned from Moscow, the tone of the Communist press began to change. Republicans, who until then had been given the derogatory nickname of '*reviralhistas*' by *Avante*, were metamorphosed into antifascists. Priority was now given to the overthrowing of fascism, at the expense of the establishment of the dictatorship of the proletariat.[64] The steps toward unifying the antifascist forces were taken via a satellite organisation of the PCP: the Portuguese League against War and Fascism, created in August 1934 and claiming to be part of the Amsterdam–Pleyel movement. The call was made around a consensual and minimal programme: amnesty for political prisoners, the fight against war and fascism, and the restoration of democratic freedoms.[65]

But it was not until February 1936 that an announcement was made about the creation of the Portuguese Popular Front (FPP),[66] composed of a dozen organisations, the list of which shows how small the gathering really was.[67] Communist organisations and their satellites constituted a majority, despite the presence of freemasons and its armed branch (the Acção Anticlerical e Antifascista) ['Anticlerical antifascist action']), of the ineffective Socialist Party[68] and of the inexpressive Republican–Socialist alliance.[69] Beside the FPP, there were still Republicans and anarchists in exile, divided up between the Madrid and Paris groups. Pável, a PCP delegate to the CI, tried to unite and integrate them to the FPP. Armando de Magalhães, executive of the PCP who came back from Moscow, was sent to Madrid in the summer of 1936. His actions led to the creation, on 18 August, of the Union of Antifascist Portuguese in Spain. It was the only organisation that succeeded in uniting radical Republicans, anarchists and Communists. However, it only existed in Madrid because of the war's constraints, and it ended up being infiltrated by the Communists. Its success in Paris was more limited due to the presence of right-wing Republican figures. Pável's efforts led, however, to the call Afonso Costa and José Domingues dos Santos sent out in January 1937 to 'every liberal and antifascist', which resulted in the creation of the FPP's Action Committee (AC), headquartered in Paris, where the PCP was more tolerated than accepted. In Paris, the AC would publish the *Unir* newspaper, press outlet of the FPP, financed by the Spanish Republic.

In Spain, a delegation of the FPP was created in Barcelona, around the *Budas*. It channelled the funds given to the FPP by the Spanish Republic and the *Generalitat* (autonomous government) of Catalonia in order to lead solidarity actions in Portugal and finance the *revolução*, whose preparation resumed at the beginning of 1937 – once the domestic and exiled groups had been contacted despite the PCP's efforts to diverge the Republicans from the 'putschist path'.

The divergences between Communists and Republicans in Portugal were insurmountable and they rendered the FPP inoperative: the former wanted to develop mass labour and set up liaison committees while the latter prioritised conspiracy. The few solidarity actions carried out with the Spanish Republicans in the name of the FPP were in fact prepared by the Republican left wing and by the anarchists, without the knowledge of the PCP (despite the individual participation of Communist militants). It was leftist Republicanism that animated the

FPP and made it come alive by using it as support for revolutionary preparations, especially in 1937 and 1938.

Conclusion

In Portugal the first steps towards antifascism were taken in the 1920s. The movement bet on propaganda, meetings and the press to raise awareness and to keep people alert, even though the shadow of fascism did not yet directly threaten Portugal. The left identified the imminent danger of the country becoming a dictatorship, the first step of a journey comprising many stages and ultimately ending in fascism. After the events of 28 May 1926, antifascism was set aside to concentrate on more immediate preoccupations. In the 1930s it reappeared in the opposition's discourse, brought back by the events in Europe and the CI directives.

The antifascist movement of the 1930s evolved following a calendar imposed by the outside, built around the creation of the FPP. Inside Portugal, it was an unusual organisation, a hybrid whose activity was directed by the Republicans, whereas from the outside it seemed to be strong around the Madrid and Paris cores. Although the PCP was the first to draw the preliminary outline of the FPP's creation, it was lost in the contradictions between the CI directives and the reality in Portugal, and did not succeed in imposing itself, especially since it remained a marginal group. Until the end of the 1930s, the regime believed the danger came from Republican groups, while the propaganda machine, especially from the outside, turned the PCP into their arch-enemy.

The disintegration of the French Popular Front put an end to the entente among Portuguese exiles. As early as November 1938, *Unir* became the Portuguese Democracy's outlet – in other words, it was a new assembly without the Communists. However, Portuguese antifascism did not wear out in the FPP. Solidarities were still able to restore unity once again when the threat of war was looming over Spain. The call from Tours in October 1939 would, despite its initial poor welcome, open the way to a new unitary organisation, the *Movimento de Unidade Nacional Antifascista* ('Movement of Antifascist National Unity'), founded in December 1943. The Second World War changed everything, introducing a new paradigm: the dichotomy between anglophiles – who supported respecting the Portuguese–British alliance – and the Axis admirers – and brought the opposition closer to those who sympathised with the dictatorship's allies.

Translated by Mathieu Franks and Sonia Izrar, revised by
Casey Sellarole

Notes

1. F. Rosas and Brandão de Brito (eds), *Dicionário de História do Estado Novo*, 2 vols, Venda Nova, 1996.
2. A. Barreto and F. Mónica (eds), *Dicionário de História de Portugal. Suplemento*, 3 vols, Porto, 1999.
3. Especially because of its assimilation to communism. Bruno Groppo, 'Fascismes, antifascismes et communismes', in M. Dreyfus and B. Groppo (eds), *Le siècle des communismes*, Paris, 2004, 739–58.
4. F. Rosas, 'Unidade antifascista', in *Dicionário de História do Estado Novo*, 991–96.
5. Groppo, 'Fascismes', 744.
6. February 1927, July 1928, April 1931, August 1931, to mention a few of the successful movements. There were a large number of attempts aborted by the police or defused by conspirators.
7. Regarding the Republic, cf. L. Bigote Chorão, *A crise da República e a ditadura militar*, Lisbon, 2009; A. Aniceto, *História de uma conspiração, Sinel de Cordes e o 28 de Maio*, Lisbon, 2000; A.J. Telo, *Ascensão e queda da I República*, 2 vols, Lisbon, 1980–1984.
8. *A Capital*, 28 October 1922.
9. Ibid., 3 November 1922.
10. A. Costa Pinto, *Os Camisas azuis. Ideologia, Elites e movimentos fascistas em Portugal, 1914–1945*, Lisbon, 1994.
11. Ibid.,'O Fascismo e a crise da Primeira República: os nacionalismos Lusitanos (1923–1925)', *Penélope, Fazer e desfazer história* 3 (June 1989), 44–62.
12. Ibid., 61.
13. P. Guimarães, 'Cercados e Perseguidos: a Confederação Geral do Trabalho (CGT) nos últimos anos do sindicalismo revolucionário em Portugal (1926–1938)', http://colectivolibertarioevora.files.wordpress.com/2013/01/cgt_anos30_pguimaraes.pdf.
14. *Seara Nova* 1 (21 October 1921).
15. Although the liberal left is predominant in *Seara Nova*, other trends are expressed. R. Fernandes, 'A Seara Nova e a Primeira República', in AA.VV., *Revistas, ideias e doutrinas. Leituras do pensamento contemporâneo*, Lisbon, 2003, 80–89.
16. E. Castro Leal, *Nação e nacionalismos. A Cruzada Nacional D. Nuno Álvares Pereira e as origens do Estado Novo (1918–1938)*, Lisbon, 1999. The Cruzada was not a fascist organisation, except during the first months of 1926, when Filomeno da Câmara and Nobre de Melon were its heads.
17. Ibid., 'A Cruzada Nacional D. Nuno Álvares Pereira e as origens do Estado Novo (1918–1938), *Análise Social* XXXIII(148) (1998), 823–51.
18. When the Cruzada called for a right reorientation of the Republic in 1921, a dispute arose with *Seara Nova*, and the antagonism remained quite strong during the following years. Jaime Cortesão, in defiance of the Cruzada, attended a conference at the Sociedade de Geografia (Geographical Society) on 9 January 1926, during which Filomeno da Câmara and Nobre de Melo

reminded how urgent it was for Portugal to do like Primo de Rivera's Spain and Mussolini's Italy and create a strong government.

19. About his role in the creation of the antifascist consciousness, see A. Reis, *Raul Proença, Biografia de um intelectual político republicano*, 2 vols, Lisbon, 2003.
20. Martinho Nobre de Melo answers back in an article entitled 'O antifascismo de Raul Poença', *Reconquista* 5 (1 April 1926), to which Raul Proença answers in 'Glorifying of Fascism', *Seara Nova* 87 (13 May 1926).
21. *Seara Nova* 77 (6 March 1926). Raul Proença published a second article on fascism in *Seara Nova* 83 (15 April 1926).
22. J. Cortesão, *A Capital*, 17 March 1926.
23. Ibid.
24. P. de Morais, *A Capital*, 16 March 1926.
25. A. Vieira, *A Capital*, 19 March 1926.
26. P. de Morais, *A Capital*, 16 March 1926.
27. J. Camoezas, *A Capital*, 19 March 1926.
28. E. Costa, *A Capital*, 18 March 1926.
29. 'A fascist revolution: here is the danger we must stand up to right now. In the whole country, opposition must get ready to fight, and not let itself be strangled by a dictatorial regime.' *A Batalha*, 12 February 1926. In his memoirs, Manual Joaquim de Sousa emphasises the necessity to organise a labour movement to fight against fascism, *Últimos tempos de acção sindical livre e do anarquismo militante*, Lisbon, 1989, 176.
30. A. Vieira, *A Capital*, 19 March 1926.
31. A. Peixe, *A Capital*, March 1926.
32. Virgílio de Sousa, João Miranda, Santos Arranha, Aleixo de Oliveira, Silva Campos and Manuel Henriques Rijo.
33. Sobral de Campos, José Tavares dos Santos, Teixeira Danton, Abel Pereira and Alberto Neves.
34. Foreseeing future history, *Seara Nova* wrote about the 'antifascist week': '[I]f one day the men gathered here came to deeply disagree on the ways to repel fascism and face the direct or indirect conditions in which it could break out in Europe and in Portugal, they would never forget the close camaraderie of its finest hours'. *Seara Nova* 80 (27 March 1926).
35. The newspaper would resurface soon after, but would be definitively banned in November 1927.
36. In 1930, their number increased to 120, and to 700 the next year, remaining stable until 1935. J. Arsénio Nunes, 'Sobre alguns aspectos da evolução política do Partido Comunista Português, após a reorganização de 1929', *Análise Social* XVII(67–68) (1981), 715–31.
37. Despite the historiographical renewal for the history of the First Republic, there is still a lack of research regarding the Republican political parties. The only one that was the subject of a monograph was the Esquerda Democrática.
38. Acção Republicana ('Republican Action') to d'Álvaro de Castro, and União Liberal ('Liberal Union') to de Cunha Leal.

39. In 1939, the outlawed Partido Democrático managed to remain organised, taking the form of an assistance commission, but deprived of its characteristic mobilisation power.
40. On the opposition inside, see H. Paulo (ed.), *Memória das oposições (1927–1969)*, Coimbra, 2010; L. Farinha, *O Reviralho. Revoltas republicanas contra a ditadura (1926–1940)*, Lisbon, 1999. On opposition in exile, see C. Clímaco, 'L'exil politique portugais en France et en Espagne, 1927–1940', Ph.D. dissertation, Université de Paris 7 Denis Diderot, 1998.
41. B. Machado, *O Militarismo*, 1927.
42. B. Machado, *A ditadura clerical-militarista em Portugal*, 1929.
43. *Le Populaire*, 18 December 1934.
44. *Le Cri des Peuples*, 10 January 1929.
45. Afonso Costa was a usual participant and speaker, at least between 1927 and 1935, at the annual 'Peace Banquet' organized by the National Council for Peace.
46. E. González Calleja, 'Más allá de la Rotonde: Los exiliados antiprimo-riveristas en París (1923–1930)', in F. Martinez López et al. (eds), *París, ciudad de acogida: el exilio español durante los siglos XIX y XX*, Madrid, 2010, 213.
47. Arquivo Nacional Torre do Tombo, Lisbon (ANTT), AOS/CO/PC-3H, p. 1, May 1932.
48. P. Díaz Morlán, *Horacio Echevarrieta, 1870–1963, el capitalista republicano*, Madrid, 1999; C. Clímaco, *Republicanos, anarquistas e comunistas no exílio (1927–1936)*, Lisbon, 2015.
49. The speeches of this conference were collected by S. Teroni and W. Klein (eds), *Pour la Défense de la culture, les textes du congrès international des écrivains*, Dijon, 2005.
50. Cortesão would not participate in this meeting due to the lack of a passport.
51. L.M. Schneider and M. Aznar Soler (eds), *II Congreso International de Escritores Antifascistas (1937): ponencias, documentos y testimonios*, Barcelona, 1979.
52. R. Proença, *Páginas de política*, Lisbon, 1972, vol. 1, 101.
53. F. Patriarca, *A questão social no salazarismo (1930–1947)*, 2 vols, Lisbon, 1995.
54. 'Intervenção de António na XII reunião plenária da Internacional Comunista', introdução e notas de J. Pacheco Pereira, *Estudos sobre o comunismo*, 0 (July 1983), 27–31.
55. B. Gonçalves, 'Duas palavras', in *Os Comunistas – Bento Gonçalves*, Porto, 1976, 119–57.
56. C. da Fonseca, 'A revolta imaginária. O operariado frente ao 28 de Maio', *Revista de História das Ideias* 7 (1985), 373.
57. Unlike other Communist parties, the Portuguese one was created from a split within the Anarchist movement.
58. Bento Gonçalves was the face of the 1929 reorganisation. He was arrested in 1930 and deported to Cape Verde, from whence he returned in 1933. He stood against the insurrectionary tactic followed by José de Sousa and the CIS. But the advanced state of the preparation did not leave him enough room for manoeuvre. Bento Gonçalves was in favour of entryism in national trade unions to influence them from within.

59. Instituto de História Contemporânea (ICS), F. 495, op. 4, d. 239 – AHS/IC, doc. 66, M. 6, cx. 1, 6 April 1934.
60. Draft letter from the Latin secretariat addressed to the Portuguese section, dated 8 November 1934, quoted in J. Arsénio Nunes, 'A formação da estratégia antifascista', *História* 17 (February 1996), 30.
61. *Avante* II(5), March 1935.
62. About Bento Gonçalves' perception of fascism and the united front's strategy evolution, see Arsénio Nunes, 'A formação', 22–33.
63. The signs of which would have been the contradictions of capitalism, the *Estado Novo*'s bankruptcy and the increasing indignation of the masses. Albino [Bento Gonçalves], 'Le Gouvernement Carmona–Salazar accélère les préparatifs de guerre au Portugal', *Correspondance Internationale* 115–16, 29 December 1934.
64. *Avante* II(13), November 1935.
65. *Avante* II(12), October 1935.
66. *Avante* II(16), February 1936.
67. On the PPF's creation, see A. Manta, *A Frente Popular Antifascista*, Lisbon, 1976, 28–29; and J. Manya, 'Le front populaire portugais entre clandestinité et exil', in Xavier Vigna (ed.), *Le Pain, la paix, la liberté*, Paris, 255–70.
68. Dissolved itself in 1933.
69. Instituto de Ciências Sociais da Universidade de Lisboa, Lisbon (ICS), F. 495, op. 10a, doc. 262 – AHS/IC, doc. 112, M 32, cx. 2, report of 23 November 1936, written in Spain by a member of the PCP's Central Committee.

References

Aniceto, A. *História de uma conspiração, Sinel de Cordes e o 28 de Maio*. Lisbon, 2000.

Barreto, A., and F. Mónica (eds). *Dicionário de História de Portugal. Suplemento*. 3 vols, Porto, 1999.

Castro Leal, E. 'A Cruzada Nacional D. Nuno Álvares Pereira e as origens do Estado Novo (1918–1938)'. *Análise Social* xxxiii(148) (1998), 823–51.

———. *Nação e nacionalismos. A Cruzada Nacional D. Nuno Álvares Pereira e as origens do Estado Novo (1918–1938)*. Lisbon, 1999.

Chorão, L. Bigote. *A crise da República e a ditadura militar*. Lisbon, 2009.

Clímaco, C. 'L'exil politique portugais en France et en Espagne, 1927–1940'. Ph.D. dissertation, Université de Paris 7 Denis Diderot, 1998.

———. *Republicanos, anarquistas e comunistas no exílio (1927–1936)*. Lisbon, 2015.

Díaz Morlán, P. *Horacio Echevarrieta, 1870–1963, el capitalista republicano*. Madrid, 1999.

Farinha, L. *O Reviralho. Revoltas republicanas contra a ditadura (1926–1940)*. Lisbon, 1999.

Fernandes, R. 'A Seara Nova e a Primeira República,' in AA.VV., *Revistas, ideias e doutrinas. Leituras do pensamento contemporâneo*. Lisbon, 2003, 80–89.

Fonseca, C. da. 'A revolta imaginária. O operariado frente ao 28 de Maio'. *Revista de História das Ideias* 7 (1985), 373–90.

Gonçalves, B. 'Duas palavras', in *Os Comunistas – Bento Gonçalves*. Porto, 1976, 121–57.

González Calleja, E. 'Más allá de la Rotonde: Los exiliados antiprimo-riveristas en París (1923–1930)', in F. Martinez López et al. (eds), *París, ciudad de acogida: el exilio español durante los siglos XIX y XX*. Madrid, 2010, 183–234.

Groppo, B. 'Fascismes, antifascismes et communismes', in M. Dreyfus and B. Groppo (eds), *Le siècle des communismes*, Paris, 2004, 739–58.

Guimarães, P. 'Cercados e Perseguidos: a Confederação Geral do Trabalho (CGT) nos últimos anos do sindicalismo revolucionário em Portugal (1926–1938)', online.

Manta, A. *A Frente Popular Antifascista*. Lisbon, 1976.

Manya, J. 'Le front populaire portugais entre clandestinité et exil', in Xavier Vigna (ed.), *Le Pain, la paix, la liberté*. Paris, 255–70.

Nunes, J. Arsenio. 'Sobre alguns aspectos da evolução política do Partido Comunista Português, após a reorganização de 1929'. *Análise Social* XVII(67–68) (1981), 715–34.

———. 'A formação da estratégia antifascista', *História* 17 (February 1996), 22–33.

Patriarca, F. *A questão social no salazarismo (1930–1947)*. 2 vols, Lisbon, 1995.

Paulo, H. (ed.). *Memória das oposições (1927–1969)*. Coimbra, 2010.

Pinto, A. Costa. 'O Fascismo e a crise da Primeira República: os nacionalismos lusitanos (1923–1925)'. *Penélope, Fazer e desfazer história* 3 (June 1989), 44–62.

———. *Os Camisas azuis. Ideologia, Elites e movimentos fascistas em Portugal, 1914–1945*. Lisbon, 1994.

Proença, R., *Páginas de política*. Lisbon, 1972, vol. 1.

Reis, A. *Raul Proença, Biografia de um intelectual político republicano*. 2 vols, Lisbon, 2003.

Rosas, F., and Brandão de Brito (eds). *Dicionário de História do Estado Novo*. 2 vols, Venda Nova, 1996.

Schneider, L.M., and M. Aznar Soler (eds). *II Congreso International de Escritores Antifascistas (1937): ponencias, documentos y testimonios*. Barcelona, 1979.

Sousa, M.J. de. *Últimos tempos de acção sindical livre e do anarquismo militante*. Lisbon, 1989.

Telo, A.J. *Ascensão e queda da I República*. 2 vols, Lisbon, 1980–1984.

Teroni, S., and W. Klein (eds), *Pour la Défense de la culture, les textes du congrès international des écrivains*. Dijon, 2005.

Cristina Clímaco is associate professor of Portuguese Modern History at the Université Paris VIII. Her research deals with the opposition to the *Estado Novo*, and specifically with the Portuguese political exiles of the 1930s. She has published numerous articles in Portuguese and non-Portuguese reviews, and the forthcoming book *Republicanos, Anarquistas e Comunistas no exílio, 1927–1936* (Lisbon, Colibri).

7

THE ARGENTINE ANTIFASCIST MOVEMENT AND THE BUILDING OF A TEMPTING DOMESTIC APPEAL, 1922–46

Andrés Bisso

An Uncommon Antifascism?

If we take a look at the images of antifascism crystallised by common sense or epics, such as the 'heroic fighting men and fighting boys of France'[1] pictured in Susan Pulsifer's poems, or the self-sacrificing soldier depicted on East German stamps,[2] we could hardly describe the Argentine antifascist movement as archetypical or even prototypical. Not only because there were comparatively very few 'fighters'[3] and a huge number of 'speakers'[4] in its ranks, but also because most of its leading activists were notable figures, even if the movement was relatively popular and enjoyed a massive following throughout the country, especially from the Spanish Civil War onwards.[5]

Indeed, Acción Argentina ('Argentine Action'),[6] the most widely recognised organisation in the pro-Allied Argentine movement, was led, among other public figures from the liberal–socialist spectrum,[7] by notables[8] such as former president of the Republic, Marcelo T. de Alvear, the president of corporate landowners, Adolfo Bioy, and the distinguished scientist (and later Nobel laureate) Bernardo Houssay.[9]

Another well-known organisation aiding the Allies, created largely through Communist and Catholic efforts, was the Junta de la Victoria ('Victory Board').[10] Its membership was limited to women (although men such as the former minister of finance, Federico Pinedo, were invited as lecturers),[11] and its leaders' compound surnames from illustrious families matched the social status of the most elegant circles of leisure and society in Argentina.[12] It was said of its local section in the city of La Plata: '[I]t would take far too long to name all the fine ladies [involved in] this exemplary crusade for solidarity'.[13]

Its notability does not mean, as we have said above, that antifascism was not popular. In this regard, we can mention the typographers who gave half of their daily wage to the Republican side in the Spanish Civil War, emphasising 'the huge international repercussions of what is happening in Spain' and advising 'all free men to participate in a concrete manner in the battle against reaction and fascism'.[14]

In fact, Argentine antifascism covered a broad social spectrum, including pro-British politicians[15] and Francophile intellectuals,[16] as well as fervent Catholics,[17] devoted Communists[18] and dissenting anarchists.[19] Contrary to Furet's view of antifascism as being irreconcilable with anti-communism,[20] challenged by other European scholars,[21] mainstream antifascism in Argentina was predominantly liberal–socialist and did not hesitate to condemn both regimes (fascist and Communist) as equally 'anti-nationalist', even when the rhetoric of 'anti-communism' was used by the dictatorial or fraudulent governments to pass repressive laws in order to attack or control the entire democratic opposition.[22] Moreover, at the beginning of Operation Barbarossa – the German invasion of the Soviet Union that ended the 'Non-Aggression Pact' period of 1939–41, which had been a traumatic experience for the antifascist community[23] – the editors of the journal *Argentina Libre* ('Free Argentina') even tried a kind of 'pro-Russian anti-Stalinism' – unaware of the possible incoherence of such a stance – by claiming 'With Russia against Hitler, in spite of Stalin' on the back cover.[24]

But the key question seems to be: why did antifascism emerge in Argentina, so far from its cradle, apparently so removed from the real problems of the country? In Leticia Prislei's words, 'How do you experience a war with an ocean in the middle?'[25] A widely shared view in national political culture[26] holds that this was indeed impossible and explains local antifascism as just an outcome of the Eurocentric political and cultural leadership of the time, obsessed with 'insignificant little right-wing groups – not all of them pro-fascist – ... that could never become the national problem par excellence. Something that did not exist was fought against, whereas *the thing that actually* did exist was silenced'.[27]

But, what was 'the thing that actually did exist'? It is undeniable that neither the Argentine Fascist Party,[28] which actually existed, nor the Argentine Social-Nationalist Party[29] had enough supporters to pose a real threat to democracy in the country. Similarly, the twelve thousand

Germans who celebrated Labour Day under a circus tent decorated with swastika flags in 1935 were not a real danger to the state,[30] and nor were the fifty thousand Italians who rejoiced on the streets of Buenos Aires over Mussolini's invasion of Abyssinia.[31] Although the antifascist movement sought and continuously proclaimed the need to ban these groups, they were not the main targets of its attacks and allusions.

Instead of identifying the enemy only with groups that willingly declared themselves fascist, Argentine antifascists built a creative image of a broader 'creole' fascism that needed to be fought,[32] and of a 'menaced nation' that ought to be defended,[33] in order to discuss what they considered as the main political, social and cultural crossroads for the country. Antifascism, as a political project, felt obliged to express (and to provide solutions to) the whole set of problems and challenges of Argentine society during the interwar period.

While the founder of the main antifascist intellectual association, Aníbal Ponce, described fascism as 'war, terror, misery … the strangulation of culture, the university turned into a barracks, the degradation and silencing of intelligence',[34] the goals and political perspectives of antifascism were to grow exponentially, especially as this movement increasingly became a gathering place for the opposition to dictatorial and fraudulent governments. During the 1930s, Argentine antifascism began to express more than a mere repudiation of Italian fascism or German Nazism, and started to mutate – without ceasing to explicitly condemn those European regimes – into a convincing appeal, a political option to unify the democratic parties of the opposition, to demand changes and defy the successive governments and also to look for ways to seize power in the country. This evolution towards a catch-it-all strategy did not happen in a hurry, but took years. In the next section we will analyse the dynamics of this process and look at the role of local politicians and exiled and migrant communities involved in the issue, from the very start of the March on Rome in 1922 to the end of the Second World War.

From Imported Fascism to Handmade Antifascism: The Utility of the Reception and Translation of a Non-native Political Appeal

At the end of the nineteenth century and during the first two decades of the twentieth century, Argentina received massive European immigration. By the 1920s migrant Italians in Argentina numbered almost two million and represented about a fifth of the total population. Bearing this in mind, it would have been surprising if fascism had failed to have an impact in Argentina from the time of its appearance in Italy.

Predictably, on 1 May 1923 (some six months after Mussolini's March on Rome) a local section of the National Fascist Party of Italy was created by Ottavio Dinale in Buenos Aires. Henceforth, Italian fascist and antifascist violence took root on the streets of the capital and other Argentine cities,[35] lasting for several years and even attracting the attention of international political leaders.[36]

In 1927, in an increasingly violent context, Socialist MP Nicolás Repetto submitted a formal question to the minister of the interior (José P. Tamborini) and the minister for foreign relations (Ángel Gallardo) in Alvear's government (who could hardly be suspected of being fascist),[37] requesting them to produce 'reports on the activities that some foreign militias are openly developing in the country'.[38] In his respectful presentation, Repetto expressed the view that those violent actions were nothing but the translation of disputes alien to the country. The existence of native fascism in Argentina was unthinkable at that moment, not only for him but also for most political actors. In less than a decade, not only Repetto but all Socialists, as well as many other politicians, intellectuals and ordinary people with other ideologies or even with no ideology at all, would change their minds and confirm the existence of 'creole' fascism.

The Socialists' official journal asserted in 1936 that 'Nazi-fascist propaganda is disseminated here by public servants: dignitaries, teachers, students, clergymen, journalists, diplomats, and even public institutions such as the Police Department and the Post Office. Openly or surreptitiously, the country is being subjected to an intense Nazi-fascist penetration'.[39] In this way, the antifascists' attempt to nationalise fascism did not strictly reflect the groups that openly supported Mussolini and Hitler, but made a more ambiguous, albeit strident, alert call (*¡Alerta!* was precisely the name of one of their journals) capable of a high degree of political mobilisation.

The communitarian migrant groups that upheld antifascism and denounced overseas fascism shared this local strategy of attacking 'creole' fascism, as it allowed them to establish the close links with Argentine political leaders that they considered indispensable to achieve their own goals. Thus, various antifascist migrant groups (Italia Libera, the De Gaulle Committee, Das Andere Deutschland and the Polish Argentine Committee, among others) could be seen in joint actions with local organisations.

Clément Moreau (Carl Meffert), a German political refugee and graphic designer, confirmed the image that local antifascism wanted to convey by creating a picture of Adolf Hitler dressed as a gaucho with a guitar and a swastika. This imaginary Hitler of the Pampas thought, according to the caption, 'this way, no one will recognise me'.[40] This was a direct attack against all Nationalist groups in Argentina, which appeared, regardless of their political basis, as mere façades for Nazi penetration. But, how did antifascism acquire an attractive, mobilising and believable meaning for the Argentines?

Perhaps the first political group to denounce the systematic infiltration of fascism even into the government was the Communist Party, which asserted that the ruling political party, Hipólito Yrigoyen's Radicalismo, had 'multiple fascists within'.[41] However, Radicalismo was not an easy target for antifascist preaching. After General Uriburu's coup d'état toppled Yrigoyen and converted Radicalismo into a resistance movement, Communist leaders were forced to acknowledge their misjudgements with respect to Radicalismo, but not to its successors in the executive, first Uriburismo and later other conservative groups such as Justismo (from Agustín P. Justo, president 1932–38), Fresquismo (from Manuel A. Fresco, governor of the Buenos Aires province, 1936–40) and Castillismo (from Ramón S. Castillo, vice president 1938–42, and president 1942–43).[42]

It was precisely because Uriburu's government undoubtedly seemed to be a 'military-fascist Junta' – accompanied by paramilitary shock troops with Italian-style uniforms, such as the Legión Cívica ('Civic Legion')[43] – that some leftist and student groups adopted a policy of domestic mobilisation based on a fascist–antifascist polarisation, in the atmosphere of increasing violence that preceded the coup and was only contained in the streets by the emergency regulations that would last until February 1932.[44] In this framework, 'the time of decisive combat' had come, and there were 'no in-betweens: either we are with fascism or we are against it. Ambiguity is, ultimately, nothing but the reinforcement of dictatorship'.[45] After Uriburu failed to counteract the popularity of Radicalismo (he was unable to prevent this party from winning the local elections of the Buenos Aires region on 5 April 1931, so he declared them null and void) and resigned under pressure from the same *justista* sectors that had helped to install him in power, antifascism increasingly spread to other groups that did not have the revolutionary passion of leftists and students, but shared its epic, intransigent and combative rhetoric against electoral fraud and the lack of political and civil liberties, which would seem even more dangerous after the emerging 'German fascism' (as Nazism was initially identified) by 1933. In this new atmosphere, and after the elections that would lead (thanks to the abstention of Radicals)

General Justo to the presidency in 1932, non-Radical antifascists used parliamentary outlets to denounce 'creole' fascism, represented by those who 'want to imitate Mussolini and Hitler, forgetting that this is country is very different from those [Italy and Germany], and that we have lived until now in full democracy, bad or good but democracy after all'.[46]

The abandonment of insurrectional tactics by Radicals and their return to the electoral competition in 1935, after three years of electoral abstention,[47] forced Conservatives to practise fraud more openly and the opposition forces to reorganise. The strategy of Popular Fronts and the outbreak of the Spanish Civil War had a significant impact on the country, where both events were translated in terms of local issues. As the Socialist writer Anderson Imbert observed: '[We have] the feeling that it is in Spain where our destiny is at stake. We have the feeling that it is in our own country, in the realm of our culture, where the millenarian struggle between old, die-hard forms and new, still unprotected forms has been renewed'.[48] The struggle for democracy seemed to be the same in both countries, even if the differences between a continent involved in a violent civil war and a nation that lived a relatively quiet daily life were glaringly obvious.[49]

The period 1935–39 was, besides, especially fruitful with regard to the building of transnational networks, particularly in the intellectual realm, allowing replication of European associations which stimulated the appearance of a new type of intellectual collective. The most successful of these new organisations[50] was undoubtedly the AIAPE (Asociación de Intelectuales, Artistas, Periodistas y Escritores – 'Association of Intellectuals, Artists, Journalists and Writers'), created by the philosopher and essayist Aníbal Ponce after a trip to France.[51]

To these intellectual gatherings and others born of parallel initiatives (such as the Comité Contra el Racismo y el Antisemitismo – CCRA – founded in 1938) must be added the aid organisations created during the Spanish Civil War, which combined, not always harmonically, the action of the Spanish Republican Embassy with the interests of local political parties, representatives of the Argentine society and various notables. In a context marked by the plurality of pro-Republican organisations and initiatives, the PEAVA (Patronato Español de Ayuda a las Víctimas del Fascismo, which replicated the PIAVA of Italian immigrants), was, together with the FOARE (Federación de Organización de Ayuda a la República Española), the reference point of the Argentine symbolic and material aid to Spanish Republicans, which continued for decades through the reception of exiles after the end of the war and denounces of the Franco regime.[52]

When the bitter news of the Republican defeat amidst profound and violent inner quarrels became known in spring 1939, it was generally blamed on the policy of appeasement adopted by France and Britain during the conflict, and democratic ideals were shaken. As the Socialist militant Josefina Marpons wrote:

> We have to gain the trust of the sceptical masses who smile on hearing the word 'democracy' after learning of the implacable behaviour of the great European democracies. Because, no matter what their future attitude may be, the current attitude of France and England towards international matters has caused as much damage to the concept of people's freedom, equality and fraternity as that of fascist Italy and Nazi Germany.[53]

In addition, the disclosure of the pact signed in August between Hitler and Stalin convinced democratic groups of the need for pan-American isolation. In that context, the presidency of Roberto M. Ortiz, who – despite its fraudulent origin – called for a standardisation of democratic institutions, helped to calm down the local issues denounced by antifascists, fuelling accusations against Axis powers and encouraging a kind of flamboyant patriotism that was sometimes damaging to German, Italian and Japanese migrants, most of whom were not involved in spying but were defined as 'foreigners, without Argentine roots, unable to assimilate the deep humanity of our moral principles, who tried, some of them unwittingly, to infect us with their anguishes, passions, unexplainable resentments, bitterness and hatreds'.[54]

When antifascism seemed to be fading as a domestic policy tool, an event occurred that made it blossom again. At the highest point of his popularity among democratic groups and soon after ordering the intervention of the Buenos Aires province, ruled by one of the most conspicuous enemies of the antifascist movement, President Ortiz fell ill, took leave in 1940 and finally died in 1942. Vice President Ramón Castillo came to power and rebuilt the fraudulent status quo. In that ebb tide of democracy, local pro-Allied organisations were born, such as the above-mentioned Acción Argentina, which, besides lamenting the occupation of France and giving support to an increasingly isolated Britain, also practised a cross-party civic ideal that strongly attracted the independent sectors of the Argentine opinion.

Meanwhile, the government reinforced its neutrality in the world war, arousing the suspicion of both the United States – belligerent since December 1941 – and the local opposition about its connivance with Nazi-fascism. In that atmosphere, Nicolás Repetto, on a visit to the United States, tried to combine foreign and internal pressure over Castillo's regime: 'In the answers to the questions posed to me [in the

United States], I always tried to leave intact the responsibility of the Argentine people, insisting that their democratic and pro-American feelings were not accurately interpreted by our government'.[55]

Following the same logic, antifascist MPs sought to indirectly target President Castillo by creating, on 20 June 1941, a Research Commission on anti-Argentine Activities, which from its first report emphasised the existence of multiple German conspiracies, and accused: '[I]t is almost superfluous to call attention to what this commission could have found out and proved ... if the National Executive Power had not created the difficulties that prevented the commission from keep acting in a straightforward way'.[56]

Paradoxically, when the 1943 military coup d'état overthrew President Castillo, a suspected philo-Nazi, the antifascist opposition – after an ephemeral moment of approval[57] – reaffirmed the connection between the new government and Nazi infiltration. By enacting restrictions on public liberties, including the closure of the antifascist groups Acción Argentina and Junta de la Victoria shortly after the start of the military regime and the banning of activities for political parties in December 1943, Democrats ended up realising that, far from being a provisional expedient for calling for new elections, the military government attempted to adopt its own policies and put off the renewal of electoral play for 'better times'.

Even when diplomatic relations with Germany were severed in 1944 and war declared in 1945, Argentine antifascist refugees in Uruguay maintained that 'the sacrifice of democracy in Argentina, which will become a reality should the democratic fiction of the military dictatorship be accepted, would allow the rebirth of totalitarianism in America'.[58] In a context of continuous tensions with the United States, the coincidences between local and international fascism seemed confirmed to antifascists, who repeatedly regretted the collaborationist spirit, 'which tries to appease the spirit of resistance to the dictatorship which remains indomitable in the conscience of the Argentine people'.[59]

After the end of the war, the ability of antifascists to spread an image of a 'fascistised' country was so overpowering that the well-known writer Ezequiel Martínez Estrada wrote a contribution to a local French-language magazine (*La Revue Argentine*) bearing the categorical title of 'L'Argentine, pays occupé' ('Argentina, occupied country').[60] In this context, democratic groups (self-proclaimed as 'the Resistance' in a clear reference to the situation in France) faced the Junta Militar, which had been established in 1943 and benefited from the potential appeal of antifascism to put the president, General Farrell, on the ropes and force him to call presidential elections. Under the effects of the early postwar euphoria that unified Stalinist Communists with Churchillian conservatives, in September 1945 Argentine antifascists and Democrats were able to gather a crowd in the March for the Constitution and Liberty; this was generally interpreted as the death certificate of the military project's aspiration to continue.

Sadly for them, just as antifascism seemed to have become a solid structure for mobilisation and participation, the traditionally 'democratic' groups were confronted with an unusual political phenomenon in the person of Colonel Juan Domingo Perón. Although this candidate represented military continuity, and Democrats had no doubts that Perón showed a 'total parity' with Adolf Hitler,[61] it proved impossible for the Unión Democrática (the coalition of *radicales, demoprogresistas,* Socialists and Communists against this rising figure) to transform the mobilising power of antifascism into the number of votes required to win the ballots.

The difference between antifascism's ideological certitudes and the electoral strength of the antifascist appeal at this crucial moment was recognised by historian Tulio Halperin Donghi in his memoirs:

> By the end of 1944, one of the exiled Italian antifascists – who refused to acknowledge that the tragic process he had experienced in Italy was being repeated in the River Plate – ... declared himself convinced that the Secretaría de Trabajo y Previsión ('Ministry of Labour and National Insurance') was boosting the popularity of the military regime far more efficiently than we had imagined ... I admit that I was less impressed by the warning than by his failure to recognise the similarity, evident to all of us, between the project of the military regime and the one implemented by Mussolini in his homeland, not because I had any doubts that this similarity was as deep as we held it to be, but because it made me fear that it would not be perceptible enough to serve as a stimulus for mobilising the opposition by tirelessly denouncing the regime, as we had hoped it would.[62]

In summary, antifascism was capable of producing this initial mobilisation, but risked presenting misleading expectations at the ballots. In contrast to the predictions of their own leaders (such as the candidate for vice president, Enrique Mosca) which gave 80 per cent of the vote to the Democratic coalition, their suprising even if relatively narrow defeat before Perón left – besides the almost entire provinces in Peronist hands and no Socialist MPs in Parliament – a profound amazement among those who had promoted the antifascist 'sacred union', and a certain incapacity among some of their members to understand the Peronist phenomenon, summarised by the reaction of Socialist leader Dardo Cúneo to the almost one million votes that the colonel had received: 'Hitler also wins elections. And that doesn't stop him from being a Nazi'.[63]

Revised by Jane Wintle Taylor

Acknowledgement

I thank Enrique Garguin for his comments and assistance on a preliminary version of this chapter.

Notes

1. S.N. Pulsifer, *L'esprit de la France. Chants de Libération – The Spirit of France. Songs of Liberation*, New York, 1944, 10.
2. In particular, Karl Sauer's 1965 commemorative series entitled *20. Jahrestag der Befreiung vom Nationalsozialismus* (Twentieth Anniversary of Liberation from Fascism), in which we can see an epic history of Communist antifascism through some stamps picturing Georg Dimitrov's trial, the International Brigades in Spain or a demonstration in favour of the unity of the Communist and Socialist parties in Germany.
3. This assertion does not overlook certain specific and, in some instances, remarkable cases of individual participation in antifascist wars (especially the Spanish Civil War and the Second World War). Perhaps one of the most interesting cases is Mica Feldman, the only woman commanding troops in the Spanish Civil War, who left us her sad and stunning memories in *Mi Guerra de España*. In this book, Feldman shows her bitterness against those who did not really get involved in the battle or watched it as spectators. Addressing a French journalist, she said: 'You came here to contemplate the civil war as spectators go to the bullring, and you even describe in beautiful articles the martyrdom of Madrid's population under the sinister bombings of the *franquista* air force. To you, the little excursion to Pinar de Húmera will be useful to send a more or less picturesque chronicle, probably merciful and full of goodwill, about a bunch of *milicianos* who have spent three weeks using dynamite against fascist machine guns and mortars' (Mica Feldman, *Mi Guerra de España*, Barcelona, 2003, 278).
4. A few of them participated not only in their own country but also abroad as 'the voice of antifascism'. A good example is the anticipated participation of three Argentine Communist writers (Raúl González Tuñón, Cayetano Córdoba Iturburu and Pablo Rojas Paz) in the Second Congress of Antifascist Writers held in Barcelona, Valencia, Madrid and Paris in July 1937. The Spanish Antifascist Alliance for the Defence of Culture informed at an early date through its newspaper of the prestige of these writers, especially González Tuñón, 'who honours with his vibrant and noble attitude the young Argentine generation'. *El Mono Azul* 1(5), 24 September 1936, 7.

5. The massive nature of antifascism was evident in the demonstration celebrating the liberation of Paris in Plaza Francia, Buenos Aires, which prompted Suzanne Langlin to say she felt 'as moved by the reaction of Argentines as by the liberation of her country', and forcing the country's most recognised writer, Jorge Luis Borges, to admit (undoubtedly with full irony) that 'a collective emotion cannot be ignoble'. Quotes taken from A. Bisso, 'La liberación de París y el fin de la Segunda Guerra Mundial con ojos bonaerenses', *Entrepasados* 34 (2008): 16. The popularity of antifascism can be seen in the thousands of subsidiary organizations that the main antifascist institutions had all over the country. We have discovered the existence of 235 local sections for Acción Argentina alone. For analyses on regional extensions and local perspectives on antifascism, see A. Bisso, 'Mímicas de guerra, costumbres de paz. Las prácticas de movilización y apelación antifascistas del Partido Socialista en el interior bonaerense durante la Segunda Guerra Mundial. Los casos de Baradero y Luján', *Ciclos en la Historia, la Economía y la Sociedad* 31/32 (2007), 79–105; A. Bisso, 'Abajo con la tiranía pueblera y totalitaria. *Mechita* o ciertas consideraciones en torno a un periódico pueblerino y ferroviario del antifascismo argentino', *Prismas* 17 (2013), 221–25; R. Pasolini, *La utopía de Prometeo. Juan Antonio Salceda: del antifascismo al comunismo*, Tandil, 2006; and H. Guzmán, 'El antifascismo en Santiago del Estero: La Brasa, 1935–1953', *Cifra* 6 (2011), online.

6. It is interesting to note that the English translation of this association's name was used at the time by its right-wing nationalist opponents. The Anglicisation of this name had the ironical purpose of insinuating that the organisation had economic or financial links with the British Embassy and to describe it as a mere branch of pro-Allied propaganda, instead of the broader objectives that Acción Argentina imposed on itself as 'a purely Argentine movement aiming to reaffirm our freedoms and to defend the country against any attempts at infiltration or conquest by any foreign power'. Extract from: 'In Defence of our Sovereignty: Foundational Manifest of Acción Argentina', in A. Bisso (ed.), *El antifascismo argentino*, Buenos Aires, 2007, 136.

7. The late interwar period was a particularly auspicious time for Socialist–liberal relationships in Argentina. The Partido Socialista's leading figures did not hesitate to accept Argentina's historical liberal tradition. As Mario Bravo, one of its prominent leaders, said, the Socialists described themselves as followers of the 1810 liberal revolution, taking up a cause that 'is paradoxical coming from the members of revolutionary parties: we must safeguard the traditions and conquests of our culture and history'. M. Bravo, 'La lucha contra el racismo es el aspecto de una lucha político-social universal', in *El pueblo contra la invasión Nazi*, Buenos Aires, 1938, 54.

8. I have analysed the 'notability' ideal of this organization in my book: A. Bisso, *Acción Argentina. Un antifascismo nacional en tiempos de guerra mundial*, Buenos Aires, 2005, chapter IV, 211–32.

9. All three were members of Acción Argentina's advisory board. The complete list of authorities can be found in ibid., 323–25.

10. On the *Junta de la Victoria*, see S. McGee Deutsch, 'Argentine Women Against Fascism: The Junta de la Victoria, 1941–1947', *Politics, Religion & Ideology* 13(2), 2012, 221–36.

11. A transcription of the mentioned lecture may be found in F. Pinedo, 'Acentuemos lo que nos une y no lo que nos separa', *La Argentina en la vorágine*, Buenos Aires, 1943, 79–84.
12. The Junta de la Victoria began its activities on 13 September 1941. Its president was Ana Rosa Schlieper de Martínez Guerrero, and its membership included the following illustrious compound surnames, among many others: María Teresa Obarrio de Pinedo, Matilde Porta Echagüe de Molinas, Margot Portela Cantilo de Parker, Silvina Ocampo de Bioy Casares and Norah Borges de La Torre.
13. Quoted in Bisso, *El antifascismo argentino*, 366.
14. *La Vanguardia*, 29 July 1936, 4.
15. The ideological range of pro-British politicians was wide and included conservatives as well as *radicales* (like Marcelo T. de Alvear, who stated that 'England was the first country that, in the uncertain hours of our nationality, when we were yet but a promise, showed faith in our destiny and granted us generous credit with London banks, enabling us to take firm initial strides toward organising our future') and Socialists (such as Nicolás Repetto, who said that 'nations that, like England, have contributed to our technical development, have also participated in the process that has placed us in a respectable position with regard to the most civilised nations in the world'). Alvear's words are quoted from L.A. Romero et al., *El radicalismo*, Buenos Aires, 1968, 303; and Repetto's phrases can be found in: 'El imperialismo inglés', *Política internacional*, Buenos Aires, 1943, 29–30. For Socialists (with an anti-imperialist tradition), the Second World War helped to improve the image of British democracy, especially blurred at the times of the Non-Intervention Committee during the Spanish Civil War and the Munich Agreement, when they were seen as 'pacifist and satisfied pirates (who) did not dare to stop Mussolini or Hitler'. E.A. Imbert, 'España en varias perspectivas', in Bisso, *El antifascismo argentino*, 446.
16. Intellectual Francophilia is evident, for instance, in these words of journalist Salazar Altamira: 'From France came the thrust of Independence, followed by literary culture and almost all artistic culture'. G.S. Altamira, 'Trois paysages caractéristiques et huit promenades à travers l'Argentine', in *Regards sur l'Argentine*, Buenos Aires, 1939, 101.
17. As we can see in J. Zanca, *Cristianos antifascistas*, Buenos Aires, 2013.
18. The most important body of work on Argentine Communist antifascism is Ricardo Pasolini's research. Besides other articles and books quoted in these footnotes, see his 'Intelectuales antifascistas y comunismo durante la década de 1930. Un recorrido posible: entre Buenos Aires y Tandil', *Estudios Sociales* 26 (2004), 81–116; and *Los marxistas liberales. Antifascismo y comunismo en la cultura argentina*, Buenos Aires, 2013.
19. Works on anarchist antifascism in Argentina are quite sparse. An exception is M.E. Bordagaray, 'Luchas antifascistas y trayectorias generizadas en el movimiento libertario argentino (1936–1955)', *Cuadernos de H Ideas* 7(7) (2013). Digital version.
20. François Furet, *Le passé d'une illusion*, Paris, 1995, 453.
21. As Mercedes Yusta states on the basis of her Spanish research, 'antifascism became an essential component of Communist political culture between

the 1930s and 1940s; but it is impossible to reduce antifascism, as deeply anti-Communist writers such as François Furet did, to a mere strategy of international Communism to attack social democracy'. M. Yusta, 'La construcción de una cultura política femenina desde el antifascismo (1934–1950)', in A. Aguado and T. Ortega (eds), *Feminismos y antifeminismos. Culturas políticas e identidades de género en la España del siglo XX*, Valencia, 2011, 254.

22. As Eduardo Laurencena, a member of the 'anti-personalist Radicalism' movement, said in an address to Congress: 'Mister President: we have seen that both Communism and fascism, the latter in its two forms, Italian and German, constitute one single and identical regime, differing only in their external and secondary manifestations, but essentially one and the same thing at the root; that this regime, of a totalitarian nature, is doctrinal and organically dictatorial and despotic, and establishes government by a party, a group or an individual, not out of transitory or accidental necessity, but as a system ... Having reached this irrefutable conclusion, we have a deep concern to learn whether only Communism is to be persecuted, leaving the way clear for fascism and pseudo-fascism to act'. In M. Bravo, L. De la Torre and E. Laurencena, *La democracia contra el fascismo*, Buenos Aires, 1937, 275. A similar position was held in France in 1938 by the Catholic antifascist François Goguel, as quoted in J. Droz, *Histoire de l'antifascisme en Europe, 1923–1939*, Paris, 1985, 209.

23. On this period in Argentina, see our article 'La división de la comunidad antifascista argentina (1939–1941). Los partidos políticos y los diferentes grupos civiles locales ante el Pacto de No Agresión entre Hitler y Stalin', *Reflejos* 9 (2000–2001), 88–99.

24. *Argentina Libre*, 26 June 1941, 12.

25. L. Prislei, *Los orígenes del fascismo argentino*, Buenos Aires, 2008, 118.

26. J.A. Ramos, *Breve historia de las izquierdas en Argentina*, Buenos Aires, 1990, vol. 2.

27. Ibid., 53. Our emphasis.

28. The Argentine Fascist Party was founded in 1932 by Héctor Bianchetti in Avellaneda, a suburban town near Buenos Aires. It suffered a split in 1934–35 that promoted the formation of the 'Fascist Forces Front' (later 'Fascist National Union') in Córdoba. C. Buchrucker, *Nacionalismo y peronismo*, 2nd edn, Buenos Aires, 1999, 176.

29. We have detected the existence of a 'Social-Nationalist Force' that figures as a paramilitary group (alongside the Legión Cívica [Civic Legion]), whose dissolution was requested by the Porteño council in a 1933 resolution (*Versiones taquigráficas del Concejo Deliberante de la Ciudad de Buenos Aires*, 19 May 1933, 728).

30. R.C. Newton, *El cuarto lado del triángulo. La 'amenaza Nazi' en la Argentina*, Buenos Aires, 1995, 108.

31. See Prislei, *Los orígenes del fascismo argentino*, 43–74.

32. Guillermo Salazar Altamira wrote that 'there are hundreds of thousands of Argentines who belong to the "fifth column" ... and they are not aware of it. It is essential that they know it, understand it, to get enrolled on *the other*

side'. G.S. Altamira, 'Radiografía de la Quinta Columna', in *El antifascismo*, 303.

33. The idea of a 'menaced nation' and the country as a 'minefield' can be found in the book by the radical congressman, A. Lanús, *Campo Minado*, Buenos Aires, 1942. The pathetic tone adopted by many authors of this period was also used by Lanús, as in: 'One afternoon, after the fall of Singapore and the landing of Japanese troops on Java, when all or most of the news of the war seemed to serve only to aggravate our misgivings, I was watching a group of children play, among whom was my son. If Germany wins, I thought, the children of people like myself holding a defined outlook on the barbarism of their political regime will probably never play again. My son, who is still small … will play no more … All the children in the world will cease to be children'. Lanús, *Campo Minado*, 7.

34. A. Ponce, 'Condiciones para la Universidad Libre', in *1918–1998. La reforma universitaria*, Buenos Aires, 1998, 49.

35. On the immediate impact of fascism in Argentina through the Italian community and its violent derivations, see M.V. Grillo, 'La llegada del *manganello. Los fascistas a la conquista de la Associazione Reduci di Guerra Europea 1924–1926'*, in L.A. Bertoni and L. de Privitellio (eds), *Conflictos en democracia*, Buenos Aires, 2009, 171–90 and footnotes, 233–34. On Italian antifascism in Argentina, see another text by M.V. Grillo, 'El antifascismo italiano en Francia y Argentina: Reorganización política y prensa (1922–1930)', in J. Casali de Babot and M.V. Grillo (eds), *Fascismo y antifascismo en Europa y Argentina – Siglo XX*, Tucumán, 2002, 73–98; and P.R. Fanesi, 'El antifascismo italiano en Argentina (1922–1945)', *Estudios Migratorios Latinoamericanos* 4(12) (August 1989), 319–54.

36. The international Socialist icon Karl Kautsky, for instance, wrote a greeting to the journal *La Vanguardia* expressing that 'the Argentine Socialists, through their propaganda, should achieve not only that their country's workers become more cultivated and better suited for their organization to fulfil its historical mission and solve the riddle of its own destiny, but also prevent Italian workers from becoming submerged in the moral degradation with which the [fascist] dictatorship threatens them'. *La Vanguardia*, 28 June 1936, 17.

37. Despite the position of the above-mentioned minister Gallardo, who as former ambassador to Italy had pointed out in 1922 that fascism had been 'beneficial' to Italy, and despite an attempt by the Socialist journal *La Vanguardia* (11 February 1923, 2) to suggest that Alvear privately relished Mussolini's propaganda films, it was clear that, beyond the government's attempt to avoid obstructing relations with the Italian regime, the figure of President Alvear and his way of holding power was very distant from that of the *Duce*. On the Philo-fascist attitude of Gallardo and Italo-Argentine relations in this period, see F. Finchelstein, *Transatlantic Fascism: Ideology, Violence, and the Sacred in Argentina and Italy, 1919–1945*, Durnham, NC and London, 2010, 51–52.

38. *Diario de Sesiones de la Cámara de Diputados*, 15 June 1927, vol. 1, 639.

39. *La Vanguardia*, 25 August 1936, 1.

40. C. Moreau, *Mit dem Zeichenstift gegen dem Faschismus*, Berlin, 1980, 30.

41. 'Yrigoyenismo y fascismo', in Bisso, *El antifascismo argentino*, 188.
42. Thus, during his lecture at a 1938 Communist Party Conference, Luis Sommi asserted 'the fascist menace is not an invention of ours. It comes from the socio-political and military reality of the world from which Argentina cannot escape'. L. Sommi, 'La salvación de la democracia', ibid., 191.
43. As Marcus Klein has written: '[D]espite its independent standing, the new organisation maintained close contacts with the government, and especially the group of nationalist officers around the provisional president ... officers of the Army supervised the enrolment of new members, a process that the Ministry of the Interior organised ... Facts indicate, then, that the Legión was only nominally based on a civilian initiative, and that Lavalle [one of its founders] had therefore acted as a front man for the new regime'. M. Klein, 'The Legión Cívica Argentina and the Radicalisation of Argentine Nacionalism during the Década Infame', *Estudios Interdisciplinarios de América Latina y el Caribe* 13(2) (July–December 2002), online.
44. On growing political violence on the streets, and the debates on how to control it, see M. González Alemán, '¿Qué hacer con la calle? La definición del espacio público porteño y el edicto policial de 1932', *Boletín del Instituto de Historia Argentina y Americana Dr. Emilio Ravignani* 34 (January 2012), online.
45. 'Compañeros estudiantes. Comité Estudiantil contra el Fascismo y el Imperialismo', in Bisso, *El antifascismo argentino*, 104.
46. Julio Gonzalez Iramain's words. *Versiones taquigráficas del Concejo deliberante de la Ciudad de Buenos Aires*, 19 May 1933, 728.
47. In those years of dictatorship and fraud we can count the following uprisings, named after their most renowned leaders: Gregorio Pomar, Severo Toranzo, the Kennedy brothers, Atilio Cattáneo and Roberto Bosch.
48. E.A. Imbert, 'España en varias perspectivas', in Bisso, *El antifascismo argentino*, 447.
49. Roberto Arlt, a famous chronicler of those times, wrote: 'It could be Paris, Berlin, London or Prague ... Everyone is talking about the damned war. They talk about the war from the morning when they are on their way to the bathroom and meet in the corridor, till the night, when they furtively go off to bed, exhausted, to lie in sorrow ... When I think of the terror hidden in all those breasts ... I feel grateful for the invisible light that brought me to life on this civilised corner (*rincón pavimentado*) of the planet'. R. Arlt, 'Un argentino piensa en Europa (16 de septiembre de 1938)', in *Aguafuertes porteñas*, Buenos Aires, 2003, 216–17.
50. The influence of intellectuals in the antifascist movement can hardly be underestimated, especially that of the group AIAPE – see R. Pasolini, 'El nacimiento de una sensibilidad política. Cultura antifascista, comunismo y nación en Argentina: Entre la A.I.A.P.E. y el Congreso Argentino de la Cultura, 1935–1955', *Desarrollo Económico* 179 (2005), 403–33; J. Cane, 'Unity for the Defense of Culture': The AIAPE and the Cultural Politics of Argentine Antifascism, 1935–1943', *The Hispanic American Historical Review* 77(3) (1997), 443–82; A. Bisso and A. Celentano, 'La lucha antifascista de la Asociación de Intelectuales, Artistas, Periodistas y Escritores (AIAPE)

(1935–1943)', in H.E. Biagini and A.A. Roig (eds), *El pensamiento alternativo en la Argentina del siglo XX*, Buenos Aires, 2006, vol. 2, 235–65; and M.A. Devés, 'El papel de los artistas en la Asociación de Intelectuales, Artistas, Periodistas y Escritores (AIAPE). Representaciones, debates estético-políticos y prácticas de militancia en el antifascismo argentino', *A contracorriente* 10(2) (2013), 126–50.

51. Ponce proved the French influence when he rejoiced that the Bulletin of the 'Comité de Vigilance' in Paris had given 'an entire page' to the local association. A. Ponce, 'El primer año de AIAPE', in Bisso, *El antifascismo argentino*, 120.
52. On this question, see D. Schwarzstein, *Entre Franco y Perón*, Barcelona, 2001.
53. *La Vanguardia*, 1 May 1939, 9.
54. C.A. Leiva, 'Un llamado a la realidad', in *Maná*, June 1940.
55. N. Repetto, *Impresiones de los Estados Unidos*, Buenos Aires, 1943, 7.
56. *Informe N°1 de la Comisión Investigadora de Actividades Antiargentinas* (1941), 79.
57. A few days after the military coup, the Socialists of Baradero (a middle-sized town in the Bonaerense province) were still debating its meaning and saying that '[t]he revolution of 4 June was not for the benefit of Nazi-Fascist *criollo* 'Nazionaloids' … it was a revolution by the people and for the people – healthy, uncontaminated – who, driven to chaos by the fraudulent *criollo* nationalists, found in the Argentine Army a body of worthy men ready to raise their swords and defend the country's Republican institutions'. *La Democracia*, 1 August 1943.
58. G. Korn, *La Resistencia Civil*, Montevideo, 1945, 117.
59. G. Korn, 'El colaboracionismo', in Bisso, *El antifascismo argentino*, 226.
60. E. Martínez Estrada, 'L' Argentine, pays occupé', *La Revue Argentine* 33 (1945), 45–47.
61. Abogados Democráticos, 'El nazismo del candidato imposible', in Bisso, *El antifascismo argentino*, 243.
62. T. Halperín Donghi, *Son memorias*, Buenos Aires, 2008, 149–50.
63. *Antinazi* 2(56), 21 March 1946, 4.

References

Altamira, G.S. 'Trois paysages caractéristiques et huit promenades à travers l'Argentine', in Commission Argentine de Cooperation Intellectuelle (ed.), *Regards sur l'Argentine*. Buenos Aires, 1939.
Arlt, R. 'Un argentino piensa en Europa (16 de septiembre de 1938)', in *Aguafuertes porteñas*. Buenos Aires, 2003, 216–17.
Bisso, A. *Acción Argentina. Un antifascismo nacional en tiempos de guerra mundial.* Buenos Aires, 2005.
——— (ed.). *El antifascismo argentino*. Buenos Aires, 2007.
———. 'Mímicas de guerra, costumbres de paz. Las prácticas de movilización y apelación antifascistas del Partido Socialista en el interior bonaerense

durante la Segunda Guerra Mundial. Los casos de Baradero y Luján'. *Ciclos en la Historia, la Economía y la Sociedad* 31/32 (2007), 79–105.

———. 'La liberación de París y el fin de la Segunda Guerra Mundial con ojos bonaerenses'. *Entrepasados* 34 (2008), 16.

———. 'Abajo con la tiranía pueblera y totalitaria. *Mechita* o ciertas consideraciones en torno a un periódico pueblerino y ferroviario del antifascismo argentino'. *Prismas* 17 (2013), 221–25.

Bisso, A., and A. Celentano. 'La lucha antifascista de la Asociación de Intelectuales, Artistas, Periodistas y Escritores (AIAPE) (1935–1943)', in H.E. Biagini and A.A. Roig (eds), *El pensamiento alternativo en la Argentina del siglo XX*. Buenos Aires, 2006, vol. 2: 'Obrerismo, vanguardia, justicia social (1930–1969)', 235–65.

Bordagaray, M.E. 'Luchas antifascistas y trayectorias generizadas en el movimiento libertario argentino (1936–1955)'. *Cuadernos de H Ideas* 7(7) (2013).

Bravo, M. 'La lucha contra el racismo es el aspecto de una lucha político-social universal', in *El pueblo contra la invasión Nazi*. Buenos Aires, 1938, 50–54.

Bravo, M., L. De la Torre and E. Laurencena. *La democracia contra el fascismo*. Buenos Aires, 1937.

Buchrucker, C. *Nacionalismo y peronismo*. 2ⁿᵈ edn. Buenos Aires, 1999.

Cane, J. 'Unity for the Defense of Culture': The AIAPE and the Cultural Politics of Argentine Antifascism, 1935–1943'. *The Hispanic American Historical Review* 77(3) (1997), 443–82.

Devés, M.A. 'El papel de los artistas en la Asociación de Intelectuales, Artistas, Periodistas y Escritores (AIAPE). Representaciones, debates estético-políticos y prácticas de militancia en el antifascismo argentino'. *A contracorriente* 10(2) (2013), 126–50.

Droz, J. *Histoire de l'antifascisme en Europe. 1923–1939*. Paris, 1985.

Fanesi, P.R. 'El antifascismo italiano en Argentina (1922–1945)'. *Estudios Migratorios Latinoamericanos* 4(12) (August 1989), 319–54.

Feldman, M. *Mi Guerra de España*. Barcelona, 2003.

Finchelstein, F. *Transatlantic Fascism: Ideology, Violence, and the Sacred in Argentina and Italy, 1919–1945*. Durham, NC and London, 2010.

Furet, F. *Le passé d'une illusion*. Paris, 1995.

González Alemán, M. '¿Qué hacer con la calle? La definición del espacio público porteño y el edicto policial de 1932'. *Boletín del Instituto de Historia Argentina y Americana Dr. Emilio Ravignani* 34 (January 2012), online.

Grillo, M.V. 'El antifascismo italiano en Francia y Argentina: Reorganización política y prensa (1922–1930)', in J. Casali de Babot and M.V. Grillo (eds), *Fascismo y antifascismo en Europa y Argentina – Siglo XX*. Tucumán, 2002, 73–98.

———. 'La llegada del *manganello*. Los fascistas a la conquista de la Associazione Reduci di Guerra Europea 1924–1926', in L.A. Bertoni and L. de Privitellio (eds), *Conflictos en democracia*. Buenos Aires, 2009, 171–90.

Guzmán, H.D. 'El antifascismo en Santiago del Estero: La Brasa, 1935–1953'. *Cifra* 6 (2011), 11–25.

Halperín Donghi, T. *Son memorias*. Buenos Aires, 2008.

Klein, M. 'The Legión Cívica Argentina and the Radicalisation of Argentine Nacionalism during the Década Infame'. *Estudios Interdisciplinarios de América Latina y el Caribe* 13(2) (July–December 2002), 5–30.

Korn, G. *La Resistencia Civil*. Montevideo, 1945.

Lanús, A. *Campo Minado*. Buenos Aires, 1942.

Martínez Estrada, E. 'L' Argentine, pays occupé'. *La Revue Argentine* 33 (1945).

McGee Deutsch, S. 'Argentine Women Against Fascism: The Junta de la Victoria, 1941–1947'. *Politics, Religion & Ideology* 13(2) (2012), 221–36.

Moreau, C. *Mit dem Zeichenstift gegen dem Faschismus*. Berlin, 1980.

Newton, R.C. *El cuarto lado del triángulo. La 'amenaza Nazi' en la Argentina*. Buenos Aires, 1995.

Pasolini, R. 'Intelectuales antifascistas y comunismo durante la década de 1930. Un recorrido posible: entre Buenos Aires y Tandil'. *Estudios Sociales* 26 (2004), 81–116.

———. 'El nacimiento de una sensibilidad política. Cultura antifascista, comunismo y nación en Argentina: Entre la A.I.A.P.E. y el Congreso Argentino de la Cultura, 1935–1955'. *Desarrollo Económico* 179 (2005), 403–33.

———. *La utopía de Prometeo. Juan Antonio Salceda: del antifascismo al comunismo*. Tandil, 2006.

———. *Los marxistas liberales. Antifascismo y comunismo en la cultura argentina*. Buenos Aires, 2013.

Pinedo, F. 'Acentuemos lo que nos une y no lo que nos separa', in *La Argentina en la vorágine*. Buenos Aires, 1943.

Ponce, A. 'Condiciones para la Universidad Libre', in AA.VV. *1918–1998. La reforma universitaria*. Buenos Aires, 1998.

Prislei, L. *Los orígenes del fascismo argentino*. Buenos Aires, 2008.

Pulsifer, S.N. *L'esprit de la France. Chants de Libération – The Spirit of France. Songs of Liberation*. New York, 1944. Bilingual text (French translation, Émile George Henno).

Ramos, J.A. *Breve historia de las izquierdas en Argentina*. Buenos Aires, 1990, vol. 2.

Repetto, N. *Impresiones de los Estados Unidos*. Buenos Aires, 1943.

Romero, L.A., et al. *El radicalismo*. Buenos Aires, 1968.

Schwarzstein, D. *Entre Franco y Perón*. Barcelona, 2001.

Yusta, M. 'La construcción de una cultura política femenina desde el antifascismo (1934–1950)', in A. Aguado and T. Ortega (eds), *Feminismos y antifeminismos. Culturas políticas e identidades de género en la España del siglo XX*. Valencia, 2011, 253–82.

Zanca, J. *Cristianos antifascistas*. Buenos Aires, 2013.

Andrés Bisso is professor of Argentine and Latin American History at the University of La Plata, Province of Buenos Aires, Argentina. He holds a Ph.D. on American History from the University Pablo de Olavide (Spain) and is associate researcher for the CONICET (Argentina). He is particularly interested in the interface between sociability and politics during the interwar period, and has published three books on this topic: *Acción Argentina. Un antifascismo nacional en tiempos de guerra mundial* (2005); *El antifascismo argentino* (2007); and *Sociabilidad, política y movilización. Cuatro recorridos bonaerenses (1932–1943)* (2009). He is currently researching a book on the history of the Argentine Scout Movement and its links with politics from its origins to the ending of the Second World War.

8

WOMEN AND ANTIFASCISM

Historiographical and Methodological Approaches

Isabelle Richet

Until recently, in the historiography of Italian antifascism 'silence has been the usual treatment accorded to women', to borrow French historian Michèle Perrot's apt phrase.[1] In her major 2008 historiographical essay, Patricia Gabrielli noted that women tended to disappear in the 'temple of virility' that was Italian antifascism and, when they did appear in this masculine universe, it was most of the time in the figure of the 'mater dolorosa' or the 'sacrificial widow'.[2] This is even more the case for the literature on the Resistance, which represents the bulk of the historiography on antifascism, as if the twenty years of the regime had simply been a preamble leading to the eighteen months of resistance to Nazi-fascism, a more glorious period whose symbolic figure was the armed partisan, the epitome of 'manly heroism'.[3]

According to official figures, however, Italian women played a substantial part in the antifascist opposition, including in its armed phase. Among the roughly 200,000 Italians officially listed as members of the Resistance, there were 35,000 partisan women engaged in the armed struggle and 20,000 women patriots (who actively took part in the Resistance without bearing arms).[4] Approximately 70,000 women joined the Gruppi di Difesa della Donna ('Women's Defence Groups') set up by the antifascist organisations to mobilise women in civil society, 2,750 were executed by firing squads, 4,500 were killed in action, 4,400 were arrested and 3,000 were deported.[5] It is more difficult to find precise figures for the *Ventennio* (the twenty years of the fascist regime) because the forms of action adopted by women did not always fit the bureaucratic criteria for identification as an opponent to the regime. In the fascist police records, women accounted for 5 per cent of the files; 5,000 were listed in their own names (and not as 'wife' or 'mother' of an antifascist) and 748 were tried by the Special Tribunal. These numbers are small and they raise a problem tackled by the recent historiography regarding the definition of the contours of antifascism during the *Ventennio* which I propose to present and analyse in what follows.

In apparent contradiction to Gabrielli's statement, there is today a long list of works dedicated to women in the Resistance and feminine antifascism, but many of them are autobiographical testimonies often written in an emotional and sacrificial vein,[6] and Gabrielli can rightly conclude that there has been a 'missed encounter between women's history, gender history and the history of antifascism'.[7] This is due to the fact that most of these works, although they did play an important role in making antifascist women visible, rarely asked the most relevant questions about their motivation for joining the struggle, the particular forms they gave to their opposition to the regime and the link – or the lack of link – they established between the struggle to free the country from the dictatorship and the struggle for women's emancipation.[8] These are the questions that the more recent research has tried to address, thereby offering a more complex image of antifascism. It is thereby also contributing to a renewal of the historiography made necessary by the crisis of the 'antifascist paradigm' due to the collapse of the First Republic of which it had been the keystone, and the revisionist offensive underway in Italian political and academic circles.[9]

In order to grasp the methodological problems the most recent researchers have been confronted with, it is important to identify the reasons for the 'silence' and the shortcomings of the research carried out in the postwar period. The most important problem is connected with the sources, which, as we know, 'incorporate sexual inequality and marginalise or undervalue feminine sources'.[10] Most of the sources of the history of antifascism deal with the political space occupied by men.[11] This is the case of the fascist sources built on the assumption that women could not be autonomous political subjects. It is also the case of the sources collected by the antifascist groups whose male leaders shared similar assumptions. Another reason is the 'autobiographical modesty' of women activists. Patricia Gabrielli refers to 'ego atrophy' in reference to *Esilio*, Vera Modigliani's autobiography in which the author hides behind the action of her husband, the Socialist MP in exile Giuseppe Modigliani, and constantly devalues her own political commitment.[12] However important they may have been, the autobiographies of Communist female activists (Camilla Ravera, Teresa Noce, Marina Sereni) tended to build an ideal-type of the Communist woman, and to subsume the fight for gender equality in the membership of the Communist Party, supposed to be, in itself, emancipatory.[13] As for the women of the Giustizia e Libertà (GL) movement (Ada Gobetti, Joyce

Lussu, Barbara Allason), they did speak in their own names in their autobiographies and testified to a political commitment that was equal to that of men; but, as we shall see later, in a context where it was important for antifascism to stress its unity, most of them chose to be gender blind.

Another cause for the historiographical silence about women has to do with the battle for the control over the memory of antifascism, which has also worked to the detriment of female activists.[14] The victors have strived to impose the memory of the armed combatants as the only legitimate one, thereby ignoring all the other forms of opposition to the regime.[15] Last but not least, the experience of female activists told the story of rebellious women who had challenged – often without being aware of it – traditional gender roles, and such images became embarrassing in the postwar context where traditional family values and the domestic virtues of women ruled supreme.[16]

On the whole, therefore, in the historiography of the first postwar period, women's participation in the antifascist struggle was for the most part ignored. When women were mentioned they were presented as subordinates who brought a soft touch in a tough manly world – 'a soothing maternal caress' according to a Communist Party leader.[17]

From the 1970s, with the emergence of social history 'from the bottom up' and women's history, feminine antifascism finally became a legitimate fully fledged research topic. This new phase was ushered in by the publication of Anna Maria Bruzzone and Rachele Farina's work *La Resistenza taciuta*, in 1976. It revealed the importance and the great diversity of women's roles, in addition to direct participation in the armed struggle: organization of civil protests in the communities; handling of communication networks; propaganda in the workplace and the marketplace. When they did not take up arms, they were an essential linchpin between the struggle of military groups and civil society. This book opened the floodgates and led to an avalanche of works reconstructing the feminine Resistance in all the regions of Italy.[18] These studies restored visibility to antifascist women, yet a majority of them were not entirely satisfactory. They were not based on rigorous archival work, and tended to make an uncritical use of testimonies and remain essentially narrative with little analysis.[19] However, Bruzzone and Farina had started to ask embarrassing questions, in particular about the haste with which antifascist leaders had wanted to send women back home after the war, and the little contribution the antifascist struggle had made to the emancipation of women. They also stressed the need to broaden the notion of

Resistance beyond the armed struggle and to study more precisely the motivations of antifascist women, many of whom did not simply follow a father, a brother or a husband. This, of course, raised the question of sources and the need to legitimise documents sometimes disregarded or devalued by historians, such as private letters and diaries that provide a wealth of information and tend to ignore ideological rigidities but focus on the complex experiences of actors.[20] Their call to study more diffuse forms of resistance found an echo in a new historiographical trend that insisted on the need to study 'the antifascists rather than antifascism'.

It is not possible here to discuss extensively the cause and consequences of the crisis of the antifascist paradigm in Italy, which is dealt with in more detail elsewhere in this volume by Filippo Focardi, Stéfanie Prezioso and Enzo Traverso. Suffice it to say that, on the one hand, its legitimising function whittled away with the collapse of the First Republic in the early 1990s and, on the other hand, it endured a frontal assault from various revisionist forces.[21] In reaction to this attack, several historians (including Guido Quazza and Leonardo Rapone) called upon researchers not to respond defensively but rather to seize this opportunity to look at antifascism 'as a series of still open, unresolved questions rather than a solid block of certitudes'.[22] Quazza, but also Rapone and Giovanni De Luna, drew attention to the civil and cultural – and not just political – roots of opposition to the regime, and they insisted on the need to multiply and cross sources in order to study concrete subjects rather than abstract ideas. They also introduced the new notion of 'existential antifascism' – that is, a feeling of opposition that did not flow from an ideological stance but was rooted in living conditions. Rapone described this 'existential antifascism' as 'a set of attitudes that was not directly political but represented attempts to conquer autonomous spaces, to reintroduce a degree of pluralism, without though leading to acts of open opposition'.[23] According to De Luna, this universe of protest rooted in the workplace and the community had until then remained in the shadows, and to limit oneself to the study of organized political actions meant 'setting the threshold of antifascism too high and eliminating all the options that were not directly connected to a formal political choice'.[24] De Luna concluded that for this new approach focusing on day-to-day existence under the dictatorship, the 'history of women became a priority',[25] and his book, *Donne in oggetto. L'antifascismo nella società italiana* (1995) is a key work in the more recent historiographical research. In it, De Luna looks at the role of women as a key to the understanding of existential antifascism in general.

The phrase '*Donne in oggetto*' refers to the expression used by the fascist police in reference to the women they were tailing, 'the woman in question'. De Luna based his research on the archives of the Special Tribunal that were made public only in 1990. He crossed the files of the Special Tribunal with those of the fascist police, the Caselario politico centrale (CPC), and strived to 'force them to tell a different story' by abstracting the elements of information they provided from the bureaucratic criteria used to collect them, thereby placing them in a different context. Disconnected from a narrowly political dimension, the police documents became precious sources to reconstruct the milieu in which antifascism emerged. They revealed an 'immersed reality', including 'the attitudes, modes of behaviour, lifestyles, ideas and worldviews of those Italians who did not adhere to fascism'.[26] In some ways, these documents disclosed the roots of an 'infra-political collective identity'.[27]

In dealing with these sources, De Luna was confronted with a major methodological problem: how could a collective 'history' be constructed on the basis of these individual 'stories' which multiplied specificities? He decided to combine a unified 'history' and the separate 'stories'. The first part presents thematic chapters: fascism, antifascism, women and politics, antifascists, the family, cultures. The second part presents the stories of four antifascist women, thus giving existential embodiment to the topics he selected. Other historians of antifascism and the Resistance – in France in particular – who have suggested paying more attention to the complex articulation between the individual and the surrounding world in order 'to reconstruct the real experiences' that eventually led people to become politically active in risky circumstances, have also considered biography a mandatory detour for doing so.[28]

A number of De Luna's findings are particularly interesting for our understanding of feminine antifascist activism. Using Vittoria De Grazia's fine study of 'How Fascism Ruled Women',[29] he identified a number of tensions that fuelled women's opposition to the regime, such as the tension between a certain modernity (consumerism, popular culture – the cinema, the radio, the feminine press), which encouraged women to experience new lifestyles, and the rigid rules of Fascist and Catholic morality, which tended to reinforce their traditional roles within the home. In addition, as the regime created a number of mass organisations for the regimentation of children and women, it tended to broaden the contours of the public sphere to penetrate the private sphere of family and community, thereby encouraging opposition attitudes that were not directly linked to strictly political questions. On the other hand, the restriction of the public sphere of politics also meant that the politicising process tended to take place in the private sphere, within the family and the various social networks in the community or the workplace, and only later on would find an organised outlet in the existing clandestine organisations.[30] If this explained the emergence of 'existential antifascism' among women (and men), as far as the link between antifascism and women's emancipation was concerned the balance sheet was quite ambiguous. Indeed, while in many ways the motivation for adopting oppositional attitudes was similar for men and women, for the latter entering into the public sphere represented an objective break with their traditional domestic existence.[31] However, most of the time this did not lead to a subjective challenge of traditional gender roles. The strict moral values promoted by the Communist leadership forced activist women to adhere even more strictly to traditional roles in order to convey a reassuring image of devoted spouses and mothers.[32] This attitude was shared by most of the clandestine groups, who asked their women members to behave 'normally' – which meant to act in accordance with the prevalent norms regulating gender roles.[33]

A number of other studies have focused more particularly on gender issues, trying to assess to what extent participation in Resistance activities challenged traditional gender roles. In her book, *Fenicotteri in volo*, Patricia Gabrielli studied the process that led some women to become Communist activists, and the impact of their political commitment on their awareness of gender inequity. 'Flying Flamingos' (*Fenicotteri in volo*) was the term used for the women activists who seconded the party organizers, maintained the communication networks of the clandestine Communist groups and connected military action to protests in civil society.[34] While confirming the existential roots of their political engagement, Gabrielli concluded that these women did not see their activism as a challenge to traditional gender roles but, on the contrary, as an extension and/or a protection of their roles as dutiful mothers or spouses.[35]

While enriching our understanding of women's political participation in the struggle against the Mussolini regime, both De Luna and Gabrielli illustrated the cultural backwardness of antifascism regarding the emancipation of women, and the missed shift from an 'objective' to a 'subjective' challenge of traditional gender hierarchies. On the other hand, additional studies of women in the Resistance that have tried to determine whether traditional gender identities were altered by the participation in the armed struggle have concluded that, in some instances, women were able to move away from 'housewifery tasks' within the movement and to adopt a diversity of new roles.[36]

A recent study by Swiss historian Noemi Crain Merz has tried to explain the missed encounter between the fight against the dictatorship and the fight against women's oppression. In *L'illusione della parità. Donne e questione feminile in Giustizia e Libertà e nel Partito d'Azione,*[37] Noemi Crain Merz has tried to answer the following question: Why did the antifascist movement that most emphasised the connection between liberty, equality and justice (i.e. Giustizia e Libertà and the Action Party) prove to be one of the most backward on the issue of gender equality, despite the presence among its members of powerful figures of emancipated women such as Ada Gobetti, Barbara Allason, Joyce Lussu and Marion Rosselli?

Her study focuses on Gobetti and Allason, two modern young women from Turin who joined the antifascist struggle very early on and played a major role during the *Ventennio* and in the armed struggle. As the leaders of GL and the Action Party shared the gender prejudices of all the other party leaders – even more so, perhaps, because of their bourgeois background – she has focused her attention on the women themselves in order to make sense of their rather paradoxical position. On the one hand, they did not seem to be interested in the feminine question, even denying that such a question existed until very late in the war. They professed a belief in universal emancipation and considered 'man' as a gender neutral category. The emancipation of 'man' would therefore automatically entail the emancipation of women. On the other hand, they insisted on the differences between the sexes. While they expected to be treated as equal in the male-dominated political sphere, they insisted on the different gender roles assigned to men and women in the private sphere, which, in their view, remained the privileged space for the self-realisation of women.

They did not perceive that the respect and admiration for their action expressed by the men of their rather privileged bourgeois liberal milieu did not alter their deep-seated conviction that women did not possess the rational intelligence or qualities required for political action. Because they denied the fact that there was a 'woman question' in Italy, they did not blame their party for remaining silent on this issue. Because they believed that men and women should play different roles, they never questioned the fact that there were no female leaders in GL or the Action Party, or that no women never signed articles in the party press. At the end of the war, when the Action Party set up separate women structures deprived of any decision-making power, they did not understand that it was a way of getting rid of the problem while pretending to address it. Parity was really an illusion within the Action Party, and its 'egalitarian postulate proved to be a means for consolidating a traditional and conservative division of gender roles'.[38] Most of the women of the Action Party (the main exception being Joyce Lussu)[39] did not understand that the role they would be granted in the public sphere would always be determined – and limited – by the assumption that their 'feminine nature' was more suited to their duties in the private sphere. And indeed, the party was not enthusiastic about women's suffrage (granted in 1946) and strongly recommended that women should not use it to step out of their proper role as the Action Party leader Ferruccio Parri, then prime minister, admonished them: 'You should not try to duplicate the same things that men do in the political, social and intellectual domains ... You should look for a field of action that is most suited to feminine nature, a role for which women have been prepared from time immemorial ... The problems of education and social assistance, the problems of maternity are yours, and so are the problems of childhood, of modern relief or ancient charity'.[40]

My own research on Marion Cave Rosselli, the British-born wife of the leader of Giustizia e Libertà Carlo Rosselli, confirms this tension, within left-liberal antifascism, between women's potential as political activists and their assigned role in the private sphere. Marion Cave was educated in a Labour family and influenced by the feminist ideas of the British suffragist movement. As a student in Florence, she witnessed the rise of the Mussolini regime, and under the influence of Gaetano Salvemini she joined the early antifascist movement in that city, where she met and married Carlo Rosselli. First in Milan and then in the internal exile island of Lipari, she was a fully fledged participant in the antifascist struggle and played a major role in the organisation of her husband's flight from Lipari. Once in exile in France, though, she rapidly understood that her role would be confined to family duties, and she increasingly resented being cut off from active political activity. While this was the case for many antifascist women in exile, as Patricia Gabrielli demonstrated in her study *Col freddo nel cuore*, Marion Rosselli was one of the few who were fully aware of these gender inequities, and she openly expressed her discontent.[41]

What can we conclude from this survey of the recent historiography concerning women and antifascism? At a general level, it confirms what Joan Scott had intuited, namely that using the analytical category of gender would entail 'rewriting history'.[42] In this respect, the understanding that the experience of women's opposition to fascism was an essential key for giving substance to the concept of 'existential antifascism' has been of particular interest. Regarding the presence and activities of women in the antifascist opposition and the Resistance, the large number of narrative studies have clearly established the important and diversified role they played during this crucial period of Italian history. On the other hand, what this participation meant for gender relations is far from straightforward. Indeed, one conclusion we can draw is that feminine antifascism was not necessarily 'feminist' in the sense that it did not always – or even often – challenge the traditional gender relations that prevailed in Italian society or in the opposition groups themselves. In some respect, it even reinforced them by justifying participation in the struggle in the name of the caring and nurturing qualities that supposedly defined feminine nature. Even when they resented the double standard applied within the opposition groups, women often adopted a 'gender blind' attitude in order not to divide the antifascist camp. As for those women who claimed equal participation in the public sphere of politics, they also adhered to the notion of separate spheres and different gender roles.[43] As various studies have noted, between the two world wars, an 'equality' feminism based on the universality of certain rights coexisted with a 'difference' feminism based on women's specific roles and contributions.[44] Italian feminist antifascism clearly belonged to the second category, and 'possible contradictions between equality in the public sphere and rights and duties in the private sphere were not resolved'.[45]

Notes

1. Michele Perrot, *Les femmes ou les silences de l'histoire*, Paris, 1998, iv.
2. Patrizia Gabrielli, *Tempio di virilità. L'antifascismo, il genere, la storia*, Milan, 2008, 8–13.
3. Ibid.; Simona Colarizi, 'Problemi storiografici sul fuoruscismo e sull'antifascismo socialista all'estero', in Francesca Taddei (ed.), *L'emigrazione socialista nella lotta contro il fascismo (1926–1939)*, Florence, 1982, 1; Giovanni De Luna, *Donne in Oggetto: l'antifascismo nella società italiana, 1922–1939*, Turin, 1995, 20.
4. Jane Slaughter, *Women and the Italian Resistance*, Denver, 1997, 33; Perry R. Wilson, 'Saints and Heroines: Re-writing the History of Italian Women in the Resistance', in Tim Kirk and Anthony Elligot (eds), *Opposing Fascism: Community, Authority and Resistance in Europe*, Cambridge, 1999, 180.
5. De Luna, *Donne in Oggetto*,19; Berardo Taddei, *Donne processate dal Tribunale speciale, 1927–1943*, Verona, 2008; Anna Bravo (ed.), *I Gruppi di Difesa della Donna, 1943–45*, Rome, 1995; A. Grissi, 'Un percorso a ritroso: le donne al confino politico, 1926–1943'. *Italia Contemporanea* 226 (2002), 31–59 ; Ibid., 'Confinate politiche contro la guerra', in D. Gagliani (ed.), *Guerra, Resistenza, Politica. Storie di donne*. Reggio Emilia, 2006, 47–54.
6. Rita Carrani (ed.), *Le donne e la Resistenza. Rassegna bibliográfica*, Coordinamento femminile azionale dell'ANPI, Rome, 1994; Marina Addis

Saba, *Partigiane. Tutte le donne della Resistenza*, Milan, 1998 ; Carla Capponi, *Con cuore di donna : il Ventennio, la Resistenza a oma, Via Rasella. I ricordi di una protagonista*, Milan, 2009 ; Laura Capobianco (ed.), *Donne tra memria e storia*, Naples, 1993; Dianella Gagliani (ed.), *Guerra, resistenza politica. Storie di donne*, Reggio Emilia, 2006 ; D. Gagliani, E. Guerra, L. Mariani and F. Tarozzi (eds.), *Donne, Guerra, Politica. Esperienze e memorie della Resistenza*, Bologna, 2000.

7. Gabrielli, *Tempio di virilità*, 8.

8. Slaughter, *Women and the Italian Resistance*, 2–3; Delfin Tromboni (ed.), *Donne contro: protagonismo delle donne e soggettività femminile tra guerra, fascismo e Resistenza*, Ferrara, 1996, 18.

9. Angelo Del Boca (ed.), *La storia negata. Il revisionismo e il suo uso politico*, Vicenza, 2009.

10. Perrot, *Les femmes ou les silences*, iv; Linda Giuva, 'Ricerche di genere e archivi: quali strumenti?', *Agenda della Società italiana delle storiche* 12 (1994); Antoinette Burton, 'Finding Women in the Archive', *Journal of Women's History* 20(1) (2008).

11. Anne Morelli, 'Exhumer l'histoire des femmes exilées politiques', *Sextant* 26 (2009), 7–16; Elisa Signori, 'L'antifascismo come identità e scelta di vita. Joyce Lussu dal fuoruscismo alla resistenza', in Luisa Maria Plaisant (ed.), *Joyce Lussu. Una donna nella storia*, Cagliari, 2003, 13–32; A. Fanciullacci, 'Nelle carte d'archivio: immagini di donne tra fascismo, antifascismo e resistenza', in A. Contini and A. Scatigno (eds.), *Carte di donne. Per un censimento regionale della scrittura delle donne dal XVI al XX secolo*, Rome 2005 ; Patricia Gabrieli, 'Biografie femminili e storia politica delle donne', *Italia Contemporanea*, 200, (September 1995), 492–509 ; Patricia Gabrieli, *Scenari di guerra, parole di donne. Diari e memorie nell'Italia della Seconda Guerra mondiale*, Bologna, 2007.

12. Vera Modigliani, *Esilio*, Milan, 1945; Gabrielli, *Tempio di virilità*, 22; Sara Galli, *Le tre sorelle Seidenfeld. Donne nell'emigrazione politica antifascista*, Florence, 2005, 13–17; Camilla Ravera, *Diario di Trent'anni, 1913–1943*, Rome, 1973; Wilson, 'Saints and Heroines', 180.

13. B. Guidetti Serra, *Compagne. Testimonianza di partecipazione politica femminile*, Turin, 1977; Teresa Noce, *Rivoluzionaria professionale*, Milan, 1977; M.Sereni, *I giorni della nostra vita*, Rome, 1956; C. Ravera, *Diario di Trent'anni*, Rome, 1973.

14. A. Swenson, 'Memory, Gender and Antifascism in France and Britain in the 1930s', in Sylvia Paletschek and Sylvia Kraut (eds), *The Gender of Memory*, Frankfurt, 2008, 125–46; L. Casalino, 'Politica e cultura nell'Italia repubblicana: memoria e interpretazioni della Resistenza nella galassia azionista', *Laboratoire italien*, 3 (2002), 118–34.

15. Alberto De Bernardi, 'L'antifascismo: una questione storica aperta', in A. De Bernardi and P. Ferrari (eds), *Antifascismo e identità europea*, Rome, 2004, xvii.

16. Gabrielli, *Tempio di virilità*, 73.

17. Franca Pieroni Bortolotti, *Le Donne nella Resistenza antifascista e la questione feminile in Emilia Romagna*, Milan, 1978, 267; Gabrielli, *Tempio di virilità*, 33.

18. Carrani, *Le donne e la Resistenza*.

19. Wilson, 'Saints and Heroines', 181–87; Slaughter, *Women and the Italian Resistance*, 53–63.
20. Patrizia Gabrielli, 'Présence et absence des femmes dans l'émigration antifasciste italienne en France', *Sextant* 26 (2009), 17; C. De Maria, 'Tra Pubblico e private. Carte personali, legami affettivi e impegno politico', *Storica* 32 (2005), 135–56.
21. Del Boca, *La storia negata*.
22. Guido Quazza, *Resistenza e storia d'Italia. Problemi e ipotesi di ricerca*. Milan, 1975 ; Ibid. 'L'antifascismo nella storia italiana del Novecento'. *Italia Contemporanea* 178 (1990), 5–16 ; Leonardo Rapone, 'L'italia antifascista', in G. Sabbatucci and V. Cidoto, *Storia d'Italia*, vol. 4, *Guerra e fascismo*. Rome and Bari, 1997, 501–59; Ibid. *Antifascismo e società italiana*. Milan, 1999.
23. Ibid.
24. De Luna, *Donne in Oggetto*, 26.
25. Ibid., 10; Giovanni De Luna, 'Ruoli e identià delle donne nell'antifascismo'. *L'impegno* XV(1) (April 1995).
26. Ibid., 26–27.
27. Ibid., 10.
28. Robert Belot, *Aux frontières de la liberté. S'évader de France sous l'Occupation*, Paris, 1998; Robert Belot, 'La biographie entre mémoire et histoire, affect et concept', in Antoine Coppolani and Frédéric Rousseau, *La biographie en histoire. Jeux et enjeux d'écriture*, Paris, 2007, 57; Guillaume Piketty, *Pierre Brossolette, un héros de la Résistance*, Paris, 1998; Guillaume Piketty, 'Résistance, biographie et écriture intime', in Coppolani and Rousseau, *La biographie en histoire*, 68–79; Simone Lässig, 'Biography in Modern History', in Volker R. Berghahn and Simone Lässig (eds.), *Biography between Structure and Agency*, New York and Oxford, 2008, 1–11.
29. Vittoria De Grazia, *How Fascism Ruled Women*, Berkeley, CA, 1992.
30. De Luna, *Donne in Oggetto*, 117.
31. Ibid., 132.
32. Patrizia Gabrielli, 'Donne nell'antifascismo', *Italia Contemporanea* 202 (March 1996), 110; Slaughter, *Women and the Italian Resistance*, 16.
33. De Luna, *Donne in Oggetto*, 103.
34. Patrizia Gabrielli, *Fenicoteri in Volo: Donne comuniste nel ventennio fascista*, Rome, 1999, 43.
35. Ibid., 14.
36. Tromboni, *Donne contro*; A. Bravo and A.M. Bruzzone, *In Guerra senza armi. Storie di donne, 1940–45*, Rome and Bari, 1995; Giorgio Vecchio, *La Resistenza delle donne, 1943–45*, Milan 2010.
37. Noemi Crain Merz, *L'illusione della parità. Donne e questione femminile in Giustizia e Libertà e il Partito d'Azione*, Milan, 2013. The title translates as 'The Illusion of Parity: Women and the Women's Question in GL [Giustizia e Libertà, 'Justice and Freedom'] and the Action Party'.
38. Crain Merz, *L'illusione della parità*, 161.
39. Joyce Lussu, 'La questione femminile e il Partito d'Azione', in L. Mercuri (ed.), *L'azionismo nella storia d'Italia*. Ancona, 1988 ; Maria Casalini, *Le donne della sinistrra, 1944–48*, Rome 2005, 153 ; Luisa Maria Plaisant, L.M. (ed.). *Joyce Lussu. Una donna nella storia*. Cagliari, 2003.

40. Quoted in Crain Merz, *L'illusione della parità*, 149 and 161.
41. Isabelle Richet, 'Marion Rosselli, la fuga da Lipari e lo sviluppo dei circuiti antifascisti in Gran Bretagna', in Alessandro Giacone and Eric Vial (eds), *I Fratelli Rosselli, l'antifascismo e l'esilio*, Rome, 2011, 74–88; and 'Marion Cave Rosselli and the Transnational Women's Antifascist Networks', *Journal of Women's History* 24(3), 117–39; Patrizia Gabrielli, *Col freddo nel cuore. Uomini e donne nell'emigrazione antifascista*, Rome, 2004.
42. Joan W. Scott, 'Gender: A Useful Category of Historical Analysis', *American Historical Review* 91(5) (December 1986), 1053–75; Joan W. Scott, 'Rewriting History', in Margaret Higonnet et al., *Behind the Lines: Gender and the Two World Wars*, New Haven, CT, 1987; Joan W. Scott, *Gender and the Politics of History*, New York, 1988.
43. Slaughter, *Women and the Italian Resistance*, 106.
44. Angela Kershaw and Angela Kimyongür, *Women in Europe between the Wars*, Aldershot, 2007, 13; Karen Offen, *European Feminism 1700–1950: A Political History*, Stanford, CA, 2000, 353–54; Francesca De Haan, et al. (eds). *Women's Activism: Global Perspectives from the 1890s to the Present*. London, 2013; S.K. Kent, *Making Peace: The Reconstruction of Gender in Interwar Britain*, Princeton N.J., 1993; Kevin Passmore (ed.), *Women, Gender and Fascism in Europe, 1919–1945*, Manchester, 1003.
45. Slaughter, *Women and the Italian Resistance*, 106.

References

Addis Saba, M. *Partigiane. Tutte le donne della Resistenza*. Milan, 1998.

Belot, R. *Aux frontières de la liberté. S'évader de France sous l'Occupation*. Paris, 1998.

———. 'La biographie entre mémoire et histoire, affect et concept', in A. Coppolani and F. Rousseau (eds), *La biographie en histoire. Jeux et enjeux d'écriture*. Paris, 2007, 56–67.

Berghahn, V.R., and S. Lässig (eds). *Biography between Structure and Agency*. New York and Oxford, 2008.

Bortolotti, F. *Le donne nella Resistenza antifascista e la questione feminile in Emilia Romagna*. Milan, 1978.

Bravo, A., and A.M. Bruzzone. *In Guerra senza armi. Storie di donne, 1940–45*. Rome and Bari, 1995.

Bravo, A. (ed.). *I Gruppi di Difesa della Donna, 1943–55*. Rome, UDI, 199.

Bruzzone, A.M., and R. Farina (eds). *La resistenza taciuta*. Turin, 2003.

Burton, A., 'Finding Women in the Archive'. *Journal of Women's History* 20(1) (2008).

Capponi, C. *Con cuore di donna: il Ventennio, la resistenza a Roma, Via Rasella. I ricordi di una protagonista*. Milan, 2009.

Capobianco, L. (ed.). *Donne tra memoria e storia*. Naples, 1993.

Carrani, R. (ed.). *Le donne e la Resistenza. Rassegna bibliográfica*. Rome, 1994.

Casalini, M. *Le donne della sinistra, 1944–48*. Rome, 2005.

Casalino, L. 'Politica e cultura nell'Italia repubblicana: memoria e interpretazioni della Resistenza nella galassia azionista'. *Laboratoire italien* 3 (2002), 118–34.

Colarizi, S. 'Problemi storiografici sul fuoruscismo e sull'antifascismo socialista all'estero', in F. Taddei (ed.), *L'immigrazione socialista nella lotta contro il fascismo (1926–1939)*. Florence, 1982.

Crain Merz, N. *L'illusione della parità. Donne e questione femminile in Giustizia e Libertà e il Partito d'Azione*. Milan, 2013.

De Bernardi, A. 'L'antifascismo: una questione storica aperta', in A. De Bernardi and P. Ferrari (eds), *Antifascismo e identità europea*. Rome, 2004.

De Grazia, V. *How Fascism Ruled Women*. Berkeley, CA, 1992.

De Haan, F., et al. (eds). *Women's Activism: Global Perspectives from the 1890s to the Present*. London, 2013.

Del Boca, A. (ed.), *La storia negata. Il revisionismo e il suo uso politico*. Vicenza, 2009.

De Luna, G.. 'Ruoli e identià delle donne nell'antifascismo'. *L'impegno* XV(1) (April 1995).

———. *Donne in Oggetto: l'antifascismo nella società italiana, 1922–1939*. Turin, 1995.

De Maria, C. 'Tra Pubblico e private. Carte personali, legami affettivi e impegno politico'. *Storica* 32 (2005), 135–56.

Fanciullacci, A. 'Nelle carte d'archivio: immagini di donne tra fascismo, antifascismo e resistenza', in A. Contini and A. Scatigno (eds), *Carte di donne. Per un censimento regionale della scrittura delle donne dal XVI al XX secolo*. Rome, 2005.

Gabrielli, P. 'Biografie femminili e storia politica delle donne'. *Italia Contemporanea* 200 (September 1995), 492–509.

———. 'Donne nell'antifascismo'. *Italia Contemporanea* 202 (March 1996), 99–112.

———. *Fenicoteri in Volo: Donne comuniste nel ventennio fascista*. Rome, 1999.

———. *Col freddo nel cuore. Uomini e donne nell'emigrazione antifascista*. Rome, 2004.

———.*Scenari di guerra, parole di donne. Diari e memorie nell'Italia della Seconda Guerra mondiale*. Bologna, 2007.

———. *Tempio di virilità. L'antifascismo, il genere, la storia*. Milan, 2008.

———. 'Présence et absence des femmes dans l'émigration antifasciste italienne en France'. *Sextant* 26 (2009), 45–57.

Gagliani, D. (ed.). *Guerra, resistenza politica. Storie di donne*. Reggio Emilia, 2006.

Gagliani, D., E. Guerra, L. Mariani and F. Tarozzi (eds), *Donne, Guerra, Politica. Esperienze e memorie della Resistenza*. Bologna, 2000.

Galli, S. *Le tre sorelle Seidenfeld. Donne nell'emigrazione politica antifascista*. Florence, 2005.

Giuva, L. 'Ricerche di genere e archivi: quali strumenti?'. *Agenda della Società italiana delle storiche* 12 (1994).

Grissi, A. 'Un percorso a ritroso: le donne al confino politico, 1926–1943'. *Italia Contemporanea* 226 (2002), 31–59.

———. 'Confinate politiche contro la guerra', in D. Gagliani (ed.), *Guerra, Resistenza, Politica. Storie di donne*. Reggio Emilia, 2006, 47–54.

Guidetti Serra, B. *Compagne. Testimonianza de partecipazione politica femminile.* Turin, 1977.

Kent, S.K. *Making Peace: The Reconstruction of Gender in Interwar Britain.* Princeton, NJ, 1993.

Kershaw, A., and A. Kimyongür. *Women in Europe between the Wars.* Aldershot, 2007.

Lässig, S. 'Biography in Modern History', in V.R. Berghahn and S. Lässig (eds), *Biography between Structure and Agency.* New York and Oxford, 2008, 1–11.

Lussu, J. 'La questione femminile e il Partito d'Azione', in L. Mercuri (ed.), *L'azionismo nella storia d'Italia.* Ancona, 1988.

Modigliani, V. *Esilio.* Rome, 1945.

`Morelli, A. (ed.). 'Exhumer l'histoire des femmes exilées politiques'. *Sextant* 26 (2009), 7–16.

Noce, T. *Rivoluzionaria professionale.* Milan, 1977.

`Offen, K. *European Feminism 1700–1950: A Political History.* Stanford, CA, 2000.

Passmore, K. (ed.). *Women, Gender and Fascism in Europe, 1919–1945.* Manchester, 2003.

Perrot, M. *Les femmes ou les silences de l'histoire.* Paris, 1998.

Piketty, G. *Pierre Brossolette, un héros de la Résistance.* Paris, 1998.

———. 'Résistance, biographie et écriture intime', in A. Coppolani and F. Rousseau, *La biographie en histoire. Jeux et enjeux d'écriture.* Paris, 2007, 68–79.

Plaisant, L.M. (ed.). *Joyce Lussu. Una donna nella storia.* Cagliari, 2003.

Quazza, G. *Resistenza e storia d'Italia. Problemi e ipotesi di ricerca.* Milan, 1975.

———. 'L'antifascismo nella storia italiana del Novecento'. *Italia Contemporanea* 178 (1990), 5–16.

Rapone, L. 'L'italia antifascista', in G. Sabbatucci and V. Cidoto, *Storia d'Italia,* vol. 4, *Guerra e fascismo.* Rome and Bari, 1997, 501–59.

———.*Antifascismo e società italiana.* Milan, 1999.

Ravera, C. *Diario di Trent'anni, 1913–1943.* Rome, 1973.

Richet, I. 'Marion Rosselli, la fuga da Lipari e lo sviluppo dei circuiti antifascisti in Gran Bretagna', in A. Giacone and E. Vial (eds), *I Fratelli Rosselli, l'antifascismo e l'esilio.* Rome, 2011, 74–88.

———. 'Marion Cave Rosselli and the Transnational Women's Antifascist Networks'. *Journal of Women's History* 24(3) (2012), 117–39.

Scott, J.W. 'Gender: A Useful Category of Historical Analysis'. *American Historical Review* 91(5) (December 1986), 1053–75.

———. 'Rewriting History', in M. Higonnet et al. (eds), *Behind the Lines: Gender and the Two World Wars.* New Haven, CT, 1987, 19–30.

———. *Gender and the Politics of History.* New York, 1988.

Sereni, M. *I giorni della nostra vita.* Rome, 1956.

Signori, E. 'L'antifascismo come identità e scelta di vita. Joyce Lussu dal fuoruscismo alla resistenza', in L.M. Plaisant (ed.), *Joyce Lussu. Una donna nella storia.* Cagliari, 2003, 13–32.

Slaughter, J. *Women and the Italian Resistance.* Denver, 1997.

Swenson, A. 'Memory, Gender and Antifascism in France and Britain in the 1930s', in S. Paletschek and S. Kraut (eds), *The Gender of Memory.* Frankfurt, 2008, 125–46.

Taddei, B. *Donne processate dal Tribunale speciale, 1927–1943*. Verona, 2008.

Trenti, F. *Il Novecento di Joyce Salvadori Lussu. Vita e azione di una donna antifascista*. Sasso Marconi, 2009.

Tromboni, Delfin (ed.). *Donne contro: protagonismo delle donne e soggettività feminile tra guerra, fascismo e Resistenza*. Ferrara, 1996.

Vecchio, G. *La resistenza delle donne, 1943–45*. Milan, 2010.

Wilson, P.R., 'Saints and Heroines: Re-writing the History of Italian Women in the Resistance', in T. Kirk and A. Elligot (eds), *Opposing Fascism: Community, Authority and Resistance in Europe*. Cambridge, 1999.

Isabelle Richet is professor emeritus of History at the Université Paris Diderot-Paris 7. Her recent publications on antifascism include: 'Marion Rosselli, la fuga da Lipari e lo sviluppo di circuiti antifascisti in Gran Bretagna', in Alessandro Giacone and Eric Vial (eds), *I fratelli Rosselli. L'antifascismo in esilio* (2011); 'Marion Cave Rosselli and the Transnational Women Antifascist Networks', *Journal of Women's History* (Autumn 2012); 'The Irresponsibility of the Outsider? American Expatriates and Italian Fascism', in Isabelle Richet and Catherine Collomp (eds), 'Voice, Exit and Freedom', special issue of the journal *Transatlantica* (June 2014, online). She is currently writing a biography of Marion Rosselli, *Marion Cave Rosselli: A Life against Mussolini* (forthcoming).

 9

THE STRAINED COURTSHIP BETWEEN ANTIFASCISM AND FEMINISM
From the Women's World Committee (1934) to the Women's International Democratic Federation (1945)

Mercedes Yusta

This contribution aims at recounting the alliances and divergences between the antifascist and feminist movements, both on an individual scale and in comparison with the development of a political culture and a common strategy against the rise of fascism. The chosen period witnessed the creation of two transnational antifascist women's organisations: the Women's World Committee against War and Fascism (1934) and the Women's International Democratic Federation (WIDF, 1945), the latter being set up after the Second World War to take over the 1934 organisation and follow in its footsteps. Through the analysis of these organisations, I aim to introduce an approach into the history of antifascist mobilisation that takes into account the gendered character, not only of the individuals that took part in the movement, but also of their organisations, discourses and strategies against the rise of fascist regimes. In addition, both the evolution of these organisations and their problematic relationships with the feminist mobilisation highlight how difficult it can be to bring together different political struggles and identities – especially when it comes to introducing the specificity of women's struggles, an issue that has often been pointed out, particularly with regard to the links between feminism and Marxism.[1]

The chapter is based on a multifarious hypothesis. Firstly, I consider that the historiography of antifascism has neglected and minimised the importance of women's involvement, which was not only numerically sizeable, but also provided the antifascist political culture with mobilisation discourses and strategies (in this regard, see Isabelle Richet's chapter in this book). Women's actions within the antifascist movement would therefore represent a women's antifascism with its own features: a kind of political subculture within antifascism that created discourses, forms of mobilisation, rituals and heroines that the whole antifascist movement would then utilise. The second part of my hypothesis concerns the intertwining of the feminist and antifascist political cultures during the earlier stages of antifascist mobilisation. While we wait for more thorough studies to be made, especially in the field of prosopography, we can still observe exchanges and intricate bonds between the feminist and antifascist militant circles. We can identify women's trajectories moving from one circle to another – discursive transfers, shared demands and strategies. Thus, in the early days of antifascist mobilisation (1933–34), an alliance between feminism and antifascism was considered not only possible, but also desirable.[2] However, there were still divisions and paradoxes, mainly because the labour movement considered feminist activists as 'bourgeois', and also because a significant number of the liberal feminists were somewhat frightened by the transnational antifascist organisations' steadfast loyalty to the Soviet Union and their close ties to national Communist parties.[3] Moreover, this temporary alliance was extremely fragile: it did not survive the change of discourse and the mutations of antifascist mobilisations at the end of the Second World War, when women's antifascism re-formed to create a transnational organisation, the above-mentioned WIDF, which would rapidly be identified with the strategic interests of the Soviet Union against the new international backdrop of the beginning of the Cold War.[4]

Those alliances were tenuous; however, I consider that women's antifascist mobilisation, in which women with feminist roots played an important role, led to the impregnation of antifascism with discourses born from a pacifist and maternalist feminist matrix, reused afterwards by the whole antifascist movement and even manipulated in the context of the Soviet strategy at the beginning of the Cold War. Investigating the genealogy and roots of those pacifist strategies and discourses should help us to get a fresher view than the oversimplified idea of an antifascism that was led from above by the Communist International (CI) with the sole aim being to further the strategic goals of the Soviet Union and the Western Communist parties. The women who strove for the antifascist cause were motivated by various intentions, but the sources, especially the publications of women's antifascist organisations, reveal that they had all analysed fascism in the light of the events that were happening in different countries, and had deemed it the main enemy to the empowerment of women.[5] Finally, I would like to stress the fact that my analysis is based on French and Spanish sources, given that both countries were very closely linked, that French women played a key role in structuring women's antifascist organisations, and that Spain had a central place in antifascist thought and mobilisation – especially in the 1930s, but also after 1945.

The Origins of Women's Antifascist Mobilisation

The birth of a feminist political tendency within the antifascist movement is almost contemporary to its institutionalisation as a transnational movement, since the Amsterdam Congress of 1932 and the 1933 Congress at the Salle Pleyel in Paris both led to the creation of the World Committee against War and Fascism (also known as the 'Amsterdam–Pleyel Movement').[6] The origins of this movement and the role the CI played in shaping it are well known. However, the efforts that Gabrielle Duchêne, who was not even a Communist Party member, put into setting up a women's branch are not as notorious. Duchêne was a feminist, a pacifist, and in 1915 – right in the middle of the First World War – she participated in the foundation of the Women's International League for Peace and Freedom (WILPF) and, shortly afterwards, founded its French section.[7] In the late 1920s, she returned from a trip to the Soviet Union. She had become a fellow traveller – but she was not a card-carrying Communist, and the path she and other women (such as the Spanish Margarita Nelken and Irene Falcón, or to some extent Isabel Oyarzábal de Palencia) followed served as a paradigm for the women who went from feminism, often with a link to the pacifist movement, to antifascism – even though some women like Irene Falcón achieved that change through open communist activism.[8] As early as January 1934, Duchêne spurred on the constitution of an International Initiative Committee that called for a 'global gathering of women': the great Women's World Congress against War and Fascism that took place in Paris in August 1934 and resulted in the creation of the Women's World Committee against War and Fascism.

Those who have studied the pacifist strategy of the Communist Party – especially Yves Santamaria – considered that this movement (be it the organisation of women or more generally the Amsterdam–Pleyel movement) was nothing but a strategy entirely made up by the CI in order to lead a massive antifascist gathering into serving the diplomatic interests of the Soviet Union, especially in case of a German attack.[9] This, however, casts aside the experience and worldview of the antifascist militants themselves, who incidentally were not all communists. In France, the creation of this movement, its strategy and its discourse, was obviously greatly influenced by the pro-Soviet strategy of the French Communist Party (PCF). Yet, other political cultures left their imprint on antifascism when it became a mass movement. Antifascism was actually a cultural melting pot of political sensibilities, and therefore one can only scrape the surface of a definition.[10]

Many feminists found an interest in antifascist activism. Christine Bard explained it as the consequence of traditional feminism running out of ideas, but also as a result of a new kind of involvement growing more appealing to the younger generations of mobilised women – one that was more global and more attuned to the present political emergencies, but which included feminist demands.[11] In France, several young women turned their feminist sensibility towards antifascist activism, even though that involved leaving their usual feminist demands, such as the right to vote, to one side in order to focus more on other means of political intervention.[12]

The participation of the WILPF, through its leader Gabrielle Duchêne, in the Amsterdam–Pleyel movement was not free of controversies. Some local sections, such as that of Lyon in 1936, even distanced themselves from the founder's political line. In fact, the participation of this feminist and pacifist organisation in the antifascist movement forced it to redefine the meaning of the concept of peace: according to Duchêne, the true task of peace defenders consisted in an 'effective, practical, ceaseless struggle against war and fascism'. The youngest activists expressed the same idea in even more drastic terms. Lucienne Leleu, secretary of the League's Marseille section, wrote to Duchêne in 1934:

> The first confusion to clear up … is above all that of refusing to see that violence may not only be found in war, but is at the base even of the present regime, and that it is not only or even mainly the result of gunshots. The revolt against war which was the basis of the League's action, if it is conscious and not merely sentimental, if it is a revolt against violence in all realms … must be a struggle against the present capitalist regime. Today a conscious pacifist must be a revolutionary.[13]

From this women's mobilisation rooted in feminism, antifascism inherited decades of thinking and both women's and feminist actions for peace. Such mobilisation went far beyond the traditionally 'female' scope of action, as it was in line with a political motivation. Although it often defended womanly values linked to motherhood – peace being a value that women defended precisely because of their ability to become mothers – the mention of motherhood (and the rights relating to it in terms of citizen participation) was mainly a means to legitimise women's intervention in politics. Antifascist women would inherit the political maternalism of their feminist elders and emphasise it. They brandished maternal values associated with the struggle against war and fascism in order to justify their intervention in the hottest political issues. These issues were not only international (such as the denunciation of the rise of fascism and of the arms race), but also national; in France, they included the fight against far right leagues, the demand for a repeal of the Daladier government's decree-laws, the fight against inflation, and support for the Popular Front – all of this at a time when French women did not have the right to vote.

Converging and Diverging Discourses and Strategies

The contents of *Femmes dans l'action mondiale* ('Women in Global Action'), a French-language newspaper published by the Women's World Committee, pointed out the tension-bearing confusions between feminist legacies and demands that the women's antifascist movement had made its own; and also that antifascist women rejected some specific aspects of feminism. Furthermore, it is interesting to note that the paper was in line with the twentieth anniversary of the declaration of the First World War, in its refusal to repeat the carnage. The pacifist and feminist legacy of Duchêne's organisation, the WILPF, appears thus as the starting point of women's antifascist mobilisation.

The newspaper was published between October 1934 and April 1939; it was essentially a blend of political commitment and women's press, a mixture that would become the trademark of the antifascist or Communist press targeting women. The contents related to both national and international political events, always in reference to the fight against fascism (and also against imperialism, especially as far as the Italian campaign in Abyssinia was concerned). They also dealt with the daily concerns of women, such as the increase of prices due to the economic crisis (the high cost of living), and the controversies surrounding women's work and their right to vote. The paper gave a blaze of publicity to concrete feminist demands, like the right for women to work (one that had been set aside in Nazi Germany, and that was threatened in France by the Laval government's decree-laws), to vote and to divorce, or even to enforce paternity claims. In connection with these typical feminist concerns, the Soviet Union was constantly presented as the world's one and only country where women's emancipation was fully accomplished: a true feminist paradise that not only guaranteed perfect equality of rights between the sexes (such as equality of duties, particularly regarding arduous work – although not many people insisted on that), but also protected women and their children, while offering childcare for female workers and the right to terminate unwanted pregnancies. Spanish Communist (from 1936 onwards) and feminist Margarita Nelken wrote these enthusiastic lines in *Femmes dans l'action mondiale* about the abortion clinics in Moscow:

> We are in the USSR: the country of socialism, of the human meaning of life. We are worlds apart from the plight of women in capitalist countries, from broken homes with countless famished children, from mothers breastfeeding while well into yet another pregnancy, and from unsafe back-alley abortions, tearing and killing.[14]

Testimonies of feminists (men or women) were called for in order to inscribe women's antifascism in the tradition and the legacy of women's mobilisation, with a specific section entitled *Femmes d'autrefois dans l'action mondiale* ('Women of the Past in Global Action'). In that publication, Victor Basch, Jean Longuet, Marcel Cachin and other famous political figures pleaded in favour of women's right to vote. The president of the League for the Rights of Man, Victor Basch, was particularly enthusiastic about women's antifascist mobilisation, which he felt would attract many more people than feminist meetings – at which he mainly saw men anyway, 'as if French women had lost interest in their fate, contrary to other countries'.[15]

In fact, the women who wrote in *Femmes dans l'action mondiale* often criticised feminism as an actual political movement. For instance, they pointed out the effects on the one hand of a political competition to attract the masses of women, and on the other hand of a Marxist analysis that believed gender solidarity did not prevent class divisions. The methods of the feminist movement were fiercely criticised; PCF leader Bernadette Cattanéo tackled the mainstream press, claiming they were

> solely interested in mockery, covering only ridiculous mock-combats and women chained to the Bastille: anything that would diminish the prestige of women and that wouldn't support their claims! And candidates that claim to defend the right to vote whilst loudly letting every one know they will never be into politics aren't any better! Wasn't it the very argument of those who opposed women's right to vote: 'women should not be allowed in politics', 'they are unable to be politicians', 'they lack political education', etc. We believe that this kind of position supports women's right to vote like a rope supports a hanged man.[16]

Yet, she also criticised the idea of an exclusively feminist position that would claim to transcend political differences:

> I once heard a feminist orator conclude her speech with: 'Woman first', and called for a sacred union of women – a position that is also completely wrong. Women don't have communities of interests, and neither

do men. Some women are ironmasters, or own factories – and their lux-
urious lifestyles are made possible by other women's misery and hard
labour. Some women can't be against the slums they own, and therefore support the female workers who inhabit them. The wives of country
squires won't defend those of the sharecroppers and small farmers they
exploit. The wife of a big trust owner can't be on the same side as the
wife of a small shop owner; their trust is ruining and leading towards
bankruptcy.[17]

The main point of divergence between feminism and antifascism
concerned the difficulty of considering gender and class inequalities
as a single issue – which would end up overthrowing this somewhat
shaky alliance. Feminism was relegated to its condition of being a bourgeois ideology (in the Marxist sense of 'false consciousness'); it would
happen again, more violently, in 1945. As far as the political situation
in France in the 1930s is concerned, the large women's organisations
were starting to drag on, and got stuck into political neutrality, which,
moreover, was often inscribed in its standing rules. Many feminist organisations found it hard to make a realistic analysis of the situation
created by the rise of fascism in Germany, and some minimised the
fascist danger. At the same time, antifascist women took part in several
feminist struggles, such as defending women's right to work (threatened by the Laval decree-laws) or even the right to vote, which was
demanded many times, through numerous declarations of politicians,
including Communist Marcel Cachin.[18] Furthermore, antifascists successfully resumed peace mobilisations with a 'realistic' approach of
pacifism, attracting many feminists, most of them linked to the WILPF:
with regard to this organisation's national conference of 1936, Christine
Bard pointed out that 'the league is now first and foremost antifascist'.[19]
It was, however, the events of 1936 – the election of Popular Front governments in both France and Spain and, above all, the outbreak of the
Spanish Civil War – that acted as a catalyst for women's antifascist
mobilisation.

The Bitter Test of Antifascism: Spain

In Spain, the situation of women's antifascist mobilisation was somewhat different. Although Spanish women had obtained the right to vote
as early as 1931, the right wing had won the legislative elections of 1933.
Since these were the first elections in which women could vote, they
were blamed for the left's defeat and accused of having resoundingly
voted in favour of the Catholic right under their confessors' influence.

Both feminist Clara Campoamor (defender of women's right to vote at the Spanish Parliament in 1931) and María Lejárraga (a feminist and Socialist) claimed that it was an error of judgement. The real problem lay in the fact that the female proletariat did not vote because the left did not bother to rally them to its cause.[20] The combination of an atmosphere of mistrust towards the right (whose leader, Gil Robles, did not hide his admiration for the rise of Nazism in Germany, and he attended the Nazi Party Conference in 1933) with the creation of the first Spanish fascist organisations, clearly inspired by Mussolini's regime, with revolutionary excitement sparking up amongst the labour parties (especially the Spanish Socialist Workers' Party – PSOE), quickly lit the antifascist flame.[21] The women who led feminist organisations, members of both the Republican and the Socialist parties, saw an opportunity to rally the masses of women who had been forgotten by traditional parties. Many were present at the beginning of the women's antifascist mobilisation, therefore representing a wide range of political beliefs.[22]

When, early in 1934, a delegate of Gabrielle Duchêne got in touch with the Spanish Communists, and more precisely with Dolores Ibárruri, to set up a Spanish branch of the Women's World Committee, the Communists easily agreed to team up with the feminists (both Republicans and Socialists) to create the Spanish antifascist women's movement known as 'Mujeres contra la Guerra y el Fascismo'. Although feminist claims appear to be much more discreet in the movement's publications (*Mujeres* and *Compañera*) than in their French counterpart, it is important to remember that long-standing feminists – such as Margarita Nelken, Isabel Oyarzábal de Palencia and even the historical feminist Belén Sarraga – participated in it. So did Irene Falcón, who seemed to be the true organiser of the women's antifascist movement (more than *Pasionaria* herself), and who insisted in her memoirs on the influence the ideas of her friend Margarita Nelken had on her philosophy.[23]

In Spain, women's antifascism immediately developed into confrontational activism. During the Congress that took place in Paris in 1934 (which would give birth to the Women's World Committee), Spain sent a delegation of twelve women who represented the left's entire political spectrum, from Republicanism to Communism. Immediately afterwards, on 22 August, their first public action was a demonstration in Madrid. Both anti-militarist and anti-colonialist, it was against the call-up of reservists for the war in Morocco. Both the demonstration and the Civil Guard's repression that followed were echoed in *Femmes dans l'action mondiale*.[24] According to the column published in *Mundo Obrero* by the PCE, bourgeois women also took part in this protest against the 'imperialist war'.[25] But the event that served as the catalyst of this women's antifascist movement was the October Revolution of 1934. In Asturias, the uprising against the Lerroux conservative government took the form of an armed insurrection led by an alliance of Communists, anarchists and Socialists. We do not know the real part the organisation of antifascist women took in the events. They were nevertheless banned, and some of their leaders, including *Pasionaria* herself and the socialist MP Veneranda Manzano, were imprisoned. On the other side of the Pyrenees, the events in Spain were proof – if they needed any more – that fascism represented a real danger, even to states that were not governed by an openly fascist regime. Accounts of repression in Asturias, especially against women, were published in *Femmes dans l'action mondiale*; they were often written by Margarita Nelken. The links of antifascist and transnational solidarity among women tightened on both sides of the border and, like the Italians who had been seeking refuge in France since 1923, the Spaniards who fled repression by the Lerroux government were treated as antifascist refugees. In 1934, Spain thus became the scene of an armed conflict between fascism and antifascism.[26]

For the Spanish feminists and/or antifascists, October 1934 marked a historic turning point when radical choices had to be made. The women's antifascist movement did not disappear. On the contrary, it survived in different forms, reappearing after the Popular Front's victory in February 1936 as the Agrupación de Mujeres Antifascistas (Antifascist Women's Group). The tone was set; pacifist feminism was now replaced by a combative spirit, even though antifascist women, and especially Dolores Ibárruri, still claimed a feminist political agenda – although she always refused to be considered as 'feminist'. In the pages of the *Mujeres* journal, *La Pasionaria* thus demanded 'the right to work, equality of wages, protection for mothers, enforced fatherhood, the right to divorce without being legally or financially held back, the right to abort, the creation of day nurseries, schools, kindergartens, canteens and after school care, the exclusion of any unsanitary work and the right to take up a position of responsibility within a context of fair competition with men'.[27] This is a familiar programme, as it is almost the same that Bernadette Cattanéo had proposed in the pages of *Femmes dans l'action mondiale*.[28]

Moreover, moderate feminists had been traumatised by the violence used by the Asturian miners, and distanced themselves from antifascism. On the other hand, the ranks of the women's organisation fed on young activist girls who found an interest in politics when the Popular Front won the elections.[29] On the other side of the border, before the

Civil War even broke out, Spain was considered as a model of anti-fascist mobilisation. The presence and visibility of women during the election campaign was interpreted as a sign of the power of women's antifascism. As historical socialist and MP for the Seine region Jean Longuet said about the victory of the Popular Front: 'In 1934 in Spain, women were blamed for the left wing's defeat in the 1933 elections! What a splendid response they just gave to those who feared the influence of the Church. ... I therefore believe that Spain's example is the clear proof that women's votes can favour proletarian parties'.[30]

This point of view was shared by Communist leader Marcel Cachin, who, during an interview with *Femmes dans l'action mondiale*, said that the victory of the Popular Front in Spain proved that 'when a massive social movement shakes society, women instinctively understand. Yes, Spanish women, like men, have freed the country from fascism. French women will certainly not act any differently'.[31] However, the argument was slightly different from the one used by the feminists: the right for women to vote, yes, but in the name of antifascism.

The fact remains that what Cachin believed to be a victory against fascism turned out rather fragile, since the coup that triggered the Spanish Civil War occurred only five months after the Popular Front's victory. That was the beginning of a true battle against fascism, arms in hand. On the Republican side, women had already been rallied by the Agrupación de Mujeres Antifascistas and by the anarchist women's organisation Mujeres Libres, and they would take part in the struggle with an enthusiasm that would soon become both legendary and cumbersome. The Civil War was also a high point of international solidarity for the more committed antifascist feminists; in the words of Gabrielle Duchêne, 'If we remain neutral we become accomplices of fascism'.[32]

The Fragile Nature of the Alliances, and the 1946 Breach

The work of Mary Nash, among others, helped to popularise the subject of women's antifascist mobilisation during the Spanish Civil War, and I refer to her studies with regard to the participation of women on the Republicans' war effort in the period 1936–39.[33] As far as the relationship between antifascism and feminism is concerned, it is important to recall that the coup and the beginning of the war – which took the form of an anarchist revolutionary process in the Republican zone – implied that an alliance with a 'bourgeois' feminism, which had been distancing itself from antifascism anyway, was not possible anymore. However, the antifascist revolutionary process gave anarchist women the opportunity to develop their most sophisticated and revolutionary efforts in favour of women's emancipation: whether it was through the Mujeres Libres organisation, or because of the policy favouring sexual and reproductive rights led by anarchist Federica Montseny as a minister of health. In this context, an antifascist mobilisation (with anarchist tendencies) truly merged with radical feminist ideals.[34] The experience was short-lived however, as it did not survive the Republican defeat: unlike their Communist counterparts, who eventually appropriated the word 'antifascist', anarchist women were not able to reorganise after the defeat.

To push the analysis of the relations between feminism and antifascism further, we must focus briefly on the resurgence of women's antifascism at the end of the Second World War. The impossibility of reinstating former alliances with feminism (no matter how fragile or ephemeral they were) seems to be a clear marker – amongst others – of the mutations the antifascist discourse and mobilisation had experienced. In November 1945 at the Maison de la Mutualité in Paris, barely a few months after the end of the Second World War, women from over sixty countries renewed the world gathering that had taken place eleven years earlier. This meeting saw the birth of a new international female organisation, the Women's International Democratic Federation, which reproduced the antifascist women's alliance of 1934. Historical antifascists and feminists such as Gabrielle Duchêne, Cécile Brunschwicg and Dolores Ibárruri were present, and, more importantly, so were members of the Resistance from several countries who had directly experienced fascism and Nazism and their most brutal practices: prisons, camps, repression and extermination. For these women, the nemesis of fascism was the Soviet Union's Red Army – and to a lesser degree, the national resistance movements, in which Communists played a leading role. This was a moment, both brief and extraordinary, of antifascist union that seemed able to lead to a new political order.[35]

The Women's International Democratic Federation, which, according to some accounts, had been created on the initiative of Soviet women,[36] was led on from its origins by a 'fellow traveller' and former member of the Resistance, Eugénie Cotton (who, in a way, took over Gabrielle Duchêne's role in the 1930s). With the aid of the Federation, antifascist women's actions were made possible – they helped to create this new political order, the fruit of the victory over fascism. The newly acquired right for women to vote became a major political weapon that helped to achieve these goals. The Federation declared that its aims were to maintain peace in Europe, prevent the resurgence of fascism and defend the rights of women as 'mothers, workers and citizens', in an order that revealed the organisation's priorities.[37] After playing a rather secondary role in the antifascist women's mobilisation during the 1930s, maternalism became the centre of attention: the whole mobilisation of the WIDF was done in the name of women's involvement, as mothers, in the public sphere. Thus, the mobilisation of antifascist women took a conservative turn with the beginning of the Cold War.[38]

But the biggest clash between antifascist women and feminism took place on a political level. Following the example of the newly created WIDF, the important pre-war women's and feminist organisations (the International Council of Women, the International Alliance of Women, and the Women's International League for Peace and Freedom) reorganised, and convened conferences of a federative nature, thus competing with the WIDF on mobilising masses of women. The WIDF had openly gone to great lengths to federate women's progressive organisations throughout the world, and that meant no other independent women's organisation could exist in the same field.

During the summer of 1946, the large feminist organisations' conferences were intended to revive these organisations after the disruption of the war. Representatives of the WIDF were sent to inform the Federation's executive committee about when such congresses were to be held. The reports cast a light on unambiguous observations: the 'forces of reaction' were manipulating feminist organisations in order to weaken the women's progressive movement represented by the Federation. The International Alliance of Women was then called 'suffragists who know nothing about life',[39] while the WILPF – which had organised the gathering of antifascist women in 1934 – was called 'undemocratic and on the verge of fascism' because of its president's anti-Soviet position.[40] An incident took place during the WILPF Conference: the Czech, Bulgarian, Spanish, French and Yugoslav delegates left the room after the Norwegian delegate had intervened, criticising Soviet intervention in the Baltic states. This reflected how the Continent's geopolitical division was reproduced within the women's movement.[41] The synthesis of the new organisation of feminists by Dolores Ibárruri offers a good insight into the WIDF's position at the time:

> While the Federation found an echo and an enthusiastic reception among progressive women [*sic*], the latent forces of anti-democracy and defeated fascism claim, with misleading instructions, that they can raise one or more international women's organisations to challenge the Federation. Those new organisations would be submissive to their reactionary manoeuvres and ready to slow down, decompose or disintegrate the great

women's democratic movement, whose real, living and active expression is our Federation.[42]

At that time, the WIDF had obviously turned the page on feminism – a feminism some leaders of the WIDF, such as *Pasionaria*, had been denouncing for years for being too bourgeois and too remote from the interests of working-class women. Indeed, women who held positions of leadership in Communist parties and pro-Soviet organisations had remained stuck with the definition of a 'bourgeois feminism', distant from the real interests of the female masses. Thus, from within the WIDF's executive committee, Ibárruri strongly affirmed: 'We are not feminist women. We are women who fight for freedom and for democracy. We know that women taking part in the fight for freedom and for democracy will help them to resolve any problem that they might face'.[43]

Far away from the 'suffragists' retrograde fight',[44] the women of the WIDF focused their struggle on denouncing the remnants of fascism, and on the fight for peace in the name of women's ancestral combat 'for children's peace and happiness'.[45] But what is particularly striking is the speed at which the antifascist discourse evolved in the women's organisation: within a few months, it changed target and accused the Western powers' policies of being the main threat to world peace. The United States and Britain had been thanked during the 1945 Conference for contributing to the defeat of fascism, but they were now being accused of fascism, which at that time was synonymous with 'anti-Soviet'. The women of the WIDF accomplished real political work: in the name of their dual status as women and antifascists, they tirelessly denounced the US presence in South East Asia, the international indulgence towards Franco's Spain, the delay in the de-Nazification of Germany and the de-fascistisation of Italy, the arms race and the threat of the atomic bomb. At the same time, however, they combined this critique of Western politics, that was often more than justified, with an increasingly sectarian position towards the Soviet Union and the 'new democracies', presented as an example of good practice regarding the defence of freedom, the rights of women and children, and, above all, world peace.

*

Having been crafted by the women's organisation in a melting pot of antifascism and feminism, the pacifist discourse became a key propaganda weapon in the political and cultural clashes that marked the beginning of the Cold War. During the summer of 1948, the Cominform thus launched a political strategy of pacifist rallying in order to present the USSR as the champion of world peace. In 1948 and 1949, respectively, the World Congress of Intellectuals for Peace in Wroclaw and the World Committee of Partisans for Peace in Paris convened, launching the World Conference for Peace. To a great extent, this movement followed the mobilisation strategies, discourses and formulas that the women's antifascist movement had developed since the 1930s in the melting pot that was antifascism and feminism. Geopolitical changes related to the Cold War's outbreak travestied the legacy of feminist pacifism and even of antifascism. However, neither the ambiguity nor the potential of this marriage between antifascism and feminism (which led to the creation of the WIDF in 1945) would wear out in this strategy of confrontation between the two superpowers. Much of the energy of these women would be channelled into anti-colonial struggles of the so-called 'Third World', where the WIDF represented an important tool for the empowerment of many women who campaigned for both national liberation and for their emancipation as women. The 'southbound' migration of discourses and strategies of women's antifascism, which became anti-imperialist and feminist, is a story that is yet to be written.[46]

Translated by Mathieu Franks and Sonia Izrar, revised by
Casey Sellarole

Notes

1. Carol Ehrlich, 'The Unhappy Marriage of Marxism and Feminism: Can It Be Saved?', in Lydia Sargent (ed.), *Women and Revolution*, Boston, 1981; Batya Weinbaum, *The Curious Courtship of Women's Liberation and Socialism*, Boston, 1978.
2. Christine Bard, *Les filles de Marianne. Histoire des féminismes, 1914–1940*, Paris, 1995; Mercedes Yusta, 'La construcción de una cultura política femenina desde el antifascismo (1934–1950)', in Ana Aguado and Teresa Ortega (eds), *Feminismos y antifeminismos. Culturas políticas e identidades de género en la España del siglo XX*, Valencia, 2011, 253–81.
3. Marilyn J. Boxer, 'Rethinking the Socialist Construction and International Career of the Concept of "Bourgeois Feminism"', *American Historical Review* 112(1) (2007), 131–58.
4. 'Réinventer l'antifascisme au féminin: la Fédération Démocratique Internationale des Femmes et le début de la Guerre Froide', *Témoigner entre histoire et mémoire. Revue pluridisciplinaire de la Fondation Auschwitz*, nº 104, Dossier 'L'antifascisme revisité. Histoire – Idéologie – Mémoire', 2009, 91–104.

5. Johanna Alberti, 'British Feminists and Anti-fascism in the 1930s', in Sybil Oldfield (ed.), *This Working-Day World: Women's Lives and Culture(s) in Britain, 1914–1945*, London, 2003, 112–24; Julie Gottlieb, 'Varieties of Feminist Response to Fascism in Inter-War Britain', in Nigel Copsey and Andrzej Olechnowicz (eds), *Varieties of Anti-Fascism: Britain in the Inter-War Period*, Basingstoke, 2010, 101–18.
6. Yves Santamaria, 'Un prototype toutes missions: le Comité de lutte contre la guerre, dit "Amsterdam–Pleyel"', 1932–1936', *Communisme* 18–19 (1988), 71–97.
7. Emmanuelle Carle, 'Women, Anti-fascism and Peace in Interwar France: Gabrielle Duchêne's Intinerary', *French History* 18(3) (2004), 291–314; Norman Ingram, 'Gender and the Politics of Pacifism: Feminist Pacifism and the Case of the French Section of the Women's International League for Peace and Freedom', in Eva Schöck-Quinteros et al., *Politische Netzwerkerinnen: Internationale Zusammenarbeit von Frauen, 1830–1960*, Berlin, 2007, 267–85.
8. Irene Falcón, *Asalto a los cielos. Mi vida con Pasionaria*, Madrid, 1996.
9. Santamaria, 'Un prototype toutes missions'.
10. Bruno Groppo, 'Fascismes, antifascismes et communismes', in Michel Dreyfus et al. (eds), *Le siècle des communismes*, Paris, 2000, 502; Gilles Vergnon, *L'antifascisme en France, de Mussolini à Le Pen*, Rennes, 2009.
11. Christine Bard, 'La crise du féminisme en France dans les années trente', *Les cahiers du CEDREF* [online] 4–5 (1995), accessed 27 February 2010, http://cedref.revues.org/291.
12. Sîan Reynolds, 'The Lost Generation of French Feminists? Anti-fascist Women in the 1930s', in *Women's Studies International Forum* 23(6) (December 2000), 679–88. See Louis-Pascal Jacquemond, 'Irene Joliot-Curie, une féministe engagée?', *Genre & Histoire* [online] 11 (Autumn 2012), http://genrehistoire.revues.org/1796.
13. Norman Ingram, *The Politics of Dissent: Pacifism in France, 1919–1939*, Oxford, 1991, 275 and 277.
14. 'La protection de la mère et de l'enfant en URSS – les cliniques d'avortement (par Margarita Nelken)', *Femmes dans l'action mondiale* 20 (20 April – 5 May 1936).
15. *Femmes dans l'action mondiale* 14 (November–December 1935).
16. Bernadette Cattanéo, 'Notre route…', *Femmes dans l'action mondiale* 9, 15 May – 15 June 1935.
17. Ibid.
18. 'Égalité des droits politiques: les opinions de Marcel Cachin (sénateur de la Seine, directeur de l'Humanité) et de Bossoutrot (le grand aviateur, candidat du parti radical-socialiste)', *Femmes dans l'action mondiale* 20 (20 April – 5 May 1936).
19. Bard, *Les filles de Marianne*, 299.
20. Clara Campoamor, *El voto femenino y yo. Mi pecado mortal*, Barcelona, 1981. María Martinez Sierra (María Lejárraga), *Una mujer por caminos de España. Recuerdos de propagandista*, Buenos Aires, 1952.
21. See chapter in this volume by Hugo García.
22. Yusta, 'La construcción de una cultura política femenina'.

23. Falcón, *Asalto a los cielos*.
24. 'Les Espagnoles aux prises avec la Garde Civile', *Femmes dans l'action mondiale* 2 (October 1934).
25. '¡Abajo la guerra imperialista! Imponente manifestación de mujeres contra la guerra y el fascismo', *Mundo Obrero*, 25 August 1934.
26. 'Contre le fascisme, aide et droit d'asile', *Femmes dans l'action mondiale* 3 (November 1934).
27. Dolores Ibárruri, 'Organicemos a la mujer para la lucha', *Mujeres. Portavoz de las mujeres antifascistas* 3 (1 May 1936), 2.
28. Bernadette Cattanéo, 'Si les femmes votaient', *Femmes dans l'action mondiale* 19 (6–20 April 1936).
29. Danièle Bussy Genevois, 'Citoyennes de la Seconde République', in Marie-Aline Barrachina et al. (eds), *Femmes et démocratie. Les Espagnoles dans l'espace public (1868–1978)*, Nantes, 2007, 129–45.
30. *Femmes dans l'Action Mondiale* 19 (6–20 April 1936).
31. Ibid. 20 (20 April – 5 May 1936).
32. Ingram, *The Politics of Dissent*, 310.
33. Mary Nash, *Defying Male Civilisation: Women in the Spanish Civil War*, Denver, 1995.
34. Martha A. Ackelsberg, *Free Women of Spain: Anarchism and the Struggle for the Emancipation of Women*. Bloomington, IN, 1991.
35. Geoff Eley, *Forging Democracy: The History of the left in Europe, 1850–2000*, Oxford and New York, 2002.
36. Renée Rousseau, *Les femmes rouges. Chronique des années Vermeersch*, Paris, 1983.
37. *Contre le fascisme, pour la paix et le bonheur, réalisons l'Union des Femmes de tous les pays! Premier Congrès National Paris, 17–20 June 1945*, Union des Femmes Françaises, Paris, 1945, 35–36.
38. Mercedes Yusta, *Madres coraje contra Franco. La Union de Mujeres Españolas en Francia, del antifascismo a la guerra fria*, Madrid, 2009.
39. 'Informe de Charlotte Muret sobre el Congreso de la Alianza Internacional de Mujeres. Lausanne, 19 agosto 1946', Organizaciones de mujeres, box 118, file 5, Archivo Histórico del PCE, Madrid.
40. 'Discussion relative au rapport de Dolores Ibárruri sur la réorganisation des associations féminines internationales.' Journée du 14 octobre 1946. Organizaciones de mujeres, box 116, file 10, Archivo Histórico del PCE (French original).
41. Ibid.
42. 'Informe de Dolores Ibárruri en el C. E. de Moscú (septiembre 1946) sobre la reorganización de organizaciones de mujeres como la Alianza Internacional de Mujeres o la LIFPL', Organizaciones de Mujeres, box 116, file 10, Archivo Histórico del PCE.
43. 'Comité Exécutif de la FDIF. Intervention de Mme Dolores Ibárruri. Stockholm, 20 au 24 septembre 1947.' Organizaciones de mujeres, folder 116, file 10, Archivo Histórico del PCE (French original).
44. Michelle Riot-Sarcey, *Histoire du feminisme*, Paris, 2002, 96.
45. Ibid.

46. Jadwiga Pieper Mooney, 'Fighting Fascism and Forging New Political Activism: The Women's International Democratic Federation (WIDF) in the Cold War', in Jadwiga E. Pieper Mooney and Fabio Lanza (eds), *Decentering Cold War History: Local and Global Change*, London, 2012: 52–72; Francisca de Haan, 'Eugénie Cotton, Pak Chong-ae, and Claudia Jones: Rethinking Transnational Feminism and International Politics', *Journal of Women's History* 25(4) (2013), 174–89.

References

Ackelsberg, M.A. *Free Women of Spain: Anarchism and the Struggle for the Emancipation of Women*. Bloomington, IN, 1991.

Alberti, J. 'British Feminists and Anti-fascism in the 1930s' in S. Oldfield (ed.), *This Working-Day World: Women's Lives and Culture(s) in Britain, 1914–1945*. London, 2003, 112–24.

Bard, C. 'La crise du féminisme en France dans les années trente'. *Les cahiers du CEDREF* 4–5 (1995), online.

———. *Les filles de Marianne. Histoire des féminismes, 1914–1940*. Paris, 1995.

Boxer, M.J. 'Rethinking the Socialist Construction and International Career of the Concept of "Bourgeois Feminism"'. *American Historical Review* 112(1) (2007), 131–58.

Bussy Genevois, D. 'Citoyennes de la Seconde République', in M.-A. Barrachina et al. (eds), *Femmes et démocratie. Les Espagnoles dans l'espace public (1868–1978)*. Nantes, 2007.

Campoamor, C. *El voto femenino y yo. Mi pecado mortal*. Barcelona, 1981.

Carle, E. 'Women, Anti-fascism and Peace in Interwar France: Gabrielle Duchêne's Itinerary'. *French History* 18(3) (2004), 291–314.

Ehrlich, C. 'The Unhappy Marriage of Marxism and Feminism: Can It Be saved?', in L. Sargent (ed.), *Women and Revolution*. Boston, 1981.

Eley, G. *Forging Democracy: The History of the Left in Europe, 1850–2000*. Oxford and New York, 2002.

Falcón, I. *Asalto a los cielos. Mi vida con Pasionaria*. Madrid, 1996.

Gottlieb, J. 'Varieties of Feminist Response to Fascism in Inter-War Britain', in N. Copsey and A. Olechnowicz (eds), *Varieties of Anti-Fascism: Britain in the Inter-War Period*. Basingstoke, 2010, 101–18.

Groppo, B. 'Fascismes, antifascismes et communismes', in Michel Dreyfus et al. (eds), *Le siècle des communismes*. Paris, 2000.

Haan, F. de. 'Eugénie Cotton, Pak Chong-ae, and Claudia Jones: Rethinking Transnational Feminism and International Politics'. *Journal of Women's History* 25(4) (2013), 174–89.

Hähnel-Mesnard, C. (ed.). *Témoigner entre histoire et mémoire. Revue pluridisciplinaire de la Fondation Auschwitz*, nᵒ 104, Dossier 'L'antifascisme revisité. Histoire – Idéologie – Mémoire', 2009.

Ingram, N. *The Politics of Dissent: Pacifism in France, 1919–1939*. Oxford, 1991.

Jacquemond, L.-P. 'Irene Joliot-Curie, une féministe engagée?'. *Genre & Histoire* 11 (Autumn 2012), online.

Martinez Sierra, M.. (María Lejárraga). *Una mujer por caminos de España. Recuerdos de propagandista*. Buenos Aires, 1952

Nash, M. *Defying Male Civilisation: Women in the Spanish Civil War*. Denver, 1995.

Pieper Mooney, J. 'Fighting Fascism and Forging New Political Activism: The Women's International Democratic Federation (WIDF) in the Cold War', in J.E. Pieper Mooney and F. Lanza (eds), *De-centering Cold War History: Local and Global Change*. London, 2012, 52–72.

Reynolds, S. 'The Lost Generation of French Feminists? Anti-fascist Women in the 1930s', *Women's Studies International Forum* 23(6) (December 2000), 679–88.

Riot-Sarcey, M. *Histoire du feminisme*, Paris, 2002.

Rousseau, R. *Les femmes rouges. Chronique des années Vermeersch*. Paris, 1983.

Santamaria, Y. 'Un prototype toutes missions: le Comité de lutte contre la guerre, dit "Amsterdam–Pleyel", 1932–1936'. *Communisme* 18–19 (1988), 71–97.

Vergnon, G. *L'antifascisme en France, de Mussolini à Le Pen*. Rennes, 2009.

Weinbaum, B. *The Curious Courtship of Women's Liberation and Socialism*. Boston, 1978.

Yusta, M. *Madres coraje contra Franco. La Union de Mujeres Españolas en Francia, del antifascismo a la guerra fria*. Madrid, 2009.

———. 'La construcción de una cultura política femenina desde el antifascismo (1934–1950)', in A. Aguado and T. Ortega (eds), *Feminismos y antifeminismos. Culturas políticas e identidades de género en la España del siglo XX*. Valencia, 2011, 253–81.

Mercedes Yusta is full professor of Spanish History at the Université Paris VIII and member of the Institut Universitaire de France. She has published numerous books and articles on resistance to the Franco dictatorship, antifascist political culture and the political activism of Spanish women in the twentieth century. Her latest book is *Madres coraje contra Franco. La Unión de Mujeres Españolas en Francia, del antifascismo a la Guerra Fría* (Madrid, Cátedra, 2009).

PART TWO

POLITICAL USES, MEMORY WARS AND REVISIONISM FROM 1945 TO THE PRESENT

10

FROM *ANTIFASCISTAS* TO **PAF**

Lexical and Political Interpretations of American International
Brigaders in Spain during the Second World War

Robert S. Coale

Two thousand eight hundred Americans served in the International
Brigades (IB), predominantly in the anglophone Fifteenth Brigade.
Approximately two-thirds were members of the Communist Party
of the United States of America (CPUSA) or the Young Communist
League, the remaining third were Socialists, liberal democrats or from
other progressive backgrounds.[1] Once in Albacete, however, on their
military identity card, they were required to describe their political
party simply and invariably as '*Antifascista*'. In the following pages we
will study the ways in which, over the ensuing years, the term would
be used and interpreted by the American veterans of the International
Brigades.

From a purely lexical standpoint there does not seem to be a clear
definition for the term 'antifascist'. The *Webster's New World Dictionary
of the American Language* does not include the word 'antifascism', although it does show a definition for 'anti-Semitism'. The same work,
however, defines fascism as:

> (1) n. The doctrines, methods, or movement of the Fascisti. (2) a system of
> government characterized by rigid one-party dictatorship, forcible sup-
> pression of opposition, private economic enterprise under centralised
> governmental control, belligerent nationalism, racism, and militarism,
> etc. first instituted in Italy in 1922. (3) a. A political movement based on
> such doctrines and policies. b. fascist behavior. See also Nazi.[2]

Logically then, anyone opposed to one or all of these policies could
consider himself an antifascist in a generic sense. We will see, however, that the meaning attached to the concept by American IB volunteers was more complex. Under this banner the Americans served in

Spain from Jarama in February 1937 until withdrawn by decision of Prime Minister Juan Negrín at the end of September 1938. They became known as the Lincolns, from the name given to their first battalion, and were present on many fronts and in different capacities, from soldiers to doctors and nurses to drivers and mechanics. It was in Spain, in fact, that they honed their antifascism.

Some historians, such as Cecil Eby,[3] argue that the term 'antifascist' was adopted mainly to whitewash the overwhelming predominance of Communists in the brigades. While membership in the party was widespread amongst volunteers, that rigid interpretation denies the fact that there were different motivations for heading to Spain. Communists were antifascists, but so were men and women who claimed other affiliations. This was also true of volunteers from other countries. Communist Party or youth organisation membership accounted for a maximum of 58 per cent of the French contingent, the largest of any nationality at approximately nine thousand volunteers.[4] Here also, *antifascisme* was not an abstract label, but rather a reflexion of political tensions of the period and was heartfelt across party lines.[5] For Rémi Skoutelsky, who has studied this contingent in depth, there were undeniably two dimensions to the French concept of *antifascisme*: one was domestic, a struggle against the extreme right wing at home, and the other was international – hostility towards Mussolini, Hitler and then Franco.[6] Similar concerns apply to the American volunteers. Some cite a desire to fight Hitler or Mussolini, whereas others stress home-grown American racism and injustice as their motivations. In fact, beginning in 1934–35, the Communists were supporting the Popular Front policy, in France, Spain, the United States and across the globe, in order to create a wider base of appeal. Underlining those efforts of the CPUSA to reach out, Peter Carroll states that:

> the influence of the Popular Front ... [was far reaching]. By linking a radical outlook to familiar American values, the Communist movement literally popularised awareness of the dangers of fascism to world peace. Indeed, most future Lincoln volunteers joined the Communist Party or one of its affiliated groups during the era of the Popular Front.[7]

Given the varied backgrounds of the American contingent, this policy fitted like a glove. The party was active on issues such as ending Jim Crow laws and racial discrimination, demanding better rights and paid vacations for workers, strengthening unions, and fighting evictions, for example. These were all policies that appealed to different sectors of the radical movement much beyond the limits of the CPUSA. More than a catchy phrase in order to camouflage the dominance of the Communist

Party, the term antifascist was an expression of the reality of the Popular Front and the appeal of its struggles in a wider arena.

In December 1937, a veterans' association was established in New York, with the stated objectives of assisting wounded volunteers with medical care, supporting Republican Spain, and aiding 'the peace and antifascist movement'.[8] This organisation, known as the Veterans of the Abraham Lincoln Brigade, or simply VALB, became a rallying point for former Lincolns and their causes. Even over the last tragic months of the Second Spanish Republic, between the end of 1938 and the early months of 1939, from across the Atlantic the former American IBers continued to labour on behalf of their Spanish antifascist comrades. Their efforts – for example, attempting to lift the arms embargo, picketing the Italian Embassy in Washington to denounce Mussolini's intervention, and endeavouring to hire a ship to transport Spanish Loyalist refugees from North Africa to Latin America – prove that their antifascism continued after their repatriation, a fact that highlights their struggle as a global one whose defining characteristics were not limited to Spain.[9]

The signing of the Molotov–Ribbentrop Pact, in August 1939, inaugurated a strenuous period for VALB. Echoing the new Communist Party line, the war in Europe was labelled 'The Second Imperialist War' in *The Volunteer for Liberty*, the official bulletin published for and by veterans.[10] Notwithstanding the apparent policy change, the word 'antifascist' did not disappear entirely from print. An article focusing on European IB veterans interned in France appeared in the bulletin in early 1940. It is interesting to note that the reference to fascism and antifascists are still set in a Spanish context, but used here to underline the difference between the war that ended on 1 April 1939 and the one that began six months later:

> The presence of these prisoners in the concentration camps is a constant embarrassment to the French Government. No one will now believe that the present war in Europe is a continuation of Spain's struggle against fascism. If it were, these tested anti-fascist fighters would be treated as heroes, not as common criminals![11]

This strict party line seconded by VALB was a disappointment to some veterans who severed ties with the organisation completely, but others remained active and managed to show their disagreement in original fashion.

Jack Shafran, veteran Lincoln brigader and party member since 1933, was dissatisfied with the policy because he saw the Second World War as a continuation of the struggle begun in 1936. Bucking the party line, he voluntarily joined the US Army in the spring 1941. Although castigated for it, his excellent record in Spain protected him. He even annoyed comrades by wearing his new uniform to veterans' events and anti-war demonstrations.[12] Such independent action was a rarity, and it was not until after June 1941 that many Lincoln veterans began volunteering for service in the armed forces, a trend that increased after the United States declared war in December. Unbeknownst to all but a few high-ranking Communists, while the party was denouncing an Imperialist War, Milton Wolff was recruiting IBers living in the United States for covert operations in Europe on behalf of British intelligence.[13] Well before the German invasion of the Soviet Union, many saw, at least unofficially, that the continuation of their antifascism would lead them to participate actively in the Second World War. In fact, once the ambiguity vanished due to the German invasion of the USSR, at least 425 ex-Lincolns served in the armed forces of the United States between 1941 and 1945. Another one hundred joined the Merchant Marine.[14]

A number of ex-Lincolns had positive initial experiences in the army and discovered that many soldiers were interested to learn from their tempering. Lou Gordon, who volunteered several months prior to Pearl Harbor, found he was sought out by both enlisted men and officers alike. In a letter from October 1941 he wrote:

> The command here knows I was in Spain and it does not work to my disadvantage. In fact, I was kept over in this training camp as part of the cadre ... Most of the men and officers, with some exceptions naturally, have a very healthy attitude on the Spanish war and discuss it freely.[15]

In another letter a few weeks later he informed VALB that, due to its popularity, he had been obliged to establish a waiting list to read *Men in Battle* (1939), the chronicle of the Americans in Spain by Lincoln novelist and future member of the Hollywood Ten Alvah Bessie, and that his captain was 'thrilled and shocked' by it. He requested VALB to send him a copy of *In Place of Splendor* written by Constancia de la Mora, former head of the Foreign Press Office in Loyalist Spain and wife of Ignacio Hidalgo de Cisneros, commander of the Loyalist Air Force.[16] In the same letter, Gordon also mentioned participating in a public debate on Hemingway's *For Whom the Bell Tolls* (1940).[17] It is apparent from these comments and requests that he did not hide his participation in the Spanish conflict. In fact, it seems to have been an open topic that interested many, at least for the moment, although we do not know if, while in uniform, Gordon openly referred to himself as an antifascist.

Other lucky veterans had similar experiences early in the American war effort. A select few found their way into combat units and fought on the front lines as early as 1942, earning praise, commendations, battlefield commissions and notoriety. These men somehow managed to join the armed forces without their prior service in Spain attracting special attention. The cases of Robert Thompson and Herman Bottcher, who had been officers in Spain, are well known. In the Asian–Pacific theatre of operations, between the two, they won three Distinguished Service Crosses, the second highest military award in the United States, just under the Congressional Medal of Honor.

As months went by and more veterans volunteered or were drafted into service, they corresponded frequently with the VALB office in New York. Some indications of their experience in Spain became apparent in amusing ways. Although few veterans had become fluent in Castilian, two years of contact with the local language appear to have left a mark on their phraseology. Lincoln veteran letters are sprinkled with Spanish words such as *hola, amigo, camarada, hasta luego, hasta la vista, avión* and *vino*. More often than not, in place of a closing salutation in English, letters end with *salud, salud y victoria, salud y República* and even an amusing reminder of the shortages endured in their previous service, *salud y tabaco*. This use of Spanish, by men who were far from fluent in the language, became a code and a bond shared by the few who had previously taken steps to thwart the rise of fascism. A couple of Spanish words sufficed to remind them of their common antifascist roots and illustrate their uniqueness.

Some veterans found that, in addition to combat experience, an odd expression or two and a vigorous antifascism, their service in Spain left them with a few ingrained habits that were potentially troublesome, especially for those who had not made their previous commitment well known. Ed Lending included the following anecdote in a letter written in January 1943. He mentioned that he thought he would be a model soldier if he were not so absent-minded. Speaking of a recent inspection he wrote:

The door flew open. In strode the Top Sarge, Two Looeys, and the Battery Captain.

'Attention!' I barked as I snapped into same and saluted briskly.

Holding the salute, I sounded off stentorially, 'Sir, Private Lending in charge of Hut 13'.

I saw consternation capture every face in the hut – officers and bunkmates! For what couldn't have been more than 10 seconds – but what felt like many hours – I was just deeply bewildered.

AND THEN I KNEW...

> The brisk salute I was holding ended in a clenched fist. So help me modesto.

> Thus ended the cosy anonymity I had been enjoying. What probably saved my soul from being dispatched by the firing squad at dawn was the fact that I reported I.B. experience at the induction center. So it was on my service record which had been transmitted here and my explanation was plausible, if not relished.[18]

By the time Lending's Popular Front salute, a physical manifestation of his antifascism, had involuntarily drawn the attention of his commanders, a considerable number of ex-Lincolns had entered the service, and, unlike earlier enlistees, as early as the spring 1942 many began to complain that they were not receiving equal treatment. As the months passed and the grievances accumulated, the veterans became convinced that they were suffering from specific discrimination in the armed forces due to their previous antifascist stance.

The case of William Aalto is a powerful example. Aalto had commanded the successful guerrilla raid in May 1938 that liberated 308 Loyalist prisoners from the fortress of Corchuna in Motril, Andalusia. He joined the US Army in late 1941. In March of the next year he wrote to a former veteran who also had served with the guerrillas in Spain:

> I have asked insistently verbally to be put into combat and then last month made a written request volunteering for combat duty in reconnaissance citing honestly my experience and the fact that I had a good record in the Spanish Army.

> But it seems I am on the FBI shit-list or else the Army's own black list. I have been kept here, used as a line corporal without the rank, etc.; while other guys, just as capable or even less, have gone on into regular divisions from this training center ...

> It seems here at least, that if you fought against Hitler in Spain, you are regarded as an enemy.[19]

Similarly, in a letter to Moe Fishman in August 1942, Dan Fitzgerald expressed his frustration and bewilderment at the army's refusal to allow him to attend bombardier training, despite achieving high test scores. Like Aalto, he was sure he was being discriminated against specifically because of his past. The following excerpt from one letter illustrates the plight and desires of many disregarded ex-Lincolns yearning for another crack at their enemies and baffled by the army's unwillingness to use their skills. In addition to denouncing an injustice, he went further and identified those he saw as obstructing social and military progress on many fronts. This revealing passage presents both military and political aspects of the antifascist struggle. On the one hand there was a war to win, but unfortunately there were also those at home who were undermining the endeavour:

> Why the hell should I be denied a job I am qualified for just because I am a militant anti-fascist? The rightfully necessary laws and regulations against the 5th column are being subverted by appeasers and defeatists to wreck morale, and [the] fighting unity of our army ... We are fighting a 2 front war. One, against the axis armies, and secondly against all appeasing, defeatist, confusionist policies that hamstring our efforts for Victory – for example the fight against Jim Crow, for a mixed regiment, for the 2nd Front, for production, etc. etc.[20]

Another Lincoln veteran, John Lucid, received a different type of special treatment. It was not the lack of access to a combat unit, but rather the company he was forced to keep that dissatisfied him most. He was relegated to a quartermaster unit in the remote Camp Ripley in Minnesota, which was filled with undesirable elements, mainly draftees of German and Italian ancestry who did not hide their anti-Semitism or their esteem for the Axis powers. He wrote:

> Altho I knew the outfit here was a Quartermaster company, even truck driving or warehousing is better than sitting on your ass – if you can't stay in a combat outfit. However, I hadn't looked forward to being in the Wehrmacht.[21]

As an ex-Lincoln he could not accept being banished to such a remote base and condemned to spend the war with such an objectionable crowd. Actually, several other comrades from Spain ended up in the same camp, a fact that illustrates that Lucid's exclusion was hardly an isolated incident. His further remarks attest to his exasperation:

> So, naturally it is necessary that these Nazi sympathisers and so on be put on ice. I would even say they are getting too good a deal here, as most of them are quite glad to be out of danger. There is little enough to do, and the sonsofbitches are far from downhearted. But of course [we], the handful of antifascists, want to do our part in the war and hate like hell to rub elbows with such a bunch.[22]

Both Lucid and Fitzgerald refer specifically to their antifascism in their denunciation of a system that they perceived to be working against them, a situation that was preventing them from carrying out the role they deemed prepared to accept. Both ex-Lincolns used the term 'antifascist' in contraposition to the Nazi sympathisers, the Fifth Column, the appeasers and the defeatists they had seen amongst them. They believed in action, but were being 'put on ice' and, in some cases, forced to serve with those they saw as their enemies.

The number of cases grew and a pattern was soon seen. Milton Wolff was convinced by early 1943 that the discrimination was not by chance or accident, but rather an explicit ban on sending Lincoln veterans overseas.[23] Like others had surmised earlier, the IB veterans were singled out for limited service exclusively on the mainland. Those who had been accepted into special services or Officer Candidate School were systematically held back, despite high examination scores and enthusiastic recommendations from their commanding officers. John Gates, former political commissar of the Fifteenth International Brigade, summed up the situation in a 1943 letter: 'While our armed forces are preparing for the invasion of Europe, I have been assigned the task of supervising spring cleaning and the planting of grass'.[24]

The official response to complaints at the time was to point to the cases of Herman Bottcher and Robert Thompson, their combat exploits and the medals they had earned in New Guinea, as proof that the claims of discrimination were unfounded. However, recent historical research has debunked that interpretation and has proved that the systematic discrimination against the ex-Lincolns was part of official policy against 'potentially subversive personnel'.[25]

This political scheme made poor use of an exceptional group of men who had rare first-hand experience fighting against the weapons and tactics of the German and Italian armies, but who were mistrusted due to their left-wing politics. The term used to identify them, however, carried more of a chronological than a political connotation. They were singled out as 'Premature Anti-Fascists', or PAF. According to this curious label, they were suspect, perhaps not for having fought fascism, but rather for having done so a bit too early. As we have illustrated, this policy of segregation and discrimination continued well after the Soviet Union entered the war with the Allies against Nazi Germany, a confirmation of its inherently political basis, despite the seemingly chronological veneer of the reprimand.

The Lincoln veterans in the United States armed forces did not limit their complaints to letters to the VALB office. They had attempted to resolve their problems through proper channels, but had got nowhere. Faced with official immobility, Daniel Fitzgerald, in the letter quoted above, urged the VALB executive board to take the matter up as early as August 1942.[26] Others made similar suggestions over the following months. Accordingly, in the spring of 1943, Jack Bjoze, then chairman of VALB, travelled to Washington where he requested that the Lincoln veterans be given the privilege of serving on the battlefield. Three Congressmen formally called upon the War Department to look into and resolve the matter, but Secretary of the Army Robert Patterson refuted the complaints as unfounded rumours. The matter received widespread attention only after a syndicated columnist, Drew Pearson, denounced the apparent policy in the *Washington Post*.[27] Shortly after the story broke, the sergeant turned gardener, John Gates, mentioned: 'The ... column stirred up a lot of understandable comment here. The reaction was one of surprise, bewilderment and anger'.[28] This remark tends to confirm earlier statements by Lou Gordon that Lincoln veterans were respected, and even supported, by their fellow soldiers who did not understand why experienced men were not granted active frontline duty. Due to the sudden and unexpected publicity, limitations affecting the veterans began to recede. Soon afterwards, many Lincoln veterans saw their requests for transfers accepted. Finally, many found themselves assigned to front line combat units in Europe and the Pacific, just as they had desired.

Once abroad and in combat, the former Lincolns continued to correspond with the VALB office to recount their adventures. Whereas in their letters written stateside to denounce discrimination, references to their prior experience were cloaked in neutral language – for example 'Spain', 'the Spanish Army' or 'I.B. experience' appear more frequently than the term 'antifascist' when recounting conversations with their commands – once returned to the front, however, they seem to have been transformed. Although now members of US Army, they naturally recalled their previous battles. Their correspondence was now peppered with references to the antifascist struggle of their earlier war. One veteran who fought in North Africa wrote of his happiness at being back in the fight: 'I wouldn't miss this present experience for anything in the world. It's a continuation of our former experiences'.[29]

Lieutenant Larry Cane, the only Lincoln veteran to wade ashore in Normandy on 6 June 1944, described his role in the breakout near St. Lô, for which he was subsequently awarded a Silver Star, as follows: 'We went into the action riding the tanks – you know the way the Russians do it in the movies. If you were at Fuentes de Ebro, you saw the 24th Battalion [of the Fifteenth Brigade] try to pull the same stunt'.[30] Dan Fitzgerald, in trying to explain the muddy conditions in France in the late autumn of 1944, wrote: 'Right now am in mud and all its miseries – very much like Jarama, only the intensity is such that one is unable to express it adequately'.[31]

For the ex-Lincolns who managed to see combat, participating in the destruction of Nazi Germany and Imperial Japan were thrilling moments which perhaps compensated to some extent for their defeat in Spain. Furthermore, finding comrades who shared the same interpretation of the war and similar ideals was a rare and special experience that they highly appreciated. A letter that Archie Brown wrote to his wife from Germany reveals the difference between the average comrade in arms and a superb one that went beyond defeating the enemy:

> When I joined up with this company I found some people who not only didn't have use for Heinies as such – but were anti-Fascists. They seem to understand what has happened. I'm going to like being with this company. They share everything between themselves – packages, food, etc. It reminds me so much of the Brigaders.[32]

The Lincoln brigaders considered themselves antifascists in Spain and also in the Second World War. Reading between the lines of many letters, it is apparent that the term 'antifascist' meant something more than simply identifying an enemy. It implied a different mindset, an 'understanding' of the reasons the war had to be waged and won. It also meant adopting comradely behaviour. These key factors, expressed in different forms, are repeated often in veterans' writings and interpretations of events. To the Lincoln veterans, not every combat soldier fighting the Axis powers was automatically an antifascist. It was a label that had to be earned, an honour that was extended sparingly.

Dan Fitzgerald, despite not gaining access to bombardier school, did end up seeing a considerable amount of combat between 1942 and 1945. As first a private and then a sergeant in the Ninth Infantry Division, he fought in North Africa, Sicily, France and Germany. In fact, he is probably one of the Lincoln veterans with the longest combat record in the Second World War. On his trek, he occasionally came across Spanish Loyalist exiles and IB veterans, events he duly mentioned in letters to New York. On one memorable page, he linked his present situation to an episode in Spain and then recounted meeting former Spanish sailors now in a different line of work. 'We are doing a Jarama' was his way of describing the stalled front in Tunisia at the time. He then further strengthened the connection to his first war: 'Ran into a bunch of former *marineros* now with the English commandos – seems that they are doing partisan work. Good boys *who know the score*'.[33] Here again we see the idea of grasping the reasons and objectives of the war as a paramount concern that separates a few special combatants from the average soldier. Several months later, he met more Loyalist exiles, not surprising considering the thousands who had sought refuge in French North Africa at the close of the Civil War in 1939. After the victory at Bizerte in May 1943, he mentioned other Spanish refugees in Tunisia: 'The spirit of these anti-fascists is grand, a tonic to the humdrum of life and faint hearts'.[34]

Milton Wolff, whose Second World War career was varied and adventurous, summarised his disappointment with the OSS in an autobiographical novel manuscript describing those years, the title of which is, unsurprisingly, *The Premature Anti-Fascist*. The following excerpt spells out that merely defeating the Axis powers was not the only concern, and echoes comments of other ex-Lincolns:

> Goff had called from Virginia telling me that I had gotten him and Aalto and the others into this OSS deal and here they were in training along with a motley assortment of characters, monarchists, capitalists, and such, characters dispossessed by the Nazi occupiers of their respective countries, whose only motive was to recapture their former possessions and positions of power – possibly as fascistic as their usurpers, *definitely not anti-fascist in the same way as our bunch.*[35]

For Dan Fitzgerald, Milt Wolff, Archie Brown and other Lincoln veterans, their version of an antifascist was a rarity in the army. Such a soldier was more than just an enemy of the Axis. He was determined, politically astute, and showed solidarity with his comrades. It is interesting to note that this definition does not seem to be related to any particular party affiliation, but rather more to the manner in which the battle was carried out and how its final objective was interpreted.

As victory in Europe approached, yet another distinction between ex-Lincolns and the average Allied soldier, not to mention the Allied Command, appeared and can be considered another element in their definition of an antifascist. These men obviously felt that since their stance as antifascists began in the war against Franco, the struggle could not end simply because the Allies were about to win the war against Berlin. They had to carry on until the despised *Generalísimo* was ousted and democracy returned to Spain. In December 1944, Leonard Lamb, then VALB executive secretary, formalised the postwar objectives of the organisation and their determined stance in an interview with Art Shields: 'This war must not come again … That means that the Franco regime must not be left to sow the seeds of fascism in Europe and Latin America. The veterans are determined to help bring freedom to Spain in order to make freedom safe for the rest of the world'.[36]

The Second World War ended with the defeat of Nazi Germany, Fascist Italy and Imperial Japan. The Lincoln veterans were proud to have participated in the victory, but were saddened that the removal of Franco was not on the agenda. Despite this setback, they continued their particular struggle against fascism in different forms over the postwar years. In an article from 1946, Milt Wolff celebrated the recent victory and honoured the role that IB veterans across Europe had played in the liberation of their respective homelands such as Norway, France, Denmark, Poland, Greece, Italy and Germany. He also echoed the goal of ridding Spain of the Franco regime, and adroitly used terminology born of the victories in Europe and Japan to link the future of Spain to the recent campaigns, and to encourage one more effort:

> There can be no question of our IB'ers [sic] resting on their laurels while fascism still exists in Spain... or elsewhere. They and we have shared in our V-E and V-J days ... Now, all together, we fight alongside the men and women of Spain for a V-Spain day ... but soon. The next convention of the IB's must take place in MADRID![37]

In fact, the truth that the International Brigade veterans were unable to celebrate the return of democracy and peace to Spain until after the death of the hated dictator was a great disappointment. As far as the American IB veterans were concerned, the changes in the postwar political arena turned their (premature) antifascism into a serious social handicap. Government efforts to suppress their radical agenda such as investigations by the House Un-American Activities Committee and by the infamous Senator Joseph McCarthy silenced many left-wingers and forced others to go underground. Accordingly, the paths taken by IB veterans after 1945 were varied, but they remained convinced antifascists.

One ex-Lincoln who had spent two years as a prisoner of war was Milt Felsen. In his memoirs he remembered his thoughts at the close of the Second World War, and of his urge to find a new method to further his beliefs: 'Part of me wanted to continue the search for answers. Was my anti-Fascism just another way to justify war? I didn't think so. I knew I would do it all over again. But that was a kind of cop-out too. There must be a way to oppose war *and* fascism, both at the same time'.[38]

In fact, Felsen was not alone. Many other veterans furthered their political beliefs in this period by shifting their activities. Having witnessed and participated in two armed conflicts, they now chose, instead, to protest war. In this way, the declarations of Leonard Lamb in December 1944, when he warned of a fascist threat in Latin America if Franco were allowed to continue governing in Spain, foreshadowed VALB's concerns. The Lincoln veterans continued to press for change in Spain, but at the same time they began to protest postwar military and political involvement by the United States abroad. As decades passed, their antifascism, born of the struggles at home and in Spain, would evolve into political activism and campaigns such as those against the Vietnam War and American meddling in Latin America.

From *antifascista*, to Premature Anti-Fascist, to Allied soldier and then even to *anti-imperialista*, the fight of the Lincoln brigaders was long and sinuous. What began in Spain was eventually carried over on a global scale between 1941 and 1945, and then beyond. Over the troubled decades of the 1930s and 1940s the meaning behind the word coined in Spain was used in different places and contexts and given various interpretations, but to the veterans the objectives were plain to see and the comrades were easily identified. As Boris Razon found when interviewing International Brigade veterans in 2001, they did not define their antifascism, rather to them it was obvious – a spontaneous reaction to the situation of the 1930s. A result of a long-term political commitment or a visceral reaction, it was never questioned as it seemed to explain itself.[39]

Notes

1. Peter N. Carroll, *The Odyssey of the Abraham Lincoln Brigade: Americans in the Spanish Civil War*, Stanford, CA, 1994, 19.
2. David B. Guralnik (ed.), *Webster's New World Dictionary of the American Language*, New York, 1972, 508.
3. Cecil Eby, *Between the Bullet and the Lie: American Volunteers in the Spanish Civil War*, New York, 1969, 19.
4. Rémi Skoutelsky, *L'Espoir guidait leurs pas: Les volontaires français dans les Brigades internationales, 1936–1939*, Paris, 1998, 332.
5. Skoutelsky, *L'Espoir guidait leurs pas*, 175–76.
6. Rémi Skoutelsky, 'Les volontaires français des Brigades internationales: Patriotisme et/ou intérnationalisme', in Serge Wolikow and Annie Bleton-Ruget (eds), *Antifascisme et Nation: Les gauches européenes au temps du Front populaire*, Dijon, 1998, 92.
7. Carroll, *The Odyssey*, 50.
8. Ibid., 219.
9. Ibid., 223.
10. *The Volunteer for Liberty* III(4) (April 1941), 2.
11. 'Conference sets tasks to free I.B. Veterans', *The Volunteer for Liberty: Organ of the Veterans of the Abraham Lincoln Brigade* [*circa* April 1940], 2.
12. Carroll, *The Odyssey*, 244.
13. Ibid., 244–48.
14. Ibid., 252.
15. Lou Gordon to 'Gentlemen', 13 October 1941. Abraham Lincoln Brigade Archives, Collection 69, 'Complaints of Discrimination during World War Two'. Tamament Library, New York University (hereafter: ALBA Col. 69).
16. Soledad Fox Maura, *Constancia de la Mora: esplendor y sombra de una vida española del siglo XX*. Salamanca, 2008, 31.
17. Lou Gordon to Moe [Fishman], 3 November 1941. ALBA Col. 69.
18. Peter N. Carroll, Michael Nash and Melvin Small (eds), *The Good Fight Continues: World War II Letters from the Abraham Lincoln Brigade*, New York, 2006, 60.
19. William Aalto to 'Goof' [probably fellow veteran Irving Goff], 8 March 1942. ALBA Col. 69.

20. Dan Fitzgerald to Moe [Fishman], 29 August 1942. ALBA Col. 69.
21. Carroll, Nash and Small, *The Good Fight Continues*, 71.
22. Ibid., 72.
23. Milton Wolff to Elsie, 18 April 1943. ALBA Col. 69.
24. John Gates to Jack Bjoze, 22 April 1943. ALBA Col. 69.
25. Carroll, *The Odyssey*, 262.
26. Dan Fitzgerald to Moe Fishman, 29 August 1942. ALBA Col. 69.
27. Carroll, *The Odyssey*, 263.
28. John Gates to Jack Bjoze, 22 April 1943. ALBA Col. 69.
29. Alexander Schwartzman to 'Vets', 2 February 1943. *The Good Fight Continues*, 156–57.
30. Larry Cane to Harold Smith, 5 October 1944. *The Good Fight Continues*, 204.
31. Dan Fitzgerald to Harold Smith, 24 October 1944. *The Good Fight Continues*, 205.
32. Archie Brown to Esther 'Hon' Brown, 12 March 1945. *The Good Fight Continues*, 211–12.
33. Dan Fitzgerald to Jack Bjoze, 13 March 1943. ALBA Col. 69 (our emphasis).
34. Ibid., 1 July 1943. ALBA Col. 69.
35. Milt Wolff, 'The Premature Anti-Fascist', manuscript, 102. The Milt Wolff Papers. Abraham Lincoln Brigade Archives, Collection 170. Tamiment Library, New York University (our emphasis).
36. Art Shiels, 'Heros of Two Wars Against Fascism', *The Worker*, 10 December 1944, 6–7.
37. Milton Wolff, 'The International Brigaders', *The Volunteer for Liberty* 6(12) (April 1946), 2.
38. Milt Felsen, *The Anti-Warrior: A Memoir*, Iowa City, 1989, 243.
39. Boris Razon, *Le temps d'un espoir*, mémoire de D.E.A. d'Histoire, Université de Paris I Panthéon Sorbonne, 2001, 68.

References

Carroll, P.N. *The Odyssey of the Abraham Lincoln Brigade: Americans in the Spanish Civil War*. Stanford, CA, 1994.

Carroll, P.N., M. Nash and M. Small (eds). *The Good Fight Continues: World War II Letters from the Abraham Lincoln Brigade*. New York, 2006.

Eby, C. *Between the Bullet and the Lie: American Volunteers in the Spanish Civil War*. New York, 1969.

Felsen, M. *The Anti-Warrior: A Memoir*. Iowa City, 1989.

Fox Maura, S. *Constancia de la Mora: esplendor y sombra de una vida española del siglo XX*. Salamanca, 2008 [English edn: *Constancia De La Mora in War and Exile: International Voice for the Spanish Republic*, Brighton, Sussex, 2006].

Guralnik, D.B. (ed.). *Webster's New World Dictionary of the American Language*. New York, 1972.

Razon, B. *Le temps d'un espoir*, mémoire de D.E.A. d'Histoire, Université de Paris I Panthéon Sorbonne, 2001.

Skoutelsky, R. *L'Espoir guidait leurs pas: Les volontaires français dans les Brigades internationales, 1936–1939*. Paris, 1998.

Skoutelsky, R. 'Les volontaires français des Brigades internationales: Patriotisme et/ou intérnationalisme' in Serge Wolikow et Annie Bleton-Ruget (dirs), *Antifascisme et Nation: Les gauches européenes au temps du Front populaire*. Dijon, Éditions Universitaires de Dijon, 1998.

Wolff, M. 'The International Brigaders', *The Volunteer for Liberty* 6(12) (April 1946).

Robert S. Coale is a professeur d'université (professor) of Hispanic studies at the Université de Rouen. He is a member of the Board of Governors of the Abraham Lincoln Brigade Archives and a contributor to *The Volunteer*. His research interests include the Spanish Civil War, the International Brigades, in particular the American contingent, the exile of Spanish Loyalists and their participation in the liberation of France. His current project deals with autobiographical accounts of the tumultuous twentieth century penned by Spanish exiles.

🎸 11

AN ANTIFASCIST POLITICAL IDENTITY?

On the Cult of Antifascism in the Soviet Union and
post-Socialist Russia

José María Faraldo

In this chapter I explore the uses and abuses of the concepts of 'fascism' and 'antifascism', with a focus on their persistence after the fall of Soviet system. The use of antifascism as a weapon against the opposition was frequent in the Soviet Union throughout the Communist era. Indeed, the public discourse during State Socialism was rich in ideologemes of hostility, hate-words such as 'revisionist', 'imperialist', 'bourgeois', 'cosmopolite', 'Trotskyite' and – of course – 'fascist'.[1] The Soviet Union developed after 1945 a political discourse of legitimation based upon the ideology of 'antifascism'.[2] Although there was an evident link between the old pre-war and postwar antifascism, it was really a new, different phenomenon. Discourses and rituals with their origins in the Spanish Civil War and in the politics of the Popular Fronts of the 1930s were merged to show that there were real reasons, of a defensive nature, for the dominion of the Communist Party. However, the foundational experience for this kind of antifascism was the Second World War, or rather the cult around this war. This legitimising construct lives on long after the end of the Soviet Union.

Fascism, Antifascism and the *Maidan* Revolution

In February 2014 a wave of protests in Ukraine, especially in the capital city of Kiev, against the president, Viktor Yanukovych, brought about a political revolution in the country. Protests began with marches against the president's decision not to sign an agreement with the European Union, but there was a wide consensus on denouncing corruption and economic stagnation.[3] On 20 February, after violent clashes at the *Maidan*, or Independence Square, with almost a hundred casualties, a provisional government took power formed by right-wing, centrist and moderate nationalist parties with ambivalent support from some right-wing radicals (the so-called 'Right Sector').[4]

Although the anti-Yanukovych protests had a broad social base, the composition of the new government, and some political errors committed by parliament (such as a bill banning Russian as co-official language, and the election of some neo-fascists to second-rank posts), immediately alienated many people in the east and south of the country. These parts of Ukraine were heavily Russian-speaking and more deeply influenced by the Soviet heritage than the central and western regions. Soon certain groups in Crimea began demonstrating against the so-called 'fascist regime' in Kiev, referring to the government that had arisen from the revolution. From the beginning, this government was considered illegal and illegitimate by many citizens in the south and west of the country, who had been brought up with the cult of antifascism and the sanctification of the fallen heroes of the Second World War.[5] At first, the situation was especially dangerous in Crimea. Some official buildings were seized and groups of Russian nationalists began to take actions in a dynamic that the weak central power in Kiev was unable to oppose. A covert Russian invasion ('the little green men'), combined with a fake referendum, resulted in the illegal annexation of Crimea and Sebastopol to Russia.

During this time, Russian president Vladimir Putin alleged that the danger of 'fascist organisations' seizing power in the capital, Kiev, was the main reason for acting on Crimea. He said he wanted to 'protect' Crimea's inhabitants against the 'fascists'. On 18 March 2014 Putin delivered a speech legitimating Russia's annexation of Crimea and Sebastopol.[6] The speech gave his version of the facts that led to the occupation of the territory, saying:

> I would like to reiterate that I understand those who came out on *Maidan* with peaceful slogans against corruption, inefficient state management and poverty. The right to peaceful protest, democratic procedures and elections exist for the sole purpose of replacing the authorities that do not satisfy the people. However, those who stood behind the latest events in Ukraine had a different agenda: they were preparing yet another government takeover; they wanted to seize power and would stop short of nothing. They resorted to terror, murder and riots. Nationalists, neo-Nazis, Russophobes and anti-Semites executed this coup. They continue to set the tone in Ukraine to this day.[7]

No matter how freely Russian Nazis may act in Russia, demonstrating and prosecuting foreigners, the problem for Vladimir Putin was that 'neo-Nazis' and 'anti-Semites' were on their own in the Ukraine. The presence of alleged Nazis in the government and in the streets of Ukraine was the best legitimation for his policy of imperial comeback.[8]

In the same speech, talking about Crimea, Putin said: 'I repeat, just as it has been for centuries, it will be a home to all the peoples living there. What it will never be and do is follow in Bandera's footsteps!' Putin thus used a well-established stereotype about the Ukraine: Stepan Bandera (1909–59), a Soviet public enemy, was the leader of the 'Ukrainian Rebel Army' (UPA), an interwar organisation of Ukrainian nationalists. Bandera was mainly to blame for taking Ukrainian nationalism towards right-wing radicalism and ethnic-cleansing politics during the 1940s.[9] The stereotype of the 'Banderites' (Bandera's followers) was still worse: they were alleged Nazi collaborators and, therefore, traitors to the Soviet people during the war. In this way Putin said he was 'saving them from the new Ukrainian leaders who are the ideological heirs of Bandera, Hitler's accomplice during World War II'.[10]

However, the accusations against the movement of the *Maidan* as being 'fascist' or 'fascist-led' were not new.[11] Still during the 'Orange Revolution' – the protests against the fraudulent Viktor Yanukovych's election in 2004 – pro-Russian media used the words 'orange fascists' in order to attack the pro-European demonstrators.

Since the beginning of the new wave of protests at the end of 2013, Communist organisations in the country have been using these terms for abusing the *Maidan*. In February 2014, the Communist deputies proposed a law 'forbidding neo-Nazi and neo-Fascist ideology', aimed to attack the many *Maidan* groups using right-wing or Ukrainian nationalist emblems.[12] *Kommunist*, the journal of the Ukrainian Communist Party, displayed a title in white letters on a red background with the Spanish phrase '*No pasarán*'.[13] On the same page were pictures of a demonstration by Eastern Ukrainian Communists with banners like 'No fascism! No nationalism!' Other illustrations showed the burning of a puppet with the face of Stepan Bandera.[14]

But the underlying idea was more complex than that, and beyond the voters or supporters of the Communists. As one author put it, the image of the *Maidan* that exists in the minds of many southern and eastern Ukrainians is that 'neo-fascists from western Ukraine want to force homosexuality throughout the whole [of] Ukraine, ruin the economy and spread anarchy with the support of the United States'.[15]

Anti-Ukrainian narratives disguised as antifascism have had a long tradition. In the Imperial Russian conception of Russia, the Ukrainians were 'little brothers', almost children who had to be taken care of by the Russians.[16] It was the image of a peasant folk, speaking a comic dialect and without an intelligentsia of its own. When the Ruthenian and then Ukrainian nationalism[17] came into being, the Russian imperial intellectuals developed a concept of Ukrainians as fanatical nationalists, anti-Russians and, still, little brothers.[18] This concept passed without transformation to the Bolsheviks, who had done everything during the Civil War to combat attempts for Ukrainian independence. In part, the succession of Stalinist waves of terror against the Ukraine had to do with this idea of Ukrainians as zealous nationalists, and the Communists' effort to destroy or discipline them. Stalinist imperialism, although allowing – and even promoting – ethnic differentiation, was above all Great-Russian. 'Ukraine and the other non-Russian republics remained distinctly different, albeit decidedly "junior brothers", in a Soviet family of nations.'[19]

But it was during the Second World War that the stereotype was strengthened, with Bandera's temporary cooperation with the Nazis and later, in the aftermath of the war, with Ukrainian armed resistance against the Soviets. The 'Banderites' stereotype was long lasting and was used, and abused, throughout Soviet times.[20] Firmly ingrained in the memory practices centred on the Second World War, prejudices against Ukrainian nationalism penetrated deep into Ukrainian society. And this was because Ukrainian nationalism was identified in a straight line with fascism.[21]

Soviet Constructs of Fascism

Pavel Tschornich's 'Historical-etymological Dictionary' (1993) defines the word 'fascism' as 'a form of open terrorist dictatorship of the most reactionary, chauvinist and aggressive part of the imperialist bourgeoisie, directed to the destruction of democracy, to the establishment of a regime of deep reaction and to the preparation of wars of aggression'.[22] This is, of course, the orthodox Marxist–Leninist view of the concept, drafted by Grigori Zinoviev, Georgi Dimitrov and the Communist International during the 1920s and 1930s.[23] The term quickly entered Russian political language. Vladimir Lenin used the word 'fascists' (*'fashisty'*) in an article published in 1921 and 'fascism' in another piece the next year.[24] The word appeared in *Pravda*, the party's newspaper, over and over again after 1922.[25] The satiric writers Ilia and Petroff used 'fascists' in 1923 in an opinion article for a Moscow newspaper.[26] The word became commonplace for attacking rival political movements

– not only those of a properly fascist nature – during the second half of the 1920s.[27] As David Priestland has written: 'the Comintern's sectarian "class against class" policy of 1928 was founded on a profound misinterpretation of Western politics. It assumed that the workers of the West were becoming more revolutionary; that capitalism was on the verge of collapse; and that fascism – the last gasp of a dying bourgeoisie – was a fleeting phenomenon that would soon crumble along with capitalism'.[28] Because fascism did not want to crumble, Communists were forced to change their politics without changing the definition of the problem. Not even during Hitler's rise to power in Germany, when it was clear that many workers turned to National Socialism, did the Comintern change its views on fascism.[29]

It is true that Communist intellectuals and politicians were the first to see fascism as a transnational phenomenon. For them, fascism was a global response by the bourgeoisie as a class to the socialist revolution of the future. It was a 'terrorist dictatorship of capital', and therefore combating fascism was seen as a general, international and, ultimately, collaborative task. Although the Soviet conception of fascism never really changed, after 1933 the harsh reality of the destruction of the German Communist Party led the Soviet Party to promote a new practical alliance with left-wing parties and movements.[30] Antifascism was, at this point, a tool to build consensus among Communists outside the Soviet Union and to mobilise the Western intelligentsia and left-wing unions for the defence of the Soviet Union. This was always one of the most important issues within the foreign policy of the USSR, which, to achieve this goal, used all the means available to the Communist movement as well those traditional to foreign policy. But in the 1930s this became essential, as there seemed to be a real danger of being attacked by Poland or Germany, and the international position of the Soviet Union was still weak.[31]

The practice of accusing someone of being a fascist as a way to delegitimise them began with the strategy against European social democrats in the interwar period. The so-called 'social-fascists' should be destroyed as 'traitors' to the working class.[32] Already in 1922, an article in *Pravda* attacked 'revisionists' for being only 'a step away from fascism'.[33]

The reconciliation with the social democrats under the 'Popular Front' strategy did not diminish the hate-speech against 'fascists', who were labelled as the Communist Party of the USSR wanted to define them. But, for a while, the target of these attacks was to change. The desperate situation of the Communists in Germany after 1933 and Hitler's seizure of power called for some kind of unity with other left-wing forces. Thus, *Pravda* spoke of the 'courage of the antifascists'.[34] 'Fascism' became again more specific as a form of invective, directed at real fascist movements. However, during the 'Great Terror' in 1937 people were most commonly subjected to repression under (false) accusations of being spies, Trotskyites or/and fascists. As a headline of *Pravda* clearly described it, 'There are no differences between fascists, Trotskyites and Zinovievites'.[35]

Popular Front's antifascism had a chance to break into the consciousness of the Soviet people by coinciding with the activism of world public opinion for the Spanish Republic during the Spanish Civil War. At a meeting of the executive committee of the Comintern, as early as 23 July 1936, Georgi Dimitrov spoke about the possibility of using the Spanish conflict for propaganda purposes.[36] Daniel Kowalsky speaks of 'five fundraising drives' and all 'sprung directly from the initiatives of the ECCI or CPUSSR'.[37]

Despite this elaborate operation, this was probably the first time in the Soviet Union when a State-run propaganda campaign about a foreign policy issue brought some kind of positive response from the population.[38] Well orchestrated by the Communist Party, the antifascist campaign took root in a popular mood of finding someone to blame for their daily hardships. Even popular culture reflected this. In a humorous 'Encyclopedia' published in the satirical journal *Krokodil*, the entry devoted to Spain defined the country as 'located on the Pyrenean peninsula, but at the moment, situated at the real centre of Europe'. The country was 'populated by Spaniards and fascist generals' and was visited by 'a lot of Fascist tourists heavily armed, mainly Germans and Italians'.[39] In this journal, the Kukryniksy – a collective of popular cartoonists – constructed from the first day of the Spanish war a catalogue of visual fascist stereotypes that they would use again during the Second World War.[40] Popular aspirations and dreams were projected against the surface of the Spanish Civil War: terrible, almost inhuman enemies were depicted on one side, and suffering, angelical victims on the other. However, the omnipresent official Soviet propaganda towards Spain moved certain people to have attitudes of resistance against it, identifying 'fascism' with a good cause because 'Franco's fascists' were beating the Communists[41] or complaining that 'your children don't see chocolate and butter, and we are sending these items to Spanish workers';[42] and even as a matter of anti-Semitism: 'In Spain there are many Yids'.[43]

'Fascism' became a common invective during these years.[44] Its abuse only stopped when, after signing the Soviet–German Non-aggression Pact, Soviet media avoided using the word.[45] Although after August

1939 there was no longer a positive image in the press of Hitler, at least not as an equal of Stalin or a 'friend' of the Soviet Union, the continuous verbal abuse and invectives against Nazi Germany – and to a lesser degree against Italy – ceased. For example, in the popular literary journal *Vokrug Sveta* ('Around the World') many articles were devoted to the Spanish war and argued against fascism until the signing of the pact.[46] After the August issue, the attacks ceased and were replaced by generic assaults against capitalism and imperialism. Also, Nikolai Shpanov's highly popular antifascist science fiction novel *The First Strike* (1939) was withdrawn from bookshops after the pact, as were many other antifascist books.[47] For a time, when the German Army and the Red Army met at the newly defined common border, within the divided and occupied Poland, the world had the impression that no one was able to stop these two totalitarian states. Soviet antifascism disappeared.

The German–Soviet pact introduced an element of distension between the fascist powers and the USSR – but only for two years, until 22 June 1941, when the Germans invaded the Soviet Union. The beginning of the confrontation is best described using, once again, a very popular Kukryniksy work: a poster showing an animalised and very mean-looking Hitler trespassing on the document of the Soviet–German Non-aggression Pact, destroying it, while a Red Army soldier stops him with a bayonet.[48] In the poster, Stalin's feeling of having been cheated was very well expressed.

As Hitler was identified with generic fascism, antifascism came to be the key concept in the war against him and his armies. Fascism was an ideology 'against humanity', 'against culture'; fascists were 'barbarians', they had 'nothing to offer to the workers'. A myriad of professional propagandists and agitators, who had fought since the revolution and throughout collectivisation for spreading the good news of Communism, translated their work into a nationalist vocabulary. Opposing fascism was now 'patriotic', as it had been during the Spanish Civil War, the 'Patriotic Antifascist War', as it was called.[49] This use crystallised, years after the conflict, in a real cult of the war.

Constructing the Cult of Antifascism

The Soviet state that survived Nazi barbarism built up its new identity and legitimacy on the traumatic war of 'national liberation'.[50] Soviet identity was shaped upon the image of the Red Army soldier who 'liberated Europe from the scourge of fascism'. Indeed the Red Army veterans were the only real mass movement in the Soviet Union during the

Stalin era and afterwards, at least until the environmental movements of the 1970s and 1980s.[51] But this was also united in a joint sequence with the martyrdom of civilians and with the fight of the Soviet partisans, understood as the embodiment of the Soviet people.

Nevertheless, the construction of an antifascist cult was not immediate. Just after the liberation of the territories, the first war remembrance policies were implemented. In some places this occurred even before the end of the conflict. Monuments were erected, commemorative tablets were set, and writers and historians began to write about the causes and developments of the war. The triumph of the USSR in the war also brought about the occupation and re-occupation of many territories: the Baltic states, Belarus and Western Ukraine, Moldavia and Bessarabia, Transcarpathia and East Prussia. These occupations were to mean a firm commitment to re-Sovietisation in a Stalinist sense. Very soon, and from 1944 in some regions, the first monuments were built and the first commemorative plaques were erected. All this was part of a heroic narrative of victimisation that displayed a closed model of war cult: the USSR alone had defeated the 'Fascist-Hitlerite' enemy with the great sacrifices and efforts of the Soviet peoples.[52] The USSR had also taken upon its shoulders the heroic task of liberating the occupied peoples of Eastern and Central Europe, who, as true brothers, were deeply grateful for that and seized every occasion to show it. The emphasis, however, was not on war but on overcoming, on reconstruction, on the search for a new order and a lasting peace, which was now threatened by the Anglo-American enemies.

In the Baltic countries and in Western Ukraine, there was a major operation of concealment, dissolution and distortion of the history of the period 1939–45, above all of the Soviet invasions. Nationalists in all these countries were accused of fascism, collaborationism and of promoting the return of the interwar dictatorships. The public discourse was that the Soviet Union had liberated the Baltic peoples and the Ukrainians from Nazi oppression. Nationalists, especially the *Banderotsy* – the Ukrainians – and the 'Forest brothers' – the Baltics – were the epitome of all evil and to blame for all attacks and, in fact, in alliance with their exiles, were continually trying to destroy the Soviet power and the peace of the Soviet peoples.[53]

The official interpretation of the Second World War was laid down by Stalin and his inner circle (especially Molotov, as Commissar for Foreign Affairs). A myriad of publications codified the new understanding of the conflict and its origins, constructing a typology of discourses that would prove long lasting. The victory over Nazi Germany was now displayed as a triumph over the West, and this linked to a kind of generic 'antifascism'. In the famous anti-Western pamphlet 'Falsifiers of History' – apparently supervised by Stalin himself – the Nazi–Soviet Pact 'appears to be a regrettable necessity to preserve Soviet security, forced on Russia by Western recalcitrance and duplicity, and certainly in no sense an alliance with the warmongering Nazis'.[54] Historians, fighting against 'false' interpretations, also found that 'Cosmopolitans' in the USSR together with 'Wall Street and its agencies' might 'falsify and distort the world historical role of the Russian people in the construction of a socialist society and in the victory over the enemy of mankind – German fascism in the Great Patriotic War'.[55]

In this way, the new fascist power was 'the West'. The United States was said to be in a 'process of fascistisation', and some authors even believed that an 'American Gestapo' and a 'police regime' existed in the United States.[56] This idea of the West – especially the United States and West Germany – as representing a kind of fascism was cultivated in a particularly intense way during late Stalinism, but would have a long, uninterrupted lifespan.

When, in 1956, Khrushchev pronounced his famous speech against Stalin at the 25th Congress of the Communist Party of the USSR, he changed all the rules.[57] During the brief explosion of freedom of 1956, there were some attempts at shaping an alternative memory of the war.[58] But the end of certainties produced new necessities. With the conclusion of the period of reforms and, finally, with the fall of Khrushchev in 1964, began a period in which the Communist elites were devoted to strengthening patriotism.[59] What was important was no longer the Utopia of building Socialism, but taking pride in the defeat of the fascists and in liberation from the foreign yoke. The people, the nation, legitimately proud of having driven out the occupier, were now the subject of politics, defined of course by the party as its vanguard.

The myth of the Great Patriotic War adopted then its classic form.[60] Since 1964, gigantic monuments to the Motherland were built all over the USSR, such as those in Kiev and Volgograd (Stalingrad). Paintings, statues, murals and all kinds of artworks were displayed in the public sphere for remembering the war; monuments and art works that were spread in multicolour albums and books, as a form of privatising public art.[61] War veterans, who were now reaching retirement, began to receive social benefits and special distinctions. Celebrations of war anniversaries took on supreme importance. Monuments, museums, cemeteries and memory sites associated with the conflict emerged everywhere. The social cohesion that could no longer be achieved by proclaiming Utopia through a future of Communism was sought now through remembrance of victory and the sufferings of the past.[62]

In historiography, as in popular history, a very important genre in the USSR, the construction of an image of fascism was clear: 'From the outset, Soviet authors, when researching fascism shortly after its rise in Europe, viewed their task not only with professional commitment but considered it as a social and political duty'.[63] In this context, the Politburo decided – in 1965, shortly after sending Khrushchev into retirement – to promote a monumental history of the war which would mark the path for all further writing about the conflict until the beginning of perestroika.[64]

This antifascist memorial policy was well received by the population, not only because it was rooted in real sufferings and family experiences, but because it allowed very different feelings and narratives to be expressed, which had hitherto been hidden or even forbidden. For Lisa Kirschenbaum, war narratives 'drew on experiences remembered by individuals while providing those who lived through the war with compelling and uplifting frameworks for narrating – and therefore remembering – their own experiences'.[65] Although the Communists' historical discourses had always used elements of the traditional nationalist narratives to create their own constructs of the past and of future prospects, they had not gone beyond the use of patriotism coupled with a progressive view of history.[66] The use of the heroic struggle of the Second World War provided an opportunity to integrate into everyday life the framework of traditional national feelings. Movies such as *The Cranes Are Flying* (Mikhail Kalatozov, 1957), *Ballad of a Soldier* (Grigori Chukhras, 1959), *Ivan's Childhood* (Andrei Tarkovsky, 1962) and the epic series *Liberation* (Yuri Ozerov, five films, 1970–71) helped to shape a very emotional view of the war that fit very well with many Soviet citizens' own experiences.[67]

This was not a unique or general process, but a programme deliberately developed by the state over time, and especially after 1968, when the promise of reforms within European Communism and the consolidation of socialist consumerism came to an end. This affected national identities: antifascism was now merged with nationalism, because 'Sovietness was a potent idea that inspired inhabitants of Ukraine not only to criticise Khrushchev but also to voice demands of the state and articulate various understandings of what it meant to be a good Soviet citizen'.[68] And, of course, this was true not only for Ukraine, but also for the whole of the Soviet Union.

People could now identify themselves through antifascism because fighting against fascism also meant defending their own national identity.[69] Thus, 'while some scholars have argued that the cult of World War II was cynically manufactured by the Communist regime for its own propaganda purposes, other researchers maintain that the war was a transformative experience for the Russian people and that the memory of that ordeal continues to be bound closely with their national self-conception'.[70] Possibly both views are true: the official memory policies merged with popular feelings.[71]

The Soviet leadership displayed many different media in order to construct those memory policies, as we have seen before, in very different ways and at different times. However, such diverse media uses were thought to be part of a *Gesamtkunstwerk*, a total artwork, as Soviet identity discourses might be described.[72]

At all events, this construct proved very powerful and, in some countries, especially Russia, Belarus and the Ukraine, it has survived political changes since the 1990s.

The Return of Soviet Antifascism

After the fall of the Soviet Union in 1991, the worldview of many ex-Soviet citizens broke down. The old truths were gone and there was nothing new to replace them.[73] Ethnic nationalism and religion, strange New Age theories and old sectarian fantasies occupied the place of the former Soviet identity. This all meant, of course, a huge change in the appreciation of the Second World War. In post-Soviet countries, conflicts over the origin of the Communist regime and the consequences and forms of the regime's output have altered in some way the cult to the war, and it is in the context of these conflicts that they have settled the transformations of the image of the Second World War. Sometimes, the war itself has become less important or has been subject to discussions about the proper Communist regime and the repressions and mortalities it caused. The world war played an important role in the independence of several countries and in their present relations with Russia, especially as a tool to accuse the 'other' or to enhance victimisation conductive to political benefits.[74]

The end of Communism came to the USSR at a time when the Western world entered a historical stage characterised by the 'globalisation' of historical memory (the extension to all societies and throughout all sectors of the society of the need to create narratives of identity based on traumas or past experiences with collective value), and by the proliferation of 'memory wars' (or the conscious construction of counter-narratives intended to replace hegemonic discourses, or at least make these narratives more plural).

In this context, there were signs that allowed the belief that events in Russia were in line with those in the rest of the world: for example, the assumption of responsibility for the crimes against other peoples of the Soviet era (indeed, under President Boris Yeltsin Russia recognised aspects such as the Katyn executions of 1940 and the secret Hitler–Stalin Pact protocols). The transformations of the war cult, which had begun during the perestroika, had now every opportunity to deploy. The end of censorship and the end of Communist rule allowed new expressions of the memory of the world war, and these might possibly have produced a decay of the Soviet antifascist legitimation, and a new narrative[75] – but they did not.

It is true, however, that, for example, during the celebrations of the 50th anniversary of the *Pobieda* ('Victory' of the war) in Moscow in 1995, an equestrian monument to Marshal Zhukov was unveiled. This Russian military officer, who had been humiliated by successive high-ranking Soviet *apparatchiks*, had enjoyed an undeniable popularity, which increased after his death, among the people. Zhukov represented the national dignity of Russian military opposition to Stalin who, by that time, had begun to be seen through the prism of the repression.[76]

However, the trauma of economic and social collapse in 1991 and the financial disaster of the late 1990s, just when it seemed that the worst was over, led the Russian population to make a positive assessment of its Communist past. It was a review that had nothing to do with nostalgia of a political nature, but with a sense of economic stability, social security and, at the same time, a legitimate feeling of national pride.[77] This was connected to a Socialist country that had arisen, not from the October Revolution, which had lost almost all its appeal, but from Victory in the Great Patriotic War.

This feeling was exploited and encouraged by the shift that Russian politics took from Vladimir Putin's rise to the presidency. A true revolution in the construction of a historical memory that was, in some respects, a return to the Brezhnev era, but otherwise assumed and associated fragments of Russian history that had been veiled and turned into a taboo by the Soviet regime: for example, the Tsars and the Orthodox Christianity. In this construction of a collective identity discourse rooted in the memory of a glorious past, a substantial role was granted to the memory of the Second World War.[78] As Elizabeth A. Wood puts it, 'by making World War II the central historical event of the twentieth century, Putin and his handlers have chosen an event of mythic proportions that underlines the unity and coherence of the nation, giving it legitimacy and status as a world power'.[79] That led to some rehabilitation of Stalin himself. In 2007, for instance, a survey by the Levada Centre in Moscow disclosed that up to 28 per cent of Russians agreed with the statement: 'No matter what mistakes and crimes are attributed to Stalin, what matters is that under his leadership people emerged victorious from the Second World War'.[80] And, in a wave of Second World War patriotism after the invasion of Crimea in 2014, voices in Russia claimed that the Russian city of Volgograd should change its name again to the glorious 'Stalingrad'. Although the intention of any such a change was to remember the Second World War battle and not the dictator, it is inevitable that it would have honoured Stalin as well as the battle.[81]

Under President Putin the mythology of the Patriotic War was remade; the Stalinist national anthem was recovered (with a different text); and anniversaries were celebrated with solemn military parades and re-enactments involving heavy artillery displays. The memory of the war was used as a weapon against other nations: Germany was accused of trying to erase the past, the Baltic countries and Poland were branded as ungrateful for not recognising that Russia – identified with the USSR – had liberated them from fascism.[82] Thus, the specific, nationalist and victimised 'antifascist' political identity of the Socialist society formed in Brezhnev's times remains essentially the core memory in Russia.

The situation in Ukraine was slightly different. When this country had been part of the Soviet Union, it had participated in the same form of antifascist memories of war as the rest of the state. But after 1991 there had been a radical reversal of official policy towards the war. As we have seen, nationalist *Banderites* were soon rehabilitated. Legally, this rehabilitation was only in terms of their participation in the fight against the Germans, while no consensus was reached regarding the meaning of their struggle towards independence in Ukraine, because the left considered them as traitors.[83] The official memory policy in Ukraine, especially after the 'Orange Revolution' of 2004, had been to favour the interpretation of the Second World War as a struggle of the Ukrainian people against the German and Russian occupiers.[84] That this view was very problematic and could only be applied to a part of the territory was made clear in February 2014 with the events in Crimea and the beginning of the civil war at the Donbass.[85]

Antifascism in post-Soviet Ukraine was embedded in the conflict between left and right, between pro-Soviet Communist activists and Ukrainian nationalists, between post-Soviet nostalgia and UPA glorification. As Anton Shekhovtsov, a researcher on Ukrainian right-wing organisations, writes, 'until 2010, "antifascism" was primarily used as

a form of self-identification by an element of Ukraine's left-wing movement, as well as being employed by the far right groupuscules to refer
to their left-wing opponents'.[86]

But things changed after the beginning of Yanukovich's second
term (2010–14). Various 'antifascist' groups (World without Nazism;
International Antifascist Front) were founded in the Ukraine by
pro-Russian politicians as undercover pro-Russian organizations,
clearly inspired by Putin's methods for handling political opponents
in Russia. Thus, antifascist discourses began to be used in a general
attack against all Ukrainian opponents to Yanukovich's policies. The
official pro-Soviet Ukrainian Communist Party, although formerly in
the opposition, also increasingly adopted such discourses. The rise of
an ultra-right-wing party called *Sbovoda* ('Liberty') in West Ukraine offered a good excuse for a renewed antifascism.

The consistency with which the Kremlin sustained the antifascist
discourse after the *Maidan* revolution and the beginning of Russia's
armed intervention in Ukraine might be perceived as rhetorical, but it
clearly seems to be part of a wider imperial strategy.[87]

Memories of Antifascism

The process of identity construction is always performed in a given historical context, where political imperatives and social memories play
a key role. Social memory is, of course, socially formed, and there are
decisive schemes in political power that influence the decision-making
process, selecting historical events and their meaning to a given society in order to build some kind of cooperative memory. In the present
case, the antifascist memory of the Second World War was formed in
a context of war and social revolution, linked to incredible violence,
transformations of all kinds and the establishment of a dictatorship.[88]

The postwar Soviet State succeeded in constructing a political
identity based upon the antifascist fight during the Second World
War. This antifascism was formed under the hierarchical structure of
power of the state Socialist dictatorship. In this context, by definition,
this conception of antifascism was closed and unique. A significant
portion of the population, however, yearned to make explicit their
postwar trauma and to express their self-identification needs as a society, which led to the popular acceptance of antifascism as the political legitimation of a given identity. There was also a construction of
memory from below, an independent civil society activity, but it arose
entirely from a particular decision and accompanied by the guidance

that it should be assimilated and disseminated by the lower echelons of the public spheres. The path of this antifascism was marked from the beginning.

Although the end of Socialism provided the opportunity for constructing a much more plural and multifaceted discourse, the truth is that in many of the successor countries – the Baltics and Ukraine, above all – and over the last twenty years, an official model of world war memory has been developing that falls within the framework of the fight against Communism. This has influenced the memory of the Second World War and has transformed it into a pathetic, victimised, defeatist memory, where there is always another who betrays and occupies, and in which only part of the population are considered as 'true patriots'. This has been particularly evident in the Baltic states, but there have been attempts to do this in other post-Soviet countries.

Putin's Russia has built an imperial memory, taking some of the oldest Soviet fragments and processing them into a narrative with a clear political mission. The story is presented like this. Russia, successor to the USSR, is not to blame for the Second World War; its armies, with great suffering, saved Europe. There was no occupation by the Soviet Union: the Baltic states, Belarus, Moldova and Ukraine all joined the USSR voluntarily. The collapse of the USSR was a move prompted by the West along with 'traitors' from within. The construction of the memory of occupation in the Baltic and Ukraine was organised by nationalist-fascists and Russophobes. Historians gladly help (or are forced to by the circumstances) to build that narrative. Thus controversies are only apparently scientific. The Russian War memory, which is equal to the memory of antifascism, is fed today by hundreds of fantasy writers, patriotic movies and television series.[89]

The use of 'antifascism' in the Soviet Union was connected to its political abuse. As every opponent was accused of being 'fascist', the term lost any specific meaning. It remained a universal negative characteristic, without a possible definition, only a bundle of attributes with which to blame every opponent. Thus, it is easy to see how both the official and the popular antifascism that originated in the Soviet Union might now be used for legitimating an invasion and a military intervention: Ukraine. And this explains, too, why many inhabitants of the regions of Eastern Ukraine were ready to fight against their own army and – probably – against their own interests: because Soviet antifascism was not really a left-wing methodology for dismantling a right-wing political movement or resisting dictatorships based on such movements, but a tool for combating generic enemies while reaffirming a self-identity.

Notes

1. 'Ideologeme' is defined – through Bakhtin, Lotman and Kristeva – as 'the semiotically minimal unit of ideological discourse'. See W. Nöth, 'Semiotics of Ideology', in *Semiotica* 148(1/4) (2004), 11–21.
2. Foucault defines 'discourse', 'treating it sometimes as the general domain of all statements, sometimes as an individualisable group of statements, and sometimes as a regulated practice that accounts for a certain number of statements'. See M. Foucault, *The Archeology of Knowledge and the Discourse on Language*, New York, 1972. We follow the last definition.
3. By the end of 2013, even in the Eastern Regions traditionally linked to Russia, more than 50 per cent of the people wanted to be in the European Union (69 per cent in Western Ukraine). http://www.pravda.com.ua/ news/2013/11/18/7002362/ (accessed 20 May 2014). See too, S. Yekelchyk and O. Schmidtke (eds), *Europe's Last Frontier? Belarus, Moldova, and Ukraine between Russia and the European Union*, New York, 2008.
4. See G. Simon, 'Staatskrise in der Ukraine. Vom Bürgerprotest für Europa zur Revolution', *Osteuropa* 1(64) (January 2014), 25–41; Simon Geissbühler (ed.), *Kiew – Revolution 3.0. Der Euromaidan 2013/14 und die Zukunftsperspektiven der Ukraine*, Hannover, 2014.
5. D. Marples, *Heroes and Villains: Creating National History in Contemporary Ukraine*, Budapest, 2007.
6. See the official Russian version at www.kremlin.ru; I quote from the English version on the same site: http://eng.kremlin.ru/transcripts/6889 (accessed 14 May 2014).
7. Ibid.
8. On Putin, see M. Geshen, *The Man Without a Face: The Unlikely Rise of Vladimir Putin*, London, 2012.
9. See J. Armstrong, *Ukrainian Nationalism*, New York, 1963; A.J. Motyl, *The Turn to the Right: The Ideological Origins and Development of Ukrainian Nationalism, 1919–1929*, Boulder, CO, 1980.
10. http://eng.kremlin.ru/transcripts/6889 (accessed 24 May 2014).
11. See, for example, this analysis: http://www.kyivpost.com/opinion/op-ed/ new-eastern-europe-the-fascism-of-patriots-and-anti-fascism-of-ban-dits-327629.html (accessed 30 May 2014).
12. *Kommunist, Organ tsentralnogo komiteta Kompartii Ukrainy*, N. 10 (1673), 12 February 2014, 1.
13. Ibid., N. 11 (1674), 14 February 2014, 1. Indeed the antifascist discourses in the Ukrainian political culture have been growing in the last years. See, for example, G. Kriuchkov, *Fashizm v Ukraine: ugroza ili real'nost'?*, Kharkov, 2008.
14. D.R. Marples, 'Stepan Bandera: The Resurrection of a Ukrainian National Hero', in *Europe–Asia Studies* 58(4) (2006), 555–66; E. Narvselius, 'The "Bandera Debate": The Contentious Legacy of World War II and Liberalisation of Collective Memory in Western Ukraine', *Canadian Slavonic Papers* 54(3/4) (2012), 469–90.

15. M. Lelich, 'The Soviet Union versus the EuroMaidan', *New Eastern Europe* 2 (2014), 25–35.
16. S. Velychenko, 'The Issue of Russian Colonialism in Ukrainian Thought: Dependency, Identity and Development', *Ab imperio* 1 (2002), 323–66.
17. Very broadly it might be said that 'Ruthenian' was the first Ukrainian nationalism in the Austrian part of the country, while 'Ukrainian' came into being as a wider concept of nation, towards central and eastern Ukraine. See T. Snyder, *The Reconstruction of Nations: Poland, Ukraine, Lithuania, Belarus, 1569–1999*, New Haven, CT, and London, 2003.
18. S. Yekelchyk, *Ukraine: Birth of a Modern Nation*, New York, 2007; S. Yekelchyk, *Stalin's Empire of Memory: Russian–Ukrainian Relations in the Soviet Historical Imagination*, Toronto, 2004.
19. Yekelchyk, *Stalin's Empire of Memory*, 5.
20. M. Dobson, '"Show the Bandits No Mercy!" Amnesty, Criminality and Public Response in 1953', in P. Jones (ed.), *The Dilemmas of De-Stalinisation: Negotiating Cultural and Social Change in the Khrushchev Era*, London, 2006, 21–40.
21. It is not that the 'integral nationalism' of the Ukrainian radical nationalists did not share some characteristics of fascism. See G. Motyka, *Ukraińska partyzantka 1942–1960: Działalność Organizacji Ukraińskich Nacjonalistów i Ukraińskiej Powstańczej Armii*, Warsaw, 2006; and J.M. Faraldo, *La Europa clandestina. Resistencia contra las ocupaciones nazi y soviética (1938–1948)*, Madrid, 2011.
22. P. Jakovlevich Tschornich's *Istoriko-etimologitscheskii slovar sovremmiennogo ruskogo jazyka*, Moscow, 1993, vol. 2, 305. The same definition, with some changes, came in the three main editions of the *Bolshaya sovetskaya entsiklopediya* (The Great Soviet Encyclopaedia). See the internet edition (based on the third, 1969–78): http://bse.sci-lib.com/article115466.html (accessed 24 October 2014). For a general view of Soviet political language, see D. Fel'dman, *Terminologiia vlasti: sovetskie politicheskie terminy v istoriko-kul'turnom kontekste*, Moscow, 2006.
23. Dimitrov's famous speech at the Seventh Congress of the Comintern with his definition of 'fascism' in Dimitrov, *Izbranniie proizhvedeniya*, vol. 1, 377. See also J. Degras, *The Communist International 1919–1943 Documents*, London, Vol. I (1919–1923), 1971, 421–22; K. McDermott and J. Agnew, *The Comintern: A History of International Communism from Lenin to Stalin*, Basingstoke, 1996, 131.
24. V.I. Lenin, 'O prodovol'stvennom naloge', *Polnie Sabranie Sochinenii*, vol. xliii, 235. See too, 'Zamietki publitsista', *Polnie...*, vol. xliv (1922), 422.
25. Some examples: 'Beschinstva fashistov', *Pravda*, 24 September 1922, 3 (first time as a headline); 'Fashistikii pogrom v Kremone, 17 July, 1922, 3; 'Polozhenie v Italii', *Pravda*, 29 July 1922, 3. 'Fashisti u Vlasti', *Pravda*, 31 October 1922, 1; 'Fashism', *Pravda*, 3 November 1922, 2.
26. Ilia and Petrov, 'Moskva, strashnoi bulbar', *Sabranie Sochineniia*, t. v, 7 November 1923, 7.
27. On Soviet conceptions of fascism until the 1950s, see N.P. Bystrov, 'Ideologema "fashism" v sovietskoi publitsistike 1920-x - nachala 1950-x

gg'. (Ph.D. dissertation at the Russian State University for Humanities, Moscow, 2009).

28. D. Priestland, *Red Flag: A History of Communism*, New York, 2009, 185–86.
29. See G.M. Adibekov (ed.), *Politbiuro CK RKP(b)-VKP(b) I Komintern. 1919–1943 gg. Dokumenty*, Moscow, 2004, especially 626–29.
30. S.G. Payne, 'Soviet Anti-Fascism: Theory and Practice, 1921–45', *Totalitarian Movements and Political Religions* 4(2) (Autumn 2003), 1–62.
31. J. Haslam, *The Soviet Union and the Struggle for Collective Security in Europe, 1933–39*, New York, 1984.
32. 'Sotsial-imperialisti i prosto imperialisty', *Pravda*, 8 October 1927, 1.
33. 'Ot reformizma do fashisma adin shag', *Pravda*, 24 September 1922, 3.
34. 'Muzhestvo antifashistov', *Pravda*, 15 January 1935, 3.
35. 'Niet raznitsy mezhdu fashistami, trotskistami I zinovievtsami', *Pravda*, 21 August 1936, 1.
36. RGASPI, f. 495, opis 18, dela 1101, quoted by D. Kowalsky, *Stalin and the Spanish Civil War*, chapter 4, 'The Campaigns of Solidarity in the USSR', paragraph 7, http://www.gutenberg-e.org/kod01/frames/fkodimg.html (accessed 24 October 2014).
37. Ibid., paragraph 25.
38. On Soviet propaganda, see the classic P. Kenez, *The Birth of the Propaganda State: Soviet Methods of Mass Mobilization, 1917–1929*, Cambridge and New York, 1985. On Stalinist times, see also S. Davies, *Popular Opinion in Stalin's Russia: Terror, Propaganda and Dissent, 1934–1941*, Cambridge, 1997.
39. *Krokodil*, 30 October 1936, 8.
40. See, for example, *Krokodil*, 30 October 1936, 14. On this collective see: M.V. Kuprijanov, P.N. Krylov and N.A. Sokolov, *Kukryniksy – grafika: 1941–1945*, Moscow, 2006.
41. G.T. Rittersporn, 'Le régime face au carnaval. Folklore non conformiste en URSS dans les années 1930', in *Annales. Histoire, Sciences Sociales* 2 (2003), 471–96, here 477.
42. S. Fitzpatrick, *Everyday Stalinism: Ordinary Life in Extraordinary Times: Soviet Russia in the 1930s*, Oxford, 1999, 171. Very similar in Davies, *Popular Opinion*, 67.
43. Davies, *Popular Opinion*, 87.
44. Iu V. Galaktionov, *Germanskii fashism v zerkale istoriografii 20-40-x godov*, Kemerovo, 1996.
45. W. Leonhard, *Betrayal: The Hitler–Stalin Pact of 1939*, New York, 1989; B.H. Bayerlein, *'Der Verräter, Stalin, bist Du!' Vom Ende der internationalen Solidarität. Komintern und kommunistische Parteien im Zweiten Weltkrieg 1939–1941* (with N. Lebedeva, M. Narinskij and G. Albert), Berlin, 2008.
46. For example, in February 1939 they published a tale about Spanish soldiers and an article presenting Spanish children's drawings on the war. See *Vokrug Sveta* 2 (February 1939), 30–32.
47. The novel tells the story of a future war between Hitler and the Soviet Union. However, some Soviet institutions, as for example the theoretical journal 'Bolshevik', still defended *The First Strike*, and Shpanov did not fall in disgrace. See V.A. Tokarev, 'Soviet'skaya voennaya utopia kanuna

vtoroy mirovoi', *Evropa* 1 (2006), 97–161; V.A. Tokarev, *Totalitarnaya antitsi-pat'sia*, Moscow, 2001.

48. Kukryniksy, 'Let Us Ruthlessly Crush and Destroy the Enemy', 1941, http://www.moma.org/collection/browse_results.php?criteria=O%3AAD%3AE%3A37855&page_number=1&template_id=1&sort_order=1 (accessed 24 October 2014).

49. X.M. Núñez and J.M. Faraldo, 'The First Great Patriotic War: Spanish Communists and Nationalism, 1936–1939', *Nationalities Papers* 37(4) (July 2009), 401–24.

50. N. Tumarkin, *The Living and the Dead: The Rise and Fall of the Cult of World War II in Russia*, Basic Books, 1995.

51. M. Edele, *Soviet Veterans of the Second World War: A Popular Movement in an Authoritarian Society, 1941–1991*, Oxford and New York, 2008.

52. The words 'Germany' and 'Germans' were meticulously avoided, above all because of the important place of the German Democratic Republic in the Socialist world system. See J.M. Faraldo, 'Die Hüterin der europäischen Zivilisation. Kommunistische Europa-Konzeptionen am Vorabend des Kalten Krieges (1944–1948)', in J.M. Faraldo, P. Gulińska-Jurgiel and C. Domnitz (eds), *Europa im Ostblock. Vorstellungen und Diskurse*, Vienna and Cologne, 2008, 91–110.

53. T. Stryjek, 'Wojna po wojnie raz jeszcze. II wojna światowa i powojenne podziemie antysowieckie we współczesnej polityce wobec pamięci i w historiografii Litwy, Łotwy, Estonii, Białorusi i Ukrainy', in A.F. Baran et al., *Wojna po wojnie Antysowieckie podziemie w Europie Środkowo-Wschodni*, Gdansk and Warsaw, 2012, 410–616.

54. T.J. Uldricks, 'War, Politics and Memory: Russian Historians Reevaluate the Origins of World War II', *History & Memory* 21(2) (Fall/Winter 2009), 60–82, here 61. The quoted book: *Falsifikatory istorii (Istoricheskaia spravka)*, Moscow, 1948.

55. Editorial, 'On the Tasks of Soviet Historians in the Struggle with Manifestations of Bourgeois Ideology', *Voprosy Istorii* 2, 1949, quoted in R.V. Daniels, *A Documentary History of Communism in Russia, Lebanon, Vermont*, 1993, 241.

56. Efim A. Rovinskii, *Fashizatsia politicheskogo stroia v stranach amerikano-an-gliiskogo bloka*, Moscow, 1952; V.N. Minaev, *Amerikanskoe gestapo*, Moscow, 1950; V.N. Minaev, *Fashitsko-politseiskii rezhim v Soediennich Shtatach Amerikii*, Moscow, 1952.

57. See P. Jones, *The Dilemmas of De-Stalinisation*, 2006, especially the Introduction.

58. A. Weiner, 'The Empires Pay a Visit: Gulag Returnees, East European Rebellions, and Soviet Frontier Politics', *Journal of Modern History* 78(2) (2006), 333–76.

59. M. Dobson, *Khrushchev's Cold Summer: Gulag Returnees, Crime, and the Fate of Reform after Stalin*, Ithaca, NY, 2009.

60. H. Altrichter, 'Der Große Vaterländische Krieg. Zur Entstehung und Entsakralisierung eines Mythos', in H. Altrichter, K. Herbers and H. Neuhaus (eds), *Mythen in der Geschichte*, Freiburg, 2004, 471–93.

61. See examples in L. Ivanovich, *Pamitniki slavy i bessmertiia*, Moscow, 1971; and in O.I. Sopotsinskii, *Velikaia otechestviennaia Voiina v proizvedieniiach sovetskich chudozhnikov. Zhivopis, Skultura, Grafika*, Moscow, 1979.

62. See the whole issue of the journal *Osteuropa* 4–6 (April–June 2005), entitled 'Kluft der Erinnerung. Russland und Deutschland 60 Jahre nach dem Krieg'.

63. S.G. Allenov and A.A. Gaklina, 'Germanskii Fashism i ieio epoche', *Politeia* 3(66) (2012), 32–45.

64. J. Hösler, 'Aufarbeitung der Vergangenheit? Der Große Vaterländische Krieg in der Historiographie der UdSSR und Rußlands', *Osteuropa. Zeitschrift für Gegenwartsfragen des Ostens* 55 (2005), N. 4–6, 115–25, here 117. See also R.D. Markwick, *Rewriting History in Soviet Russia: The Politics of Revisionist Historiography, 1956–1974*, Basingstoke, 2001, especially 209–19; V.M.K. Kulish, 'Sovetskaia istoriografiia Belikoii Otiechesviennoii voiny', in *Sovietskaia Istoriografiia*, Moscow, 1996, 279–83.

65. L.A. Kirschenbaum, *The Legacy of the Siege of Leningrad, 1941–1995*, New York, 2006, 8.

66. A.S. Tuminez, *Russian Nationalism since 1856*, Oxford, 2000.

67. See L. Karl, '"Von Helden und Menschen". Der Zweite Weltkrieg im sowjetischen Spielfilm und dessen Rezeption in der DDR, 1945–1965'. Ph.D. dissertation, Eberhard-Karls-Universität, Tübingen, 2002; J. Woll, *Real Images: Soviet Cinema and the Thaw*, London and New York, 2000.

68. Z. Wojnowski, 'De-Stalinization and Soviet Patriotism: Ukrainian Reactions to East European Unrest in 1956', *Kritika. Explorations in Russian and Eurasian History* 13(4) (Fall 2012), 799–829.

69. And antifascism was often used as a discursive weapon in international relations until the perestroika. As examples: F.I. Novik, *Neofashizm v FRG: podiiemy i porazheniya (1949–1974)*, Moscow, 1976; B. Lopukhov, *Neofashizm — opasnost' dli'a mira*, Moscow, 1985; V.V. Pustogarov, *Neofashizm i mezhdunarodnaya bezoapasnots*, Moscow, 1989.

70. Uldricks, 'War, Politics and Memory', 60.

71. On the deep popular roots of the cult, see A. Weiner, *Making Sense of War: The Second World War and the Fate of the Bolshevik Revolution*, Princeton, NJ, 2001.

72. This is, of course, a reference to B. Groys, *The Total Art of Stalinism: Avant-Garde, Aesthetic Dictatorship and Beyond*, Princeton, NJ, 1992, although Groys speaks about Stalinism.

73. In my opinion, the best account of the end of the Soviet Union, and after, is S. Kotkin, *Armageddon Averted: The Soviet Collapse, 1970–2000*, Oxford and New York, 2001 (updated edition 2008).

74. W. Jilge, 'Post-Soviet Ukrainian Narratives on World War II', in E. Barkan, E.A. Cole and K. Struve (eds), *Shared Memory – Divided Memory: Jews and Others in Soviet-Occupied Poland, 1939–1941*, Leipzig, 2007, 103–31; E.-C. Onken, 'The Baltic States and Moscow's 9 May Conmemoration: Analysing Memory Politics in Europe', *Europe–Asia Studies* 1 (2007), 23–46; K. Brüggemann and A. Kasekamp, 'The Politics of History and the "War of Monuments" in Estonia', *Nationalities Papers* 3 (2008), 425–48.

75. For a first re-evaluation in Russia, G.A. Bordiugov and F. Bomsdorf (eds), *60-Letie okonchaniia Vtoroi Mirovoi i Velikoi Otechestvennoi: Pobediteli I pobezhdennye v kontekste politiki, mifologii i pamiati. Materialy K Mezhdunarodnomu Forumu (Moskva, Sentiabr 2005)*, Moscow, 2005.

76. A. Langenohl, 'Die Erinnerungsreflexion des Grossen Vaterländischen Krieges in Russland zum fünfzigsten und sechzigsten Jahrestag des Sieges (1995 und 2005)', in *Jahrbuch für historische Kommunismusforschung*, 2005, 68–80.

77. Maya Nadkarni and Olga Shevchenko, 'The Politics of Nostalgia: A Case for Comparative Analysis of Post-Socialist Practices', *Ab Imperio* 2 (2004), 487–520.

78. J. Hösler, 'Der "Große Vaterländische Krieg" in der postsowjetischen Historiographie', in L. Karl and I.J. Polianski (eds), *Geschichtspolitik und Erinnerungskultur im neuen Russland*, Göttingen, 2009, 237–48. On other uses of the war: D.R. Marples, *'Our Glorious Past': Lukashenka's Belarus and the Great Patriotic War*, Hannover, 2014.

79. E.A. Wood, 'Performing Memory: Vladimir Putin and the Celebration of World War II in Russia', *The Soviet and Post-Soviet Review* 38 (2011), 172–200, here 174.

80. See B. Dubin, 'Erinnern als staatliche Veranstaltung. Geschichte und Herrschaft in Russland', *Osteuropa* 58(6) (2008), 62.

81. http://www.theguardian.com/world/2014/jun/08/stalingrad-name-may-return-to-russian-city (accessed 2 July 2014).

82. See, for example, the discussion about the Sovietization of the Baltics in a leading Russian historiographic journal, where Stalinist theses of 'liberation' were spread. R.X. Simoniian and T.M. Kochegarova, 'Sobuitiia 1939–1940 godov v massovom coznanii nasieleniia stran Baltii', *Novaia i noveishaia Istoriia* 3 (2009), 19–33. There are, of course, other, more liberal debates; see, for example, the journal *Neprikosnoviennii zapac. Debaty o politikie i kulturie*, special issue 'Sovietskoie proshloie: mezhdu politikoi pamiati i realnoi politickoi', 2(64) (2009).

83. K.V. Korostelina, 'Mapping National Identity Narratives in Ukraine', *Nationalities Papers* 41(2) (2013), 293–315.

84. V. Ishchenko, 'Fighting Fences vs Fighting Monuments: Politics of Memory and Protest Mobilization in Ukraine', *Debatte* 19(1–2) (2011).

85. V. Hryner, 'Gespaltene Erinnerung. Der Zweite Weltkrieg im ukrainischen Gedenken', *Osteuropa* 55(4–6) (2005), 88–102.

86. http://anton-shekhovtsov.blogspot.com.es/2015/03/the-uneasy-reality-of-antifascism-in.html#more (accessed 20 March 2015).

87. http://www.thedailybeast.com/articles/2015/02/08/anti-nazi-group-secretly-helping-kremlin-rebuild-russian-empire.html

88. Weiner, *Making Sense of War*.

89. S. Norris, *Blockbuster History in the New Russia: Movies, Memory and Patriotism*, Bloomington, IN, 2012.

References

Adibekov, G.M. (ed.). *Politbiuro CK RKP(b)-VKP(b) I Komintern. 1919–1943 gg. Dokumenty*. Moscow, 2004.

Allenov, S.G., and A.A. Gaklina. 'Germanskii Fashism i ieio epoche'. *Politeia* 3(66) (2012), 32–45.

Altrichter, H. 'Der Große Vaterländische Krieg. Zur Entstehung und Entsakralisierung eines Mythos', in H. Altrichter, K. Herbers and H. Neuhaus (eds), *Mythen in der Geschichte*. Freiburg, 2004, 471–93.

Armstrong, J. *Ukrainian Nationalism*. New York, 1963.

Bayerlein, B.H. '*Der Verräter, Stalin, bist Du!*' Vom Ende der internationalen Solidarität. *Komintern und kommunistische Parteien im Zweiten Weltkrieg 1939–1941*. Berlin, 2008.

Bordiugov, G.A., and F. Bomsdorf (eds). *60-Letie okonchaniia Vtoroi Mirovoi i Velikoi Otechestvennoi: Pobediteli I pobezhdennye v kontekste politiki, mifologii i pamiati. Materialy K Mezhdunarodnomu Forumu (Moskva, Sentiabr 2005)*. Moscow, 2005.

Brüggemann, K., and A. Kasekamp. 'The Politics of History and the "War of Monuments" in Estonia'. *Nationalities Papers* 3 (2008), 425–48.

Bystrov, N.P. 'Ideologema "fashism" v sovietskoi publitsistike 1920-x - nachala 1950-x gg'. Ph.D. dissertation, Russian State University for Humanities. Moscow, 2009.

Daniels, R.V. *A Documentary History of Communism in Russia, Lebanon*. Vermont, 1993.

Davies, S. *Popular Opinion in Stalin's Russia: Terror, Propaganda and Dissent, 1934–1941*. Cambridge, 1997.

Degras, J. *The Communist International 1919–1943 Documents*. London, Vol. I (1919–1923), 1971.

Dobson, M. '"Show the Bandits No Mercy!" Amnesty, Criminality and Public Response in 1953', in P. Jones (ed.) *The Dilemmas of De-Stalinisation: Negotiating Cultural and Social Change in the Khrushchev Era*. London, 2006, 21–40.

———. *Khrushchev's Cold Summer: Gulag Returnees, Crime, and the Fate of Reform after Stalin*. Ithaca, NY, 2009.

Dubin, B. 'Erinnern als staatliche Veranstaltung. Geschichte und Herrschaft in Russland'. *Osteuropa* 58(6) (2008), 57–65.

Edele, M. *Soviet Veterans of the Second World War: A Popular Movement in an Authoritarian Society, 1941–1991*. Oxford and New York, 2008.

Faraldo, J.M. 'Die Hüterin der europäischen Zivilisation. Kommunistische Europa-Konzeptionen am Vorabend des Kalten Krieges (1944–1948)', in J.M. Faraldo, P. Gulińska-Jurgiel and C. Domnitz (eds), *Europa im Ostblock. Vorstellungen und Diskurse*. Vienna and Cologne, 2008.

———. *La Europa clandestina. Resistencia contra las ocupaciones nazi y soviética (1938–1948)*. Madrid, 2011.

Fel'dman, D. *Terminologiia vlasti: sovetskie politicheskie terminy v istoriko-kul'turnom kontekste*. Moscow, 2006.

Fitzpatrick, S. *Everyday Stalinism: Ordinary Life in Extraordinary Times: Soviet Russia in the 1930s*. Oxford, 1999.

Foucault, M. *The Archeology of Knowledge and the Discourse on Language*. New York, 1972.

Galaktionov I.V. *Germanskii fashism v zerkale istoriografii 20-40-x godov*. Kemerovo, 1996.

Geissbühler, S. (ed.). *Kiew – Revolution 3.0. Der Euromaidan 2013/14 und die Zukunftsperspektiven der Ukraine*. Hannover, 2014.

Geshen, M. *The Man Without a Face: The Unlikely Rise of Vladimir Putin*. London, 2012.

Groys, B. *The Total Art of Stalinism: Avant-Garde, Aesthetic Dictatorship and Beyond*. Princeton, NJ, 1992.

Haslam, J. *The Soviet Union and the Struggle for Collective Security in Europe, 1933–39*. New York, 1984.

Hösler, J. 'Aufarbeitung der Vergangenheit? Der Große Vaterländische Krieg in der Historiographie der UdSSR und Rußlands'. *Osteuropa. Zeitschrift für Gegenwartsfragen des Ostens* 55 (2005), N. 4–6.

———. 'Der "Große Vaterländische Krieg" in der postsowjetischen Historiographie', in Lars Karl and Igor J. Polianski (eds), *Geschichtspolitik und Erinnerungskultur im neuen Russland*, Göttingen, 2009.

Hryner, V. 'Gespaltene Erinnerung. Der Zweite Weltkrieg im ukrainischen Gedenken'. *Osteuropa* 55(4–6) (2005), 88–102.

Ishchenko, V. 'Fighting Fences vs Fighting Monuments: Politics of Memory and Protest Mobilization in Ukraine'. *Debatte* 19(1–2) (2011).

Ivanovich, L. *Pamitniki slavy i bessmertiia*. Moscow, 1971.

Jilge, W. 'Post-Soviet Ukrainian Narratives on World War II', in E. Barkan, E.A. Cole and K. Struve (eds), *Shared Memory – Divided Memory: Jews and Others in Soviet-Occupied Poland, 1939–1941*. Leipzig, 2007.

Jones, P. *The Dilemmas of De-Stalinisation*. London and New York, 2006.

Karl, L. '"Von Helden und Menschen…". Der Zweite Weltkrieg im sowjetischen Spielfilm und dessen Rezeption in der DDR, 1945–1965'. Ph.D. dissertation, Eberhard-Karls-Universität, Tübingen, 2002.

Kenez, P. *The Birth of the Propaganda State: Soviet Methods of Mass Mobilization, 1917–1929*. Cambridge and New York, 1985.

Kirschenbaum, L.A. *The Legacy of the Siege of Leningrad, 1941–1995*. New York, 2006.

Korostelina, K.V. 'Mapping National Identity Narratives in Ukraine'. *Nationalities Papers* 41(2) (2013), 293–315.

Kotkin, S. *Armageddon Averted: The Soviet Collapse, 1970–2000*. Oxford and New York, 2001.

Kowalsky, D. *Stalin and the Spanish Civil War*. (Gutenberg-e.) New York, 2004. Electronic book.

Kriuchkov, G. *Fashizm v Ukraine: ugroza ili real'nost'?* Kharkov, 2008.

Kulish, V.M.K. 'Sovietskaia istoriografiia Belikoii Otiechesviennoii voiny', in *Sovietskaia Istoriografiia*. Moscow, 1996.

Kuprijanov, M.V., P.N. Krylov and N.A. Sokolov. *Kukryniksy – grafika: 1941–1945*. Moscow, 2006.

Langenohl, A. 'Die Erinnerungsreflexion des Grossen Vaterländischen Krieges in Russland zum fünfzigsten und sechzigsten Jahrestag des Sieges (1995 und 2005)', in *Jahrbuch für historische Kommunismusforschung*, 2005.

Lelich, M. 'The Soviet Union versus the EuroMaidan'. *New Eastern Europe* 2 (2014), 25–35.

Leonhard, W. *Betrayal: The Hitler–Stalin Pact of 1939*. New York, 1989.

Lopukhov, B. *Neofashizm—opasnost' dli'a mira*. Moscow, 1985.

Markwick, R.D. *Rewriting History in Soviet Russia: The Politics of Revisionist Historiography, 1956–1974*. Basingstoke, 2001.

Marples, D.R. 'Stepan Bandera: The Resurrection of a Ukrainian National Hero'. *Europe–Asia Studies* 58(4) (2006), 555–66.

———. *Heroes and Villains: Creating National History in Contemporary Ukraine*. Budapest, 2007.

———. *'Our Glorious Past': Lukashenka's Belarus and the Great Patriotic War*. Hannover, 2014.

McDermott, K., and J. Agnew. *The Comintern: A History of International Communism from Lenin to Stalin*. Basingstoke, 1996.

Minaev, V.N. *Amerikanskoe gestapo*. Moscow, 1950.

———. *Fashitsko-politseiskii rezhim v Soediennich Shtatach Amerikii*. Moscow, 1952.

Motyka, G. *Ukraińska partyzantka 1942–1960: Działalność Organizacji Ukraińskich Nacjonalistów i Ukraińskiej Powstańczej Armi*. Warsaw, 2006.

Motyl, A.J. *The Turn to the Right: The Ideological Origins and Development of Ukrainian Nationalism, 1919–1929*. Boulder, CO, 1980.

Nadkarni, M., and O. Shevchenko. 'The Politics of Nostalgia: A Case for Comparative Analysis of Post-Socialist Practices', *Ab Imperio* 2 (2004), 487–520.

Narvselius, E. 'The "Bandera Debate": The Contentious Legacy of World War II and Liberalisation of Collective Memory in Western Ukraine'. *Canadian Slavonic Papers* 54(3/4) (2012), 469–90.

Norris, S. *Blockbuster History in the New Russia: Movies, Memory and Patriotism*. Bloomington, IN, 2012.

Nöth, W. 'Semiotics of Ideology'. *Semiotica* 148(1/4) (2004), 11–21.

Novik, F.I. *Neofashizm v FRG: podiiemy i porazheniya (1949–1974)*. Moscow, 1976.

Núñez, X.M., and J.M. Faraldo. 'The First Great Patriotic War: Spanish Communists and Nationalism, 1936–1939'. *Nationalities Papers* 37(4) (July 2009), 401–24.

Onken, E.-C. 'The Baltic States and Moscow's 9 May Conmemoration: Analysing Memory Politics in Europe'. *Europe–Asia Studies* 1 (2007), 23–46.

Payne, S.G. '*Soviet Anti-Fascism: Theory and Practice, 1921–45'*. *Totalitarian Movements and Political Religions* 4(2) (Autumn 2003), 1–62.

Priestland, D. *Red Flag: A History of Communism*. New York, 2009.

Pustogarov, V.V. *Neofashizm i mezhdunarodnaya bezoapasnots*. Moscow, 1989.

Rittersporn, G.T. 'Le régime face au carnaval. Folklore non conformiste en URSS dans les années 1930'. *Annales. Histoire, Sciences Sociales* 2 (2003), 471–96.

Rovinskii, E.A. *Fashizatsia politicheskogo stroia v stranach amerikano-angliiskogo bloka*. Moscow, 1952.

Simon, G. 'Staatskrise in der Ukraine. Vom Bürgerprotest für Europa zur Revolution'. *Osteuropa* 1(64) (January 2014), 25–41.

Simoniian, R.X. and T.M. Kochegarova. 'Sobuitiia 1939–1940 godov v massovom coznanii nasieleniia stran Baltii'. *Novaia i noveishaia Istoriia* 3 (2009), 19–33.

Snyder, T., *The Reconstruction of Nations: Poland, Ukraine, Lithuania, Belarus, 1569–1999*. New Haven, CT, and London, 2003.

Sopotsinskii, O.I. *Velikaia otechestviennaia Voiina v proizvedieniiach sovetskich chudozhnikov. Zhivopis, Skultura, Grafika*. Moscow, 1979.

Stryjek, T. 'Wojna po wojnie raz jeszcze. II wojna światowa i powojenne podziemie antysowieckie we współczesnej polityce wobec pamięci i w historiografii Litwy, Łotwy, Estonii, Białorusi i Ukrainy', in A.F. Baran et al. (eds), *Wojna po wojnie Antysowieckie podziemie w Europie Środkowo-Wschodni*. Gdansk and Warsaw, 2012.

Tokarev, V.A. *Totalitarnaya antitsipat'sia*. Moscow, 2001.

———. 'Soviet'skaya voennaya utopia kanuna vtoroy mirovoi'. *Evropa* 1 (2006), 97–161.

Tschornich, P.J. *Istoriko-etimologitscheskii slovar sovremmiennogo ruskogo jazyka*. Moscow, 1993, vol. 2, 305.

Tumarkin, N., *The Living and the Dead: The Rise and Fall of the Cult of World War II in Russia*. Basic Books, 1995.

Tuminez, A.S. *Russian Nationalism since 1856*. Oxford, 2000.

Uldricks, T.J. 'War, Politics and Memory: Russian Historians Reevaluate the Origins of World War II'. *History & Memory* 21(2) (Fall/Winter 2009).

Velychenko, S. 'The Issue of Russian Colonialism in Ukrainian Thought: Dependency, Identity and Development'. *Ab imperio* 1 (2002), 323–66.

Weiner, A. *Making Sense of War: The Second World War and the Fate of the Bolshevik Revolution*. Princeton, NJ, 2001.

———. 'The Empires Pay a Visit: Gulag Returnees, East European Rebellions, and Soviet Frontier Politics'. *Journal of Modern History* 78(2) (2006), 333–76.

Wojnowski, Z. 'De-Stalinization and Soviet Patriotism: Ukrainian Reactions to East European Unrest in 1956'. *Kritika. Explorations in Russian and Eurasian History* 13(4) (Fall 2012), 799–829.

Woll, J. *Real Images: Soviet Cinema and the Thaw*. London and New York, 2000.

Wood, E.A. 'Performing Memory: Vladimir Putin and the Celebration of World War II in Russia'. *The Soviet and Post-Soviet Review* 38 (2011), 172–200.

Yekelchyk, S. *Stalin's Empire of Memory: Russian–Ukrainian Relations in the Soviet Historical Imagination*. Toronto, 2004.

———. *Ukraine: Birth of a Modern Nation*. New York, 2007.

Yekelchyk, S., and O. Schmidtke (eds), *Europe's Last Frontier? Belarus, Moldova, and Ukraine between Russia and the European Union*. New York, 2008.

José M. Faraldo is associate professor of Modern History at the Complutense University of Madrid. He has worked at the European University Viadrina, in Frankfurt/Oder (Germany) and at the Center of Research on Contemporary History (ZZF), in Potsdam (Germany). He has researched extensively about nationalism, European unity, visual and popular culture in former Communist countries, and comparative history of fascism and communism, with special attention to resistance. His current project is a history of Communist secret police in Eastern Europe, focusing on the cases of the Soviet Union, East Germany, Poland and Romania. His recent publications include: *Europe, Nation, Communism: Essays on Poland* (2008); *La Europa clandestina. La Resistencia contra las ocupaciones nazi y soviética (1938–1948)* (2011); *Reconsidering a Lost Intellectual Project: Exiles' Reflections on Cultural Differences* (2012) [with Carolina Rodríguez-López (eds)].

❧ 12

THE BURDEN OF THE REAR-VIEW MIRROR
Myth and Historiography of Republican Antifascism in France
Gilles Vergnon

In a speech about fascism during the 1928 Labour and Socialist International Congress in Brussels, six years after Mussolini's coming to power, Emile Vandervelde, Belgian president of the organisation, spoke of two distinct sides of Europe separated by a diagonal line running from Kowno in Poland to Bilbao in Spain, 'one Europe led by steam-horses, the other by live ones; one ruled by Parliaments, the other by dictators'.[1] Defining fascism as the exclusive purview of 'second-rate Europe' and calling it a 'successful Boulangist movement', a 'type of Bonapartism morally inferior to even the second issue of Bonapartism', he established clear boundaries around the phenomenon. These geographical limits (Eastern and Middle Europe) and social boundaries (a product of 'the ruling classes' growing fearfulness') seemed to exclude any future expansion of fascism towards Western Europe's industrialised countries. Fascism was delineated as an avatar of nineteenth-century authoritarianism of the likes of Bonaparte or Boulanger.

Much later, at the end of the twentieth century, in November 1997, an 'Antifascist Book Fair' was held in Gardanne in the Bouches-du-Rhône region of France, stronghold of the National Front party. Amongst the thirty-two speakers invited were several famous names, most notably writer Edmonde Charles-Roux and editor Alexandre Adler, French historians Pierre Broué and Madeleine Rebérioux, and German historian Albrecht Betz.[2] During their intervention, one suggested to reserve a part of the territory to 'inveterate LePenists' where 'they could run around freely, goose-step, inaugurate squares to the memory of Pétain and streets to that of Touvier, listen to mass in Latin, and all that silly business they enjoy so much'.[3] The National Front was thus described as the last avatar of a generic syncretic 'extreme right wing', likened to the Vichy government, extreme Catholicism or even Nazism with the mention of 'goose-stepping'.

Both examples are perfect illustrations of how to use your rear-view mirror in politics. As we all know, a rear-view mirror is an instrument that allows one to look back without turning around in order to better control one's driving. And true enough, it is a common, even useful practice, beyond automobiles, to look behind in order to understand the particulars of a certain situation or political, social or cultural movement. The issue here is that one does that *without turning around*, thereby validating representations that we have inherited and repeated as such – in this case, appraising Italian fascism under the lens of Bonapartism or Boulangism, and judging today's 'radical right' through the prism of historical fascism. Marx used to call this phenomenon the 'poetry of the past' and called upon his fellow men to shed this bad habit.

This chapter will be the occasion to question the renewal of Republican antifascism in France after 1945 in two consecutive cycles: the 'Cold War Cycle', from 1947 to the end of the Algerian War in 1962, and the more recent (unfinished) cycle relating to the rise and settlement of the National Front in the French political landscape since 1983. French 'Republican antifascism', even though it was foreshadowed in the 1920s, only took its definitive shape through the 'great fear of Republicans',[4] which followed the riots of 6 February 1934, and it can be defined as follows:

> It is a type of discourse, a collective statement that could be represented spatially by a three-sided object: the *defence* of the Republic and of the labour movement – both the protective walls and the marching wings – *through* the union of left-wing parties, *for* a social Republic and for peace.
>
> It is also a repository of collective actions comprising both street actions and a whole array of political rituals, mostly imported from the political life in Weimar Germany (the raised fists, the militarisation of political formations, the three arrows designed by Sergei Chakhotin for the German Social Democratic Party (SPD) and later reused by the SFIO for its logo).[5]

Both elements were mobilised in February 1934 against the cluster of nationalist-leagues, from Croix-de-Feu (Cross of Fire) to the Jeunesses Patriotes ('Patriotic Youth') to Francistes. But the very concept of fascism was reduced to a new avatar, that of 'the eternal White' (Maurice Agulhon), a character the French left-wing parties have known very well since the nineteenth century: anti-parliamentary, authoritarian, bellicose, a representative of the owning class. That is the reductive definition that was used in a mass of literature, articles and leaflets, and was also summarised in a film commissioned by the French Communist Party in 1936: Jean Renoir's *La Vie est à nous* ('Life Belongs to Us'), where the figure of the archetypal fascist was a Croix-de-Feu and served the '200 families' along with the foreign fascist powers. And the trick worked, no doubt turning 1930's Republican antifascism into a real 'rallying myth', as Georges Sorel would have put it.[6]

In order to accurately describe such an impeccable success, we first have to mention the European context: the looming threat of Nazi Germany combined with general authoritarian dynamics running throughout most of the Continent, from Portugal to Austria, from Romania to Poland. The title of Daniel Guérin's book, *La Peste brune* ('The Brown Plague'), clearly refers to this type of 'generic fascism', which also responds to a similar worldview on the other side of the political spectrum, amongst the real or so-called 'fascists'. Robert Brasillach, for instance, devoted a whole chapter of *Notre Avant-Guerre* ('Our Pre-war') to giving a 'grand tour' of European fascism, in his search for the *homo fascista*, from the Rexist Party in Belgium to the Legion of Archangel Michael in Romania, without forgetting of course the Spain of Falange.[7]

But we must also address the context within France itself, where the various left-wing parties, despite being divided and implementing different partisan or diplomatic strategies, shared one same Republican *credo* to which the French Communist Party (Parti Communiste Français, PCF) rallied with great fanfare in 1935. It was a generation shaped and moulded by the Dreyfus affair that drew the outlines of antifascism, which was often experienced as a revival of the founding event: Victor Basch, founder and chairman of the League for the Rights of Man (born 1863), the three initiators of the Watchfulness Committee of Antifascist Intellectuals (Comité de vigilance des intellectuels antifascistes, CVIA) from the oldest (Alain, born 1868) to the youngest (Paul Rivet, born 1876) or Léon Blum himself (born 1872), all started their political careers defending Captain Dreyfus. Finally, the cluster of nationalist groups against which they mobilised was likened to a type of 'fascism' described restrictively in terms of content and extensively in terms of practices. That probably does not reflect the reality as it is understood today by historians ('futuro-centrism', 'modernity', belligerence and imperialism) but it does reflect a system of representation where fascism equalled traditional authoritarianism and Bonapartism. As a matter of fact, the centre of gravity of the leagues – Taittinger's Patriotic Youth and Colonel La Rocque's *Croix-de-Feu* – was quite close to that representation. Fascism as 'imagined' and partially fantasised by the French left was similar to its main point of reference.

The 'rallying myth' therefore mobilised the people of the 1930s against an overly simplistic, extensive and mythical fascism. After the

Liberation, the myth also grew bigger from the legacy of the Second World War and the Resistance. As former communist journalist Dominique Desanti said about his own career, 'to be antifascist meant first and foremost to beat the Nazis'.[8] After 1945, 'fascism' referred to Hitler, to the Nazis, and for the next thirty-odd years, to the 'Dachau–Buchenwald–Ravensbrück' trinity. As a consequence, antifascism and the Resistance, or 'new Resistance', were the same thing: the antifascist character was someone who joined the struggle against that 'dirty war' or against the *fachos*, in line with the protesters of 12 February 1934 who were already then forerunners of the Resistance. Emmanuel d'Astier thus wrote in the newspaper *Libération*, in 1964, with no worry of anachronism: '[T]he people of Paris wrote the first chapter of the French Resistance in February 1934 and never needed a temporary Brigadier General to invite us to do so'.[9] That very same antifascism, both inherited (from the Front Populaire) and enriched (by the war and by the Resistance), would later reappear in 1945 in two successive cycles.

Antifascist Cycles after the War

Antifascism was first recycled against the Gaullist Alliance of the French People (Rassemblement du peuple français, RPF) between 1947 and 1950, then against the Poujadists in 1956, then against Charles de Gaulle's return to power[10] thanks to the 'ultra' movement of French Algeria in May 1958, then against the same 'ultras' in the guise of the Secret Army Organisation (Organisation Armée Secrète, OAS) in 1961–62. Each of those episodes showed a re-emergence of the fascist branding, the mottos and the type of actions practised before the war.

The RPF, the Poujadists ('Poujadolf', 'Maréchal Poujade') and the 'ultras' of French Algeria were all branded as fascists. The 1934 slogan, 'fascism shall not pass', would be chanted again in May 1947 before the Salle Wagram as it was hosting an 'anti-Communist' rally, in Paris in 1956 against a Poujadist meeting, in May 1958 against General de Gaulle's return to power, and again in April 1961 against the generals who supported the coup in Algiers – this time with a slight variation, 'military fascism shall not pass'. Just like in 1934 with the CVIA and the web of local committees that covered every part of the territory at that time, 1958 saw the re-creation of a Committee for the Defence of the Republic, and 1961 the constitution of the Antifascist Union's League of Action, with, in the case of the latter, local committees of various names that were more significant than originally thought.[11] Finally, the protests of 12 February 1934 were commemorated down in the streets until

1951, when the commemorations were banned by the police; they were thereafter replaced by meetings. However, this 'antifascist revival', although it does illustrate a quasi-ideal or typical use of the rear-view mirror, did not work, contrary to its predecessor. The reasons behind that failure were the context and the fact that it was impossible to unite the various left-wing parties, divided between 'Atlanticist' socialists and Soviet Union fanatics. Another reason was the subject: Gaullism just did not lend itself to being classed as extreme right; it also presented itself as an heir to the Resistance, even as an heir to 1930s antifascism, with personalities such as André Malraux and Jacques Soustelle. The only exceptions were the 1961 and more importantly the 1962 rallies against the OAS, which brought the various left-wing parties together (as a one-off) against an adversary that fitted its own representation this time.

Regarding the second cycle, which started in 1983 against the National Front (Front National, FN) and is ongoing, the burden of the rear-view mirror is still present and its use still widespread. But this time, it is less systematic and depends on the level of analysis. A multi-scale analysis reveals the existence of three different levels of rallying and discourse: theoretical and historical references brought up against the National Front, national actions, and local rallying, with interactions between the three.

Within the 'intellectual sustenance', which fed the press and the grey literature of political organisations and in turn cascaded down to the protest organisers, five major titles were published between 1984 and 1989: *L'Effet Le Pen* ('The Le Pen Effect') by Edwy Plenel and Alain Rollat, journalists for the newspaper *Le Monde*; *Les Hommes de l'extrême droite* ('The Men of the Far Right') by Alain Rollat; *Vigilance* (Vigilance) by Marie-José Chombart de Lauwe; *Au Front* ('To the Front') by Anne Tristan, a journalist close to the Revolutionary Communist League (Ligue Communiste Révolutionnaire, LCR, Trotskist); and *Le Front National à découvert* ('The National Front Unveiled'), the first academic study of the phenomenon, a collection of analyses coordinated by Nonna Mayer and Pascal Perrineau.[12] But none of these works considered the National Front as a fascist party. On the contrary, each of the books insisted both on the novelty of the FN and on how it drew on a long history of authoritarian right-wing parties. Edwy Plenel and Allain Rollat considered it to be the 'totalitarian synthesis' of a far-right legacy that spanned from MacMahon to the OAS, without forgetting Boulangism, the fascist leagues, Vichy and Poujadism. They clearly explained why the old mottos, such as 'fascism shall not pass', would not work with them. Sociologist and former resistant,

Marie-Jo Chombart de Lauwe, spoke of a 'new right wing', whereas Anne Tristan believed the FN to represent a 'powerful, very old and very French kind of xenophobia'. Political scientist Pierre-André Taguieff preferred to use the category 'national-populism', which he had coined in previous and more confidential articles, and insisted on the novelty of the phenomenon.[13] On the contrary, local rallying systematically played around a 'neo-antifascism' reconfigured around anti-racism.[14] The latter used the whole repertoire of the 1930s and the memory of the Second World War, or rather of its repulsive components: the Shoah and Vichy.

They sang 'Le Chant des Partisans' after the Liberation, just as they chanted 'fascism shall not pass' in 1934. This is the legacy in which the new slogans coined against a new enemy were embedded. And thus, they chanted 'F for Fascist, N for Nazi, down with the FN' or 'Le Pen, fascist, racist, assassin'. As for the register of the collective actions, it mostly came straight from the 1930s, more particularly with the practice of 'counter-protests' to stop Jean-Marie Le Pen from holding a meeting, discouraging people from participating en masse, or at least to discredit it. Between those two levels, national rallies came within the framework of two consecutive and very different uses of the rear-view mirror.

In 1983, the March for Equality and Against Racism lied within the scope of the educative anti-racism directly inherited from the 1960s. One of its main spokespersons, young Toumi Djaidja from Vénissieux, explained that the aim was to 'wake up the French', a mission that was clearly accomplished as he declared having left 'thinking the French were racist' but having experienced the opposite.[15] In the same way, the chants (aside from the classics 'French or immigrants, solidarity' or 'Enough with the murders') and the banners held high ('The hunt is over, we're on our way', 'France is like a motorcycle, it needs a mixture to move forward') do not refer directly to the FN or borrow from the repertoire of antifascism. The same goes for the 'Pals' Party' organised two years later by the organisation SOS Racisme ('SOS Racism', an NGO close to the Socialist Party) on 15 June 1985 at the Place de la Concorde.[16] The register is almost the same, as shown by the intervention of SOS Racisme president Harlem Désir before the concert: 'This movement does not belong to anyone, it only belongs to you, you who are wearing our badge... you French people of all origins, from the first to the tenth generation of immigrants'.[17] On 19 August 1987, on *L'heure de vérité*, one of the leading political programmes on French television at the time, Désir once again stated those references to humanism, to the 'Human Rights Party', more than to antifascism. It was indeed all about creating the largest possible front, from Republican right-wingers (Michel Noir, Bernard Stasi, Simone Veil) to the extreme left of the political spectrum, all on the moral standpoint of anti-racism rather than on the political foundation of antifascism.

Three different registers thus coexisted at the end of the 1980s: an analytic register which focused both on the novelty of the FN and on the fact that it was embedded in a long history of 'ante-fascism'; a register of national actions all built around ethical anti-racism, deliberately trans-partisan; and finally, the local register of 'neo-anti-fascism', which attempted at reviving the practices and references of the 1930s and of the Resistance in a synthesis heavily dominated by Communist culture. As we can see, the use of the rear-view mirror, as important as it was on a local level where the militants referred to a capital of tried and tested historical references, was much more of an issue on a national level. The series of analyses of the FN links it to the family tree of Boulangism, the leagues and Vichy, all the while demonstrating that it is still a new avatar made to fit France at the end of the twentieth century. As far as the 'Beurs' March' (*Marche des Beurs*) or 'SOS Racism' are concerned, they were trying to avoid the dangers of an antifascist revival by focusing more on a unifying sense of social morals than on a dividing political discourse. But although social morals tend to bring together large numbers of people – potentially, at least – they do not rally them to a cause, while a political discourse, although divisive, can act as a strong rallying force. The joint failure of all three registers, illustrated by the results of Jean-Marie Le Pen at the first stage of the 1988 presidential election (14 per cent of the votes cast), brought about reshaping 'anti-LePenism' around two new initiatives. The *Appel des 250* ('Appeal of the 250 [personalities]'), published in May 1990 in the weekly magazines *Politis* and *Rouge*, stated that 'the rise to power of a fascist and racist party put France in great danger', and that 'Le Pen, directly following Nazi ideology, is a fascist and a racist'.[18] The text was a barely hidden remake of the appeal 'To the workers' which founded the CVIA. It was signed by 250 political figures who covered the whole spectrum of French left-wing parties, from the LCR to the Socialist Party (Parti Socialiste, PS) with a few prominent members of the Resistance (the Aubracs, Claude Bourdet, Charles Tillon and Henri Rol-Tanguy). It opened the way to a 'large national protest'. The second initiative, a 'Manifesto against the National Front', was launched in June 1990, kick-started by Jean-Christophe Cambadelis, Socialist MP for Paris. Contrary to the previous initiative, this one had its roots in governmental left-wing parties, from Lionel Jospin and Dominique Strauss-Kahn (PS) to Dominique Voynet (Green Party) and Georges Marchais (PCF). More importantly, following the analysis of Pierre-André Taguieff, the Manifesto defined the FN as 'national-populism' and tried to escape the curse of the rear-view mirror in order to create a consistent anti-LePenism rather than an ill-positioned and inefficient neo-antifascism. But its rallying capacity was too severely limited by its closeness to the Socialist Party, now become a 'governmental party', and by the weight of its references: as a few local writers said, 'national-populism shall not pass' is hard to chant... The anti-FN cycle ended abruptly after the effective dissolution of the Manifesto and of the Réseau Ras l'Front at the end of the twentieth century. It goes to show how difficult it was for the militants to absorb the 'intellectual nourishment', even when they tried to, and how impossible it was to revive historical antifascism in a context poles apart from the 1930s, marked by the disappearance of right-wing predatory dictatorships and of the 'big light in the East' and the collapse of the 'Republican ecosystem'[19] on the soil that had grown historical antifascism.

A Belated Historiography

We have no choice but to acknowledge that antifascism has not been properly studied in any of its consecutive versions and remained feebly referenced until the 1990s. None of the many studies of the Front Populaire tried to define it, as if it were an obvious phenomenon, and they did not try to explain the central role that it played in constituting the coalition either.[20] In 1985, historian Jacques Droz, in *Histoire de l'antifascisme en Europe* (A History of Antifascism in Europe), presented various antifascist movements, journals and initiatives without ever even trying to define the phenomenon.[21] Only two white stones occupy this empty space in historiography: *Fascismes français* ('French Fascisms') by Jean Plumyène and Raymond Lasierra (1963), and the remarks of Antoine Prost in a 1966 article entitled 'The Protests of 12 February 1934 in the Provinces'.[22] Plumyène and Lasierra were therefore the very first to coin the issue of French fascism and antifascism, and they made a clear difference between 'real' fascism and '*fâschisme*' as imagined by antifascists. But it was Annie Kriegel who first tried to study the issue in an intervention entitled 'Antifascism: A Typical Stalinist Myth' at a conference of the Feltrinelli foundation in 1989;[23] an intervention that would later be reused in the magazine *Commentaire*. As she attacked the work of Jacques Droz directly, referring to it as an 'erudite illustration of the Stalinist myth', she explained that the prefix 'anti' allowed a group to exist through naming its own enemy, whereas the concept of 'fascism' itself was variable. As an 'elliptical concept', it did not reach full maturity until after 1933, disappeared in 1939 then reappeared in 1941. As a concept with various shapes and forms, it was allowed to 'extend or reduce the scope of the enemy to infinity and at will', all the way to socialist or social-democrat left-wing parties. As a 'fusional concept', it implied that Nazism, 'traditionalist nationalism of the Salazar or Franco kind' and counter-revolution were one and the same. Kriegel concluded that the 'exceptional influence' of antifascism could only be explained by its flexibility, most particularly 'amongst Anglo-Saxon pragmatic yet inexperienced academics'.[24] A few years later, François Furet developed a similar opinion in *Le passé d'une illusion* (The Passing of an Illusion), about the mystification of antifascism which covered up the realities of the Stalin regime.[25] These analyses only confirmed, by reversing it, the discourse held by French Communists, especially in the 1950s when Annie Kriegel and François Furet were young. To say that fascism, and therefore antifascism, were 'geometrically variable concepts' is obviously relevant when you take into account the successive returns of the Comintern and the International Communist Movement, which alternate between open and closed periods, alliance proposals to past or future partners and shooting them on sight. But such a statement makes no sense if we look to the SFIO, to the League for the Rights of Man, or even to the Radicals, whose joint importance in 1934–36 was vastly superior to the French communists. In the same way, stating that the 'genuinely fascist regime of Mussolini did not succeed in lopping off the concept of antifascism' totally obliterated the 'first antifascism wave' of the 1920s, even though it was pretty dynamic in France and even in Belgium.[26] In 1994, as a reply to those analyses, Maurice Agulhon wrote an article entitled 'Should we rethink the history of antifascism?' and reminded us of the existence of 'a number of antifascisms' that were not Soviet manipulations.[27] The weight of Communist interpretations of antifascism, as it claimed to be at the start of it or even have a monopoly over it, had been stunting the development of a serious historiography of antifascism in France for a very long time, including with those who intended to denounce its manipulations. Only at the end of the 1990s did the historiography of antifascism start growing, with a conference organised by Serge Wolikow at the University of Dijon in December 1996 and published two years later under the title 'Antifascism and the Nation'.[28] The latter intended to question antifascism under the double light of the 'growing national acculturation of labour movements' in the 1930s and of its international dimension. Serge Berstein thus explained in a debate with Aldo Agosti and Antonio Elorza that France holds a 'sui generis antifascism' which is 'incontestably spontaneous' and 'springs from the depths of opinion', and lies within the scope of 'traditional Republican patriotism'.[29] Italian historian Agosti showed that antifascism was both 'a national priority and an international obligation', but never managed to create a common reference to all democratic powers.[30]

In a way, that is the path – mixing the history of cultural and political practices and the history of partisan strategies – that I have tried to tread in my own book, *L'Antifascisme en France*, published in 2009. In order to understand antifascism in France, we have to return its diversity and reintegrate it into the long-term history of left-wing parties and of the 'Republican idea in France',[31] of which antifascism was perhaps the last expression. The antifascist foundation of the 1930s relied on a particular context that no one can duplicate: just as you can never step twice in the same river, you cannot play the same trick twice, three times or more, when the cards and the players have changed. Political players are perfectly aware of that, despite not being able to free themselves from their old frames of mind completely, which shows both the persisting importance of the rear-view mirror and the failure to create a new scope of expectations. Although the term 'antifascism' is currently only explicitly thrown around by a minority of the radical left,[32] the shadow of this word hangs over all left-wingers who only use it for its condemnatory connotation, without using this connotation in their understanding of emerging issues that European societies face or in the context of an actual political programme.

Translated by Mathieu Franks and Sonia Izrar, revised by
Casey Sellarole

Notes

1. 'IIIe Congrès de l'Internationale ouvrière socialiste', published by the IOS secretariat, Zurich, 1928, part 2, 19.
2. *Eclairer sans brûler. Salon du livre antifasciste, Gardanne, Novembre 1997.* Texts collected by S. Roche, Arles, 1997.
3. Ibid., 79.
4. According to the syndicalist André Delmas' expression, when he was Secretary-General of the Syndicat sational des instituteurs.

5. G. Vergnon, *L'Antifascisme en France. De Mussolini à Le Pen*, Rennes, 2009; also, 'Le poing levé, du rite soldatique au rite de masse', *Le Mouvement social* 212 (July–September 2005), 77–92.

6. G. Sorel, *Réflexions sur la violence*, Paris, 1926.

7. D. Guérin, *La Peste brune, a passé par là. A bicyclette à travers l'Allemagne hitlérienne*, Paris, 1933; R. Brasillach, 'Ce mal du siècle, le Fascisme...', in *Notre Avant-guerre*, Paris, 1973, 301–62.

8. D. Desanti and J.-T. Desanti, *La Liberté nous aime encore*, Paris, 2001, 63.

9. E. d'Astier, 'Trente ans déjà. Le 6 février 1934, les fascistes donnent l'assaut à la gueuse', *Libération*, 6 February 1964. The 'temporary Brigadier General' is, of course, Charles de Gaulle, Colonel in 1940, named 'temporary' General on 25 May 1940.

10. Some examples in P. Fougeyrollas and F. George, *Un philosophe dans la Résistance*, Paris, 2001, 130; P. Robrieux, *Notre génération communiste*, Paris, 1977, 33–34.

11. R. Branche and S. Thénaud (eds), *La France en guerre 1954–1962. Expériences métropolitaines de la guerre d'indépendance algérienne*, Paris, 2008, and particularly the following chapters: M. Coppin, 'De Dunkerque à Montreuil-sur-mer: un littoral ouvrier contre la guerre d'Algérie' (198–214), and M. Coppin and A. Trogneux, 'Face au putsch' (215–19).

12. E. Plenel and A. Rollat, *L'Effet Le Pen*, Paris, 1984; A. Rollat, *Les Hommes de l'extrême droite*, Paris, 1985; M.-J. Chombart de Lauwe, *Vigilance. Vieilles traditions extrémistes et droites nouvelles*, Paris, 1987; A. Tristan, *Au Front*, Paris, 1987; N. Mayer and P. Perrineau (eds), *Le Front national à découvert*, 1989.

13. P.-A. Taguieff, 'La rhétorique du national-populisme (I)', *Cahiers Bernard-Lazare* 109 (June–July 1984), 19–38; also, 'La rhétorique du national-populisme (II)', *Mots* 9 (October 1984), 113–39.

14. Vergnon, *L'Antifascisme en France*, 170 sq.

15. *Journal télévisé*, Antenne 2, 3 December 1983, the Institut national de l'audiovisuel (INA) website, www.ina.fr (accessed 27 April 2012).

16. About the birth of SOS Racisme, see Philippe Juhem's 'SOS Racisme. Histoire d'une mobilisation apolitique. Contribution à une analyse des représentations politiques après 1981', doctoral dissertation at the Department of Political Sciences, Paris X University, 1998. It shows that, unlike the 'March', which started from below, SOS began with a small group of militants who came from the LCR, well equipped with a cultural and political capital. They intended to occupy the field of youth (both student and high school), who were empty of any militant references of the post-May 1968 years, thus creating a venture closer to Doctors Without Borders or Amnesty International than to the CVIA of the 1930s.

17. *Soir 3*, www.ina.fr (accessed 27 April 2012).

18. The call made the front page ('Le Pen is a fascist') of the weekly paper *Politis* (105, 23 May 1990). It intended to federate various sensibilities 'on the left of the left of governments'. It was cited in the LCR's weekly paper *Rouge*, 1402, 24 May 1990, and then in the monthly paper *Ras l'front*, 1, July–September 1990.

19. For this concept, see J.-F. Sirinelli, *Les Vingt décisives. Le passé proche de notre avenir 1968–1985*, Paris, 2007.

20. It is true concerning the books of J. Danos and M. Gibelin, *Juin 36*, Paris, 1952, re-edited 1972; J. Kergoat, *La France du Front populaire*, Paris, 1986; and G. Lefranc, *Histoire du Front populaire*, Paris, 1965.
21. J. Droz, *Histoire de l'antifascisme en Europe, 1923–1939*, Paris, 1985.
22. J. Plumyène and R. Lasierra, *Fascismes français*, Paris, 1963; A. Prost, 'Les manifestations du 12 février 1934 en province', *Le Mouvement social* 54 (March 1966), cited in *Autour du Front populaire. Aspects du mouvement social au XXe siècle*, Paris, 2006.
23. A. Kriegel, 'Sur l'antifascisme', *Commentaire* 50 (1990), 299–302.
24. Ibid.
25. F. Furet, *Le passé d'une illusion. Essai sur l'idée communiste au XXe siècle*, Paris, 1995.
26. See 'Préhistoire de l'antifascisme', in Vergnon, *L'Antifascisme en France*, 21–42.
27. M. Agulhon, 'Faut-il réviser l'histoire de l'antifascisme?', *Le Monde diplomatique*, August 1994.
28. S. Wolikow and A. Bleton-Ruget (eds), *Antifascisme et Nation*, Dijon, 1998.
29. S. Berstein, 'Table ronde: Front Populaire et Antifascisme en débat', in Wolikow and Bleton-Ruget, *Antifascisme et Nation*, 253–54.
30. A. Agosti, 'Round Table', in Wolikow and Bleton-Ruget, *Antifascisme et Nation*, 255.
31. C. Nicolet, *L'idée républicaine en France*, Paris, 1982.
32. Let us take a caricatural example of the Femen (a radical feminist movement) protest that suggested an 'antifascist vaccine' to voters at a polling station that Marine Le Pen was scheduled to visit (*France 3 Nord-Pas de Calais*, 25 May 2014). Now let us take the tragic example: the death of young Clément Méric, an activist of Action antifasciste, who died after being attacked by a group of skinheads on 6 June 2013.

References

Agulhon, M. 'Faut-il réviser l'histoire de l'antifascisme?'. *Le Monde diplomatique*, August 1994.

Branche, R., and S. Thénaud (eds), *La France en guerre 1954–1962. Expériences métropolitaines de la guerre d'indépendance algérienne*. Paris, 2008.

Brasillach, R. 'Ce mal du siècle, le Fascisme…', in *Notre Avant-guerre*, Paris, 1973.

Chombart de Lauwe, M.-J. *Vigilance. Vieilles traditions extrémistes et droites nouvelles*. Paris, 1987.

Danos, J., and M. Gibelin. *Juin 36*. Paris, 1952, re-edited 1972.

Desanti, D., and J.-T. Desanti. *La Liberté nous aime encore*. Paris, 2001.

Droz, J. *Histoire de l'antifascisme en Europe, 1923–1939*. Paris, 1985.

Eclairer sans brûler. Anti-fascist Book Fair, Gardanne, November 1997. Texts collected by Simone Roche. Arles, 1997.

Fougeyrollas, P., and F. George. *Un philosophe dans la Résistance*. Paris, 2001.

Furet, F. *Le passé d'une illusion. Essai sur l'idée communiste au XXe siècle*. Paris, 1995.

Guérin, D. *La Peste brune a passé par là. A bicyclette à travers l'Allemagne hitlérienne*. Paris, 1933.

'IIIe Congrès de l'Internationale ouvrière socialiste', Zurich, 1928.

Juhem, P. 'SOS Racisme. Histoire d'une mobilisation apolitique. Contribution à une analyse des représentations politiques après 1981'. Ph.D. dissertation. Paris, 1998.

Kergoat, J. *La France du Front populaire*. Paris, 1986.

Kriegel, A. 'Sur l'antifascisme'. *Commentaire* 50 (1990), 299–302.

Lefranc, G. *Histoire du Front populaire*. Paris, 1965.

Mayer, N., and P. Perrineau (eds). *Le Front national à découvert*. Paris, 1989.

Nicolet, C. *L'idée républicaine en France*. Paris, 1982.

Plenel, E., and A. Rollat. *L'Effet Le Pen*. Paris, 1984.

Plumyène, J., and R. Lasierra. *Fascismes français*. Paris, 1963.

Prost, A. 'Les manifestations du 12 février 1934 en province'. *Le Mouvement social* 54 (March 1966), in *Autour du Front populaire. Aspects du mouvement social au XXe siècle*. Paris, 2006.

Robrieux, P. *Notre génération communiste*. Paris, 1977.

Rollat, A. *Les Hommes de l'extrême droite*. Paris, 1985.

Sirinelli, J.-F. *Les Vingt décisives. Le passé proche de notre avenir 1968–1985*. Paris, 2007.

Sorel, G. *Réflexions sur la violence*. Paris, 1926.

Taguieff, P.-A. 'La rhétorique du national-populisme (I)'. *Cahiers Bernard-Lazare* 109 (June–July 1984), 19–38.

———. 'La rhétorique du national-populisme (II), *Mots* 9 (October 1984), 113–39.

Tristan, A. *Au Front*. Paris, 1987.

Vergnon, G. 'Le poing levé, du rite soldatique au rite de masse'. *Le Mouvement social* 212 (July–September 2005), 77–92.

———. *L'Antifascisme en France. De Mussolini à Le Pen*. Rennes, 2009.

Wolikow, S., and A. Bleton-Ruget (eds). *Antifascisme et Nation*. Dijon, 1998.

Gilles Vergnon is associate professor of Modern History at the Institut d'Etudes Politiques de Lyon (*Sciences-Po* Lyon). He has published books about the French Resistance (*Le Vercors. Histoire et Mémoire d'un Maquis*, 2005), the history of the left in Europe (*Les gauches européennes après la victoire nazie. Entre planisme et unité d'action*, 1997) and France (*L'antifascisme en France. De Mussolini à Le Pen*, 2009; *Le modèle suédois. Les gauches françaises et l'impossible social-démocratie*, 2015). His current research focuses on Resistance guerilla movements in Europe (1940–44) and the building of social states in Western Europe in 1945–48.

13

Did Revisionism Win?

Italy between Loss of Historical Consciousness and Nostalgia for the Past

Stéfanie Prezioso

The historian's role is to reinterpret and to revise. An ultimately unremarkable aspect of historical research, the work of revision cannot be reduced to the expansion of knowledge through discovering new documents and establishing their provenance and authenticity; revision is also the work of historical consciousness, the awareness of the distance that separates the moment in which the inquiry takes place from the past to which the object belongs.[1] To use Claudio Pavone's pertinent definition, revision is an 'ethical–cultural category, which expresses the need and even more so the obligation of all human beings, cultures and social and political groups to continuously revise their own convictions … to question themselves when the times change and the people who live through them change as well'.[2] This definition of the historian's role requires therefore accounting not only for his/her choices and values, but also for the semantic space he/she inhabits, that 'inescapable plurality of interpretations' that Jürgen Habermas noted at the time of the 'historians' controversy' (*Historikerstreit*).[3] Hence, no less so than the task of establishing facts and 'eliminating everything that belongs to fables, myths and distortions',[4] the work of revision is part and parcel of the rigorous reconstruction of historical processes.

In contrast, revisionism is neither a clear object nor a concept but, as Bruno Bongiovanni demonstrated, a 'polymorphic' and 'uneven' term, one of 'remarkable plasticity', broadly related to 'the critique of dominant orthodoxy'.[5] Rarely a term that one claims for oneself, it is most often used inside quotations marks, as if it could not fully escape the suspicion attached to its polemic and condemnatory usage.[6] There is thus a fundamental difference between revision, 'an indispensible moment of historical research', and revisionism.[7] For the latter, the re-reading of historical phenomena rests on a 'moral-historical' orientation, which aims at judging and often condemning previous interpretation in the service of a political battle – a term that must be understood broadly – or a journalistic 'scoop' that exposes 'shocking' or allegedly newly discovered documents. Bongiovanni, in fact, recommended abandoning the term, arguing that its limited heuristic usefulness did not justify the confusion it introduced. However, when the term is used in combination with the (Freudian) concepts of repression and inversion (*rovescismo*), it remains pertinent for understanding a series of phenomena that emerged in Italy and elsewhere in the West in the 1970s, intensifying through the 1980s and 1990s, and reaching their zenith in the first decade of the new millennium.[8]

Historiography depends on its context, not only because it is tied to the discovery of new documents – often in relation with the politics of archival accessibility – but also because it touches upon the complex relation that every society maintains with its past, and the unstable equilibrium in its midst between history, memory and forgetting.[9] Since 1989 (the symbolic year of the fall of the Berlin Wall and the bicentennial of the French Revolution), albeit to a varying degree, all European societies have experienced a wave of revisionism premised on anti-Communism – and its corollary anti-antifascism – as its 'historical paradigm'. This revisionism put revolutionary phenomena on trial even as it walked away from the 'debts of a past that is no longer subject to ethical evaluation'.[10] The shift was facilitated by another phenomenon that took place at the end of the 'short twentieth century', the loss of the horizon of social transformation, which some authors defined as 'the end of the postwar', associated with Francis Fukuyama's ringing declaration of 'the end of history'.[11] In Italy, this was supplemented at the beginning of the 1990s with the collapse of the political system and the disappearance of the Communist, Socialist and Christian-Democratic parties – caught in the *Tangentopoli* scandal and attacked by the judiciary machine in Operation *mani pulite* ('clean hands') – and with Silvio Berlusconi's stepping into the political arena (his so-called *discesa in campo*), allied with former neo-fascist Gianfranco Fini, and calling for a 'new Republic' to replace the 'old political class, overthrown by reality and overtaken by the times'.[12]

In the following twenty years, revisionism would plant strong roots in the Italian soil, taking advantage of the exceptional success of the push towards hegemony of what Gabriele Turi called 'the culture of the plural right-wing'.[13] It would position itself as the alternative to a so-called orthodoxy of a Marxist, Communist, 'populist-Leninist', and generally antifascist historiography, that had allegedly dominated the discipline – as well as the greater part of public opinion – in postwar Italy.[14] Raising the banner of a 'de-ideologised', 'dispassionate', and above all 'disinterested' history, the revisionist reading of the recent past, and notably of fascism, antifascism and the Resistance, would establish itself as the reassertion of a long-suppressed self-evidence.[15] Revisionism has advanced to the point that it is legitimate to ask whether it has actually won.[16]

'Liquid Times'

'Today's world no longer has any kind of stability; it is shifting, strad-dling, gliding away all the time', wrote Paul Virilio.[17] In this 'modern fluid' world, characterised by 'self-intensifying, compulsive and obses-sive modernisation', memory and history appear as a useless burden and a lure; that is especially true for history that is charged with values to be invested in the present.[18] As we are carried into the twenty-first century at the breakneck speed of a 'direct narration' that obliterates the ties between past, present and future, it seems as if little is left to those most conscious among us except to contemplate history – like the angel of history in Walter Benjamin's reading of Klee's painting *Angelus Novus* – as 'one single catastrophe, which unceasingly piles rubble on top of rubble and hurls it before his feet', unable 'to awaken the dead and to piece together what has been smashed'.[19] In a world in which the fluidity of references makes history a kind of 'blob that holds ev-erything and its opposite', destroying the past thus appears as the only alternative to political irrelevance.[20]

In this process, the media has become a true historical agent. With its numerous and varied channels, it is 'capable of imposing a certain memory on public opinion and eliciting this or that way of looking at the past'.[21] The media – and the culture industry in general – thus be-comes the site of the reification of history.[22] From this perspective, the over-mediatisation of historical themes related to fascism – in particu-lar, the Second World War and its share of horrors, as well as the cru-cial period of the European Resistance movements – goes hand in hand with our societies' loss of historical consciousness.[23] In its stead we find, as it were, the 'fascination with the sublime', that 'history without time' to which Marco Revelli has alluded in his work.[24] Since the 1980s, the extraordinary mobilisation of images, symbols and representations as-sociated with the Second World War has significantly altered the way Western societies relate to this dramatic past. This historical imaginary forms the basis of an official and media-supported instrumentalisation that produces a diffuse and sometimes unconscious self-referential perception of the traces left by the event in the present. Subject to this 'tyranny of the present', the Second World War has been purged of its most contradictory, controversial and dramatic aspects. While this observation is scarcely new, a few years ago it was still possible to encounter luminous witnesses to a different historical consciousness; by now, to borrow an image from Pier Paolo Pasolini, the fireflies have disappeared.[25]

It follows that it is impossible to reflect on the way our societies 'cultivate [their] past or bury it, reconstruct it, constitute it, mobilise it', without situating this reflection in the conditions of the 'present time' of historiographic production in the West.[26] This is a time when, as Eric Hobsbawm once wrote, 'the destruction of the past, or rather of the social mechanisms that link one's contemporary experience to that of earlier generations, is one of the most characteristic and eerie phenomena of the late twentieth century'.[27] In the wake of the 'crisis' of the models and cultural values of the 'short twentieth century', the public use of history undoubtedly contributes (as Nicola Gallerano argued) to the emergence of a historical common sense. But it is also conducive to the formation of a diffuse, implicit and inchoate sense of the past's presence in the present.[28] This past, assembled through the mediatised mobilization of utterly heterogeneous cultural references, is imaginary and counterfactual.[29]

Both representations and emotional excitation play a cardinal role in this mobilisation. What becomes important is not so much the greater or lesser plausibility of the historical account, but the articulation of a 'nostalgia for the past', the carrier wave for what Levi Della Torre dubbed the 'end of the postwar', when 'the positive idea of change is replaced by the themes of danger, decadence and pollution'.[30] The 'nostalgia for the past' works through what Michel de Certeau called composite cultural material; the use of photographs, images and stories of all kinds in a way that blurs the boundaries between fiction and reality, and between past and present – an art perfected over decades in Italy by popular magazines such as *Gente* and *Oggi*.[31] The image thus becomes one of the principal vectors of the construction of a view of the past; it is through the image, which makes historical discourse more explicit and immediately perceptible, that history is popularised. A good example is the reconstruction of the fascist regime – and conversely of the Italian partisans – in the Italian media in general, and in particular in the 'deeply national' medium of television, carrier of identity and memory. Italian television amplified the 'rehabilitative orthodoxy' of the 'good' Mussolini, becoming the propagator of a 'forgiving memory' of the regime, based on a reassuring image of a fascism presented as 'necessary' to the 'redemption of national identity' and to the subsequent struggle against Communism.[32]

The prolific journalist Bruno Vespa, who hosts the RAI television programme *Porta a Porta*, always very friendly towards Silvio Berlusconi, is the recognised master of the art of surfing the 'nostalgia for the past'. A single episode, that of 20 October 2004 dedicated to 'grandpa Benito', will suffice as an example: Romano Mussolini and his daughter Alessandra 'shared' with the public intimate details of the life of a man who was 'all about family and home' [*tutto casa e famiglia*]: 'Bruno Vespa presented us the "soap opera" of the Mussolini family', wrote Curzio Maltese in *La Repubblica* two days later, 'taking fascism off the hook by trivialising it ... two hours in the "story of an Italian", a charming and sporty guy, good husband, excellent father, affectionate father-in-law, unforgettable grandfather, who incidentally happened to be a dictator for twenty years, with the known inconveniences but one shouldn't exaggerate all that ... the '*Porta a Porta* of nostalgia' was a family get together with film clips and the emotional leafing through the photo album'.[33]

In this sense, Italian television played a role in what Gianpasquale Santomassimo calls 'the Italian ideology', namely, the 'sweetening of the [fascist] phenomenon [that] serves as a cover for a benign collective self-absolution, which is by now constitutive of Italian mass culture'.[34] This ideology, which emerged as soon as the Second World War ended, paints the picture of an Italy whose honest and industrious people wanted nothing more than to live peacefully, and, like the character of Gennaro Jovine in Eduardo de Filippo's theatre play, were waiting 'that the night shall pass' (*adda passà 'a nuttata*).[35]

The Italian media's tendency towards self-absolution grew stronger during the 1980s, the 'accursed' 1980s, the decade of Thatcher and Reagan, of the ubiquitous injunction to get rich, the imposed individualism of 'individuals without individuality', and the anti-politics that constituted from this perspective the decisive break, the beginning of the 'great leap backwards' decried by Serge Halimi.[36] As prime minister, the Socialist Bettino Craxi began attacking the traditions, history of struggle and cultural and political content of the Italian workers' movement, strongly rooted in the Communist Party, which he saw as an impediment to his projects of transformation.[37] It is thus in the 1980s that the idea of fascism 'with a human face' began circulating, together with the image of a 'blind' antifascism, allegedly insensitive to the threat posed by those other enemies of democracy (namely,

Communists), and in any event incapable of embodying what an 'authentic Republican democracy' should be.[38] Renzo De Felice started the fire in the mid-1970s with the book *Fascism: An Informal Introduction to its Theory and Practice*.[39] Interviewed by Michael Ledeen, De Felice called antifascism 'a mentality of intolerance and of ideological oppression which seeks to disqualify its opponents in order to destroy them'.[40] A decade later he repeated these accusations in two interviews in the *Corriere della Sera* with Giuliano Ferrara – who would soon become a devotee of Berlusconi – in which he made a clear distinction between democracy and antifascism, insisted that historiographical revisionism was necessary in a period of 'political innovation', and called for using it as a foundation for the second Italian Republic.[41] These debates, at once political and historiographical, have then been injected into the public space through a number of channels, such as exhibitions about the 'modernity' of fascism, docufictions produced by the RAI, and cinema that focuses on the intimate and the private – for example, Pasquale Squittieri's prototypical 1984 film *Claretta*, which tells the story of Clara Petacci, Mussolini's mistress, who was executed with him.[42]

Another threshold was crossed in 1994, after the electoral success of Berlusconi's coalition, with the massive adoption by the Italian media of a new, revisionist orthodoxy, unburdened by doubts, which relied on a historiography 'whose seriousness [was] inversely proportional to its impact on the media'.[43] This revisionist orthodoxy, although distinct from Renzo de Felice's work, would have been impossible without it, in particular the interview books, of which the most important was *Rosso e Nero*, a true 'programmatic manifesto of Italian revisionism'.[44] This new orthodoxy set itself the task of updating and rehabilitating what has been the project of the neo-fascist Movimento Sociale Italiano (MSI) since the 1950s, to bring about a reconciliation between fascist and antifascist 'memory'. The documentary *Combat Film*, shown on RAI in April 1993, a hagiographical account of the so-called 'youth of Salò' – marked the change in the political climate.[45] The film, based on footage taken by US troops between 1943 and 1946, was 'one-sided'.[46] It depicted partisans 'as machinegun-toting renegades answerable to no one except themselves', whereas the fascists, beginning with the display of Mussolini's corpse, were represented as victims. As Filippo Focardi put it, 'revisionism concerning antifascism and the Resistance thus goes hand in hand with revisionism concerning the fascist dictatorship'.[47] The Italian media not only accompanied this transformation but to an extent led it, responding to the appeal of novelty against what appeared to be a form of conservatism all the more incomprehensible since fascism was long gone.

The Culture of the 'Plural Right' against the Popolo dei morti (People of the Dead)

It is impossible to understand the success of this revisionist orthodoxy in Italy without considering the role of the upheavals that shook Italian society beginning in the early 1990s: the collapse of the Italian political system, the creation of Forza Italia, associated with the makeover of the neo-fascist MSI, which became 'Alleanza Nazionale' in 1995, and with the powerful surge, from the early 1980s, of Umberto Bossi's party, La Lega Nord. The dramatic ascendance of this new right in the twenty years that followed can be attributed to its unprecedented capacity to combine political cultures of very different lineages through the construction of a fascism-friendly 'story of origins' that appealed to all the elements that constituted it, from Bossi's Lega Nord, a party that united an obsessed regionalism with racism and with an anti-state sentiment, to Alleanza Nazionale, with its well-known neofascist moorings. The new 'plural'[48] right that rallied to support Berlusconi, ideologically cemented by anti-Communism and its corollary, anti-antifascism, would put the systematic destruction of antifascism as a political and cultural reference point high on its political agenda. And its task was facilitated by the growing remoteness of the event, with the inevitable change in perspective, by the death of its protagonists, some of whom had become its historians, and by the arrival on the Italian political scene of a generation whose parents had not experienced fascism.[49] These conditions were supplemented by what Francesco Biscone called 'the repressed of the Republic', namely, the persistence, after the Second World War, of a reactionary anti-democratic culture; it is this culture that would become fertile ground to Berlusconi's coalition.[50]

The 'plural right' that emerged in the 1990s, taking advantage of the political crisis, owed its power of persuasion to two factors: first, its ability to combine diverse political cultures, without smoothing the rough edges specific to each tradition, through the key ideological theme of an anti-Communism founded on the memory of an Italian Communist Party – a party that at one time exceeded two million members;[51] and second, the successful mobilisation of a media network (public as well as private television broadcasters, daily newspapers, journals) that set itself the task of reshaping public opinion, thus assuring it what Gabriele Turi calls a 'sub-cultural hegemony', which allowed the right to present itself as a 'non-partisan', eclectic and uniquely authentic representation of a timeless Italian culture.[52]

The consecration of historiographical revisionism in its most outrageous version serves to constitute and legitimise a new Republic with its distinctive calendars, on which a rarefied antifascism figures only in the commemorations in which the West celebrates itself.[53] This Republic requires a retroactive 'national reconciliation' that would be capable of integrating Fini's ex-neo-fascists.[54] Revisionism's 'new blockbuster historiography' shines therefore in the re-reading of the period of the Resistance, the foundational moment of the so-called First Republic.[55] One thinks of the extraordinary success of the books of an author such as Giampaolo Pansa, who self-identifies as a revisionist, on such topics as the 'lie' of the Resistance, its 'dirty war' and its 'crimes'.[56]

Beginning in the early 1990s, the Resistance was increasingly represented as the site of the attempt by 'subversive' Communist partisans to impose their dictatorship; Pansa's novels offer the most accomplished examples of this trend.[57] The Resistance became 'one violence opposing another'.[58] An often cited example is the partisans' 'summary justice', responsible for around ten thousand deaths in fascist ranks.[59] This de-contextualized reading, which relies on a historical critique of violence, assumes the status of the rediscovery of a repressed self-evidence, thus brushing aside hundreds of local and national studies of the violence of the war, of Italian society in the period, of the Resistance as a real movement inscribed in its historical time, and of the motivations but also the contradictions of the movements and militants, female and male, who proposed and embodied new orientations, who organised according to political criteria consolidated in the course of battle, and who made their painful choices in painful circumstances.[60]

In conclusion, these times of 'soft apocalypse', 'antifascism seems no longer capable of inspiring "real passions"'.[61] It is not that the debates over the role, function and moral and political value of antifascist politics in the period between the wars and their aftermath have lost their vigour, but the retroactive smoothing of the roughness inherent in every historical process has won an increasing number of adepts. The growing remoteness of this stark period of Italian and world history has the effect of accelerating the 'crisis of antifascism', most importantly by drowning the period's historiographical problematics in a 'tide of indistinction'.[62] History and memory are blurred together in a retroactive reconciliation that effectively ranks the violence of both 'totalitarian ideologies' as equal on a single 'scale of evil'. Neither worse nor better than each other, fascists and antifascists appear in this perspective as equally guilty and therefore equally innocent.[63]

This reading of history relies on similarities and analogies rather than on distinctions and comparisons, the indispensable tools of historical critique. It involves those public and political uses of history that in the last twenty years have subordinated the past to the needs of the present, but also the manner in which our societies treat and deal with their past.[64] The virulence with which antifascism and the experience of Resistance were placed on the index is thus proportional to the fear that 'the remembrance and collective redemption of the victims of past struggles' – of those dead who, in Calamadrei's words, 'we know one by one, who fell by our side, in prisons and on gallows, in the mountains and on the plains, on the Russian steppes and in the sands of Africa, on the seas and in the deserts' – would lead to a 'revolutionary critique of the present'.[65]

Today more than ever, history is made to obey the unspoken prohibition against 'calling the present into question'.[66] The 'perverse' omissions and media distortions that this prohibition puts in play are inseparable from the substitution of the opposition between democracy and anti-democracy for that between fascism and antifascism, so that democracy appears as synonymous with liberalism, and the boundaries of anti-democracy extend to encompass anything that fails to fit the liberal view of the world.[67] Taking advantage of the 'collective self-absolution' of fascism that began as soon as the war ended, and of the political, economic and cultural upheavals of the 1970s and 1980s, and also of the generational shift, the revisionist reading of history took root in the public imagination. Attached to it was an assault on the historian's craft – also in crisis, and increasingly perceived as 'the dust-covered heritage of a useless caste' – that dispensed with the whole set of values that underlie the profession, and with it, with the social function of history.[68] One can only hope that the over-the-top revisionism that Angelo D'Orsi calls '*rovescismo*' ('inversion') disappears over time from Italian mass culture.[69]

Nevertheless, in this 'liquid society' in which the past is either a burden or an opportunity for experiencing the 'fascination with the sublime', one catches oneself lamenting like Dante Livio Bianco the time when 'divisions were clear cut' and a 'sense of necessity was at the root of this idea of freedom, a calm acceptance of the fact that in the end we were outlaws of an impossible world'.[70]

Translated by Gabriel Ash

Notes

1. M. De Certeau, *L'écriture de l'histoire*, Paris, 1975.
2. C. Pavone, 'Per la storia del revisionismo', *Atti del convegno 'Mappe del 900'*, *I Viaggi di Erodoto, Rivista di cultura storica* 46 (2002).

3. J. Habermas, 'Du différent en droit. Quelques remarques sur le "pluralisme des interprétations"', in J. Habermas, *Après l'Etat–nation*, Paris, 2000, 195; M. Cuillerai, 'L'irréconcilié: l'histoire critique aux marges de l'amnistie', *L'Homme et la Société* 159 (2006), 33.

4. P. Vidal-Naquet, 'Les assassins de la mémoire', in P. Vidal-Naquet, *Les assassins de la mémoire*, 3rd edn, Paris, 2005.

5. P. Vidal-Naquet, 'Thèses sur le "révisionnisme"', in Vidal-Naquet, *Les assassins de la mémoire*, 103.

6. B. Bongiovanni, '"Revisionismo": storia e antistoria di una parola', *Passato e presente* 60 (2003), 17–28.

7. A. D'Orsi, 'Dal revisionismo al rovescismo', in A. Del Boca (ed.), *La storia negata. Il revisionismo e il suo uso politico*, Vicenza, (2009) 2010, 349.

8. Del Boca, *La storia negata*, 9; D'Orsi, 'Dal revisionismo al rovescismo'; A. Mammone, 'A Daily Revision of the Past: Fascism, Anti-Fascism, and Memory in Contemporary Italy', *Modern Italy* 11 (2006), 211–26.

9. P. Ricoeur, *La mémoire, l'histoire, l'oubli*, Paris, 2000.

10. Bongiovanni, "Revisionismo", 25; S. Luzzatto, *La crisi dell'antifascismo*, Turin, 2004; E. Traverso, 'De l'anticommunisme. L'histoire du 20e siècle relue par Nolte, Furet et Courtois', *L'Homme et la société* 140–41 (2001), 169–94.

11. E.J. Hobsbawm, *Age of Extremes: The Short Twentieth Century 1914–1991*, London, 1997; S.L. Della Torre, 'Fine del dopoguerra e sintomi antisemitici', *Rivista di storia contemporanea* 4 (1984), 437–555.

12. S. Berlusconi, 'Il discorso della discesa in campo. Per il mio Paese', 26 January 1994 (http://www.cini92.altervista.org/discorsoberlusconi.html) (accessed 19 January 2015).

13. G. Turi, *La cultura delle destre. Alla ricerca dell'egemonia culturale in Italia*, Turin, 2013.

14. S. Courtois, 'Les crimes du communisme', in S. Courtois (ed.), *Le livre noir du communisme*, Paris, 1997, 9–41; R. De Felice, *Rosso e Nero*, Milan, 1995; E. Galli della Loggia, *La morte della patria. La crisi dell'idea di nazione tra Resistenza, antifascismo e Repubblica*, Bari, 1996; Idem, 'Formes et fonctions de l'antifascisme dans la vie politique italienne. Légitimité ou Légitimation?', *Vingtième siècle* 100(4) (2008), 69–78; F. Furet, *Penser la révolution française*, Paris, 1978; F. Furet, Le passé d'une illusion, Paris, 1995. [The passing of an illusion, Chicago, 2000]

15. G. Santomassimo, 'Marxismo e storia dal solido al liquido', *Passato e Presente* 72 (2007), 138.

16. Del Boca, *La storia negata*, 9; D'Orsi, 'Dal revisionismo al rovescismo', 329–71; Mammone, 'Daily Revision of the Past', 211–26.

17. J. Armitage (ed.), *Paul Virilio: From Modernism to Hypermodernism and Beyond*, London, 2000, 48; Z. Bauman, *Liquid Times: Living in an Age of Uncertainty*, Oxford, 2007.

18. Z. Bauman, *Culture in a Liquid Modern World*, Cambridge, 2011, 21.

19. W. Benjamin, *On the Concept of History* (1940) 2005, translated by Dennis Redmond. http://www.marxists.org/reference/archive/benjamin/1940/history.htm

20. S. Pivato, 'Storia e identità giovanile', *I viaggi di Erodoto. Rivista di cultura storica* 46 (2002), 261–66.

21. P. Blanchard and I. Veyrat-Masson (eds), *Les guerres de la mémoire. La France et son histoire*, Paris, 2008, 31; M. Isnenghi (ed.), *I luoghi della memoria. Strutture ed eventi dell'Italia unita*, Bari, 1996–1997; P. Sorlin, *L'immagine e l'evento: l'uso storico delle fonti audiovisuali*, Turin, 1999.

22. E. Traverso, 'Le memorie dell'Europa. La fine del "principio speranza"', in F. Focardi and B. Groppo (eds), *L'Europa e le sue memorie. Politiche e culture del ricordo dopo il 1989*, Rome, 2013, 280.

23. E. Traverso, *Le passé mode d'emploi, histoire, mémoire, politique*, Paris, 2005.

24. M. Revelli, 'Storia e scienze sociali: una storia senza tempo per un tempo senza storia?', *Movimento operaio e socialista* 1–2 (1987), 27–44; N. Gallerano (ed.), *L'uso pubblico della storia*, Milan, 1995.

25. P.P. Pasolini, *Scritti corsari*, Milan (*Corriere della Sera*, 1 February 1975); S. Pivato uses the same image in S. Pivato, *Vuoti di memoria. Usi e abusi della storia nella vita pubblica italiana*, Bari, 2007, 41.

26. F. Hartog and G. Lenclud, 'Régimes d'historicité', in A. Dutu and N. Dodille, *L'Etat des lieux en sciences sociales*, Paris, 1993, 23.

27. Hobsbawm, *Age of Extremes*, 3.

28. Gallerano, *L'uso pubblico della storia*.

29. P. Ricoeur, *Temps et récit*, Paris, 1983–1985.

30. Della Torre, 'Fine del dopoguerra e sintomi antisemitici', 437–55; N. Gallerano, 'Fine del caso italiano? La storia politica tra "politicità" e "scienza"', *Movimento operaio e socialista* 1–2 (1987), 17.

31. G. Eley, 'Finding People's War Film: British Collective Memory and WWII', *American Historical Review* 3 (2001), 818–38.

32. M. Franzinelli, 'Mussolini, revisionato e pronto per l'uso', in Del Boca (ed.), *La storia negata*, 205; S. Serenelli, '"It was like something that you have at home which becomes so familiar that you don't even pay attention to it": Memories of Mussolini and Fascism in Predappio, 1922–2010', *Modern Italy* 18(2) (2013), 157–75; I. Veyrat-Masson, *Télévision et histoire, la confusion des genres: docudrama, docufiction et fictions du réel*, Brussels, 2008.

33. C. Maltese, 'Soap Opera Mussolini', *La Repubblica*, 22 October 2004.

34. G. Santomassimo, 'La trincea del totalitarismo', *Il Manifesto*, 3 October 2004.

35. G. De Luna, 'La Repubblica italiana nata dalla guerra', *Passato e Presente* 81 (2010), 25; E. De Filippo, 'Napoli milionaria (1945)', in *Cantata dei giorni dispari*, Turin, 1976.

36. M. Gervasoni, *Storia d'Italia degli anni Ottanta. Quando eravamo moderni*, Venice, 2010.

37. P. Morgan, '"I was there, too": Memories of Victimhood in Wartime Italy', *Modern Italy* 14 (2009), 220; P.P. Poggi, *Nazismo e revisionismo storico*, Rome, 1997; G. De Luna, *La passione e la ragione. Il mestiere dello storico contemporaneo*, Milan, 2011, 81.

38. R. De Felice, 'De Felice e il superamento dell'antifascismo', *Corriere della sera*, 8 January 1988; F. Focardi, *La guerra della memoria. La Resistenza nel dibattito politico italiano dal 1945 a oggi*, Bari, 2005, 255–58; S. Prezioso, 'Prise en otages des victimes et usages publics de l'histoire', *Amnis. Revue de civilisations contemporaines Europes/Amériques* 6 (2006), 121–34; Eadem, 'Antifascism

and Antitotalitarianism: The Italian Debate', *Journal of Contemporary History* 43 (2008), 555–72.

39. R. De Felice, *Fascism: An Informal Introduction to its Theory and Practice. An Interview with Michael A. Ledeen*, New Brunswick, NJ, 1976.

40. Ibid., 26.

41. R. De Felice, 'De Felice e il superamento dell'antifascismo', *Corriere della sera*, 27 December 1987 (and 1988, see Note 38); Focardi, *La guerra della memoria*, 252–54; G. De Luna, 'Revisionismo e Resistenza', in Del Boca (ed.), *La storia negata*; J. Jacobelli (ed.), *Il fascismo e gli storici oggi*, Bari, 1988.

42. Gervasoni, *Storia d'Italia degli anni Ottanta*; P. Dogliani, 'La Seconda guerra mondiale: le politiche della memoria in Europa', in F. Focardi and B. Groppo (eds), *L'Europa e le sue memorie*, 37; R.J.B. Bosworth and P. Dogliani (eds), *Italian Fascism: History, Memory and Representation*, New York, 1999; S. Gundle, 'Playing the Dictator: Re-enactments of Mussolini in Film and Television', *Modern Italy* 18(2) (2013), 177–95.

43. G. Corni, *Fascismo, condanne e revisioni*, Rome, 2011, 108.

44. D'Orsi, 'Dal revisionismo al rovescismo', 353; De Luna, 'Revisionismo e Resistenza', 311–12.

45. G. De Luna, *La Repubblica del dolore. Le memorie di un'Italia divisa*, Milan, 2011; G. Crainz, 'I programmi televisivi sul fascismo e la Resistenza,' in E. Collotti (ed.), *Fascismo e antifascismo. Rimozioni, revisioni, negazioni*, Bari, 2000, 463–92; S. Neri Serneri, 'A Past to Be Thrown Away? Politics and History in the Italian Resistance', *Contemporary European History* 4(3) (1995), 367–81; B. Spinelli, 'La TV e l'Italia malata', *La Stampa*, 8 April 1994.

46. Neri Serneri, 'A Past to Be Thrown Away?', 373.

47. F. Focardi, 'Il passato conteso. Transizione politica e guerra della memoria in Italia dalla crisi della Prima repubblica ad oggi', in F. Focardi and B. Groppo (eds), *L'Europa e le sue memorie*, 56.

48. G. Caldiron, *La destra plurale. Dalla preferenza nazionale alla tolleranza zero*, Rome, 2001; N. Tranfaglia, *Anatomia dell'Italia repubblicana 1943–2009*, Florence, 2010.

49. Luzzatto, *La crisi dell'antifascismo*, 11.

50. F. Biscione, *Il sommerso della Repubblica. La democrazia italiana e la crisi dell'antifascismo*, Turin, 2003.

51. P. Anderson, 'Italy. An Invertebrate Left: Italy's Squandered Heritage', *London Review of Books*, vol. 31 (12 March 2009), 5; Idem, 'An entire order converted into what it was intended to end', *London Review of Books*, vol. 31 (26 February 2009), 4; G. Caldiron, *La destra plurale*; N. Tranfaglia, *Anatomia dell'Italia repubblicana 1943–2009*.

52. G. Turi, *La cultura delle destre*, 72.

53. G. Napolitano, 'L'Italia e il D-Day', *La Repubblica*, 8 June 2014; S. Woolf, 'Fine della Patria?', *Passato e Presente* 68 (2006), 90; F. Cicchitto, 'Forza Italia, da movimento a partito di governo', presented in the seminar 'La Casa delle libertà. Radici e valori di un'alleanza nuova', Todi, 31 January – 1 February 2003; G. Turi, 'Usi e abusi della storia: storia di lotta e (ora) di governo', *Passato e Presente* 80 (2010), 104; A. Bistarelli, 'La casa delle libertà storiografiche', *Passato e Presente* 66 (2006), 5–12.

54. N. Bobbio, *De Senectute e altri scritti autobiografici*, Turin, 1996, 8; Luzzatto, *La crisi dell'antifascismo*, 51; Pavone, 'Per la storia del revisionismo'.

55. G. Rochat, 'La Resistenza', in E. Collotti (ed.), *Fascismo e antifascismo. Rimozioni, revisioni, negazioni*, Bari, 2000, 273–92.

56. G. Pansa, *La grande bugia. Le sinistre italiane e il sangue dei vinti*, Milan, 2006; Idem, *Il revisionista*, Milan, 2009; Idem, *I vinti non dimenticano. I crimini ignorati della nostra guerra civile*, Milan, 2010; Idem, *La guerra sporca dei partigiani e dei fascisti*, Milan, 2012.

57. Corni, *Fascismo, condanne e revisioni*, 96.

58. De Felice, 'De Felice e il superamento dell'antifascismo'; F. Focardi, *La guerra della memoria*, 255–58; Prezioso, 'Prise en otages des victimes', 121–34.

59. G. Crainz, 'La giustizia sommaria in Italia dopo la Seconda guerra mondiale', in M. Flores (ed.), *Storia, verità, giustizia: I crimini del XX secolo*, Milan, 2001, 162.

60. C. Pavone, *A Civil War: A History of the Italian Resistance*, London, 2013; Santomassimo, 'Marxismo e storia dal solido al liquido', 137–44; L. Baldissara and P. Pezzino, *Il massacro. Guerra ai civili a Monte Solo*, Bologna, 2009; S. Peli, *Storia della Resistenza in Italia*, Turin, 2006.

61. B. Méheust, *La nostalgie de l'occupation*, Paris, 2012, 21–22.

62. Luzzatto, *La crisi dell'antifascismo*, 12.

63. G. Santomassimo, 'Metabolizzare il fascismo', *Passato e Presente* 77 (2009), 147.

64. Ricoeur, *La mémoire, l'histoire, l'oubli*, 26.

65. De Luna, 'La Repubblica italiana nata dalla guerra', 21.

66. C. Le Bissonais, *Mémoires plurielles: cinéma et images, lieux de mémoire?*, Grâne, 2007.

67. L. Rapone, 'Antifascismo e storia d'Italia', in E. Collotti (ed.), *Fascismo, antifascismo. Rimozioni, revisioni, negazioni*, Bari, 2000, 239; E. Traverso, *L'histoire comme champ de bataille. Interpréter la violence du 20e siècle*, Paris, 2010.

68. S. Fiori, 'Una storia in crisi', *La Repubblica*, 6 February 2014.

69. D'Orsi, 'Dal revisionismo al rovescismo', 329–71.

70. D.L. Bianco, *Venti mesi di guerra partigiana nel Cuneese*, [s.l.], 1946, 8–10; L. Casalino, 'Politica e cultura nell'Italia repubblicana: memoria e interpretazioni della Resistenza nella galassia azionista', *Laboratoire italien* 3 (2002), 131.

References

Anderson, P. 'An entire order converted into what it was intended to end'. *London Review of Books*, vol. 31 (26 February 2009), 4.

———. 'Italy. An Invertebrate Left: Italy's Squandered Heritage'. *London Review of Books*, vol. 31 (12 March 2009), 5.

Armitage, J. (ed.). *Paul Virilio: From Modernism to Hypermodernism and Beyond*. London, 2000.

Baldissara, L., and P. Pezzino. *Il massacro. Guerra ai civili a Monte Solo*. Bologna, 2009.

Bauman, Z. *Liquid Times: Living in an Age of Uncertainty*. Oxford, 2007.
———. *Culture in a Liquid Modern World*. Cambridge, 2011.
Benjamin, W. *On the Concept of History* (1940) 2005. Translated by Dennis Redmond. http://www.marxists.org/reference/archive/benjamin/1940/history.htm
Bianco, D.L. *Venti mesi di guerra partigiana nel Cuneese*. [s.l.], 1946.
Biscione, F. *Il sommerso della Repubblica. La democrazia italiana e la crisi dell'antifascismo*. Turin, 2003.
Bistarelli, A. 'La casa delle libertà storiografiche'. *Passato e Presente* 66 (May–August 2006), 5–12.
Blanchard, P., and I. Veyrat-Masson (eds). *Les guerres de la mémoire. La France et son histoire*. Paris, 2008.
Bobbio, N. *De Senectute e altri scritti autobiografici*. Turin, 1996.
Bongiovanni, B. '"Revisionismo": storia e antistoria di una parola'. *Passato e presente* 60 (2003), 17–28.
Bosworth, R.J.B., and P. Dogliani (eds). *Italian Fascism: History, Memory and Representation*. New York, 1999.
Caldiron, G. *La destra plurale. Dalla preferenza nazionale alla tolleranza zero*. Rome, 2001.
Casalino, L. 'Politica e cultura nell'Italia repubblicana: memoria e interpretazioni della Resistenza nella galassia azionista', *Laboratoire italien* 3 (2002), 131.
Certeau, Michel de. *L'écriture de l'histoire*. Paris, 1975.
Corni, G. *Fascismo, condanne e revisioni*. Rome, 2011.
Courtois, S. 'Les crimes du communisme', in S. Courtois (ed.), *Le livre noir du communisme*. Paris, 1997, 9–41.
Crainz, G. 'I programmi televisivi sul fascismo e la Resistenza', in E. Collotti (ed.), *Fascismo e antifascismo. Rimozioni, revisioni, negazioni*. Bari, 2000, 463–92.
———. 'La giustizia sommaria in Italia dopo la Seconda guerra mondiale', in M. Flores (ed.), *Storia, verità, giustizia: I crimini del XX secolo*. Milan, 2001, 163–70.
Cuillerai, M. 'L'irréconcilié: l'histoire critique aux marges de l'amnistie'. *L'Homme et la Société* 159 (2006), 25–50.
De Felice, R. *Fascism: An Informal Introduction to its Theory and Practice. An Interview with Michael A. Ledeen*. New Brunswick, 1976 (first Italian edition, *Intervista sul fascismo, a cura di Michael Ledeen*, 1975).
———. *Rosso e Nero*. Milan, 1995.
De Filippo, E. 'Napoli milionaria (1945)', in *Cantata dei giorni dispari*. Turin, 1976.
Del Boca, A. (ed.). *La storia negata. Il revisionismo e il suo uso politico*. Vicenza, 2010.
Della Torre, S.L. 'Fine del dopoguerra e sintomi antisemitici'. *Rivista di storia contemporanea* 4 (1984), 437–55.
De Luna, G. *La passione e la ragione. Il mestiere dello storico contemporaneo*. Milan, 2001.
———. 'Revisionismo e Resistenza', in A. Del Boca (ed.), *La storia negata. Il revisionismo e il suo uso politico*. Vicenza, (2009) 2010, 293–328.
———. 'La Repubblica italiana nata dalla guerra'. *Passato e Presente* 81 (2010), 19–28.

————. *La Repubblica del dolore. Le memorie di un'Italia divisa.* Milan, 2011.

Dogliani, P. 'La Seconda guerra mondiale: le politiche della memoria in Europa', in F. Focardi and B. Groppo (eds), *L'Europa e le sue memorie. Politiche e culture del ricordo dopo il 1989.* Rome, 2013, 27–50.

D'Orsi, A. 'Dal revisionismo al rovescismo', in A. Del Boca (ed.), *La storia negata. Il revisionismo e il suo uso politico.* Vicenza, (2009) 2010, 329–71.

Eley, G. 'Finding People's War Film: British Collective Memory and World War II'. *American Historical Review* 3 (June 2001), 818–38.

Focardi, F. *La guerra della memoria. La Resistenza nel dibattito politico italiano dal 1945 a oggi.* Bari, 2005.

————. 'Il passato conteso. Transizione politica e guerra della memoria in Italia dalla crisi della Prima repubblica ad oggi', in F. Focardi and B. Groppo (eds), *L'Europa e le sue memorie. Politiche e culture del ricordo dopo il 1989.* Rome, 2013, 51–90.

Franzinelli, M. 'Mussolini, revisionato e pronto per l'uso', in A. Del Boca (ed.), *La storia negata. Il revisionismo e il suo uso politico.* Vicenza, (2009) 2010, 203–36.

Furet, F. *Penser la révolution française.* Paris, 1978.

————. *Le passé d'une illusion,* Paris, 1995. [The passing of an illusion, Chicago, 2000]

Gallerano, N. 'Fine del caso italiano? La storia politica tra "politicità" e "scienza"'. *Movimento operaio e socialista* 1–2 (January–August 1987), 5–25.

————. (ed.). *L'uso pubblico della storia.* Milan, 1995.

Galli della Loggia, E. *La morte della patria. La crisi dell'idea di nazione tra Resistenza, antifascismo e Repubblica.* Bari, 1996.

————. 'Formes et fonctions de l'antifascisme dans la vie politique italienne. Légitimité ou Légitimation?'. *Vingtième siècle* 100(4) (2008), 69–78.

Gervasoni, M. *Storia d'Italia degli anni Ottanta. Quando eravamo moderni.* Venice 2010.

Gundle, S. 'Playing the Dictator: Re-enactments of Mussolini in Film and Television'. *Modern Italy* 18(2) (2013), 177–95.

Habermas, J. 'Du différent en doit. Quelques remarques sur le "pluralisme des interprétations"', in J. Habermas, *Après l'Etat–nation.* Paris, 2000.

Hartog, F., and G. Lenclud, 'Régimes d'historicité', in A. Dutu and N. Dodille (eds), *L'Etat des lieux en sciences sociales.* Paris, 1993.

Hobsbawm, E.J. *Age of Extremes: The Short Twentieth Century 1914–1991.* London, 1997.

Isnenghi, M. (ed.). *I luoghi della memoria. Strutture ed eventi dell'Italia unita.* Bari, 1996–1997.

Jacobelli, J. (ed.). *Il fascismo e gli storici oggi.* Bari, 1988.

Le Bissonais, C. *Mémoires plurielles: cinéma et images, lieux de mémoire?* Grâne, 2007.

Luzzatto, S. *La crisi dell'antifascismo.* Turin, 2004.

Mammone, A. 'A Daily Revision of the Past: Fascism, Anti-Fascism, and Memory in Contemporary Italy'. *Modern Italy* 11 (2006), 211–26.

Maltese, C. 'Soap Opera Mussolini', *La Repubblica,* 22 October 2004

Méheust, B. *La nostalgie de l'occupation.* Paris, 2012.

Morgan, P. '"I was there, too": Memories of Victimhood in Wartime Italy'. *Modern Italy* 14 (2009), 217–31.

Neri Serneri, S. 'A Past to Be Thrown Away? Politics and History in the Italian Resistance'. *Contemporary European History* 4(3) (November 1995), 367–81.

Pansa, G. *La grande bugia. Le sinistre italiane e il sangue dei vinti*. Milan, 2006.

———. *Il revisionista*. Milan, 2009.

———. *I vinti non dimenticano. I crimini ignorati della nostra guerra civile*. Milan, 2010.

———. *La guerra sporca dei partigiani e dei fascisti*. Milan, 2012.

Pasolini, P.P. *Scritti corsari*. Milan, 1975.

Pavone, C. 'Per la storia del revisionismo', *Atti del convegno 'Mappe del 900', I Viaggi di Erodoto, Rivista di cultura storica* 46 (2002). Online.

———. *A Civil War: A History of the Italian Resistance*. London, 2013 (1st Italian edition, *Una guerra civile: saggio storico sulla moralità della Resistenza*, Turin, 1991).

Peli, S. *Storia della Resistenza in Italia*. Turin, 2006.

Pivato, S. 'Storia e identità giovanile'. *I viaggi di Erodoto. Rivista di cultura storica* 46 (2002), 261–66.

———. *Vuoti di memoria. Usi e abusi della storia nella vita pubblica italiana*. Bari, 2007.

Poggi, P.P. *Nazismo e revisionismo storico*. Rome, 1997.

Prezioso, S. 'Prise en otages des victimes et usages publics de l'histoire'. *Amnis. Revue de civilisations contemporaines Europes/Amériques* 6 (2006), 121–34.

———. 'Antifascism and Antitotalitarianism: The Italian Debate'. *Journal of Contemporary History* 43 (2008), 555–72.

Rapone, L. 'Antifascismo e storia d'Italia', in E. Collotti (ed.), *Fascismo, antifascismo. Rimozioni, revisioni, negazioni*. Bari, 2000.

Revelli, M.'Storia e scienze sociali: una storia senza tempo per un tempo senza storia?', *Movimento operaio e socialista* 1–2 (1987), 27–44.

Ricoeur, P. *Temps et récit*. Paris, 1983–1985.

———. *La mémoire, l'histoire, l'oubli*. Paris, 2000.

Rochat, G. 'La Resistenza', in E. Collotti (ed.), *Fascismo e antifascismo. Rimozioni, revisioni, negazioni*. Bari, 2000, 273–92.

Santomassimo, G. 'La trincea del totalitarismo'. *Il Manifesto*, 3 October 2004.

———. 'Marxismo e storia dal solido al liquido'. *Passato e Presente* 72 (2007), 137–44.

———. 'Metabolizzare il fascismo'. *Passato e Presente* 77 (2009), 145–50.

Serenelli, S. '"It was like something that you have at home which becomes so familiar that you don't even pay attention to it": Memories of Mussolini and Fascism in Predappio, 1922–2010'. *Modern Italy* 18(2) (2013), 157–75.

Sorlin, P. *L'immagine e l'evento: l'uso storico delle fonti audiovisuali*. Turin, 1999.

Tranfaglia, N. *Anatomia dell'Italia repubblicana 1943–2009*. Florence, 2010.

Traverso, E. 'De l'anticommunisme. L'histoire du 20e siècle relue par Nolte, Furet et Courtois'. *L'Homme et la société* 140–41 (2001), 169–94.

———. *Le passé mode d'emploi, histoire, mémoire, politique*. Paris, 2005.

———. *L'histoire comme champ de bataille. Interpréter la violence du 20e siècle*. Paris, 2010.

———. 'Le memorie dell'Europa. La fine del "principio speranza"', in F. Focardi and B. Groppo (eds), *L'Europa e le sue memorie. Politiche e culture del ricordo dopo il 1989*. Rome, 2013, 277–301.

Turi, G. 'Usi e abusi della storia: storia di lotta e (ora) di governo'. *Passato e Presente* 80 (2010), 101–22.

———. *La cultura delle destre. Alla ricerca dell'egemonia culturale in Italia*. Turin, 2013.

Veyrat-Masson, I. *Télévision et histoire, la confusion des genres: docudrama, docufiction et fictions du réel*. Brussels, 2008.

Vidal-Naquet, P. *Les assassins de la mémoire*, 3rd edn. Paris, 2005.

Woolf, S. 'Fine della Patria?'. *Passato e Presente* 68 (May–August 2006), 87–103.

Stéfanie Prezioso is professor of History at the Faculty of Social and Political Sciences at the University of Lausanne. Her work deals mainly with the generation of 1914, the question of political exile and the problems relating to the appropriation of historical memory and the public use of history. She is the author, in particular, of *Itinerario di un 'figlio del 1914'. Fernando Schiavetti dalla trincea all'antifascismo* (2004); *Tant pis si la lutte est cruelle! Volontaires internationaux contre Franco* (2008) (ed. with Jean Batou and Ami-Jacques Rapin); 'Antifascism and Antitotalitarianism: The Italian Debate', *Journal of Contemporary History* 43(4) (October 2008), 555–72; and *L'heure des brasiers. Violence et révolution au 20e siècle* (2011, ed. with David Chevrolet).

14

ANTIFASCISM AND THE RESISTANCE

Public Debate and Politics of Memory in Italy from
the 1990s to the Present

Filippo Focardi

As did the majority of European nations following the end of the
Second World War,[1] Italy created a new public narrative about the
war constructed around two basic premises: the first placed the entire
blame for the suffering of the war squarely on the shoulders of the Nazi
regime and its people (thus relieving the Italians of its responsibility for
the Axis war), and the second exalted the Italian Resistance as a movement supported by the entire Italian people, who were united against
the Nazi-Fascist oppressor.[2]

Due to the parties that formed the National Liberation Committee,
which led the resurgence against Germany and the Republic of Salò
(1943–45), antifascism and the Resistance became the pillars of the
new democratic Republic that rose from the ashes of fascism. In subsequent years, this base of legitimacy was threatened at various times
by the anti-Communism fomented during the Cold War.[3] However,
it was reinforced by the antifascist historiography, which, while not
in agreement on all matters, underlined the Italian people's non-in-
volvement with, if not total aversion to, the fascist regime, as well as
reaffirming the link between the antifascism of the 1920s and 1930s,
the national liberation movement of the years 1943–45, and the birth
of the Republic.

Despite the challenge in the name of anti-Communism, antifascism
and the Resistance remained a focal point for national memory in the
1950s, an era characterised by the hegemony of Christian Democrats.
It was renewed in the 1960s with the birth of the centre-left governments, which expanded to include the Socialists,[4] but was challenged
anew in the 1970s, and this time from the New Left which considered

the Resistance as a sort of revolution betrayed that still needed to be brought to a conclusion.[5] However, the government of 'national solidarity' – based on the agreement between Christian Democrat leader Aldo Moro and Communist Party leader Enrico Berlinguer – claimed this heritage, defending the 'Republic born out of the Resistance' in their fight against domestic terrorism. After the kidnapping and killing of Moro by the Red Brigades in 1978, antifascism and the Resistance were embraced by the new president of the Republic, Socialist Sandro Pertini, a charismatic and popular ex-partisan.[6]

However, the 1980s were a turning point for the legacy of antifascism and the Resistance.[7] They marked a radical departure from the previous decade, and the public memory, anchored in the Resistance and antifascism, came under fire through a historical revisionism with two main goals: criticising the Resistance and antifascism, while simultaneously softening the fascist experience in Italy. This played out on an international stage of rising tensions between the United States and the Soviet Union (the second Cold War) along with a new wave of anti-Communism that swept the globe, including Italy, where it not only involved moderate forces but the Socialist Party of Bettino Craxi as well.[8]

In this context, we find widespread attacks on the Resistance, largely of an anti-Communist nature typical of the first Cold War: the distinction between antifascism and democracy and the accusation of totalitarianism levied at the Communist Party. Furthermore, some actions carried out by the Communist Resistance (like the bombing of German soldiers in Via Rasella in Rome in March 1944, which prompted a retaliation by the Nazis at the massacre of the Fosse Ardeatine;[9] the killing of fascist philosopher Giovanni Gentile in Florence and the execution of partisans with other political affiliations like the Porzus massacre in the Friuli region)[10] marred the public image of the Resistance and the antifascist movement. Moreover, the killing of Italians by Tito's Communists at the end of the Second World War and the elimination by the Italian Communists after the liberation of political opponents and class enemies suspected of being fascists, especially in the so-called 'Triangle of Death' in Emilia, served as counterpoints to any suggestion of fascist violence.[11]

These events received continuing coverage by the conservative media and over time were obsessively published in the neo-fascist press. They were echoed in the public opinion, thanks in part to Socialist newspapers and magazines such as *L'Avanti* and *Mondoperaio*, which repeatedly took to emphasising a need to replace the fascist/antifascist paradigm with a totalitarian/anti-totalitarian one. Therefore, with the

challenge of the Communist Party (PCI), Craxi's Socialist Party legitimised traditional topics that, thus far, had been linked to the right.

There was no new significant historical research that served as a catalyst for this contemporary re-reading of the Resistance. The new interpretation of fascism was otherwise inspired by the works of Renzo De
Felice, at the time the most important Italian historian of fascism. In the
1970s, De Felice endorsed an image of Mussolini's regime as authoritarian and not totalitarian, highlighting the fact that the regime modern-
ised the country and enjoyed a broad popular consensus.[12]

On board with this 'rebranding' of the regime was a vast array of
journalists dedicated to popularising history – from Arrigo Petacco
and Antonio Spinosa to Roberto Gervaso, Giordano Bruno Guerri and,
perhaps the most important of all, Indro Montanelli. The function of
these prolific writers, exhibition curators and television guests – con-
troversially described as 'talk-show historians' – was to break down De
Felice's interpretation for the general public with the intent of creating
an authentic media 'vulgate'.[13]

This re-evaluated alleged 'fascist critics' such as Dino Grandi and
Giuseppe Bottai, and placed a humanised Mussolini at the centre of
the regime's historical image. This version of Mussolini was the embodiment of all the vices and virtues of his people. As such, he created
a regime 'in the image and likeness' of the country, characterised by
a massive dose of rhetoric (and amorous intrigues) but with minimal
violence and repression. What developed during these years was later
defined by one of the greatest scholars of fascism – De Felice's student,
Emilio Gentile – as the 'retroactive defascistisation' of the regime.[14]

The German Nazis – (wrongly) considered a perfect model of
'Totalitarianism of Steel' – were used as a point of reference to which
Italian fascism was compared, a process derived from De Felice, thus
stripping the Italian regime of its repressive traits. The comparison of
the fascist years with the Third Reich allowed Italians to distance themselves from the German experience and to redefine their regime in a
reassuring and benevolent light.

At the same time, there was no attempt to utilise De Felice's category
of consensus to examine the complex relationship between the regime
and the people. In fact, the alleged mass support from the Italian people for Mussolini, taken as a mere matter-of-fact without any critical
analysis, was used as incontrovertible proof of the regime's merits.
This flipped the previous paradigm, which depicted the Italian people as a nation of antifascists, on its head, and promoted the exact opposite view, which was no less misleading or ideological.[15] De Felice,
while at times distancing himself from the zealous supporters of this

revisionist history, played a significant role in promoting this notion to the public.

A critical moment in this shift can be seen in the interviews De Felice gave to Giuliano Ferrara, which were published in the leading Italian daily *Corriere della Sera* in December 1987 and January 1988.[16] De Felice supported institutional reforms proposed by the Socialist leader Craxi, and contended that those reforms must be accompanied by the elimination of constitutional provisions that forbade the reformation of the Fascist Party. Thus, reforms were inextricably linked with the revisionist history of the regime.

'The discussion of the renewal of the political system naturally encounters the issue of historical revisionism', affirmed De Felice, who urged that the revision be made without hesitation, due to the fact that Italian fascism was 'extraneous from the accusation of genocide' and 'out of the shadow of the Holocaust'. In order to construct a modern liberal democracy, according to De Felice, the country had to overcome 'the official ideology of antifascism'.

Criticism of the Resistance in the 1980s resulted in increasing pressure on state institutions in the 1990s to create a new public memory free from the fascist/antifascist paradigm. Once again, this effort found resonance in radical political changes. On an international scale, the collapse of the Soviet Union between 1989 and 1991 resulted in a crisis for Communism. In Italy, the disintegration of the party system of the so-called First Republic in 1992–93, shaken up by investigations of endemic corruption, lead to the disappearance or drastic reduction of all the antifascist political parties, from the Christian Democrats (DC) to the Communist Party (PCI), that had signed the constitutional pact.

Meanwhile, a solid political right, with no historical ties to either the Resistance or antifascism, was born. The new parties included the Lega Nord ('Northern League') of Umberto Bossi, Forza Italia of Silvio Berlusconi and the old Movimento Sociale Italiano (MSI), later called the Alleanza Nazionale, with neo-fascist roots. This, followed by a change in the electoral law in August 1993 that transformed the proportional system into a majority system, created a bipolar political reality with one of the two poles monopolised by forces that were either hostile to antifascism or largely extraneous to it.[17]

This triggered a political use of history thus far unseen. One of the catalysts for this 'memory war' was the centre-right government's need to legitimise MSI and its leader, Gianfranco Fini, after Berlusconi's electoral victory in March 1994. Fini's party was one of the protagonists of this success. Furthermore, for the first time in the postwar era, it was part of the ruling coalition. All the centre-right parties rallied around coalition leader Berlusconi and agreed on a policy of neutral-ising antifascism as a discriminating factor in political legitimisation/ delegitimisation.

In the public debate, like in the 1950s, a pacification or reconcil-iation of the past was promoted with the goal of creating a 'shared memory'.[18] The rhetoric of pacification called on the public to view the young Italians who aligned themselves with Mussolini following the announcement of the Italian armistice on 8 September 1943 – kindly referred to as 'The Boys of Salò' – as acting on 'good faith' and with 'ethical patriotism'.[19] This was in an effort to 'defend the national hon-our' or to at least give mutual respect to all those who died in the war, irrespective of the flag they fought under. It was said that it was nec-essary to overcome 'the counterproductive values of antifascism' and the dramatic divisions of the civil war. In the 1990s, the president of the Republic, the Christian Democrat Oscar Luigi Scalfaro, received nu-merous appeals to this end. It was followed by unsuccessful efforts in 2003 and 2008 to pass laws equating the fighters of the Social Republic of Mussolini with the other fighters of the Second World War, includ-ing the partisans[20] – that is to say, to claim 'equalisation' between fas-cists and antifascists by disregarding the radically different reasons and ideals for which they had fought.

Gianfranco Fini, author of the transformation of the MSI into the National Alliance, played an important role in the politics of memory promoted by the right. Fini's goal to form a modern right-wing govern-ment led him to close the door on the 'century of ideologies' consign-ing both fascism and antifascism to the history books (according to the political thesis presented at the National Alliance's Fiuggi Congress in January 1995). As the Socialist intellectuals tied to Craxi had already at-tempted, Fini sought to replace the fascism/antifascism paradigm with a totalitarianism/anti-totalitarianism one. At the time, this effort carried little credibility seeing that, as late as 1994, Fini had called Mussolini 'the greatest statesman of the century'.[21]

It is also important to note that with the introduction of anti-totali-tarianism as an ideological reference point, the post-fascist right, using an interpretation taken from De Felice, considered German Nazism and Communism to be totalitarian but did not consider Italian fascism as such. The condemnation of fascist anti-Semitism and of the persecu-tion of the Jews was deemed sufficient to definitively dissociate fascism from Nazi totalitarianism.

Therefore, it is not surprising that, at the end of the 1990s, Fini con-tinued his path to democratic legitimacy by first visiting Auschwitz in 1999 and then Israel in November 2003, where he condemned the 'infamous racial laws of 1938 enacted by fascism', calling them an 'absolute evil' for their co-responsibility in the Holocaust. Fini's stance on the anti-Semitic aspects of fascism caused a break in the more nostalgic factions of the party, starting with the granddaughter of the fascist leader, Alessandra Mussolini.[22] In the public arena, however, this functioned as a sort of 'purification rite' that paved the way for the dissemination of a softened image of the fascist regime, which was widespread in the 1980s, and now took on a face of blatant rehabilitation in many cases.[23] Having come to terms with the anti-Semitism of the regime, many right-wingers of MSI origins felt that they had a clean slate from where they could promote the historical merits of fascism.

This attitude has been adopted in other political and cultural expressions of the centre-right (less so among the Catholics), articulated in the most grotesque and disturbing way by Prime Minister Silvio Berlusconi, who asserted in a 2003 interview that 'Mussolini did not murder anyone. Mussolini used to send people on vacation in internal exile'.[24] Furthermore, Berlusconi added in January 2013, on the occasion of the commemoration of National Holocaust Day, that *Il Duce* did many good things aside from enacting racial laws and aligning himself with Hitler.[25]

The attacks against antifascism have also found fertile ground in public opinion, where the Resistance and national identity have been vigorously debated. This debate was fuelled by successful books from the 1990s such as *La morte della Patria* ('Death of the Homeland') by the historian Ernesto Galli della Loggia, and De Felice's *Rosso e Nero* ('Red and Black').[26] The authors argued against a common view of the Resistance; for example, both found the alliance between the antifascist parties of the National Liberation Committee to be the origin of one of the worst vices of Italian politics: the domination of partitocracy. But above all, they stigmatised 8 September 1943 (the day on which the armistice between the Italians and the Allies was announced) as the moment of 'death to the homeland', unlike the antifascist narrative which promotes the idea of 8 September as the beginning of the Italian redemption. De Felice furthered an interpretation that reduced the Resistance to a civil war between two armed minorities, fascists and antifascists, which did not involve the majority of the Italian people. All of these interpretations have found plenty of ink in the leading Italian daily newspaper, *Corriere della Sera*.

This cultural offensive, promoted by the right, definitively established a legitimate 'anti-antifascist memory' that resounded in the public square in the 1990s.[27] There was a wholesale assault on the Resistance in the print media and on television using traditional themes, already in vogue in the 1950s and the 1980s, with renewed accusations against the Communist Party and the Communist partisans for acting treacherously against other partisans, for provoking the Nazis in violent retaliation without concern for innocent citizens, for carrying out assassinations after the war on class enemies under the guise of weeding out fascists, and for being responsible – at least morally and politically – for the massacres of Italians perpetrated by the Yugoslav Communists. Another line of attack focused on the Action Party, one of the main forces on the left that inspired the Resistance.[28]

This pounding counter-narrative often pulled out old neo-fascist clichés: for instance, the centre-right newspapers published dismissive judgments of 8 September as a 'day of dishonour', and called the Resistance a nefarious 'fratricidal war'.[29] Included in the line-up were the nostalgic tributes to Mussolini as a man ready to sacrifice himself for his country by accepting the leadership of the Social Republic in an attempt to curb the German's thirst for revenge for having been betrayed – a typical theme of the neo-fascist memory, authoritatively endorsed by De Felice.[30]

This culture, with its underlying anti-Resistance sentiment, also found expression at official levels. It is significant that Berlusconi, during his first three terms as prime minister until 2006, systematically avoided the celebration of 25 April, the national holiday that marks the liberation of the country from fascism. It is also not surprising that the former prime minister and members of his party expressed a clear preference for 18 April, the day of the election victory in 1948 of the Christian Democrats over the Socialist–Communist bloc, as the true date of the birth of democracy in Italy. In fact, on many occasions they proposed replacing 25 April with this day as a national holiday.[31] The last unsuccessful attempt was in September 2011, shortly before the fall of Berlusconi's fourth government.

The centre-right, in power for most of the period 2001–11, initiated specific attempts to institutionalise their politics of memory into the public sphere. Among the most significant was an attempt to rewrite history books, which promoted the left's historiographical interpretation.[32] These efforts led to wide-scale protests and were ultimately abandoned. A more successful effort was the introduction of new place names throughout the nation. In the name of a 'reconciled past', local centre-right governments promoted the renaming of city streets, squares and public buildings after an array of fascist personalities as well as martyrs of the Foibe killings (and for the latter, they did so with the support of moderate parties on the left).[33] The last striking example

of this was the dedication of a monument in the name of the war criminal Rodolfo Graziani in a small town in the central region of Lazio, not
far from Rome.[34]

Another effective tool in the promotion of this new political culture
was national television, with the airing of TV dramas depicting historical events, the most notable being *Il cuore nel pozzo* ('The Heart in
the Well') which dramatised the Foibe massacres.[35] The culmination of
this transformation was the introduction of two new public days of remembrance: the Day of Remembrance on 10 February in memory of the
victims of the Foibe massacres and of those Italians expelled from Istria
and Dalmazia,[36] and the Day of Freedom on 9 November to commem-
orate the fall of the Berlin Wall.

The Day of Remembrance, sponsored by the National Alliance, was
approved by Parliament in 2004 with the lone dissent coming from the
Communist parties, Rifondazione Comunista and Comunisti Italiani.
This act introduced the memory of the Foibe massacres into the public
consciousness, one of the cornerstones of the neo-fascist memory. In
the early years, the tenor of the celebrations was distinctly anti-Resistance. While the dramatic events along the Eastern border at the end of
the Second World War certainly demand attention from the country,
it has thus far been done without critical analysis. Neo-fascist clichés
about the Foibe, described as being motivated by anti-Italian hatred on
the part of the Yugoslav government, have been adopted with no consideration of Italy's occupation of Yugoslavia from 1941–43, or the war
crimes committed by Italy during this period.

The second new holiday – the so-called Day of Freedom advanced
by Berlusconi's Forza Italia party – was approved by Parliament in
2005. This time, the entire centre-left coalition voted against the law.
Designed to illustrate 'the harmful effects of totalitarianism, past and
present', the celebration has a clear anti-Communist significance but
has failed to inspire the public. It is relevant to note, however, that on the
first anniversary in 2006, Forza Italia released a commemorative poster
illustrating the 'Enemies of Freedom' which featured Adolf Hitler, Josef
Stalin, Fidel Castro, Saddam Hussein and Osama Bin Laden, but omitted Mussolini, the 'dictator of the house'.[37]

The attacks on the public memory of the Resistance were both the
cause and effect of the crisis of the so-called 'antifascist paradigm',
some aspects of which had been criticised in the past by antifascist historians like Nicola Gallerano with an intent to rebuild it, not destroy
it.[38] Gallerano had, for example, questioned the presumed unanimity
of the parties of the National Liberation Committee or the stereotypical
version of popular support for the Resistance.

In response to the right-wing offensive against the Resistance, a vigorous defence of antifascism as a founding principle of the Italian Republic has been mounted since the mid-1990s. On an official level, the presidents of the Republic – Oscar Luigi Scalfaro, Carlo Azeglio Ciampi and Giorgio Napolitano – have placed limitations on right-wing requests for 'pacification'. They have agreed to piety towards all the fallen fighters, but with a clear distinction between those who fought for freedom and democracy and those who fought for the dictatorship.[39]

The legacy of the Resistance has fuelled a wave of vigorous protests 'in the streets', with the celebrations of 25 April becoming occasions for popular mobilisation. Following the election of Berlusconi in 1994, the Communist newspaper *Il Manifesto* organised a protest against the new government in Milan, and in 2002, after Berlusconi's second election victory, the trade unions organised a similar event on this day in defence of workers' rights. In 2006, numerous protests were held nationally to contest constitutional reforms promoted by the Berlusconi government, which were shot down two months later in a popular referendum.

This shows that there exists a social memory of the Resistance and that it is still alive in new generations. It also shows the existence of an 'antifascist guarantee',[40] the same as emerged in the 1960s and 1970s against the subversion of the neo-fascists and was revived in the 1990s to combat the Berlusconi government, which many saw as a threat to democracy.

Another galvanising moment in shaping public opinion was in the mid-1990s, when criminal cases were brought against Nazi war criminals, particularly with the trial in Rome against former S.S. officer Erich Priebke, one of the officials responsible for the massacre at the Fosse Ardeatine and, with other cases, subsequently tried by the military courts.[41] With the memory of the Nazi-fascist massacres still alive in the country, the antifascist memory was relaunched and became a principle weapon against proposals of 'reconciliation', which were furthered not just by the right but also by moderate leftists. The memory of these German massacres drew attention to the Italians as victims of Nazism. This indirectly hindered a re-examination of the national conscience regarding the crimes of Italian fascism, cementing a self-absolving image of Italians as 'such good people', which was firmly rooted in the country immediately after the war.[42]

But this alibi of the 'good Italian' was brought into question in the 1990s by new studies that delved into the most sordid aspects of fascist Italy: colonial violence, the persecution of the Jews and the crimes committed in the occupied territories during the Second World War.

Criticism of the stereotype of colonialism with a 'human face' found an advocate in the historian and journalist Angelo Del Boca,[43] who inspired a 2006 legislative proposal by the Italian Communist Party to dedicate a day to remember the victims of Italian colonialism,[44] followed by another proposal by the Communists to remember all victims of fascism.[45] The electoral debacle of the radical left in 2008 effectively ended these initiatives.

Efforts to defend and reinforce the antifascist public memory managed to counter but not to eliminate the antifascist crisis, failing to construct a 'regenerative reading of the Resistance paradigm'.[46] The new historiographical interpretation developed in 1991 by Claudio Pavone put forth a three-pronged interpretation of the Resistance: a war of national liberation, a civil war and a class war.[47] This definition was not adequately developed by the left in the public debate, and ended up being partially co-opted and distorted by the right to show that even the antifascist historiography defined the Resistance as a civil war.

In contrast to the anti-Berlusconi movement, the opposite can also be seen: a number of politicians, intellectuals and journalists from the Socialists, Communists and even old extra-Parliamentary leftists switched sides, particularly to Berlusconi's Forza Italia party, where they played an active role in the revisionist battle over memory.[48]

Renowned antifascist journalist Giampaolo Pansa is an important example of this. Pansa did not choose to be politically tied to the right but with his books, which sold hundreds of thousands of copies, he was one of the main architects of the controversy against the Resistance, which was conducted in an increasingly acrimonious atmosphere. His most successful book, *Il sangue dei vinti* ('The Blood of the Vanquished'), published in 2003, intertwined narrative fiction and historical journalism to paint a bleak portrait of the violence that partisans perpetrated against the fascists after the war. Hailed by right-wing newspapers, the 'Dan Brown of Italian History' (as Pansa has been called by British historian Philip Cooke)[49] portrayed the Resistance as a useless and ruthless civil war that continued after 1945 by the will of the Communist Party, which was motivated by class hatred and revolutionary ideals.

Alongside these two poles – strict opposition and 'betrayal' – there has emerged a left that is willing to revise the antifascist memory in the name of being open to compromise. A move towards an agreement with the right has mainly come from the current majority of the ex-Communist Party, transformed first into the Partito Democratico della Sinistra ('Democratic Party of the Left', PDS) and then the Democratici di Sinistra ('Democrats of the Left', DS) and finally merging with the Catholics of former Prime Minister Romano Prodi into the

Partito Democratico ('Democratic Party', PD). It was precisely the ruling class who led the post-Communist transition who have shown a willingness to listen, more than others, to entreaties from the right to build a 'shared memory', seeing it as common ground on which to cement the new bipolar political reality.[50]

In May 1996, on the occasion of his inauguration as President of the Chamber of Deputies, Luciano Violante, a former magistrate and Democratic Party MP, made a speech to the chamber that had a huge impact on the public debate. Violante expressed hope that the memory of the Resistance could finally become a shared 'national value'. To this end, he invited the public to listen to the feelings of the adversaries of the Resistance 'to understand, without falsified revisionism, the motives for which thousands of young men, when all was lost, sided with Salò and not on the side of rights and freedoms'.[51] In this way he opened a dialogue with the right to overcome 'conflicting memories'. Another step in this direction was a meeting between Violante and Gianfranco Fini in Trieste in March 1998 to discuss the issue of the Foibe massacres,[52] followed by the DS vote in 2004 in favour of the 'Day of Remembrance'.

The unanimous decision to establish a Holocaust Memorial Day in 2000, certainly the most important of the new public holidays, can also be read as a sign of compromise regarding memory. The law establishing the holiday has many merits and is part of a recent international trend thrusting the memory of the Holocaust on centre stage.[53] It is nevertheless important to note that the text of the law does not mention the word 'fascism' or the word 'antifascism', and it expressly provides for the memory of those who, 'even from different fields and camps', helped and protected the persecuted. As a result, the mass media teemed with the figures of 'good Italians', 'saviours of Jews', including many 'good fascists', and above all, Giorgio Perlasca, an Italian merchant who was a fascist volunteer in the Spanish Civil War, pretended to be a Spanish diplomat and saved thousands of Jews in Hungary. As noted by historian Stefano Pivato, the left's willingness to accept a plea bargain on the memory of the past resulted in a 'division of memory', leading to a sort of bartering system for the construction of the national public memory.[54] For example, the production of a drama about the Foibe killings was 'compensated by producing a documentary on the massacre at the Fosse Ardeatine'.

The push for mutual political recognition thus follows a creation, from above, of a 'shared memory'. Expunging the most uncomfortable aspects of Italian history in the twentieth century – from colonial crimes to responsibility for the actions of the Axis during the war – results in a memory founded on a national self-victimisation. It is what historian Giovanni De Luna has called the 'victimage paradigm': marked emotional content, fuelled by television shows featuring the stories of survivors or families of victims of the Foibe killings, Nazi massacres or race-related deportations that have a strong impact on the public.[55]

The actions of the president of the Republic have been fundamental in creating a national memory in Italy. Neither the bitter dispute between right and left regarding the past nor the attempts at compromise undertaken by post-Communists and post-fascists have generated a new master narrative. However, the president of the Republic has, with some success, made attempts to do so. A fundamental role in this regard was played by Carlo Azeglio Ciampi, who served as president from 1999 to 2006.[56] Concerned about both the wounds caused by the conflict between Berlusconi and the opposition and the threat to national unity by the Northern League, Ciampi initiated a process of 'citizenship education' via a politics of memory that resulted in the recovery of the Resistance as a legacy of ideals to be passed down to the younger generations and as a historical and moral capital on which to rebuild a sense of national belonging and strengthen the unity of the country.

In open disagreement with those who see 8 September as the 'death of the homeland', like Galli della Loggia, Ciampi reiterated the traditional tenet of the Resistance as a struggle for national liberation and a 'second Risorgimento'. In line with the historiographical writings of Pietro Scoppola,[57] the president proposed a broader vision of the protagonists of the Resistance, including the partisans and soldiers who took up arms against the fascists, the people who gave them protection and support, the deportees and the victims of massacres.

Ciampi managed to highlight the patriotic character of the Resistance thanks to an emphasis on the role played by the military: those who, after the armistice, fought against the Germans, as well as those deported to Germany but who refused to fight for the Social Republic (the so-called Italian Military Internees, IMI). Not by chance, Ciampi elevated the Greek island Cephalonia, scene of the worst Nazi massacre of Italian soldiers, to one of the principal sites for the memory of the Italian Resistance.

Ciampi interpreted the Resistance as a 'union of the people and the armed forces', and reaffirmed it as the origin for the Constitution and the basis for renewed patriotism in the Republic with the rediscovery of national symbols such as the flag and national anthem.[58] This is all within the framework of constructing a 'complete memory' based not only on the Resistance, but also on the Risorgimento (the nineteenth-century movement for Italian national unity), the First World War and the victims of the Foibe massacres.

Following in the footsteps of Ciampi, his successor Giorgio Napolitano, one of the leaders of the former Communist Party, praised the Risorgimento and the national-patriotic Resistance, but not without silencing the 'dark side' relating to the civil war, with particular reference to the postwar revenge killings stigmatised in Pansa's books. In the face of the political parties' growing credibility problems, the voice of the president has emerged in recent years as a focal point for a nation at the mercy of regressive dynamics and a syndrome of decline.[59]

The actions of the president of the Republic were decisive in thwarting the most radical attacks by the right seeking to abolish the 25 April Liberation Day holiday and to equate the fighters of Salò with the partisans. Liberation Day has remained in its place, even if it has lost some relevance given the emergence of antagonistic memories such as those of the Foibe massacres, and competing ones like those of the Holocaust. Even today, institutional legitimacy cannot ignore reference to the Resistance. Even Silvio Berlusconi, who, for many years, had refused to participate in commemorations of the Resistance, finally chose to celebrate 25 April for the first time as prime minister in 2009.[60] However, the links between the Resistance and antifascism and its role of democratic renewal are more and more tenuous. The word 'antifascism' itself is nearly completely absent in the speeches of Ciampi and Napolitano as if it acts as a barrier to constructing the coveted shared memory. Thus, the country that gave birth to fascist totalitarianism continues to postpone its showdown with the legacy of its dark past.

Notes

1. See T. Judt, 'The Past is Another Country: Myth and Memory in Postwar Europe', in I. Deàk, J.T. Gross and T. Judt (eds), *The Politics of Retribution in Europe: World War II and its Aftermath*, Princeton, NJ, 2000, 293–303.
2. See F. Focardi, *La guerra della memoria. La Resistenza nel dibattito politico italiano dal 1945 a oggi*, Rome and Bari, 2005, 3–18.
3. Ibid., 19–32.
4. Ibid., 41–46.
5. See P. Cooke, *The Legacy of the Italian Resistance*, Basingstoke and New York, 2011, 110ff.
6. Focardi, *La guerra della memoria*, 52–55.

7. See F. Focardi, 'Il passato conteso. Transizione politica e guerra della memoria in Italia dalla crisi della prima Repubblica ad oggi', in F. Focardi and B. Groppo (eds), *L'Europa e le sue memorie. Politiche e culture del ricordo dopo il 1989*, Rome, 2013, 51–59.

8. From 1981 to 1991, Italy was governed by the so-called *Pentapartito*, the five-party coalition government that included the Christian Democrats and the Socialist Party, but summarily excluded the Communist Party from the ruling coalition; Craxi led the government from 1983 to 1987. See S. Colarizi and M. Gervasoni, *La cruna dell'ago: Craxi, il partito socialista e la crisi della Repubblica*, Rome and Bari, 2005.

9. In the attack carried out by Communist partisans, 33 German soldiers were killed. In retaliation, the German authorities ordered 335 Italians to be shot.

10. Here, in February 1945, Italian Communist partisan units eliminated the command of the 'Osoppo' brigade, made up of Catholics and Actionists, which opposed the plan to annex Friuli Venezia Giulia cultivated by the Slovenian Communist resistance movement.

11. Cooke, *The Legacy of the Italian Resistance*, 151–54.

12. See R. De Felice, *Mussolini il duce. Gli anni del consenso 1929–1936*, Torino, 1974; Idem, *Intervista sul fascismo*, ed. M.A. Ledeen, Rome and Bari, 1975.

13. See F. Focardi, 'Il vizio del confronto. L'immagine del fascismo e del nazismo in Italia e la difficoltà di fare i conti con il proprio passato', in G.E. Rusconi and H. Woller (eds), *Italia e Germania 1945–2000. La costruzione dell'Europa*, Bologna, 2005, 91–121; G. Santomassimo, 'Il ruolo di Renzo De Felice', in E. Collotti (ed.), *Fascismo e antifascismo. Rimozioni, revisioni, negazioni*, Rome and Bari, 2000, 415–29.

14. See E. Gentile, *Fascismo. Storia e interpretazione*, Roma and Bari, 2002, VII. It should be remembered that Gentile also attributes the responsibility for the 'defascistisation' of the fascist regime to the antifascist culture, which denied for a long time the existence of an ideology of fascism, and rather considered it a simple 'house of cards' without foundation.

15. See P. Corner, 'Fascismo e controllo sociale', *Italia contemporanea* 228 (2002), 381–405; Idem, 'L'opinione popolare nell'Italia fascista degli anni Trenta', in P. Corner (ed.), *Il consenso totalitario. Opinione pubblica e opinione popolare sotto fascismo, nazismo e comunismo*, Rome and Bari, 2012, 127–54.

16. The first interview was published on 27 December 1987, and the second on 8 January 1988. Full texts in Focardi, *La guerra della memoria*, 252–58.

17. Focardi, 'Il passato conteso', 59–60.

18. Ibid., 61.

19. The expression is used in S. Woolf, 'Introduzione. La storiografia e la Repubblica italiana', in. S. Woolf (ed.), *L'Italia repubblicana vista da fuori (1945–2000)*, Bologna, 2007, 45.

20. Focardi, 'Il passato conteso', 61–62.

21. See A. Statera, 'Il migliore resta Mussolini', *La Stampa*, 1 April 1994.

22. See A. Mattioli, *'Viva Mussolini!'. La guerra della memoria nell'Italia di Berlusconi, Bossi e Fini*, Milan, 2011, 49–67. After serving as Foreign Minister in 2004 and President of the House in 2008, Fini broke with Berlusconi in 2010. Fini eventually arrived at a complete condemnation of the Fascist

regime and the Republic of Salò; however, he gradually lost political power, disappearing from the political scene after the elections in February 2013.

23. See S. Pivato, *Vuoti di memoria. Usi e abusi della storia nella vita pubblica italiana*, Rome and Bari, 2007, 91.

24. Interview given on 27 August 2003 to the British newspaper *The Spectator*. See P. Franchi, 'Cavaliere, ripassi un po' di storia', *Corriere della Sera*, 13 September 2003.

25. 'Berlusconi: Mussolini fece bene', in *Repubblica*, 28 January 2013.

26. See E. Galli della Loggia, *La morte della patria*, Rome and Bari, 1996; and Renzo De Felice, *Rosso e nero*, ed. P. Chessa, Milan, 1995.

27. See A. Del Boca (ed.), *La storia negata. Il revisionismo e il suo uso politico*, Vicenza, 2009.

28. See C. Novelli, *Il Partito d'Azione e gli italiani. Moralità, politica e cittadinanza nella storia repubblicana*, Milan, 2000, VII–XXIII.

29. Focardi, *La guerra della memoria*, 66–68.

30. See R. De Felice, *Mussolini l'alleato. La guerra civile 1943–1945*, Turin, 1997.

31. Focardi, 'Il passato conteso', 67. The word *foibe* refers to the sinkholes typical to the Kras region shared by Italy, Slovenia and Croatia. After the Italian armistice in September 1943 and then in the spring of 1945, many Italians were killed and thrown into these pits. The word is commonly used to talk about all the Italian victims of Yugoslavian violence, even if the majority died in Yugoslavian internment camps. The number of Italian victims is controversial. The more reliable estimates speak of four to five thousand deaths, mostly fascists but also antifascists who opposed the Yugoslavian annexation. See P. Pupo and R. Spazzali, *Foibe*, Milan, 2003.

32. See L. Baldissara, 'Di come espellere la storia dai manuali di storia. Cronache di una polemica autunnale', *Il Mestiere di Storico* II(2001), 62–86.

33. Focardi, *La guerra della memoria*, 69–70.

34. See G.A. Stella, 'Il Mausoleo della crudeltà', *Corriere della Sera*, 30 September 2012.

35. See V. Delle Donne, 'Il film sulle foibe commuove l'Italia', *Il Secolo d'Italia*, 8 February 2005.

36. See P. Pallante (ed.), *Il giorno del ricordo. La tragedia delle foibe*, Rome, 2010.

37. See O. Pivetta, 'Dittatori, Berlusconi salva Mussolini', *L'Unità*, 8 November 2005, and an online version of the poster at http://eang.blog.kataweb.it/files/photos/uncategorized/1107manifesto.jpg (accessed 31 October 2014).

38. See N. Gallerano, 'Critica e crisi del paradigma antifascista', *Problemi del Socialismo* 7 (1986), 106–33.

39. Focardi, *La guerra della memoria*, 62–64.

40. Sergio Luzzatto, *La crisi dell'antifascismo*, Turin, 2004, 63.

41. Having been acquitted in the first trial in August 1996, the decision was appealed by the prosecution and Priebke was condemned fifteen years in prison in July 1997. After a second appeal, he was sentenced to life in prison in March 1998 but, due to his age, was placed under house arrest. He died in Rome at the age of 100 in October 2013.

42. See F. Focardi, *Il cattivo tedesco e il bravo italiano. La rimozione delle colpe della seconda guerra mondiale*, Rome and Bari, 2013.

43. See A. Del Boca, *Italiani brava gente?*, Neri Pozza, 2005.
44. Draft Law n. 1845 for the 'establishment of a Memorial Day in memory of the African victims during the Italian colonial occupation', presented on 23 Oct. 2006, by the Deputy Jacopo Venier.
45. Draft law n. 1982 for the 'establishment of a Memorial Day for the victims of Fascism', presented on 24 Nov. 2006, by the Deputy Severino Galante and others.
46. See T. Baris, 'Amnesie, conflitti e politiche della memoria', in *Gli Italiani in guerra. Conflitti, identità, memorie dal Risorgimento ai nostri giorni*, vol. iv – vol. 2, M. Isnenghi and G. Albanese (eds), *Il Ventennio fascista: la Seconda guerra mondiale*, Turin, 2008, 732.
47. See C. Pavone, *Una guerra civile. Saggio storico sulla moralità nella Resistenza*, Turin, 1991.
48. Among the most notable: Giuliano Ferrara, Gianni Baget Bozzo, Paolo Guzzanti, Paolo Liguori, Ferdinando Adornato and Renzo Foa. There has not been a study on the change of alliances by individuals of the left, most importantly the Socialists, to the centre-right, or the effect this had in the political and cultural arena.
49. Cooke, *The Legacy of the Italian Resistance*, 181.
50. Focardi, 'Il passato conteso', 75.
51. Full text of Violante's comments in Focardi, *La guerra della memoria*, 285–86.
52. See L. Mattina (ed.), *Democrazia e nazione. Dibattito a Trieste tra Luciano Violante e Gianfranco Fini*, Trieste, 1998.
53. The text of the law in Focardi, *La guerra della memoria*, 289–90.
54. Pivato, *Vuoti di memoria*, 122.
55. See G. De Luna, *La Repubblica del dolore. Le memorie di un'Italia divisa*, Milan, 2011, 82ff.
56. Focardi, *La guerra della memoria*, 94–107; B. Thomassen and R. Forlenza, 'Re-narrating Italy, Reinventing the Nation: Assessing the Presidency of Ciampi', *Journal of Modern Italian Studies* 5 (2011), 705–25.
57. See Pietro Scoppola, *25 aprile. Liberazione*, Turin, 1995.
58. See P. Peluffo, *La riscoperta della Patria*, Milan, 2012 (first edition 2008), 166–70 and 204–12.
59. Focardi, 'Il passato conteso', 83–85.
60. 'Silvio omaggia i partigiani e li seppellisce', in *Libero*, 26 April 2009. It was clearly an attempt by Berlusconi to use the holiday to his political advantage by celebrating it as 'Festival of Freedom'. However, it showed how the right could not avoid mentioning the Resistance as a source of institutional legitimacy.

References

Baldissara, L. 'Di come espellere la storia dai manuali di storia. Cronache di una polemica autunnale'. *Il Mestiere di Storico* 2 (2001).
Baris, T. 'Amnesie, conflitti e politiche della memoria', in *Gli Italiani in guerra. Conflitti, identità, memorie dal Risorgimento ai nostri giorni*, vol. IV – vol. 2, M.

Isnenghi and G. Albanese (eds), *Il Ventennio fascista: la Seconda guerra mondiale*. Turin, 2008.

Colarizi, S., and M. Gervasoni. *La cruna dell'ago: Craxi, il partito socialista e la crisi della Repubblica*. Rome and Bari, 2005.

Cooke, P. *The Legacy of the Italian Resistance*. Basingstoke and New York, 2011.

Corner, P. 'Fascismo e controllo sociale'. *Italia contemporanea* 228 (2002), 381–405.

———. 'L'opinione popolare nell'Italia fascista degli anni Trenta', in P. Corner (ed.), *Il consenso totalitario. Opinione pubblica e opinione popolare sotto fascismo, nazismo e comunismo*. Rome and Bari, 2012.

De Felice, R. *Mussolini il duce. Gli anni del consenso 1929–1936*. Turin, 1974.

———. *Intervista sul fascismo*, ed. M.A. Ledeen. Rome and Bari, 1975.

———. *Rosso e nero*. ed. P. Chessa, Milan, 1995.

———. *Mussolini l'alleato. La guerra civile 1943–1945*. Turin, 1997.

Del Boca, A. (ed.). *Italiani brava gente?* Neri Pozza, 2005.

———. *La storia negata. Il revisionismo e il suo uso politico*. Vicenza, 2009.

De Luna, G. *La Repubblica del dolore. Le memorie di un'Italia divisa*. Milan, 2011.

Focardi, F. 'Il vizio del confronto. L'immagine del fascismo e del nazismo in Italia e la difficoltà di fare i conti con il proprio passato', in G.E. Rusconi and H. Woller (eds), *Italia e Germania 1945–2000. La costruzione dell'Europa*. Bologna, 2005.

———. *La guerra della memoria. La Resistenza nel dibattito politico italiano dal 1945 a oggi*. Rome and Bari, 2005.

———. *Il cattivo tedesco e il bravo italiano. La rimozione delle colpe della seconda guerra mondiale*. Rome and Bari, 2013.

———. 'Il passato conteso. Transizione politica e guerra della memoria in Italia dalla crisi della prima Repubblica ad oggi', in F. Focardi and B. Groppo (eds), *L'Europa e le sue memorie. Politiche e culture del ricordo dopo il 1989*. Rome, 2013.

Gallerano, N. 'Critica e crisi del paradigma antifascista'. *Problemi del Socialismo* 7 (1986), 106–33.

Galli della Loggia, E. *La morte della patria*. Rome and Bari, 1996.

Gentile, E., *Fascismo. Storia e interpretazione*. Rome and Bari, 2002.

Judt, T. 'The Past is Another Country: Myth and Memory in Postwar Europe', in I. Deàk, J.T. Gross and T. Judt (eds), *The Politics of Retribution in Europe: World War II and its Aftermath*. Princeton, NJ, 2000, 293–303.

Luzzatto, S. *La crisi dell'antifascismo*. Turin, 2004.

Mattina, L. (ed.). *Democrazia e nazione. Dibattito a Trieste tra Luciano Violante e Gianfranco Fini*. Trieste, 1998.

Mattioli, A. *'Viva Mussolini!'. La guerra della memoria nell'Italia di Berlusconi, Bossi e Fini*. Milan, 2011.

Novelli, C. *Il Partito d'Azione e gli italiani. Moralità, politica e cittadinanza nella storia repubblicana*. Milan, 2000.

Pallante, P. (ed.). *Il giorno del ricordo. La tragedia delle foibe*. Rome, 2010.

Pavone, C. *Una guerra civile. Saggio storico sulla moralità nella Resistenza*. Turin, 1991.

Peluffo, P. *La riscoperta della Patria*, 2nd edn. Milan, 2012.

Pivato, S. *Vuoti di memoria. Usi e abusi della storia nella vita pubblica italiana*. Rome and Bari, 2007.

Pupo, R., and R. Spazzali. *Foibe*. Milan, 2003.

Santomassimo, G. 'Il ruolo di Renzo De Felice', in E. Collotti (ed.), *Fascismo e antifascismo. Rimozioni, revisioni, negazioni*. Rome and Bari, 2000.

Thomassen, B., and R. Forlenza. 'Re-narrating Italy, Reinventing the Nation: Assessing the Presidency of Ciampi'. *Journal of Modern Italian Studies* 5 (2011), 705–25.

Woolf, S. 'Introduzione. La storiografia e la Repubblica italiana', in S. Woolf (ed.), *L'Italia repubblicana vista da fuori (1945–2000)*. Bologna, 2007.

Filippo Focardi is associate professor of Modern History at the University of Padua, Italy. He has published widely on the memory of fascism, the Italian Resistance and the Second World War; the punishment of Italian and German war criminals; the reparations for the Italian victims of Nazism; and the politics of memory of the European Union. His publications include the books *La guerra della memoria. La Resistenza nel dibattito politico italiano dal 1945 ad oggi* (2005); *Criminali di guerra in libertà. Un accordo segreto tra Italia e Germania federale 1949–55* (2008); and *Il cattivo tedesco e il bravo italiano. La rimozione delle colpe della seconda guerra mondiale* (2013).

15

IN SEARCH OF THE LOST NARRATIVE

Antifascism and Democracy in Present-Day Spain

Javier Muñoz Soro

The Parable of the Exterminating Angel

On 16 July 2011 the Coordinadora Antifascista de Albacete ('Antifascist Coordination Committee of Albacete') held a meeting in order to 'to pay tribute to the historical memory of antifascism'. Among the activities scheduled were the 'faithful remembrance of the crimes committed by the fascist side' and the 'feats' performed during the Civil War of 1936–39 by the Frente Popular ('Popular Front'), commemorating 'all those who fought for a proletarian Spain and against a regime that was clearly opposed to the interests of the working classes and in favour of the bourgeoisie'. The meeting closed with a summons to 'all those who consider themselves as anti-Francoists' to participate in the antifascist mobilisation, since, as attendees were reminded, 'fascism is still present in our lives, a form of fascism represented today by capitalism in all its forms'.

This meeting took place on a hill close to Valdepeñas, in the region of La Mancha, near the remains of a monumental sculpture erected in 1964 by Juan de Ávalos, the author of the sculptures at the Valle de los Caídos ('Valley of the Fallen'), the burial site of General Franco, some thirty miles north-west of Madrid. In 1964, the dictatorship was conducting a propaganda campaign with the slogan '25 Years of Peace', in an attempt to seek fresh sources of legitimacy for its rule – peace, order and progress – alongside the original claim to legitimacy which it never renounced: its victory in the Civil War.

The monumental, 15-metre-high sculpture represented one of the archangels of Saint Michael, chief of the celestial legions, wielding a mighty sword in the shape of a cross and flanked by two vertical shafts of stone, squarely meeting fascist tastes, with the following inscription at the base: 'In perpetual memory of the martyrs of the Crusade'. According to the chroniclers of the period, the statue was conceived as 'a monument to victory and peace', and at its inauguration ceremony the minister of the interior, General Camilo Alonso Vega, warned of the need to remain vigilant against renewed attempts by Communism to 'mount a revolution in Spain'.[1]

The general was not far wrong on that occasion, since on the highly significant date of 18 July 1976 (the 40th anniversary of the Nationalist rising that started the Civil War), the Grupos de Resistencia Antifascista Primero de Octubre (GRAPO, 'First of October Antifascist Resistance Groups') set off a bomb under the monument. As a result of the explosion, the exterior copper layer was lost, revealing the sculpture's inner structure of iron, which involuntarily rendered it as a work of contemporary art.

Antifascist Unity and Two Cases of Totalitarianism

We can use this parable to make some observations on antifascism in Spain and its present day political uses, as well as on the efforts made to construct an antifascist collective memory and the public debates they have triggered. As this is a chapter of a collective work, I will endeavour to keep within the limits of the Spanish case and its peculiarities, although as we shall see it cannot be understood in isolation from Europe and the debates on the history, the content and the political ethics of antifascism.

The Spanish case, in fact, serves as a paradigm for the concept of 'antifascism': namely, the historical development of an operational, but at the same time ideological and cultural, political unity in opposition to fascism. The Spanish Civil War may have become the foundational myth of international antifascism, but the rifts it caused lay the grounds for refuting the idea of antifascist unity.[2] Ferran Gallego has written about a 'cultural space under construction', which suffered severe setbacks such as the events of May 1937 in the Republican zone, while Hugo García considers that the course of the Spanish left is best understood as one of unity, which is more in tune with the idea of antifascist political culture.[3]

The difficulties faced by this new political culture to overcome the traditional cultures of the Spanish left – libertarian, republican, socialist and Communist – did not cease with the end of the war in April 1939. From that point on, disputes over the respective responsibilities for the defeat became increasingly frequent, and shortly afterwards the Pact between Nazi Germany and the Soviet Union did away with any chances of antifascist solidarity.[4] With the invasion of the USSR two years later, antifascist discourse returned with renewed vigour among Spaniards in exile, who took pains to present a united image to the Allied powers with a view to the defeat of the Axis and the anticipated downfall of Franco.

In June 1942, following the instructions of the Comintern, the PCE (Spanish Communist Party) promoted the Unión Nacional Española (UNE, 'Spanish National Unity'), but with little success. In November 1943, Socialists from the Spanish Socialist Workers' Party (PSOE), along with Republicans, Catalan and Basque nationalists, founded the Junta Española de Liberación (JEL, 'Spanish Liberation Junta').[5] These were the groups that, together with the anarcho-syndicalist union CNT (Confederación Nacional del Trabajo, or 'National Confederation of Labour'), set up the Alianza Nacional de Fuerzas Democráticas (ANFD, 'National Alliance of Democratic Forces') in 1944, which was joined by the PCE in February 1946. On the tenth anniversary of the electoral victory of the Frente Popular in February 1936, anti-Francoist unity appeared to be regaining strength.[6]

However, discrepancies over which strategy to adopt continued to hinder the initiatives in favour of unity: whether to create a resistance organisation, in the style of the group set up by De Gaulle in France, or to restore Republican institutions; whether to continue with the guerrilla fight, following the failed invasion across the Pyrenees in 1944; or whether to seek the support of monarchist generals to topple Franco. In fact, the conversations held from 1945 onwards between the ANFD and the monarchists – among whom was José María Gil Robles, leader of the main Catholic right-wing party during the Republic – to seek a negotiated end to the dictatorship caused a rift with the CNT and deep divisions within the Socialists.[7]

The Communists soon abandoned the ANFD and were excluded from all united anti-Francoist platforms until 1976, but not from the Republican governments in exile. They were also excluded from other initiatives, such as the famous pro-European meeting held in Munich in 1962, despite the fact that the PCE had by then become the most powerful organisation of the anti-Franco struggle within Spain. The militant anti-Communism of the PSOE (which, at its latest party conference, had prohibited participation in organisations with the PCE), as well as the one of liberal Republicans like Salvador de Madariaga, and of exiled former militants of the Partido Obrero de Unificación Marxista (POUM, a Trotskyist party that had been outlawed by the Republic following the events of May 1937), prevented the consolidation of an antifascist culture among opponents of the dictatorship. During the long years of the Cold War, some of the above collaborated with anti-Communist institutions such as the Congreso por la Libertad de la Cultura ('Congress for Cultural Freedom'), funded by the CIA, without compromising their anti-Francoist activism.[8]

In 1951 the leading anarchist newspaper in exile, *Solidaridad Obrera*, stated that the foremost problem for those in exile was to 'establish responsibilities for having lost the war', and asked: 'How can antifascist unity be possible when the antifascist individual without a party must necessarily pact with antifascists who are backed by a party, and who are prisoners of their leaders...?'[9] A motion on the 'Antifascist Front' was approved at the Second Conference of the CNT in exile, held in Toulouse in September 1961. This document clearly stated the limits of the 'pact among forces characterised by objectives and methods that are not only divergent but opposed', exclusively aimed at overthrowing the Spanish 'totalitarian regime' in order to 'restore, in its place, fundamental political, syndicalist and citizenship rights', but in no event to go any further in developing democratic institutions. This pact was to be inspired by an 'antifascist, rather than merely anti-Francoist, principle'; that is to say, it could not encompass 'Communist or fascist totalitarian parties'.[10]

However, a short time before this, the CNT had failed in its negotiations to join the Unión de Fuerzas Democráticas (UFD, 'Union of Democratic Forces') founded in 1961 by the PSOE and the Christian Democrats within Spain, who were led by Manuel Giménez Fernández, a former right-wing minister during the Republic. Thus anti-Francoist unity was delayed, paradoxically, until after the death of the dictator in 1975.

Reconciliation versus Antifascism

In fact, the idea of bringing disenchanted Francoists into an agreement to end the dictatorship, even forsaking a Republican regime, constituted the main division among those in exile and, from the late 1950s and early 1960s, between Spaniards in exile and those in Spain. The idea was associated, implicitly at first and later explicitly, with the notion of reconciliation. It was not, as in the case of Italy during the same period, a matter of convergence with Catholic antifascists at a time of serious institutional crisis, but rather of reconciliation with the monarchists, ex *falangistas* (members of the fascist party Falange

Española) and Catholics against whom they had fought tooth and nail on the battlefields and, what was worse, behind the lines.

Reconciliation was not, despite the tenets of the current antifascist discourse, a Francoist narrative, as Francoism never renounced its victory as a source of legitimacy, not even after it began speaking of peace. This was a narrative, eventually becoming 'the' narrative, of the defeated left, derived from the Socialist leader Indalecio Prieto's call for national consensus in 1942 and his negotiations with the monarchists in 1948 for a transition to a constitutional monarchy. It was also reflected in the 'National Reconciliation policy' adopted by the PCE in 1956 and the demand for a 'comprehensive amnesty embracing all responsibilities deriving from the Civil War' issued at its Fourth Congress in 1960. The concept was also present when leaders in exile and from the opposition within the country met in Munich in 1962 in the name of reconciliation, and explicitly renounced violence on the road to democracy.[11]

Not even the majority of the radical 'new left' that sprang up in the 1960s regarded the key to their struggle against the dictatorship (and, still less, to their social project) as their antifascist identity and continuity with the Republican past (again, in stark contrast with Italy in the same period).[12] However, certain Communist organisations that emerged in response to the PCE's ideological revisionism and national reconciliation policy did so, especially the Maoists of the Partido del Trabajo de España (PTE, 'Spanish Labour Party'), the Organización Revolucionaria de Trabajadores (ORT, 'Workers' Revolutionary Organization') and the Basque Movimiento Comunista (MC, 'Communist Movement'). The latter self-defined as 'an antifascist group ... deeply marked by the experience of war [and] defeat', but where antifascism was construed in such a generic manner as its opposite, fascism, identified with the oligarchy and imperialism.[13]

But the antifascism of these organisations was inoperative, constrained by the contradictory calls 'to the antifascist mass struggle' (or an 'Antifascist Front policy') and the actions of a radicalised, minority vanguard.[14] This contradiction was further highlighted within organisations that opted for violence, such as GRAPO, authors of the attack on the Valdepeñas archangel, who referred to the Civil War as the 'National Revolutionary War'; or the Frente Revolucionario Antifascista y Patriota (FRAP, 'Revolutionary Patriotic Antifascist Front'), amongst whose founders figured Julio Álvarez del Vayo, a former minister of the Republic and commissioner-general of the Republican Army during the Civil War. Similarly, the Basque terrorist group ETA established clearer links between its 'war' against Francoist Spain and the one that the *gudaris* or Basque Nationalist soldiers had fought in 1936–39.[15]

This process of ideological accumulation had a certain influence on the historic left-wing parties. Having practically disappeared from PCE discourse since the 1950s, Communist newspapers such as *Mundo Obrero* and *Nuestra Bandera* began using the term 'antifascist' again during the final years of the dictatorship.[16] On the 50th anniversary of the party's foundation, general secretary of PCE Santiago Carrillo recalled the Frente Popular experience as something far more important than a mere political coalition, but 'in fact, a new political formation', that should be the model for a new alliance between labour and culture in the transition to socialism. There was still, however, a more pressing aim, namely amnesty and the restoration of political freedoms, that determined a provisional alliance, 'albeit with forces with a class significance opposed to our own'.[17]

The isolation of the radical left deepened following the death of the dictator in November 1975, both owing to the poor electoral results obtained by the parties that presented themselves in the first democratic general election in June 1977 (in all cases less than 1 per cent) and to the repression and growing loss of social legitimacy of the terrorist groups. In the meantime, the PCE of *La Pasionaria* kept the Republican flags concealed at its meetings while accepting the symbols of the monarchy, and Santiago Carrillo declared to journalists that 'the Civil War is a historical fact and already belongs to the past'.[18] In 1977 the Amnesty Law was passed at the initiative of the left-wing parties in Parliament, and after the largest popular mobilisation seen during that period.[19] This law freed thousands of political prisoners, but at the same time granted pardons for the human rights abuses committed by civil servants and members of the security forces.[20]

Almost a decade later, in 1986, on the 50th anniversary of the outbreak of the Civil War, Felipe González, the president of a PSOE government with an absolute majority, remembered those who had contributed 'to the defence of freedom and democracy in Spain', but 'with respect for those who, from different positions to those of a democratic Spain fought for a different society, for which many have also sacrificed their lives'.[21] The interpretation of the war as a collective tragedy in which all were equally to blame, and the resulting need for reconciliation as a starting point for a peaceful and democratic coexistence, became the dominant narrative in the Spanish transition process.

Francoism and Anti-Francoism

While the transition to democracy was carried out in the name of reconciliation and symmetry between the 'two Spains' – that 'were not so distinct, so distant' as stated in an editorial published in the newspaper *El País* in 1978[22] – the Francoism/anti-Francoism argument ceased to be relevant. In contrast with Germany, it was not a question of overcoming two totalitarianisms. The PCE had been the main force of the democratic opposition, and its leader, Santiago Carrillo, showed notable moderation and pragmatism in accordance with the new 'Eurocommunism' slogan. Furthermore, few in Spain perceived Francoism as a fascist regime; it was, perhaps at most, an authoritarian regime with 'limited pluralism', according to the well-known definition by political scientist Juan J. Linz.[23] The focus was no longer on fascism versus antifascism, but on 'relegating to the recesses of memory' a fratricidal war, together with the reasons given by both sides to fight it.[24]

Paradoxical as it may seem, overcoming anti-Francoism was an explicit aim of the parties that had taken part in the fight against Franco. One leading PCE figure, Ramón Tamames, declared that 'the best thing we can do for the future is to forget our Francoisms and anti-Francoisms. It is a sterile argument'.[25] This was reinforced by the sociologist Víctor Pérez Díaz: the controversy was irrelevant to the 'real Spain' and 'civil society', the true protagonist of the successful transition to democracy, which was only 'loosely committed to the experience of Francoism and anti-Francoism'.[26] The poor results obtained by the conservative Alianza Popular (AP, 'People's Alliance', later renamed the Partido Popular or 'People's Party') and the PCE in the elections of 1977, appeared to confirm this. Even Picasso's *Guernica*, a worldwide icon of antifascism, returned to Spain in 1981 transformed into 'a symbol of reconciliation'.[27]

The Francoist/anti-Francoist argument had become identified with others that divided the political and intellectual world during the transition process: past/future, ideology/politics, rupture/reform. In parliamentary debates and in the media, anti-Francoism was increasingly linked to nostalgia for an illusion, to ideological radicalism, to a dangerous political revolutionism and even to the violence exercised by extreme left-wing terrorist groups that had not disarmed after the death of the dictator. 'Franco and Francoism must be left to historians', affirmed one of the best-known historians of the period, Javier Tusell, coinciding with the psychiatrist Carlos Castilla del Pino: 'We must amnesty Francoism; and then, write its history'.[28] Both had taken part in the opposition to the regime.

The choice between looking to the future and civil education in historical memory, present in other European post-fascist transitions,[29] was also made in Spain. Renowned intellectuals upheld the morality of democracy, with an interest in 'how' rather than merely 'what', and their concern lay in the social legacy left by the dictatorship, especially among the 'silent masses' classified by the sociologist Amando de Miguel as 'sociological Francoism'.[30] These legacies were traceable in undemocratic behaviour such as a penchant for intriguing and conspiring, the absence of dialogue, irregular law enforcement, weak incentives as regards responsibility, and a political praxis aimed at holding power while turning a deaf ear to social demands. Many believed that the dictatorship still cast a long shadow over democracy, and this assumption is still the keystone of the antifascist discourse in Spain.

Anti-Francoism, in any case, had ceased to be the antithesis of Francoism, to become its consequence. As Manuel Vázquez Montalbán wrote, 'resistance was not a virtue, the virtue of a methodical critique, but a vice inherited from our anti-Francoist past'.[31] The disappearance of Francoists necessarily implied the same of anti-Francoists too, as another author, Pier Paolo Pasolini, had written a few years earlier about Italy. The antifascist narrative seemed to have been definitively left behind.

Historical Memory and Antifascism

Nevertheless, in the mid-1990s, the memory of the war and the dictatorship returned with force in the political debates. Public debate over this issue amongst journalists, writers, political scientists and historians became common in Spain, as it had earlier in other European countries.

Up to that point, Spanish historiography had been relatively united in the task of reconstructing a 'scientific' canon – albeit strongly influenced by historical materialism – that was opposed to the clumsy propaganda of Francoism. The Transition to democracy and the end of censorship caused a boom of works on the recent past, especially on the Civil War, but the traumatic memory of the violence was marginalised from the political debate, as we have seen, as a result of the process later called 'pact of silence'. In fact, this strategy was not very different from the one that had been adopted in Western Europe during the Cold War,[32] and that lasted until it was called into question in the 1960s by new factors ranging from generational renewal and, in the case of Italy, the consequences of a serious political and institutional crisis.

In the case of Spain, historiographical divisions have been linked above all to the change of political scenario after a decade and a half of Socialist rule when the right-wing Partido Popular ('People's Party') won the elections in 1996.[33] Other interlinked factors were added to this political opportunity, such as the arrest of former Chilean dictator Augusto Pinochet in London in 1998 by order of the Spanish judge Baltasar Garzón, and the subsequent legal orientation of the debate on the Spanish dictatorship under the influence of 'transitional justice' initiatives in Chile and Argentina; also, the massive ceremonies of beatification of the Catholic 'martyrs' in the Civil War, such as the one held in Rome in 2001. The first historiographical overviews of the Civil War and Francoist repression that called into question the narrative of the 'two Spains' involved in a 'collective tragedy', were challenged in the late 1990s by a highly successful publicity drive in terms of media presence and sales, epitomised by Pío Moa's *Los mitos de la Guerra Civil* (2003). These works simply recovered the old Francoist myths on the topic, and have thereby been described as 'neo-Francoist pseudo-revisionism'.[34]

In addition, the same years witnessed the emergence of a social movement that, under the banner of 'historical memory', demanded that the state offer dignity, reparation and justice to the victims of Francoism – above all, the first exhumations from mass graves of victims of Francoist repression, which led to the foundation in 2000 of the Asociación para la Recuperación de la Memoria Histórica (ARMH, 'Association for the Recovery of Historical Memory'). A large social demand for stories on these topics arose in this way, in particular stories on violence during the war and the dictatorship that have multiplied in recent years, whether as books, special issues of journals, lectures or conference papers.

The combination of these trends has resulted in a Spanish version of the *Historikerstreit* focused on issues such as the limits of Republican democracy, the causes of the war, the nature of violence behind the lines and the postwar repression, the exile, the contribution to democracy of ex-Francoist intellectuals and the numerical and political importance of anti-Francoism. Pro-Francoist pseudo-revisionism has gradually been excluded from this struggle due to its marginal position in the academic field, even if it holds solid institutional bases of power as was proved by the controversial 'Spanish Biographical Dictionary' sponsored by the Royal Academy of History.[35]

In the academic sphere, one sector stands by the demands of the movement of 'historical memory' and has been accused of being 'partisan' or 'militant' in defending the Second Republic as a democratic experience and as a source of legitimacy for Spanish democracy today.

Considerable differences exist, however, between historians who use memory in a more political way, ignoring the boundaries between historical interpretation and moral assessment, and a much larger sector of historians with different political views that cannot be summarily identified with a coherent and politically operational antifascist paradigm. This current of opinion transcends the boundaries of academic history, and has been responsible for some intellectual and civic initiatives in the last few years, such as the manifesto 'With pride, modesty and gratitude'.[36] Heated debates in the media have continued, and historians have not remained aloof.

The accusation of 'revisionism', in its pejorative Marxist sense, makes little sense in the case of Spain, where the antifascist legitimacy of other post-fascist democracies, such as Italy, has not existed and hence cannot be broken. It is therefore directed against the historians who have called into question the political myth of a democratic and antifascist Republic, highlighting the regime's deficit of legitimacy, its politics of exclusion and its high levels of conflict and violence.[37] This interpretation is explicitly aligned with the contribution of historians such as François Furet, Stéphane Courtois, Ernst Nolte and Renzo De Felice, even though it claims a 'scientific character' opposed to what it considers political uses of a 'partisan' or 'memorialist' history, framed by an 'anti-Francoist paradigm'.[38] But the so-called 'academic revisionism' also harbours an underlying political assumption: the legitimacy of the present Spanish democracy stems from the Transition that culminated in the Constitution of 1978, and by no means from a Republic that would have failed as a democratic experiment.[39]

Antifascism or Revolution

Antifascist memory is socially built, institutionalised and linked to present political interest of an evocative and mythical nature.[40] Antifascism does not appear to take up a prominent place in a study conducted by Federica Luzi on the family identity of the children of Spanish exiles, but occupied instead by a moral universe composed of humanistic and progressive values. In her research, the category 'antifascism' appears in the narratives most closely committed to activating collective memory, often within associations, in an attempt to create a shared memory among the descendants of those who, as mentioned, had been divided by profound ideological conflicts. An 'invented' Republic, divested of its more conflictive aspects, became a mythical age, a unifying symbol and a moral excuse for the present.[41]

Thus the Republic acts in Spain as a myth bringing antifascist memory together over and above ideological differences. It also has a mobilising power, as it becomes a political model and a moral reference point supporting certain aspirations in the present, particularly those that call for greater democratic representation and an ethical regeneration of politics. Not only is historical continuity upheld through exemplary lessons, but these reach beyond political education. There is also a need to acknowledge and sustain the legitimacy stemming from the victims' suffering and the fight against modern barbarism represented by fascism, totalitarianism and racism.

The memory built in this way leads to a European framework in which the war, the recollection of the crimes of fascism and the Holocaust are present in any project aiming to consolidate a common ethical and civil identity based on democracy, freedom, equality and tolerance. It is a framework, however, in which antifascism is in crisis, refuted by an anti-antifascist culture that holds it responsible for the feebleness of civic patriotism and the lack of a strong national identity, and for concealing the crimes committed by Communist totalitarianism and by partisans in a European civil war, far removed from the myth of a people's liberation movement.[42]

It is precisely in the acknowledgement as victims in the defence of the values of freedom and democracy that the moral legitimacy and political functionality of antifascism are determined today. To return to the parable of the angel, when the antifascist orator vindicates 'the memory of those who fought for a proletarian Spain and against a regime that was clearly opposed to the interests of the working classes and in favour of the bourgeoisie', we can harbour reasonable doubts regarding the recipient of the action – that is to say, whether it refers to the military and civilian rebels who rose up against the legal Republican authority, or to this self-same Republican and bourgeois authority.

Historians such as Santos Juliá and Fernando del Rey have pointed out the difficulty involved in considering as 'democratic' the combined forces represented at the time by the Frente Popular, and reminded us of the revolutionary process that was set in motion after July 1936 in the zone that was 'formally faithful' to the Republic.[43] The violence present during that process cut short any 'victimist' narrative on behalf of the Republicans, and ruled out the idea of a more or less legitimate antifascist violence, as its aim would not have been the defence of the Republic but rather of a revolution of the industrial workers and peasants.[44]

Therefore the question remains: how should the violence in the Republican zone be conceptualised, and how does it fit into the antifascist narrative? Recent studies make it difficult to maintain the thesis of spontaneity, lack of control, and revanchism, usually called on not to justify the use of terror in the Republican rearguard but to attenuate its political dimension and explain the impotence of the Republic to prevent it.[45] Does this amount to regarding both sources of violence as equal? Many historical studies have argued that a 'politicide' was committed in the rebel zone and continued after the end of the war, something that Paul Preston has gone so far as to describe as a 'Spanish Holocaust'.[46] Nevertheless, an essential part of the antifascist discourse involves denouncing the dangers of equidistance, of placing both sides on an equal standing, leaving unscathed a hypothetical 'third Spain' that remained free from violence and defended liberal democratic values.[47]

The 'Regime of 78'

The heart of the matter is the Transition, with a capital T. The control over this process by Francoist elites and the army, the high level of violence, the symbol of institutional continuity represented by the monarchy imposed by Franco, the absence of transitional justice for crimes committed under the dictatorship, and the lack of memory policies acknowledging exiled citizens and the victims of Francoism are the arguments most frequently used to refute the narrative of an 'exemplary Transition' put together by its protagonists. The 'antifascist narrative' argues, instead, that the Transition was not as peaceful as it is generally held to be, that it did not make a clean break with Francoism and that it did not incorporate antifascism as a central element of democratic culture, in contrast to other European countries.

In the words of historian Ricard Vinyes, during the Transition the state launched an attack on Spaniards' 'historical memory', depriving citizens of it and stripping the establishment of a constitutional state at the end of the dictatorship of its ethical foundation and popular roots. A law, a myth and a narrative were imposed in their place: the Amnesty Law of 1977, 'that legally established equal impunity', the myth of 'an exemplary transition' and a narrative based on oblivion, silence and an 'ideology of reconciliation' that, in fact, equated 'the Francoist executioners with their victims'. In a word, it was a functional 'good memory' built on equidistant ethics.[48]

Therein lies the origin of the Spanish democratic culture, tainted by authoritarianism: 'the regime of '78' (a reference to the 1978 Constitution) denounced by Podemos, the new party which won 8 per cent of the vote at the 2014 European elections and has become one of the country's three main political forces, according to recent voting intention polls. Thereby the political scientist Juan Carlos Monedero, one of the founders of Podemos, refutes the idea of an 'exemplary Transition' as the founding moment of a modern democracy comparable to those of other European countries, stating that, on the contrary, Spanish democracy was 'founded on genocide'. This author blames the legacy of the dictatorship for the country's weak democratic culture, characterised by a deferential attitude to power and an uncritical acceptance of leadership, a patrimonial attitude towards the public domain, scarce civic education, apoliticism and corruption.

For Monedero, 'the source from which sprang Spanish democracy was 14 April 1931 [the founding date of the Second Republic]', and the democratic regeneration required in order to meet the standards reached in Europe could only be achieved by establishing links with an antifascist legitimacy: 'Only through recovering the historical transformative capacity of the Spanish people shall we find the path upon which to pursue our transformation'. Antifascist ideology has thus acquired a utopian dimension, given that memory 'may bear today its emancipating fruits in favour of a dense democracy', for a citizenship that is critical and 'mobilised in defence of its rights, up to date in the use of critical and objective media, educated, well read, knowledgeable in the performing arts, secular, respectful of intellectual activity and striving to support a progressive cultural task'. Thus, 'the place that in 1939 was called Spain' was like a looking glass in which Spaniards should recognise themselves and build a better society.[49]

All these issues are complicated by further cleavages, in particular regarding generational renewal and nationalist claims. As for the first, the demand for historical memory has been linked to the 'generation of grandchildren', the offspring of those who did not experience the Civil War at first hand. It is curious to note that this same factor is mentioned among the causes of the crisis of antifascism in Italy since the mid-1990s, at precisely the time when it flourished in Spain. Antifascism is expressed in a generational key, as each 'own generation' strives to find, in Monedero's terms, 'the theme of its time'. This translates as 'claiming what their parents had ignored' and reviewing the narrative of the Transition drawn up by the 'perpetrators of memoricide', who were mostly 'descendants of the winning side'. In addition, the generation that occupied the leading roles during the Transition held important positions in political, financial and cultural power, 'reached posts of responsibility very early in their careers and did not learn to step down from them', thus becoming a 'barrier generation' preventing access to a younger generation.[50]

The national question creates another cleavage in Spanish antifascist discourse: Catalonia and the Basque Country were the sole regions that had written a historical narrative different from the 'official' indulgent version of Francoism and the Transition, which largely explains the vitality of their civil society and nationalist mobilisation. This assumption is twofold. First, their nationalist movements seek in their defeat and the Francoist repression, which they identify with Spanishness, a part of their historical legitimacy. It does not seem a coincidence that most documentaries based on testimonies of Republican victims of Francoist repression or in exile have been produced by Catalonia's regional television channel.[51] To give another example, the Law on Memorial Democràtic de Catalunya ('Catalonia's Democratic Memory') provides that 'the current democratic system has its most immediate roots in the Republican memory and in anti-Francoism', but one of the shortcomings of the Transition was 'the institutionalisation of silence and the relegation from memory of democratic traditions and their players'. The law concludes that 'the memory of the past and social education' are 'factors of political identity and national pride'.[52] Second, antifascism may ultimately be a common principle upon which to refound the Spanish nation, the only way to halt the secessionist aspirations of those territories, a patriotic and regenerationist tool.

Anti-system Antifascism

Antifascism, therefore, does not consist merely of the circumstantial union of a broad political front in the struggle against fascism, understood as a historical phenomenon, nor solely in a claim to democratic legitimacy in the fight for the Republic and, subsequently, for those in exile and anti-Francoism. There is yet a further Antifascism with a capital A that upholds a political ideology, according to the distinction made by Giovanni Orsina with regard to the Italian situation,[53] though less well defined and articulate in the Spanish case. This ideological antifascism, as well as interpreting the democratisation of Spain as an imperfect process owing to its failure to make a clean break from the dictatorship, understands fascism as a 'political constant', masked by new forms of social control and capitalist exploitation.

This interpretation of fascism also allows two readings that, in turn, differentiate the ideological orientation of these tiny left-wing and anti-system groups. The first envisages fascism in accordance with Marxist–Leninist orthodoxy as an instrument in the hands of the dominant classes within a context of economic crisis or as a threat to their social mobilisation interests. The emphasis falls on maintaining continuity with historical fascism: 'Antifascism as part of the proletarian struggle must be anti-capitalist in nature, and always highlight the classist nature of fascism, which makes it an instrument of the bourgeoisie'.[54] The second reading, of a libertarian outlook and influenced by the reflections made by the New Left since the 1960s, interprets fascism as intrinsic to modernity, to bureaucratic rationality and to the daily functioning of the capitalist system, associated in these historical times to neoliberalism, independently of the political juncture. It sees fascism and capitalism as two sides of the same coin, together with 'other ways of managing power in which the function of the state is understood as necessary'.[55] This view is identified especially with the authoritarian behaviour of institutions under democratic systems, but also theorises on the emergence of a 'comprehensive fascism produced by society rather than by the state', defined as 'postmodern fascism' or 'demo-fascism'.[56]

The immediate aim of all the above groups is to combat the growth of a racist, xenophobic and populist extreme right, in Spain and throughout Europe, and remove its 'mask of democratic respectability'.[57] This is especially true as these lines are written in 2014, when an economic crisis and cuts in welfare are encouraging the rise of fascism under socio-economic conditions that, in certain aspects, are reminiscent of those in the 1930s during the Great Depression.[58] As stated in the declaration of the International Antifascist Congress held in Berlin in April 2014:

> In Germany and beyond, neo-fascist and right-wing populist parties are moving into position; everywhere in Europe they are using the current crisis to regroup their forces. Given the Euro-crisis and the social devastation it has wrought, they judge that they are in a good position to strengthen national and xenophobic arguments and discourses. The antifascist movement has found it hard to analyse this rightward lurch in Europe.[59]

For these groups, unity is not an easy matter when, for example, some still remember the 'social revolution' carried out during the Spanish Civil War as opposed to the 'counter-revolutionary work' of Stalinist and social-democrat 'traitors' in May 1937.[60] However, since the mid-1990s these groups have gradually converged through antifascist collectives and coordination initiatives, many of which formed the Coordinación Antifascista del Estado Español ('Spanish State Antifascist Coordination Group'), or the refounded Federación Ibérica de Juventudes Libertarias (FIJL, 'Iberian Federation of Libertarian Youth').[61] Under the famous Civil War slogan '*No pasarán*' ('They shall not pass!'), they have multiplied their social networks, characterised by a strong presence on internet and cyber-activism, as well as through initiatives, meetings and conferences against fascism and racism. Examples are those celebrated at the Universidad Complutense de Madrid in November 2013, which resulted in an assault on a number of conservative student associations, and those held in Barcelona in June 2014.[62]

One of the most recent initiatives along these lines was the drafting of the *European Antifascist Manifesto*, signed in Spain by more than three hundred intellectuals, trade union representatives and activists in political and social movements. The Manifesto declares that 'the antifascist fight has to construct an alternative vision of society, diametrically opposite to the one defended by the extreme right': solidarity, tolerance and fraternity, rejection of the oppression of women, respect for the right to differ, internationalism and the defence of humanistic and democratic values.[63] The poet Marcos Ana, who spent twenty-three years imprisoned under the Francoist regime, attended the presentation of the document.

The quest for historical memory takes on a special relevance in the light of the strategy adopted by these antifascist coordination groups. Firstly, in order to escape the dynamic of street-level confrontation favoured by 'urban tribes', self-labelled as antifascist, this is considered counterproductive and favours their 'criminalisation' by the authorities.[64] And secondly, in order to avoid using the term 'fascist' in vain, and, of course, to turn antifascist unity into a strategy for mobilising the masses.

Conclusion: The Ongoing Construction of an Antifascist Memory

In Spain, the transition to democracy failed to settle the major narratives of confrontation originating in the Civil War, as it may have appeared at some point, and twenty years later the Transition itself has been called into question for the absence of reparations' policies for the victims and challenged by a powerful narrative regarding 'unfinished democracy', as well as the political continuities and inertias inherited from the dictatorship.[65] By the mid-1990s, a new antifascist discourse started to denounce the Transition's attempt to reconcile the 'two Spains' and to impose a shared official memory, an attempt that was leading, paradoxically, to the crisis of antifascism in Italy in the very same years.[66]

The Socialist governments of José Luis Rodríguez Zapatero (2004–11) attempted to adopt these new demands to their political agenda with initiatives such as the so-called Ley de memoria histórica ('Law of Historical Memory') and the new primary school subject Educación para la ciudadanía ('Education in Citizenship'). Two symbolic representations of this policy were the government's project to remove Franco from the Valley of the Fallen, turning it into 'a place of peace and reconciliation', and the order to remove Franco's equestrian statue in Madrid, placed at a short distance from the statues of the Socialist leaders of the Republic Indalecio Prieto and Francisco Largo Caballero, and the monument to the Constitution of 1978.

After taking power in December 2011, the Partido Popular has halted all those initiatives, including the exhumation of mass graves in which thousands of victims of the Francoist repression are still buried. In a multi-tiered discourse directed at a wide range of potential audiences, the PP has made compatible the non-condemnation of Francoism in Parliament with repeated claims that the Transition represents the foundational moment of Spain's democracy.

As we have seen, antifascism was reduced to a rhetorical status in the discourse of Republicanism in exile when Franco's dictatorship managed to survive the defeat of European fascism, and consolidated from the late 1940s. The exiled Republicans, in fact, were more divided than united by the memory of defeat and the debate over the respective responsibilities for this defeat, as well as by renewed anti-Communism during the Cold War period. The possibility of a real antifascist political praxis was complicated by the tendency of many anti-Francoists, especially within the organisations of the non-Communist left in exile and the Christian-Democratic groups, to equate the two totalitarian systems, fascism and Communism. Impulses towards unity were stronger inside the country, where in the 1960s the PCE became the main force of the clandestine opposition to the dictatorship, but even so we cannot equate antifascism directly with anti-Francoism.

The call for a national reconciliation of the leaders of anti-Francoist organisations, including the Communist Party, was instead a unifying factor, but in the opposite direction to antifascism as a political strategy. For the same reason, we cannot attribute to Francoism the notion of equidistance upon which the transition from dictatorship to democracy was based, that is to say a 'pact of silence' regarding the Republican past and the crimes of Francoism, which was legally protected by the Amnesty Law of 1977. The narrative of reconciliation came from the anti-Francoist left. But nearly forty years after the death of the dictator this does not seem enough for the new generations, whose memory of the war has been transmitted to them exclusively through books or passed down from family history.

In the midst of a severe institutional, social and economic crisis, the memory of a more or less 'invented' Republic, and the cause of justice for the victims of Francoist repression, have become an operational political tool, as was recently illustrated by the profusion of Republican flags at the demonstrations following the abdication of King Juan Carlos I in June 2014. We should not confuse nostalgia for an idealised Second Republic and the anti-Franco struggle with a politically operative antifascism comparable to the one that since the 1960s has conditioned the political praxis and even the institutions in Italy. The Franco dictatorship and the Spanish Transition took place in very different historical circumstances. However, since the mid-1990s a generic antifascism has reappeared with force in Spanish political vocabulary, denouncing the right in power and its continuities with Francoist culture, and calling for the revision of the exemplary narrative of the Transition and of some key elements of the institutional, political and economic system, in an international context marked by the end of the Communist utopia.

Notes

1. *ABC* (Madrid), 17 November 1964.
2. A. Kramer, 'The Cult of the Spanish Civil War in East Germany', *Journal of Contemporary History* 39(4) (2004), 531–60.
3. F. Gallego, *Barcelona, mayo 1937: la crisis del antifascismo en Cataluña*, Madrid, 2007; H. García, 'La República de las pequeñas diferencias: cultura(s) de izquierda y antifascismo(s) en España, 1931–1939', in M. Pérez Ledesma and R. Cruz (eds), *Historia de las culturas políticas en España y América Latina*, Madrid, 2015, vol. 4, 207–37. See also the chapter by Hugo García in this volume.
4. E. Treglia and L.C. Hernando, 'Dopoguerra e ritorno al socialfascismo. La politica del PCE e la sua lettura della Guerra Civile durante il biennio del Patto Molotov–Ribbentrop', in E. Acciai and G. Quaggio (eds), *Un conflitto che non passa: storia, memoria e rimozioni della guerra civile spagnola*, Pistoia, 2012, 107–24.
5. A. Mateos, *Historia del antifranquismo*, Barcelona, 2011, 73–81.
6. 'En el décimo aniversario del 16 de febrero', *Mundo Obrero. Boletín del Partido Comunista de España en Francia*, Toulouse, 16 February 1946; '¡Que triunfe la unidad republicana!', *España Popular*, México, 15 February 1946.
7. Á. Herrerín, *La CNT durante el franquismo*, Madrid, 2004; L.C. Hernando, *El PSOE y la monarquía*, Madrid, 2013.

8. O. Glondys, *La Guerra Fría cultural y el exilio republicano español*, Madrid, 2012.

9. F. Alaiz, 'Problemas de base en el exilio', *Solidaridad Obrera*, Paris, 23 June 1951.

10. *CNT*, Toulouse, 17 September 1961.

11. J. Muñoz Soro, 'La reconciliación como política. Memoria de la violencia y la guerra en el antifranquismo', *Revista de Historia Jerónimo Zurita* 84 (2009), 113–33.

12. J. Mark, N. Townson and P. Voglis, 'Inspirations', in. R. Gildea, J. Mark and A. Warring (eds), *Europe's 1968: Voices of Revolt*, Oxford, 2013, 72–103.

13. C. Laíz Castro, *La izquierda radical en España durante la transición a la democracia*, Madrid, 2000.

14. 'Comunicado público de la 1ª conferencia de nuestro Partido', *Mundo Obrero Rojo. Órgano central del Partido del Trabajo de España*, 7 March 1975; 'Lo ocurrido el 20 de noviembre', *En lucha. Órgano central de la Organización Revolucionaria de Trabajadores (ORT)*, 1 (January 1974).

15. Muñoz Soro, 'La reconciliación como política', 113–33.

16. In a quantitative analysis, *España Popular* (México) used this on 121 occasions in 1945 but only once in 1966; *Mundo Obrero* (the organ of the Central Committee), 44 times in 1976 and 27 in 1975, but only once in 1960; *Nuestra Bandera* (the party's 'ideological education' magazine) did so 26 times in 1975 and 21 in 1974, but just once in 1966, 1967 and 1968.

17. 'Ayer el Frente Popular… ¿Y hoy?', *Nuestra Bandera* 63 (January 1970).

18. *Pueblo*, Madrid, 31 December 1976.

19. P. Aguilar, 'La amnesia y la memoria: las movilizaciones por la amnistía en la transición a la democracia', in M. Pérez Ledesma and R. Cruz (eds), *Cultura y movilización en la España contemporánea*, Madrid, 1997, 327–57.

20. *BOE* 248, 17 October 1977, 22765–66.

21. *El País*, Madrid, 18 July 1986.

22. Editorial, 'Los vencidos piden la palabra', *El País*, 2 December 1978.

23. J.J. Linz, 'Una teoría del régimen autoritario. El caso de España', in M. Fraga (ed.), *La España de los años setenta*, Vol. III. *El Estado y la Política*, Madrid, 1974, 1467–1531.

24. Santos Juliá, 'Echar al olvido. Memoria y amnistía en la transición', *Claves de Razón Práctica* 129 (2003), 14–24.

25. Ramón Tamames, 'Lo mejor, olvidar la polémica estéril', *Diario 16*, 20 November 1979, 9.

26. V. Pérez Díaz, 'Un análisis de las elecciones: Negociación, a los 40 años impotencia política', y 'Una salida honorable del franquismo', *El País*, 17 and 19 July 1977. The author's thesis in *La primacía de la sociedad civil*, Madrid, 1993.

27. J. Tusell, 'El final de la transición', *El País*, 11 September 1981.

28. J. Tusell, 'El General Franco, dos años después', *Ya*, 23 November 1977; C. Castilla del Pino, 'Democracia: una primera expectativa', *El País*, 24 June 1977.

29. L. La Rovere, *L'eredità del fascismo. Gli intellettuali, i giovani e la transizione al postfascismo, 1943–1948*, Turin, 2008.

30. A. de Miguel, *La sociología del Franquismo: análisis ideológico de los minis-tros del régimen*, Barcelona, 1974; A. de Miguel, *La herencia del franquismo*, Madrid, 1976.

31. 'Sobre la memoria de la oposición antifranquista', *El País*, 26 October 1988.

32. H. Lübbe defined it in 1983 as a 'pact of silence' (*kollektives Beschweigen*); Á. Lozano, *Anatomía del Tercer Reich. El debate y los historiadores*, Barcelona, 2012, 18.

33. P. Aguilar, 'Presencia y ausencia de la Guerra Civil y del franquismo en la democracia española. Reflexiones en torno a la articulación y ruptura del *pacto de silencio*', in J. Aróstegui and F. Godicheau (eds), *Guerra Civil, mito y memoria*, Madrid, 2006, 245–94.

34. Among the former, Santos Juliá (ed.), *Víctimas de la Guerra Civil*, Madrid, 1999; among the latter, P. Moa, *Los orígenes de la Guerra Civil Española*, Madrid, 1999 See E. Moradiellos, 'Critical Historical Revision and Political Revisionism: The Case of Spain', *International Journal of Iberian Studies* 21(3) (2008), 219–29.

35. J.L. Ledesma, 'El *Diccionario Biográfico Español*, el pasado y los histori-adores', *Ayer* 88 (2012), 247–65; Á. Viñas (ed.), *En el combate por la historia. La República, la Guerra Civil, el franquismo*, Barcelona, 2012.

36. Read online at http://www.pce.es/leon/Memoria/070406.htm (accessed 4 March 2015).

37. M. Alvarez Tardío and F. del Rey (eds), *The Spanish Second Republic Revisited: From Democratic Hopes to Civil War (1931–1936)*, Brighton, Sussex, 2012.

38. F. del Rey, 'Revisionismos y anatemas. A vueltas con la II República', *Historia Social* 72 (2012), 155–72. See the debates between P.C. González Cuevas, I. Saz, F. del Rey, G. Ranzato and J.L. Ledesma in *Historia del Presente* 17 (2011) and 22 (2013).

39. M. Álvarez Tardío, *El camino a la democracia en España: 1931 y 1978*, Madrid, 2005.

40. P. Aguilar, *Políticas de la memoria y memorias de la política*, Madrid, 2008, 64–65.

41. F. Luzi, 'La reinvención de la identidad colectiva de los descendientes de los refugiados españoles. El antifascismo como instrumento de legit-imación de la memoria del exilio en Francia y en Europa', *Migraciones y Exilios* 13 (2012), 33–44.

42. L. Baldissara, 'Antifascismo', in A. De Bernaldi and S. Guarracino (eds), *Il Fascismo*, Milan, 1998, 149–56.

43. F. del Rey, 'Trampas de la memoria antifascista', *El Mundo*, 22 March 2007, 4–5.

44. Santos Juliá, '¿Una memoria antifascista?', *El País*, 26 April 2008.

45. Among others, J. Ruiz, *The 'Red Terror' and the Spanish Civil War: Revolutionary Violence in Madrid*, New York, 2014; J.L. Ledesma, 'Una retaguardia al rojo. Las violencias en la zona republicana', in F. Espinosa (ed.), *Violencia roja y azul. España, 1936–1950*, Barcelona, 2010, 147–247; F. del Rey, 'Por tier-ras de La Mancha: Apuntes sobre la violencia revolucionaria en la Guerra Civil española (1936–1939)', *Alcores* 11 (2011), 223–63; M. Thomas, *The Faith*

and the Fury: Popular Anticlerical Violence and Iconoclasm in Spain, 1931–1936, Brighton, Sussex, 2013.

46. P. Preston, *The Spanish Holocaust: Inquisition and Extermination in Twentieth-Century Spain*, New York, 2012. See also P. Anderson, *The Francoist Military Trials: Terror and Complicity, 1939–1945*, New York, 2010.

47. F. Espinosa (ed.), *Violencia roja y azul. España, 1936–1950*, Barcelona, 2010; or F. Sánchez Pérez's preface to *Los mitos del 18 de julio*, Barcelona, 2013.

48. R. Vinyes (ed.), *El estado y la memoria: gobiernos y ciudadanos frente a los traumas de la historia*, Barcelona, 2009, 25.

49. J.C. Monedero, *La Transición contada a nuestros padres. Nocturno de la democracia española*, Madrid, 2nd edn. 2013, pp. 22, 33, 43, 65–66, 187 and 238–39.

50. Ibid., 59–63, and 14 for the presentation by historian Emilio Silva, founder of the first Asociación de Recuperación de la Memoria Histórica.

51. J. Labanyi, 'Historias de víctimas: la memoria histórica y el testimonio en la España contemporánea', *Iberoamericana* VI(24) (2006), 87–98.

52. Law 13/2007, of 31 October, on the Memorial Democràtic.

53. G. Orsina, 'Quando l'Antifascismo sconfisse l'antifascismo. Interpretazioni della Resistenza nell'alta cultura antifascista italiana, 1955–1965', *Alcores* 11 (2011), 109–27.

54. Plataforma Antifascista Zamora, 2010, 'Antifascismo. El peligro reformista y el camino a seguir', http://old.kaosenlared.net/media/18/18253_1_Antifascismo_2C___el___pe.pdf (accessed 3 March 2015).

55. 'No basta con vencer al fascismo. Análisis libertario del fascismo y el antifascismo', Juventudes Libertarias de Madrid-Federación Ibérica de Juventudes Libertarias (FIJL), Madrid, 2014.

56. P. García Olivo, 'Demofascismo', 2006, in www.lahaine.org/index.php?p=18154 (accessed 4 March 2015); Gustavo Roig, 'Lógica antifascista: ¿sumar, restar, multiplicar o dividir?', *Diagonal* 51 (2007).

57. D. Karvala (ed.), *No pasarán… aunque lleven trajes. La lucha contra la extrema derecha hoy*, Barcelona, 2010.

58. V. Navarro, 'Los orígenes del fascismo en Europa, antes y ahora', *Público*, Madrid, 27 May 2014.

59. http://crisisracism.noblogs.org/material-eng/information-text (accessed 3 March 2015).

60. 'Lo que es y lo que no es el 19 de julio', Grupo Bandera Negra-Federación Ibérica de Juventudes Anarquistas (FIJA), Madrid, 2014.

61. http://antifa.es; http://juventudeslibertariasmadrid.wordpress.com (this, and the following sites, accessed 19 September 2014).

62. http://unitatcontraelfeixisme.org.

63. http://antifascismeuropa.org/manifiesto/en.

64. 'Construir antifascismo', Izquierda Anticapitalista, www.anticapitalistas.org/spip.php?article28629.

65. J. Rodrigo, *Cruzada, paz, memoria. La guerra civil en sus relatos*, Granada, 2013, 105. On the major narratives, see Santos Juliá, *Historias de las dos Españas*, Madrid, 2004.

66. S. Luzzatto, *La crisi dell'antifascismo*, Turin, 2004.

References

Aguilar, P. 'La amnesia y la memoria: las movilizaciones por la amnistía en la transición a la democracia', in M. Pérez Ledesma and R. Cruz (eds), *Cultura y movilización en la España contemporánea*. Madrid, 1997, 327–35.

———. 'Presencia y ausencia de la Guerra Civil y del franquismo en la democracia española. Reflexiones en torno a la articulación y ruptura del *pacto de silencio*', in J. Aróstegui and F. Godicheau (eds), *Guerra Civil, mito y memoria*. Madrid, 2006.

———. *Políticas de la memoria y memorias de la política*. Madrid, 2008.

Álvarez Tardío, M. *El camino a la democracia en España: 1931 y 1978*. Madrid, 2005.

Álvarez Tardío, M., and F. del Rey (eds). *The Spanish Second Republic Revisited: From Democratic Hopes to Civil War (1931–1936)*. Brighton, Sussex, 2012.

Anderson, P. *The Francoist Military Trials: Terror and Complicity, 1939–1945*. New York, 2010.

Baldissara, L. 'Antifascismo', in A. De Bernaldi and S. Guarracino (eds), *Il Fascismo*. Milan, 1998, 149–56.

Espinosa, F. (ed.). *Violencia roja y azul. España, 1936–1950*. Barcelona, 2010.

Gallego, F. *Barcelona, mayo 1937: la crisis del antifascismo en Cataluña*. Madrid, 2007.

García, H. 'La República de las pequeñas diferencias: cultura(s) de izquierda y antifascismo(s) en España, 1931–1939', in M. Pérez Ledesma and R. Cruz (eds), *Historia de las culturas políticas en España y América Latina*. Madrid, vol. 4, 2015, 207–37.

Glondys, O. *La Guerra Fría cultural y el exilio republicano español*. Madrid, 2012.

Hernando, L.C. *El PSOE y la monarquía*. Madrid, 2013.

Herrerín, Á. *La CNT durante el franquismo*. Madrid, 2004.

Juliá, S. (ed.). *Víctimas de la Guerra Civil*. Madrid, 1999.

——— 'Echar al olvido. Memoria y amnistía en la transición'. *Claves de Razón Práctica* 129 (2003), 14–24.

———. *Historias de las dos Españas*. Madrid, 2004.

Karvala, D. (ed.). *No pasarán… aunque lleven trajes. La lucha contra la extrema derecha hoy*. Barcelona, 2010.

Krammer, A. 'The Cult of the Spanish Civil War in East Germany'. *Journal of Contemporary History* 39(4) (2004), 531–60.

Labanyi, J. 'Historias de víctimas: la memoria histórica y el testimonio en la España contemporánea'. *Iberoamericana* VI(24) (2006), 87–98.

Laíz Castro, C. *La izquierda radical en España durante la transición a la democracia*. Madrid, 2000.

La Rovere, L. *L'eredità del fascismo. Gli intellettuali, i giovani e la transizione al post-fascismo, 1943–1948*. Turin, 2008.

Ledesma, J.L. 'Una retaguardia al rojo. Las violencias en la zona republicana', in F. Espinosa (ed.), *Violencia roja y azul. España, 1936–1950*. Barcelona, 2010, 147–247.

———. 'El *Diccionario Biográfico Español*, el pasado y los historiadores', *Ayer* 88 (2012), 247–65.

Linz, J.J. 'Una teoría del régimen autoritario. El caso de España', in Manuel Fraga (ed.), *La España de los años setenta*, Vol. III. *El Estado y la Política*. Madrid, 1974, 1467–1531.

Lozano, Á. *Anatomía del Tercer Reich. El debate y los historiadores*. Barcelona, 2012.

Luzi, F. 'La reinvención de la identidad colectiva de los descendientes de los refugiados españoles. El antifascismo como instrumento de legitimación de la memoria del exilio en Francia y en Europa'. *Migraciones y Exilios* 13 (2012), 33–44.

Luzzatto, S. *La crisi dell'antifascismo*. Turin, 2004.

Mark, J., N. Townson and P. Voglis. 'Inspirations', in R. Gildea, J. Mark and A. Warring (eds), *Europe's 1968: Voices of Revolt*. Oxford, 2013, 72–103.

Mateos, A. *Historia del antifranquismo*. Barcelona, 2011.

Miguel, A. de. *La sociología del Franquismo: análisis ideológico de los ministros del régimen*. Barcelona, 1974.

———. *La herencia del franquismo*. Madrid, 1976.

Moa, P. *Los orígenes de la Guerra Civil Española*. Madrid, 1999.

Monedero, J.C. *La Transición contada a nuestros padres. Nocturno de la democracia española*. 2nd edn. Madrid, 2013.

Moradiellos, E. 'Critical Historical Revision and Political Revisionism: The Case of Spain'. *International Journal of Iberian Studies* 21(3) (2008), 219–29.

Muñoz Soro, J. 'La reconciliación como política. Memoria de la violencia y la guerra en el antifranquismo'. *Revista de Historia Jerónimo Zurita* 84 (2009), 113–33.

Orsina, G. 'Quando l'Antifascismo sconfisse l'antifascismo. Interpretazioni della Resistenza nell'alta cultura antifascista italiana, 1955–1965'. *Alcores* 11 (2011), 109–27.

Pérez Díaz, V. *La primacía de la sociedad civil*. Madrid, 1993.

Preston, P. *The Spanish Holocaust: Inquisition and Extermination in Twentieth-Century Spain*. New York, 2012.

Rey, F. del. 'Por tierras de La Mancha: Apuntes sobre la violencia revolucionaria en la Guerra Civil española (1936–1939)'. *Alcores* 11 (2011), 223–63.

———. 'Revisionismos y anatemas. A vueltas con la II República'. *Historia Social* 72 (2012), 155–72.

Rodrigo, J. *Cruzada, paz, memoria. La guerra civil en sus relatos*. Granada, 2013.

Roig, G. 'Lógica antifascista: ¿sumar, restar, multiplicar o dividir?'. *Diagonal* 51 (2007).

Ruiz, J. *The 'Red Terror' and the Spanish Civil War: Revolutionary Violence in Madrid*. New York, 2014.

Sánchez Pérez, F. (ed.). *Los mitos del 18 de julio*. Barcelona, 2013.

Tamames, R. 'Lo mejor, olvidar la polémica estéril', *Diario 16*, 20 November 1979, 9.

Thomas, M. *The Faith and the Fury: Popular Anticlerical Violence and Iconoclasm in Spain, 1931–1936*. Brighton, Sussex, 2013.

Treglia, E., and L.C. Hernando. 'Dopoguerra e ritorno al socialfascismo. La politica del PCE e la sua lettura della Guerra Civile durante il biennio del Patto Molotov–Ribbentrop', in E. Acciai and G. Quaggio (eds), *Un conflitto che non passa: storia, memoria e rimozioni della guerra civile spagnola*. Pistoia, 2012.

Viñas Á. (ed.). *En el combate por la historia. La República, la Guerra Civil, el fran-quismo.* Barcelona, 2012.
Vinyes, R. (ed.). *El estado y la memoria: gobiernos y ciudadanos frente a los traumas de la historia.* Barcelona, 2009.

Javier Muñoz Soro is associate professor of Modern History at the Faculty of Political Sciences of the Complutense University of Madrid, having previously worked at the University of Cagliari (Italy). He is particularly interested in the history of culture, intellectuals and the media in Spain during the Franco dictatorship and the transition to democracy, as well as in Spanish–Italian relations since 1945. He has published the book *Cuadernos para el Diálogo. Una historia cultural del segundo franquismo* (2006) and numerous articles in Spanish and Italian academic journals. His current research project focuses on the concept of post-fascism from a European transnational perspective.

16

Dictatorship and Revolution

Disputes over Collective Memory in Post-Authoritarian
Portugal

Manuel Loff and Luciana Soutelo

When analysing collective memory of the recent past, one must consider what has become known as 'historical revisionism'. We are not specifically talking about its historiographic dimension, but rather the broad social and political phenomenon active in potentially every contemporary society. Historical revisionism can be defined in its three main scopes: apologetic tendencies over Nazi-fascist regimes and, broadly, twentieth-century right-wing dictatorships; interpretations focused on redistributing historical responsibility for war, reversing social and historiographical consolidated views, thus converting oppressors into victims; and reinterpretations of political and social revolutions and upheavals, revolutionary processes, movements and organisations, in order to depict them as criminal. Historical revisionism operates in very differing cases and almost regardless of historical contexts. In this sense, Enzo Traverso perceives it as 'an ethical-political turn' in the way of understanding the past.[1]

The Portuguese (and Spanish, for that matter) process of coming to terms with a dictatorial past since the 1970s is of clear interest because, if not for any other reason, it evolved while other European societies were confronted with a 'return of the repressed', 'a third and fourth stage' (according to Henry Rousso) of the post-1945 remembrance of Nazism, Holocaust and collaboration. Clashes in the late 1970s and the 1980s over attempts to historicise National-Socialism and the Holocaust (the West German 1986 *Historikerstreit*), De Felice's critique of an Italian anti-fascist version of Fascism, controversy over French Holocaust negationism and revisionism, and the Vichy regime's nature and genocidal responsibilities were, *grosso modo*, contemporary to the Portuguese Revolution (1974–76) and to the Spanish democratic transition (1976–78), as well as to the first stages of Iberian democracies.

In the case of Portugal, a social revolution followed the fall of a 48-year-long dictatorship. Consequently, two revisionist trends emerged: on the one hand was an attempt to dilute the repressive nature of Salazar's dictatorship and to minimise its social costs, while on the other was an attempt to condemn the 1974 Revolution for its radicalism. These two trends usually appear together and it is hard to find them apart: many interpretations of the dictatorship are read retrospectively and comparatively in order to highlight the excesses of the 1974–76 revolutionary period; this therefore allows for very negative interpretations of the Revolution opposed to a whitewashed[2] version of the dictatorship. Historical revisionism emerged as a social phenomenon in the Portuguese public sphere at the end of the 1980s, its peak being reached in the mid-1990s and more specifically at the Revolution's twentieth anniversary in 1994. Hostile discourses regarding the Revolution progressively unfolded in an attempt to build up a social atmosphere in which 'mild' interpretations of the dictatorship became commonplace. This process explains why historical revisionism is a fundamental feature in understanding the public disputes over the memory of Portuguese dictatorship in the last decades.

Revolution and Memory: Repression and Resistance Logos and the Specificity of Colonial War

The 25 April 1974 military coup by the 'Armed Forces Movement' (Movimento das Forças Armadas, MFA) almost overnight produced a revolutionary political break-up with the past. Democracy was, in the Portuguese experience of the 1970s, a consequence of both a military coup and a social revolution. The transitional process towards a fully institutionalised democracy would last until April 1976, when a new Constitution was passed. The Portuguese revolution took place during the nineteen months leading up to November 1975. Unlike most other transitions from dictatorship to liberal-democratic regimes, especially the remaining ones that Samuel Huntington equivocally assembled into what he called a 'third wave of democratisation',[3] the Portuguese transitional model met every condition in order to produce a clear rupture with the authoritarian past, politically as well as socially, economically and culturally. Left-wing political culture, in the post-1968 context, was becoming clearly predominant in a society where industrialisation, war[4] and massive emigration forced the Portuguese to (re)politicise their perception of the world.[5]

That clear ideological hegemony of the left was present in the definition of *Estado Novo*, the Portuguese dictatorship of 1926–74, as a 'fascist' regime in every legal document passed in the first years of democracy (including the 1976 Constitution). 'Fascist repression' was the legal definition of the political police's activity, and thus of Salazarism and its oppressive nature: 'crimes systematically perpetrated against the Portuguese people', 'arbitrary and inhumane action', 'terrorist activities' and 'institutionalised crime'. Criminal procedures against those responsible for such crimes became 'imprescriptible'[6] – a legal principle which remains formally effective, though in fact never evoked.

The social expression of the memory of the victims of Salazar's repression was very intense throughout the revolutionary period, drawing a first stage in the post-1974 process of remembering dictatorship. It was their moment to finally express their grievances and for people to hear and pay tribute to them, although there was inevitable political competition between the different organisations and their respective symbolic cultures. This necessarily implied recognising the role of Communist and, to a lesser extent, far-left militants (in the final stage of the dictatorship), as they were the ones, in metropolitan Portugal, who suffered the most at the hands of the political police (Polícia Internacional de Defesa do Estado, PIDE, renamed Direção-Geral de Segurança, DGS, in 1969). *Edições Sociais*, close to the Communist Party (PCP), created a collection specifically dedicated to *Episódios da Resistência Antifascista*. A few Socialists and Republicans published their own autobiographical accounts regarding the resistance. At any rate, most of these memorial recollections had already circulated underground during the 1960s.[7] A special place was dedicated to memorial accounts of political prisoners, both Communists and anarchists, who had survived the concentration camp of Tarrafal (1936–54).[8] In 1978, thirty-two coffins were transferred from Tarrafal to Lisbon; this was probably the largest public tribute to antifascist resistants in the entire democratic period.

The military who, together with civilian leaders, ran the country until 1976, payed their own tribute to the military victims of the dictatorship: General Humberto Delgado, a Salazarist dissident who became the opposition presidential candidate in 1958, was trapped in Spain in 1965 and murdered by the Portuguese political police, and posthumously reintegrated into the air force in 'public recognition of his virtues and valour'.[9] Furthermore, every 'penalty imposed upon the military in view of the facts that occurred during the invasion of the Portuguese State of India by the Indian armed forces in December 1961' were 'nullified'. These military did not comply with Salazar's orders to resist *à outrance*, and were punished and expelled from the army after being released by the Indians and sent back to Portugal.[10]

Nevertheless, the military origin of the democratisation process remains one of the main sources of ambiguity in social and political elaboration of the memory of the Colonial War. In this first stage of post-authoritarian remembrance, an important role was played by the massacres perpetrated by the military in the Colonial War, mostly in Mozambique, while colonial violence as a whole was fundamentally overlooked. In 1975–78, a number of underground publications produced in the last years of the dictatorship, especially those of progressive Catholic associations, were republished.[11] Soon after the Revolution and until the early 1990s, the state and the media overlooked these events. In fact, in 1976, Ramalho Eanes, by then the army's general chief-of-staff, prosecuted one of the publishers for 'abuse of the freedom of the press'[12] shortly before being elected president of the Republic. Some pieces on the massacres perpetrated in Northern Angola (1961) and in Mozambique (1972) were published in 1992–94, notably in the weekly *Expresso*, on the ex-combatants' 'culture of silence' and on one of the most obscured features of Portuguese warfare, the use of napalm. However, when the same reporters picked up some of these stories on television, the focus was no longer on African survivors but on Portuguese perpetrators. This was the case with a 1998 documentary on the massacre in Wiriyamu and other Mozambican villages (1972)[13] and with the killings perpetrated by nationalists of the União das Populações de Angola (UPA) against Portuguese settlers in Northern Angola (March–April 1961). While reporter Felícia Cabrita had chosen to portray in *Expresso*, in 1991, what she had called the 'days of rage' (reprisal massacres perpetrated by Portuguese settlers in Luanda in February, and in the Dembos territory from March to June 1961), another television documentary in 1998 showed no interest in the African victims of the Portuguese counter-massacres, but only in the Portuguese victims of the UPA violence.[14] Nine years later, the tone was clearly different in the widely celebrated documentary *A Guerra: Colonial, do Ultramar, de Libertação*, and the Portuguese war crimes were finally clearly documented.[15]

After forty years of Portuguese democracy, it is extremely difficult to find any reference to Portuguese war crimes in any History schoolbook, or in any pedagogical curriculum in any other form. And from a military official standpoint, denial was (and still is) the rule. An army Commission for the Study of African Campaigns (1961–1974),[16] headed by General Themudo Barata, was instructed in 1980 to 'systematically and thoroughly collect all documentation with historical and military potential interest' to the study of 'the African Campaigns' – deliberately avoiding the use of the 'colonial' adjective. Its publications would become the most substantial official version of the 1961–74 war prepared by a Portuguese State agency. Their authors were dealing with the 'memory of a significant part of our population', which, according to them, had suffered from an 'enormously intense emotional shock' from that 'rare, even unique, metamorphosis in the life of all people': 'a country, on its own initiative and conscious of the risk impending over its own survival, being cut off from, in a short one-and-a-half year period, 95 per cent of the territory under its sovereignty and integrated in its vital circuits for centuries'.[17]

An openly nationalistic and historically revisionist discourse pervades the five monographic volumes produced by the commission, attempting to draw a Portuguese *Sonderweg* in History, as is usually the case in such discourses. Their core ideas on how to explain the Portuguese presence in Africa, the Colonial War, the fall of the regime and decolonisation are fundamentally the same as post-1945 Salazarist literature and propaganda, produced in the assimilationist final stage of Portuguese colonialism, which depicted a non-colonialist and non-racist general context in which the 'African campaigns' should be read. There was no 'colonialism' and no 'colonies', but rather 'Overseas Provinces' (Províncias Ultramarinas) as, in fact, Salazar called them after the 1951 constitutional reform:

> Overseas territories had always been considered as parts of the Portuguese 'Fatherland', under a 'unitarian conviction of Portugal and the Portuguese', so 'compelling to the Portuguese people that its highest representatives, in the government and in Parliament, never dared throughout history to risk [to inscribe] anything against the unity of the Portuguese Nation, which was perceived as pluri-continental, in the fundamental Laws of the Nation. ... [It was] in the soul of the people and no one would dare to attempt [anything] against it.[18]

However, the Portuguese democratic state had apparently done just that fifteen years earlier. There had been no racism, but rather a 'heterogeneous structure of the Portuguese population, amongst which those living in the African territories have been included [*sic*] for centuries', and 'official Portuguese policy' had 'always' been to adapt legislation 'to [each colony's] level of development [and] to respect the values and culture of every human group and the conviviality tradition among all races'. The Africans as well as the Portuguese supported the patriotic effort to fight the 'terrorists' who had been financed and mobilised by foreign powers.[19] There was not a word regarding the massacres perpetrated by the Portuguese, nor on the 250,000 young dodgers (20 per cent of all those called up) who escaped military service.[20] Furthermore, there was nothing on 'the absence of African and mixed people in every important position, both in the private and public sectors of the colonial society, … their insignificant representation in the upper level of the educational system …, the unceasing use of forced labour, expropriation of African land as a pervasive practice, arbitrary arrests and torture, or even the massacres of entire villages',[21] as established by historical research.

Silence and Political and Social Devaluation of Resistance Memory

Social reconstruction of memory followed, as it usually does, social and political chronology. A second stage began at the end of the Revolution, in what became known (under the hegemonic political discourse produced since then) as the 'democratic normalisation'. After a complex and extremely intense political and social process, the revolutionary left (Communists and all components of the far left: Maoists, Trotskyists, progressive Catholics), including an important part of the military, were ousted from power by an amalgamated coalition ranging from moderate Socialists to a hardly compatible wide military group, including moderate left-wing as well as ultra-right neo-Salazarists, internationally supported by US and West European governments. Overthrowing the last of Vasco Gonçalves' cabinets at the end of August, this coalition prepared an almost bloodless military confrontation with a divided military left on 25 November 1975, and prevailed.

By then, decolonisation of the Portuguese colonies in Africa was finally carried out, during the politically extremely 'hot' summer[22] and autumn of 1975, which was still under complex Cold War circumstances (a South African invasion of Angola with the help of a significant part of the Portuguese settlers' elite, triggering both Cuban and American intervention), and a huge majority of the Portuguese settlers rejected the handing over of power to the African liberation movements. In December 1979, a right-wing coalition took power and for sixteen consecutive years (1979–95) its main party, the PPD (renamed *Social-Democratic* in 1976), did not leave power, although it was forced into a grand coalition led by the Socialists in 1983–85. In 1982, a constitutional reform, voted by this same political bloc, put a definite end to the revolutionary cycle, ideologically redesigning the Constitution and dissolving the last of the revolution-legitimatised acting institutional bodies (Conselho da Revolução) as a constitutional court, according to the original text of 1976. Most of its members, especially those who had been allies of the Socialist and right-wing forces in the process of defeating the radical left in the final stage of the Revolution, created the 'Associação 25 de Abril' that same year, which was committed to 'collecting, preserving and treating informative and documentary material related to the history of 25 April and the historical process preceding and following it'. Paradoxically enough, in their effort to retrieve 'the spirit of the liberating movement of 25 April 1974' (art. 3 of its Statute), these men, virtually all in military reserve, only found, up until the end of the 1980s, their former opponents of 1975 (Communists and the remains of the far left organisations) to celebrate the Revolution with.

As literature suggests in a variety of cases involving post-authoritarian social expression of the memory of oppression, the first two decades subsequent to the Revolution were a period of clear political and social devaluation of those who had opposed and resisted the dictatorship, and consequently of their commitment and their memory.

Showing a congenital sense of continuity with an uncomfortable piece of the past (the Salazar era), it is reasonable to say that leading Portuguese right-wing characters always preferred, at least until the early years of the twenty-first century, to remain silent about the dictatorship and the Colonial War. The whole cultural and social ambiance of the years that followed the end of the 1974–75 Revolution – recession, decolonisation, the rise of a post-industrial society, the structural problems of an economy undergoing a severe adaptation process following the end of a corporative-controlled economy, the end of an authoritarian modernisation process – allowed economic and political elites (both socialist and right-wing) to almost unanimously blame the revolutionary 'irresponsible hazards' for economic trouble. In fact, as often happens in most post-authoritarian societies, memory of recent political confrontation (revolution and decolonisation in the Portuguese case) gained precedence over the memory of the events that had occurred fifteen years earlier (the colonial war and mass emigration), thirty years earlier (massive delusion regarding the fraud against Delgado in the 1958 presidential election) or fifty years earlier (heavy repression in the early years of Salazar's rule). This whole picture gave Portuguese conservatives the ability to impose a politically motivated discussion on the negative legacy of the nineteen-month-long Revolution rather than discuss the forty-eight years under the *Estado Novo* regime – at least whenever it became impossible to elude the debate on Salazar, Marcelo Caetano (who succeeded him in 1968), political police, repression, corporatism, and war in Africa.

Already at the end of the 1970s, the political forces that had access to power avoided discussing the dictatorship: for Socialists committed to a moderate discourse, both inside the government (1976–78, 1983–85) or in opposition to the right-wing administrations (1979–83, 1985–95), celebrating the Revolution and elaborating on the memory of the dictatorship was almost too much of a radical left approach; for the right-wing parties, who electorally represented conservative social groups that kept and reproduced an essentially positive memory of the Salazar and Caetano years, this whole debate was embarrassing and was described as uninteresting and useless for the pursuit of economic development. Accordingly, historical legacy, of what was a wide social elite consensus over Salazar and his political paradigm, still plays a central role even today in the Portuguese upper-classes' obvious ambiguity regarding the memory of the dictatorship and their own courses of action throughout the last fifteen years of the regime. After two decades of leading the more conservative and elitist of the two major right-wing parties (CDS), Diogo Freitas do Amaral, an exceptional case among Portuguese conservative leaders,[23] complained about the intolerance of the Portuguese conservatives over the memory of Salazar's regime by stating that, from their point of view, 'it is not bearable that someone supposedly right-wing', like himself, 'criticises that regime or that era' in Portuguese history. Amaral said: 'I was convinced, but now I think I was wrong, that a huge majority of the Portuguese right was, or had sincerely become, a democratic right'.[24]

The tenth anniversary of the Revolution, in 1984, came at the worst moment of the economic crisis after the fall of the dictatorship. A negative perception of the Revolution and of the democratic system built upon it apparently concealed negative memories of Salazar's regime. In a 1984 survey,[25] no more than a third of the respondents thought that 25 April had 'improved my personal fulfilment' and around a fifth responded that it had 'improved my economic situation'; only 22.5 per cent thought the Revolution had been 'positive' for 'economic development', 24.5 per cent for 'social stability' and 26.4 per cent for 'youth prospects'. Ten years later, the proportion of positive answers to these questions had doubled or tripled. In 1984, a pervasive negative perception of the revolutionary legacy overlooked every actual data on how democracy had evidently improved mass education: no more than 33.4 per cent of the respondents thought that the revolutionary legacy on 'access to education' was positive – but by 1994, in a much better economic situation, that figure had more than doubled. In 1984, 'freedom' had seemed to be the only topic where a relatively positive consensus had been preserved about the revolutionary legacy: a huge 82.5 per cent of the respondents thought the 25 April uprising had had a 'positive effect' regarding 'freedom of speech', rising a only little to 88.4 per cent in 1994.

Furthermore, it may prove significant that some perceived those ten consecutive years (1985–95) in which Portugal was led by Aníbal Cavaco Silva's administration, known today as the Cavaquismo, as a sort of democratisation of Marcello Caetano's authoritarian modernising project for Portugal.[26] It was quite impressive, in this sense, that a significant number of Caetano's collaborators or government appointees had returned to political and economic power by this time.[27]

1989: The Emerging of Historical Revisionism as a Social and Political Phenomenon

The Berlin Wall fell and 'real socialism' collapsed in 1989, fourteen years after the end of the revolutionary expectations in Portugal, most of which were spent under right-wing governments. The social and cultural atmosphere was ripe for producing clashes between opposing memorial discourses and policies. Social sciences were already producing solid works on most of Salazar's regime dimensions, but that did not prevent prototypical revisionist controversy. In fact, 1989 (the peak of liberal-conservative Prime Minister Cavaco Silva's power and the fall of the Soviet bloc) was a crucial moment to realise how a sort of 'memory screen'[28] had been created: no public debate on the 1926–74 dictatorship became possible without also discussing the 1974–75 Revolution (as if both periods were historically or politically comparable), thus producing a historically confusing discourse, often clearly anachronistic. This 'eclipse' effect usually reinforces the attempt to rehabilitate the dictatorship, in a context of widespread acceptance of interpretations built upon the condemnation of the Revolution.[29] For the right-wingers, the Revolution upon which democracy had been built had opened the way to a short Marxist/Communist/collectivist/totalitarian dictatorship worse than Salazar's.[30] As Vasco Graça Moura summed up at the twentieth anniversary of 25 April 1974: 'Revolution did not instate freedom. It overthrew an authoritarian regime but tried to build up a totalitarian regime in its place'.[31] Indeed, in 1994, the kind of dictatorship revisionist view most current in the public sphere was one based on a 'relativising comparison' with the revolutionary period. Such arguments usually follow the same pattern as those produced in other national cases in which the fall of fascist authoritarian regimes in the 1940s allowed political and social changes in which the role of Communists and/or other left-wing radical forces was central.

Academic mainstream discourse had already evolved from a 1960s and 1970s fascist-categorisation of Salazar's *Estado Novo* towards an authoritarian, non-totalitarian and non-fascist definition that had always been predominant in Anglo-Saxon universities, especially in the United States, which had never left the authoritarian classification of the Portuguese 'benevolent' dictatorship.[32] This was at the core of the first memorial controversies, with neo-Salazarist and liberal-conservative historians and intellectuals sharing the totalitarian theory precept which denied any similarity between the *Estado Novo* and Italian and German fascism. They also applied De Felice's assumption to Portugal's case, that definition of Italian fascism until the 1970s would have been imposed by antifascists. After some theoretical/historiographical essays published in the 1960s by exiled activists (including Communist leader Álvaro Cunhal's *Rumo à Vitória*, 1965) or by scholars studying abroad, there was solid historiographical research assessing the fascist matrix of Salazar's regime in the 1930s and 1940s,[33] which rejected the already predominant authoritarian simplistic interpretation that disregarded violence, massive repression and mass mobilisation. On the other side, a neo-Salazarist discourse had some editorial success. Salazar's biographer Franco Nogueira, former minister of foreign affairs (1961–69), described the *Estado Novo* as a 'passive State, according to liberal models', opposed to 'a totalitarian State, according to Communist, fascist or Nazi models'.[34] For two monarchist law professors in 1989, only 'vileness, stupidity and dishonesty that was thrown over [Salazar's] character and his work', together with a 'hard silence, orchestrated by today's powerful men and by opinion makers', could explain the 'ingratitude' regarding Salazar.[35] In 1988, the Ministry of Education adopted the authoritarian thesis on the *Estado Novo*, and until the mid-1990s memorial controversy, silence over the Colonial War and police violence became a common practice in the Portuguese school system.[36] The very first postgraduate programme on the dictatorship opened in 1989, at the Universidade Nova de Lisboa. Meanwhile, Cavaco Silva's government hindered legislation that imposed open access to the most relevant archives of the dictatorship (personal and political archives of Salazar and the political police). When they were eventually opened, influential sociologist António Barreto proposed to dismantle the latter and turn the documents on three million people over to living individuals or their descendants. Historians reacted and he was unsuccessful.

All in all, there was a significant change in academe towards historical research on the 1926–74 period. Research as well as fiction, autobiography, film (both fiction and documentary) on these subjects has been booming since the late 1990s. The media became significantly more attentive to scientific research. Clashes between academics became more visible: in August 2012, a sort of Portuguese *Historikerstreit* broke out when Manuel Loff strongly criticised an openly revisionist and negationist essay by Rui Ramos on twentieth-century Portuguese history.[37] The controversy continued for four months, calling most twentieth-century historians and some sociologists and political scientists into the debate.

Nevertheless, unlike Spain where revisionist disputes have been public since the late 1990s, for a long time Portuguese academic historians, and basically most of the academe, have either overlooked or endorsed revisionist interpretations – however, just as happens in other European cases, the arguments and language used by academic revisionism are clearly more sophisticated than this kind of opinion commonly diffused in the media. In the case of the Revolution, the predominant analysis in historiography and political studies tends to overstress the role of political parties/organisations and the military, while underestimating the relevance of social movements to explain the historical process. Although revisionist conceptions are not developed in all of these interpretations, most of them share some of its core assertions: (1) that the impossibility of a 'transition to a parliamentary democracy without leftist revolutionary distress' was the cost imposed by 'the authoritarian regime colonial blindness'; (2) that 'the anachronism of an isolated imperial Portugal was initially replaced by the anachronism of a revolutionary and military-socialist Portugal';[38] and, of course, (3) that same thesis of a double legacy of the Portuguese democracy, as if it had been built against both right- and left-wing authoritarianism.[39] Furthermore, in the twenty-first century some extremely aggressive – and abusively *unhistorical*, for that matter – revisionist discourses are spreading throughout the public sphere led by high profile historians like Rui Ramos, whose analysis on Salazarism and the revolutionary period, despite not being endorsed by most academics (nor refuted by most of them), benefit from extensive support in the mass media.[40]

On the other hand, Salazar's centennial in 1989 became one of the few opportunities to seize a fairly official view of Portuguese right-wing political leaders on Salazar and his regime. To Freitas do Amaral, there had been 'authoritarianism, intolerance, coldness, toughness with his opponents …, personal seclusion, incapacity for dialogue, mistrust in Portuguese maturity, [and] aversion to individual liberties', but Salazar also represented 'intelligence, culture, … personal honesty, devotion to public interest, willpower, love of Portugal, capacity for government, sense of State, independence from … groups of interest, foreign powers'. While PM Cavaco Silva avoided any comment at all, one of his ministers, Dias Loureiro, praised Salazar's 'expertise' for 'making Portugal emerge from [the Spanish Civil War and the Second World War] and paying the lowest cost possible' and for his 'highly positive' financial policy at the beginning of his rule. For Loureiro, as is usual with right-wingers, it was only 'after 1945' that Salazar seemed to have 'lost touch with a modern world's vision', 'placing Portugal out of European recovery dynamics, [and] losing an ideal chance to start industrialisation', thus presuming the fascist years (1930s and the Second World War) to be Salazar's 'finest hour'. The 'Colonial War' – an expression hardly used in right-wing discourses on Salazarism – was harmful to Portuguese society, not so much for being a deliberately unacceptable policy of the regime, but because it 'further compromised Portuguese [economic] development'. Loureiro acknowledged that 're-strictions imposed on freedom of speech and on freedom of political activity, [and] the absence of a democratic organisation of society pro-duced, in fact, economic, cultural and scientific stagnation, therefore delaying our modernity'. In other words, authoritarianism and dicta-torship had not been intrinsically bad as such, but had merely an in-strumentally negative impact on economic and cultural 'development', and on progress towards achieving 'modernity'.

In contrast, on the left, Socialist Jorge Sampaio (President in 1996–2006), a student activist in the 1960s, shared with the rest of the left that 'the *Estado Novo* was the Portuguese variety, in the specific conditions of Portuguese society and in the context of its genesis …, of the wave of authoritarian and fascist regimes that swept Europe between the end of World War I and the end of World War II'. Furthermore, he pointed out the 'single party', 'corporatism', 'censorship', 'repression and political police were instruments to coerce Portuguese citizens' thoughts and ac-tions', and 'manipulation of public opinion through propaganda' were its core characteristics. But Sampaio, as well as Loureiro, underlined the 'productive and technological underdevelopment, dependence on government protection on taxation and from political protest, … ob-solete industrial and productive organisations', the sort of 'obstruc-tions that persist in Portuguese society' that had been 'originated and consolidated' by Salazar's policies. For Dias Lourenço, a communist resistant who was a political prisoner for seventeen years, Salazar 'em-bodied in Portugal the response of the most reactionary forces to the unsolvable contradictions and conflicts of the twentieth-century's first quarter'. His main concern was to point out to 'some "historians" and "biographers" who tried, behind the curtain of Portuguese "smooth traditions", to elude the inhumane nature of Salazarist fascism and to prudishly silence death by torture in police dungeons and cold-blooded executions, on the streets, … a violent suffocation of freedom and culture', 'a significant part [of which] remains to be written in Portuguese historiography'.[41]

Three years later, there was a public debate over what left-wing intellectuals described as 'dictatorship whitewashing', which was, in fact, a first stage of a larger dispute that would reach its most intense point in 1994, at the Revolution's twentieth anniversary. On 15 April 1992, the government granted pensions to two former political police inspectors for 'exceptional and relevant services rendered to the country', a gesture that could be read as economic politics of memory openly beneficial to former agents of Salazar's political police. Controversy rose and widened because this same pension had been denied in 1988 to Salgueiro Maia (one of the young captains who had led the military operations in April 1974), who died a few days earlier on 4 April. This public dispute over the pensions should be regarded as the first moment of a widespread public debate about the Portuguese dictatorship, with a significant influx of indignation and criticism.

In 1994, an exceptional profusion of Revolution celebrations was being prepared amidst memorial controversy. The situation climaxed when a commercial television station, SIC, invited one of those political police inspectors to a debate. Strong criticism emerged against clear operations intended to whitewash the dictatorship and to devalue the Revolution, which became the dominant tone on the 25 April anniversary debate. Portugal was finally experiencing the revisionist effrontery that other European countries had already been bearing for years, in an ambiance influenced by the presumption of media neutrality.[42] 'Is this pluralism?' asked Mário Mesquita. 'Does it consist in arithmetically giving air time to Salazarism and democracy, perpetrators and victims? … His Excellency, the Inspector, a citizen of the Portuguese democracy, is he worth the time given to him on Portuguese television? Or is this only about using a perverse fascination towards the *pide* [inspector] as a stratagem for television market purposes?' According to Mesquita, editor of *Diário de Notícias*, this opening of the democratic public sphere to a former torturer was the result of an extensive strategy to explain Salazarism away and to erase the boundary between dictatorship and democracy.[43]

At the same time, a self-portrait of the Portuguese as victims of war was emerging: the former combatants believed that neither society nor the state had been as morally appreciative or as legally fair as they felt they were entitled;[44] and the *retornados* (the Portuguese equivalent to the French *pieds noirs*), settlers who chose to return to Portugal, portrayed themselves as victims of decolonisation, of the Revolution and of the liberation movements in Africa. Self-victimisation impelled them to talk about their own experiences, openly asking the state and society to empathise with their feelings and their pain, as well as their legal demands. The pervading lack of determination of most of the new African states (except, perhaps, Mozambique) to develop specific memorial policies on the war from an African perspective left room for Portuguese-centred memorial policies conveyed by the Portuguese armed forces and former combatant and *retornados* associations.[45]

In fact, all those who subscribe to the narrative of the 'amputated Nation' operate inside a widespread consensus on a sort of cultural, self-indulging explanation – the *lusotropicalismo* – committed to proving a special capacity to cultural assimilationism, an alleged multi-racialism and the absence of race prejudice, a presumably fatherly attitude of Portuguese colonists. In 2001, José Leitão, the first high commissioner for Immigration and Ethnic Minorities, stated while discussing reparation demands from some African states and Afro-descendants' organisations in the UN Conference against Racism, Racial Discrimination, Xenophobia and Related Forms of Intolerance (Durban): '[I]t is illegitimate to demand official apologies from a country who decolonised, who made itself responsible for its past faults, and who has created a solidarity relationship with the Portuguese-speaking African countries'.[46] In fact, the Portuguese government overlooks, and often denies, the African tragedy and never investigated or publicised any figures about the African victims of colonial repression and the 1961–74 war, nor does it recognise any war crimes (according to national or international law: massacres, torture and killing of prisoners, chemical warfare, etc.), and never discussed any financial reparation with its five former African colonies or East Timor.

Altogether, revisionist views regarding the Revolution/decolonisation tended to penetrate more easily on Portuguese public opinion, which explains why, in the mid-1990s, this sort of interpretation can be considered as 'hegemonic memories'; nevertheless, the 'revolt of memory' of 1994 implied a widespread criticism of all revisionist trends. Consequently, it also produced a greater visibility of a globally positive assessment of the Revolution and antifascist memorial discourses. Whereas, at the twentieth anniversary of the Revolution, debate focused on the process of 'whitewashing' the memory of the dictatorship, ten years later, under another right-wing government, the controversy moved to the memory of the Revolution as such: the government slogan for the official commemorations, 'April is

Evolution', was widely criticised as it intended to suppress the rupture horizon of 25 April.

In 2006–07, Salazar was the winner on the public television station show, *Grandes Portugueses*, followed by historical Communist leader Álvaro Cunhal. Subsequently, there was debate over the programme's methods and its social relevance. Although the historical judgement underlying this result should not be taken as representative of Portuguese society as a whole, it is interesting to reflect sociologically on the media impact of electing Salazar 'the greatest Portuguese ever' and how it helps to (re)construct memory in the public sphere. In fact, it could also be argued that both the 1992 decision to reward former torturers and the revisionist upsurge of 1994 were not representative of the opinion of most Portuguese citizens.

What motivates the intensity of the debate on Portugal's recent past is the growing visibility of a revisionist discourse intended to whitewash the dictatorship, which evolved in the public sphere since the late 1980s alongside the increasing process of historical revisionism on the Revolution. It is significant that the extensive indignation that emerged in the mid-1990s against revisionist discourses was mostly against the dictatorship whitewashing, and less against the abusive and openly hostile discourses about the Revolution. This was the case until very recently; on its fortieth anniversary (2014), celebrated under the worse social and economic recession since 1984, ruling right-wing parties and neoconservative intellectuals chose to dwindle (even if temporarily) their revisionist stance in the face of a widespread revival of revolutionary symbols (songs like *Grândola, Vila Morena*, slogans like the *25 de Abril sempre!*, etc.) in rallies and different forms of public protest. Apparently, the 1974 Revolution is still a source of political inspiration for quite a number of Portuguese. This source of inspiration was strong enough to force presidential historical consultant David Justino to ask for 'values of the Revolution to be used in order to project the future, instead of searching [in the present] for identical signs of the ones we lived with before 1974'.[47]

However, a symbolic struggle is still going on among different memory discourses disputing hegemony on the process of rebuilding the past. The way each memory discourse is more or less visible reproduces a specific balance of the forces operating in this battle over memory. Memorial policies play a central role in the struggle for ideological and symbolic hegemony for the construction of the terms of perception and organisation of social reality: we either remember to preserve, or we remember to change.

Notes

1. E. Traverso, *El pasado, instrucciones de uso. Historia, memoria, política*, Madrid, 2007. See also: D. Losurdo, *Il revisionismo storico. Problemi e miti*, Rome and Bari, 1996; M. Haynes and J. Wolfreys (eds), *History and Revolution: Refuting Revisionism*, London, 2007; P.P. Poggio, *Nazismo y revisionismo histórico*, Madrid, 2006. About the origins and use of totalitarianism, see E. Traverso, 'Introduction. Le totalitarisme. Jalons pour l'histoire d'un débat', in *Le totalitarisme. Le XXe siècle en débat*, Paris, 2001; H. Rousso, 'La légitimité d'une comparaison empirique', in Henry Rousso (ed.), *Stalinisme et nazisme. Histoire et mémoire comparées*, Brussels, 1999.
2. *Branqueamento* is the word commonly used in the Portuguese public debate.
3. S.P. Huntington., *The Third Wave: Democratisation in the Late 20th Century*, Oklahoma, 1991.
4. In February and March 1961, nationalist rebellions in Angola started a Colonial War (1961–74), which soon spread to Guinea-Bissau (1963) and Mozambique (1964). Of the 920,000 Portuguese soldiers drafted, 10,000 were killed and 30,000 wounded, and it is estimated that over 100,000 returned from war with post-traumatic stress disorder (PTSD).
5. M. Loff, 'Fim do colonialismo, ruptura política e transformação social em Portugal nos anos setenta', in M. Loff and M. da C. Meireles Pereira (eds), *Portugal, 30 anos de Democracia (1974–2004)*, Porto, 2006, 153–93.
6. Law No. 8/75, 25.7.1975, passed by the Council of the Revolution (Conselho da Revolução, created in March 1975, representing every military rank, through delegate election). For transitional justice in the years following the Revolution, see I. Pimentel and M.I. Rezola (eds), *Democracia, Ditadura. Memória e Justiça Política*, Lisbon, 2013.
7. See A. Ventura, *Memórias da Resistência. Literatura autobiográfica da resistência ao Estado Novo*, Lisbon, 2001.
8. See N. Brito, *O Tarrafal na memória dos seus prisioneiros, 1936–1954*, foreword by Manuel Loff, Lisbon, 2006.
9. Decree 647/74, 21 November 1974.
10. Decree 727/74, 19 December 1974. The new provisional government recognised Indian sovereignty over Goa, Daman and Diu on 31 December 1974.
11. See, among several others, J. Amaro (ed. and comments), *Documentos secretos. Massacres na guerra colonial. Tete, um exemplo*, Lisbon [1976]; *Boletim Anti-Colonial 1 a 9*, Porto [1975].
12. See 'A mentira oficial', *Expresso-Revista*, 5 December 1992.
13. See F. Cabrita and P. Camacho, *Regresso a Wiriyamu*, SIC, 1998.
14. See F. Cabrita and P. Camacho, *Angola, 1961. O princípio do fim*, SIC, 1998.
15. J. Furtado, 'Massacres contra chacinas', in *A Guerra: Colonial, do Ultramar, de Libertação 3*, RTP, 2007.
16. See *Portaria 43/80*, 16 February 1980.
17. C.E.C.A. [*Comissão para o Estudo das Campanhas de África*], *Resenha histórico-militar das campanhas de África (1961–1974)*, vol. 1 ('Enquadramento geral'), Lisbon, [1988], 16, 7–8.
18. C.E.C.A. *Subsídios para o estudo da doutrina aplicada nas Campanhas de África (1961–1974)*. Lisbon, 1990, 30–31.

19. C.E.C.A., *Resenha histórico-militar*, 58, 54, 122.
20. See Guerra Colonial. Recrutamento, in http://www.guerracolonial.org/specific/guerra_colonial/uploaded/graficos/estatiscas/recrutamento.swf
21. G. Bender, *Angola sob o domínio português. Mito e realidade*, Lisbon, 1980, 11 [originally: *Angola under the Portuguese: Myth and Reality*, Berkeley, CA. 1976].
22. The expression *Verão quente* (hot summer) is currently used to describe that period of political and social confrontation.
23. Diogo Freitas do Amaral was one of the youngest members of the dictatorship second chamber (Câmara Corporativa) in the late years of Caetano's rule, the Christian-Democrat leader in 1974–82 and 1987–91, and a regular member of the government.
24. See *Notícias Magazine*, 9 March 2003.
25. See 'Sondagem. 25 de Abril? Claro que sim!', *Visão*, 21 April 1994.
26. See A.L. de Sousa Franco, 'A Economia', in A. Reis (ed.), *Portugal 20 anos de Democracia*, Lisbon, 1993, 170–293.
27. See M. Loff, 'Coming to Terms with the Dictatorial Past in Portugal after 1974: Silence, Remembrance and Ambiguity', in S.Troebst and S. Baumgartl (eds), *Postdiktatorische Geschichtskulturen im Süden und Osten Europas. Bestandsaufnahme und Forschungsperspektiven*, Göttingen, 2009, 79.
28. Henry Rousso talks about the French *Libération* as a 'souvenir écran' that pushes backward the memories of the 1940 defeat and the German occupation. H. Rousso, *Le syndrôme de Vichy. De 1944 à nos jours*, Paris, 1990.
29. See L. Soutelo, 'O desenvolvimento do revisionismo histórico em Portugal e a memória do Estado Novo', in I. Pimentel and M.I. Rezola (eds), *Democracia, Ditadura. Memória e Justiça Política*, Lisbon, 2013, 385–95.
30. See M. Loff, '1989 in Kontext portugiesischer Kontroversen über die jüngste Vergangenheit. Die rechte Rhetorik der zwei Diktaturen', in E. François, K. Kończal, R. Traba and S. Troebst (eds), *Geschichtspolitik in Europa seit 1989. Deutschland, Frankreich und Polen im internationalen Vergleich*, Göttingen, 2013, 396–426.
31. 'Portugal e o passado', *Diário de Notícias*, 10 April 1994. Vasco Graça Moura, one of the most representative right-wing intellectuals, was the head the National Committee for the Commemoration of Portuguese Discoveries (1988–95).
32. See L.S. Graham, D.L. Wheeler, S. Payne, P.C. Schmitter.
33. Especially Fernando Rosas' earlier works. For an *authoritarian* non-fascist interpretation of the *Estado Novo*, see the works of Manuel Braga da Cruz, João Medina, Hipólito de la Torre, António Telo, António Costa Pinto, Irene Pimentel, Filipe Ribeiro de Meneses, Jacques Georgel, Philippe C. Schmitter and Yves Léonard; and neo-Salazarists José Hermano Saraiva, Franco Nogueira, Joaquim Veríssimo Serrão and Jaime Nogueira Pinto. For a *fascist* interpretation, see the works of Manuel Loff, Fernando Rosas, Luís Reis Torgal, João Paulo Avelãs Nunes, João Arsénio Nunes, Hermínio Martins and Dawn Linda Raby; and the special case of Eduardo Lourenço, Manuel Villaverde Cabral and Manuel de Lucena, who subscribed to both interpretations on different occasions.

34. See F. Nogueira, *Salazar*, 6 vols, Oporto, 1977–1985; Idem, 'II Suplemento' to F. Nogueira, *História de Portugal (1933–1974)*, Porto, 1981.
35. M. Castro Henriques and G. de Sampaio e Melo (eds), *Salazar. Pensamento e doutrina política. Textos antológicos*, Lisbon and S.Paulo, 1989, 10–11. See also J. Nogueira Pinto (ed.), *Salazar visto pelos seus próximos (1946–68)*, Venda Nova, 1993; J. Nogueira Pinto, *António de Oliveira Salazar. O outro retrato*, Lisbon, 2007.
36. See I. Menezes et al., 'Visions of the Authoritarian Past in Citizenship Education Policies and Practices in Spain and Portugal', in R. Hedtke and T. Zimenkova (eds), *Education for Civic and Political Participation: A Critical Approach*, London, 2013, 207–24.
37. See M. Loff, 'Uma história em fascículos', and R. Ramos, 'Um caso de difamação', in *Público*, 2, 16 and 21August 2012; Rui Ramos (ed.), *História de Portugal*, Lisbon, 2009 (a weekly *Expresso* free offer in 2012).
38. A. Reis, 'Introdução' *in* A. Reis (ed.), *Portugal Contemporâneo*, V. 6, Lisbon, 1990, 8.
39. See K. Maxwell, *The Making of Portuguese Democracy*, Cambridge, 1995. For the analysis of historical revisionism in Portugal, see M.M. Cruzeiro, 'Revolução e revisionismo historiográfico. O 25 de Abril visto da história', in R. Cunha Martins (ed.), *Portugal 1974. Transição política em perspectiva histórica*. Coimbra, 2011; L. Soutelo, 'O revisionismo histórico em perspetiva comparada: os casos de Portugal e Espanha', in M. Loff, F. Piedade and L. Soutelo (eds), *Ditaduras e Revolução. Democracia e políticas de memória*, Coimbra, 2014.
40. See M. Loff, 'Estado, democracia e memória: políticas públicas e batalhas pela memoria da ditadura portuguesa (1974–2014)', in Loff, Piedade and Soutelo (eds), *Ditaduras e Revolução*. Henrique Raposo is the Portuguese equivalent of Pío Moa's or Federico Jiménez Losantos' in Spain [see his *História politicamente incorrecta do Portugal Contemporâneo (de Salazar a Soares)*, Lisbon, 2013], pushing his thesis mainly through the media and out of the academe.
41. 'Como os líderes vêem Salazar', *Expresso*, 22 April 1989.
42. M. Loff, *Salazarismo e Franquismo na época de Hitler (1936–1942)*, Oporto, 1996, 77–78.
43. 'O telemasoquismo democrático', *Diário de Notícias*, 22 April 1994, 13.
44. Former servicemen who suffered from PTSD only saw their right to state indemnities and medical attention legally recognised in 2000, after the approval of Law 46/99, already under António Guterres' Socialist administration. See *Público*, 23 June 1999 and 13 April 2000. See also L. Quintais, *As guerras coloniais portuguesas e a invenção da História*, Lisbon, 2000.
44. Half a million fled from the African colonies to Portugal in 1974–76, several hundred thousand chose to remain in Africa, but where white minority supremacy persisted: Ian Smith's Rhodesia and Apartheid's South Africa. For a historiographic appraisal, see F. Tavares Pimenta, *Angola, os Brancos e a Independência*, Oporto, 2008. For mainstream accounts, see R. Garcia, *S.O.S. Angola. Os dias da ponte aérea*, and *Os que vieram de África*, Alfragide, 2011 and 2012; A. Marques, *Segredos da decolonização de Angola*, Lisbon, 2013; in fiction, see D.M. Cardoso, *Cadernos de Memórias Coloniais*, Lisbon, 2011; and

J. Magalhães, *Os Retornados*, Lisbon, 2008; also, public TV station series *Depois do Adeus*, RTP/SP Televisão, 2012, script by I. Gomes, A. Vasques, C. Dias, J. Pinto Carneiro, L. Marques, S. Salgado and V. Monteiro, historical consultant Helena Matos.
46. *Público*, 6 September 2001.
47. *Público*, 6 December 2013.

References

Amaro, J. (ed. and comments). *Documentos secretos. Massacres na guerra colonial. Tete, um exemplo*. Lisbon [1976].

Bender, G. *Angola sob o domínio português. Mito e realidade*. Lisbon, 1980, 11 [originally: *Angola under the Portuguese: Myth and Reality*. Berkeley, CA, 1976].

Brito, N. *O Tarrafal na memória dos seus prisioneiros, 1936–1954*, foreword by Manuel Loff. Lisbon, 2006.

C.E.C.A. [Comissão para o Estudo das Campanhas de África], *Resenha histórico-militar das campanhas de África (1961–1974)*, vol. 1 ('Enquadramento geral'). Lisbon, [1988].

———.*Subsídios para o estudo da doutrina aplicada nas Campanhas de África (1961–1974)*. Lisbon, 1990.

Cardoso, D.M. *Cadernos de Memórias Coloniais*. Lisbon, 2011.

Cruz, M. Braga da. *O partido e o Estado no Salazarismo*. Lisbon, 1988.

Cruzeiro, M.M. 'Revolução e revisionismo historiográfico. O 25 de Abril visto da história', in R. Cunha Martins (ed.) *Portugal 1974. Transição política em perspectiva histórica*. Coimbra, 2011.

Franco, A.L. de Sousa. 'A Economia', in A. Reis (ed.), *Portugal 20 anos de Democracia*. Lisbon, 1993, 170–293.

Garcia, R. *S.O.S. Angola. Os dias da ponte aérea*. Alfragide, 2011.

———. *Os que vieram de África*. Alfragide, 2012.

Haynes, M., and J. Wolfreys (eds). *History and Revolution: Refuting Revisionism*. London, 2007.

Henriques, M. Castro, and G. de Sampaio e Melo (eds). *Salazar. Pensamento e doutrina política. Textos antológicos*. Lisbon and S.Paulo, 1989.

Huntington, S.P. *The Third Wave: Democratisation in the Late 20th Century*. Oklahoma, 1991.

Loff, M. *Salazarismo e Franquismo na época de Hitler (1936–1942)*. Oporto, 1996.

———. 'Fim do colonialismo, ruptura política e transformação social em Portugal nos anos setenta', in M. Loff and M. da C. Meireles Pereira (eds), *Portugal, 30 anos de Democracia (1974–2004)*. Porto, 2006, 153–93.

———. *'O nosso século é fascista!' O mundo visto por Salazar e Franco (1936–1945)*. Oporto, 2008.

———. 'Coming to Terms with the Dictatorial Past in Portugal after 1974: Silence, Remembrance and Ambiguity', in S. Troebst and S. Baumgartl (eds), *Postdiktatorische Geschichtskulturen im Süden und Osten Europas. Bestandsaufnahme und Forschungsperspektiven*. Göttingen, 2009.

———.'1989 in Kontext portugiesischer Kontroversen über die jüngste Vergangenheit. Die rechte Rhetorik der zwei Diktaturen', in E. François, K. Kończal, R. Traba and S. Troebst (eds), *Geschichtspolitik in Europa seit 1989. Deutschland, Frankreich und Polen im internationalen Vergleich*. Göttingen, 2013, 396–426.

———. 'Estado, democracia e memória: políticas públicas e batalhas pela memória da ditadura portuguesa (1974–2014)', in M. Loff, F. Piedade and L. Soutelo (eds), *Ditaduras e Revolução. Democracia e políticas de memoria*. Coimbra, 2014.

Losurdo, D. *Il revisionismo storico. Problemi e miti*. Rome and Bari, 1996.

Lucena, M. de. *A Evolução do Sistema Corporativo Português*. 2 vols. Lisbon, 1976.

Magalhães, J. *Os Retornados*. Lisbon, 2008.

Marques, A. *Segredos da decolonização de Angola*. Lisbon, 2013.

Maxwell, K. *The Making of Portuguese Democracy*. Cambridge, 1995.

Meneses, F. Ribeiro de. *Salazar: A Political Biography*. New York, 2009.

Menezes, I., et al. 'Visions of the Authoritarian Past in Citizenship Education Policies and Practices in Spain and Portugal', in R. Hedtke and T. Zimenkova (eds), *Education for Civic and Political Participation: A Critical Approach*. London, 2013, 207–24.

Nogueira, F. *História de Portugal (1933–1974)*. II Suplemento. Porto, 1981.

———. *Salazar*. 6 vols. Oporto, 1977–1985.

Pimenta, F. Tavares. *Angola, os Brancos e a Independência*. Oporto, 2008.

Pimentel, I., and M.I. Rezola (eds). *Democracia, Ditadura. Memória e Justiça Política*. Lisbon, 2013.

Pinto, A. Costa. *Salazar's dictatorship and European fascism. Problems of Interpretation*. New York, 1995.

Pinto, J. Nogueira (ed.). *Salazar visto pelos seus próximos (1946–68)*. Venda Nova, 1993.

———. *António de Oliveira Salazar. O outro retrato*. Lisbon, 2007.

Poggio, P.P. *Nazismo y revisionismo histórico*. Madrid, 2006.

Quintais, L. *As guerras coloniais portuguesas e a invenção da História*. Lisbon, 2000.

Ramos, Rui (ed.). *História de Portugal*. Lisbon, 2009.

Raposo, H. *História politicamente incorrecta do Portugal Contemporâneo (de Salazar a Soares)*. Lisbon, 2013.

Reis, A. 'Introdução', in A. Reis (ed.), *Portugal Contemporâneo*. Vol. 6. Lisbon, 1990, 7–10.

Rosas, F. *Salazar e o poder. A arte de saber durar*. Lisbon, 2012.

Rousso, H. *Le syndrôme de Vichy. De 1944 à nos jours*. Paris, 1990.

———. 'La légitimité d'une comparaison empirique', in H. Rousso (ed.), *Stalinisme et nazisme. Histoire et mémoire comparées*. Brussels, 1999.

Schmitter, Philippe C. 'The "Regime d'Exception" that Became the Rule: Forty-Eight Years of Authoritarian Domination in Portugal', in L.S. Graham and H.M. Makler (eds), *Contemporary Portugal*. Austin, TX, 1979, 3–46.

Soutelo, L. 'O desenvolvimento do revisionismo histórico em Portugal e a memória do Estado Novo', in I. Pimentel and M.I. Rezola (eds), *Democracia, Ditadura. Memória e Justiça Política*. Lisbon, 2013, 385–95.

————. 'O revisionismo histórico em perspetiva comparada: os casos de Portugal e Espanha', in M. Loff, F. Piedade and L. Soutelo (eds), *Ditaduras e Revolução. Democracia e políticas de memoria.* Coimbra, 2014.

Torgal, L. Reis. *Estados Novos, Estado Novo. Ensaios de História Política e Cultural.* 2 vols. Coimbra, 2009.

Traverso, E. 'Introduction. Le totalitarisme. Jalons pour l'histoire d'un débat', in *Le totalitarisme. Le XXe siècle en débat.* Paris, 2001.

————. *El pasado, instrucciones de uso. Historia, memoria, política.* Madrid, 2007.

Ventura, A. *Memórias da Resistência. Literatura autobiográfica da resistência ao Estado Novo.* Lisbon, 2001.

Luciana Soutelo is a researcher at the Instituto de História Contemporânea/NOVA. She holds a master's degree in Contemporary History from the Universidade do Porto (Portugal) and a bachelor's degree in History from the Universidade Federal Fluminense (Brazil). She is particularly interested in the study of collective memory and the public use of history. She has published some articles on the memory of the Portuguese Revolution and on historical revisionism, such as 'Visões da Revolução dos Cravos: *combates pela memória* através da imprensa (1985–1995)' (2012), 'As memórias do salazarismo e do franquismo no espaço público' (2013), and 'A memória pública sobre a Revolução e a ditadura em Portugal: da valorização do antifascismo ao desenvolvimento do revisionismo histórico' (2014), and was co-editor of the edited volumes *Ditaduras e Revolução. Democracia e políticas de memoria* (2014) and *A revolução de 1974–75: repercussão na imprensa internacional e memória(s)* (2014). She submitted her PhD thesis ('A memória pública do passado recente nas sociedades ibéricas. *Revisionismo histórico e combates pela memória* em finais do século XX') to the Universidade do Porto (Portugal) in December 2015 and is presently waiting to defend it.

Manuel Loff received his Ph.D. from the European University Institute (Florence) and is tenured associate professor at the University of Porto (Portugal) and coordinator of the thematic line on 'History and Memory: Collective Memories, History of the Present and Oral History' at the Instituto de História Contemporânea (Lisbon). He has taught at the Universidad Autónoma de Madrid and at the Hebrew University of Jerusalem. He has published in Portugal, Spain, Germany, Brazil and the United States, including *Ditaduras e Revolução. Democracia e políticas da memoria* (2014, co-editor); '*O nosso século é fascista!' O mundo visto por Salazar e Franco (1936–1945)* (2008); and 'Coming to Terms with the Dictatorial Past in Portugal after 1974: Silence, Remembrance and Ambiguity', in S. Troebst and S. Baumgartl (eds), *Postdiktatorische Geschichtskulturen im Süden und Osten Europas* (2010).

17

ANTIFASCISM BETWEEN COLLECTIVE MEMORY AND HISTORICAL REVISIONS

Enzo Traverso

'Revisionism' is an ambiguous concept whose meaning can change considerably according to its context and use. A short genealogy reveals that, far from being exclusively historiographical, 'revisionism' is also a political phenomenon deeply related to attitudes and statements that transcend academic boundaries and put into question the relationship of our societies with their own past. It is useful to remember that revisionism is a concept borrowed from political theory, where it arose at the end of the nineteenth century as a polemical tool in the middle of a Marxist controversy. The tenants of German orthodox Marxism – championed by Karl Kautsky – qualified the social-democratic thinker Eduard Bernstein as 'revisionist'. Bernstein had expressed his scepticism with respect to the idea of a 'collapse' (*Zusammenbruch*) of capitalism and embraced a peaceful, parliamentary transition to socialism, renouncing the project of a socialist revolution.[1] Thus, 'revisionism' meant both a theoretical and a political change, a reinterpretation of capitalism that implied a significant strategic reorientation of the German Social Democratic Party. After the birth of the Soviet Union and the transformation of Marxism into a state ideology with its dogmas and its secular theologians, the adjective 'revisionist' became a stigma directed against political adversaries within the Communist movement, accused of betrayal and complicity with class enemies. Charged with a strong ideological taste, 'revisionism' designated a 'deviation' from the orthodox line, grounded upon a wrong interpretation of the sacred texts. In the field of historical studies, it generally conserved this negative connotation, meaning both the abandonment of canonical interpretations and the adoption of new, politically controversial views.

One can observe that revisions are the 'physiological' modality of recording history. History is always written in and from the present:

our interpretations of the past are obviously related to the culture, intellectual sensitivity, ethical and political worries of our time. Each society has its own regime of historicity – its own perception of and relationship with the past – that frames and inspires its historical productions. Consequently, historiography changes with the succession of epochs, the enchainment of generations and the metamorphosis of collective memories. If our vision of the French or Russian revolutions is significantly different with respect to that of our ancestors – for instance the historians of the 1920s or 1960s – this occurs not only because we have discovered new sources and documents, but primarily because our time has a different perspective on the past. These 'revisions' constitute the natural procedure of historical investigation: far from being immutable or timeless, historiography has its own history. 'Revisionism', nonetheless, means something different; it is a notion usually referring to bad, wrong or unacceptable revisions. 'Usually' should be emphasised here because there are many types of revisionism. In a certain sense, there is a radical discrepancy between a continental European and an American conception of revisionism. The former is currently related to attempts at 'rehabilitating' fascism carried on by numerous apologetic interpretations; the latter is anti-conformist and distances itself from mainstream, conservative interpretations of Soviet history. In Europe, 'revisionist' currents are right-wing oriented; in the United States, they oppose neoconservative historical visions. In the United States, 'revisionists' are scholars such as Moshe Lewin, Arch Getty and Sheila Fitzpatrick who, from the 1970s onwards, have criticised the Cold War historiography based on the dogma of anti-Communism and have investigated the social history of the Soviet Union behind its totalitarian facade. According to Sheila Fitzpatrick, 'revisionism' is a 'scholarly strategy' whose main features she summarises in the following way: 'Iconoclasm about received ideas, scepticism about grand narratives, empiricism, and lots of hard work on primary sources'.[2] This programme (when she speaks of 'grand narratives' she refers first to Cold War conservative stereotypes) allowed enormous advances in historical knowledge. Against the traditional approaches of scholars such as Richard Pipes and Martin Malia, for whom the entire history of the USSR could be explained as the progressive display of a criminal ideology in power (Communism as a totalitarian 'ideocracy'),[3] this group of 'revisionist' historians rethought both the revolution and Stalinism, resetting them into their own context and describing them in their real dimensions. The global reinterpretation of terror and violence is among their most significant contributions. It stressed the economic role played by the Gulag, re-evaluated the number of victims – between 1.5 and 2 million

instead of 10 million, according to the purely imaginary estimation previously suggested by Robert Conquest – and analysed the uncontrolled
dynamic of the war against the kulaks during the collectivisation campaign of the early 1930s.[4]

In the last two decades, another fruitful 'revisionist' current shook
Israeli historiography. Putting into question some tenacious nationalistic – and mythical – narratives of the Arab–Israeli War of 1948, the
so-called 'new historians' (Benny Morris and Ilan Pappe are the best
known) investigated the complexity of this conflict and modified its
perception. Their works convincingly prove that this war was experienced by the citizens of the new Jewish State as a struggle for self-defence and, at the same time, was carried on by the military elite as an
ethnic cleansing campaign.[5] On the one hand, Israel fought for its survival, but on the other, it transformed this conflict into a good pretext
for expelling more than six hundred thousand Palestinians from their
land. The result was a 'revision' that re-established the historical truth:
Palestinians did not abandon their homes following a supposed injunction of the Arabic regimes; they had been banned with violence.

These few examples suffice to show that 'revisionism' is not reduc-
ible to Ernst Nolte's apologetic interpretation of National Socialism
– Auschwitz as the epilogue of Bolshevik violence reproduced by a
threatened Third Reich – or Renzo De Felice's vision of the Repubblica
Sociale Italiana (1943–45) as a patriotic sacrifice accomplished by
Mussolini in order to avoid a 'Polish' destiny of total occupation and
submission (these two interpretations will be mentioned further). Nolte
and De Felice's pleas for 'revisionism' as the 'daily bread of scientific
work' and intrinsic duty of historians do not change the highly debatable character of their own 'revisions'.[6]

In other words, there are many sorts of historical revisions: some of
them are legitimate and even necessary; others are unacceptable, even
indecent attempts to rehabilitate criminal regimes. We can discuss the
pertinence of an ambiguous and often mistakable word such as 'revisionism', but the fact remains that many historical revisions, which are
mostly qualified as 'revisionism', imply an ethical and political turn in
our vision of the past. These revisions correspond with the emergence
of 'apologetic tendencies' in historiography (Jürgen Habermas used this
formula during the German *Historikerstreit* in 1986).[7] When used in this
way, revisionism inevitably takes on a negative connotation. Clearly,
no one reproaches 'revisionist' scholars for having discovered and investigated unexplored archives or documents. If they were strongly
criticised it is rather because of the political purposes subjacent to their
interpretations. It is also clear that all forms of 'revision', whatever their

aim and impact may be, transcend the boundaries of historiography and put into question the public use of history.[8] Revisionism is a delicate topic not because it criticises canonical, dominant interpretations, but because it affects a shared historical consciousness and a feeling of collective responsibility toward the past. It always deals with foundational events such as the French and the Russian revolutions, fascism, National Socialism, Communism, colonialism and other experiences whose interpretation directly affects, far beyond our vision of the past, our vision of the present and our collective identities.

*

With respect to 'revisionism', antifascism is a study case par excellence: over the past thirty years we have been witnessing recurrent waves of 'anti-antifascist' historiographical revisions which have produced debates and virulent controversies. Periodically restarted by new generations of scholars, these campaigns have found huge echoes in the media far beyond the academic field thus becoming debatable issues for public opinion. Such disputations have taken place almost everywhere in Europe and reached a particular virulence in Italy, Germany, France and Spain.

In Italy, the 'anti-antifascist' historical revision goes back to the 1980s, when the biographer of Mussolini, Renzo De Felice, launched his plea to abandon the harmful 'antifascist paradigm'.[9] In his view, this paradigm had been a powerful obstacle to historical investigation for several decades, and it was time for young historians to leave behind such a dominant ideological framework. His claim that for decades the historical interpretation of fascism had been shaped, and sometimes replaced, by ethical and political condemnation was not incorrect. Too many scholars of postwar Italy, he lamented, had confused historical investigation with political criticism, establishing a kind of antifascist dogma that framed and limited a deeper knowledge of twenty years of fascist rule. Rejecting this 'antifascist paradigm' meant to break out of the walls of a damaging historiographical insularism – the old Benedetto Croce's vision of fascism as an Italian 'moral illness' – and to re-inscribe the regime of Mussolini into the long duration of Italian history. Surely fascism was not to be condemned; it had to be historicised like every other age or political regime and there was no reason to make an exception and surround it with a protective barrier. De Felice left a considerable body of work – notably his monumental biography of Mussolini – and today some of his achievements are commonly accepted (notably his vision of fascism as a mass totalitarianism, deepened and extended by some of his disciples).[10] Of course, the problem does not lie in the fact that De Felice reinserted fascism into the continuity of Italian history, rather that he finished by expelling antifascism from it. Fascism had its legitimate place in Italy's history, but its enemies did not. Thus, antifascism became the movement of an isolated minority, responsible for the 'death of the fatherland' and ultimately for throwing the country into a civil war that broke its national unity.[11] This debate is not yet extinguished; it regularly returns in the form of best-sellers devoted to the blind violence of partisans, from the debate on the Italian victims of the Yugoslavian Communist Resistance, the Foibe, to the polemical uses of the excellent biographies of Primo Levi.[12]

In Germany, this 'anti-antifascist' campaign reached its climax during the decade that followed its national reunification. The annexation of the GDR was conceived as a political, economic and cultural process that inevitably implied the demolition of antifascism: the legacy of the German Resistance. Due to its symbiotic links with Stalinism, and because of its institutionalisation as a state ideology in the GDR, antifascism ceased to be a contradictory, conflicting, ambiguous tradition that required critical historicising; it became a 'myth' that was hiding a totalitarian ideology.[13] Unlike the attempts to 'relativise' the Holocaust during the *Historikerstreit*, this conservative crusade finally won. Its success was not only historiographical: in Berlin, the urban landscape was remodelled, erasing almost all the vestiges of forty years of real socialism.[14]

In France, the 'revisionist' campaign never took the form of a rehabilitation of Petain's Vichy, but was instead absorbed by the general attack against Communism. In *The Passing of an Illusion* (1995), François Furet presented antifascism as the humanistic and democratic mask with which, at the time of the Popular Fronts, the USSR had extended its pernicious, totalitarian influence on the European intelligentsia.[15] In the wake of Furet, Stéphane Courtois simply ascribed antifascism to the 'black book of Communism', as an ideological tool invented in order to justify the crimes of Communism.[16] The last (and most rabid) representative of the French Cold Warriors is probably Bernard Bruneteau, a political scientist who depicts antifascism as a form of 'intellectual terrorism fabricated by the strategists of the international communist apparatus'. The purpose of such a malignant invention was 'corrupting the judgment of authentic democrats and liberals'.[17]

In Spain, 'revisionist' scholars tried to disqualify antifascism as a 'red' narrative to which they pretended to oppose an objective, neutral, uncommitted and scientifically grounded recording of history. Curiously, such a 'non-partisan' scholarship resulted in an apologetic interpretation of the Spanish Civil War, in which Franco's violence and authoritarianism became marginal features with respect to his meritorious work of preserving his country from the tentacles of Bolshevik totalitarianism. According to Pío Moa, author of several best-sellers, Franco's putsch was a Republican 'myth', because its justified military *alzamiento* had been provoked by the attempt of the Popular Front to push the Republic into the hands of communism. Moa embodies a kind of Spanish 'Noltism': like his German equivalent, he believes that Franco's violence was collateral damage in a healthy, legitimate reaction against a Bolshevik threat.[18] Moa played the role of a post-fascist outsider, but his voice found the unexpected support of a recognised scholar like Stanley G. Payne who, along with De Felice in Italy, pleaded for reinterpreting the Spanish Civil War against the Republican 'vulgate'. Thus, the outsider became a pathbreaker.[19] Recently, a new generation of conservative historians has adopted a different strategy: they do not claim Franco's innocence, but simply stress the Republicans' guilt; they do not deny the authoritarian features of Franco's dictatorship, but simply pretend that during the Civil War, the Republic did not represent a democratic alternative to fascism; they do not deny the extreme violence of Francoism, but simply stress that Republican violence was not qualitatively different and was even anterior (like Nolte's Bolshevik *prius*). Unlike Moa, they do not try to rehabilitate Franco, but stress that violence started before 1936, carried out by the left. The Spanish tragedy, they conclude, lies in the fact that the defenders of the Republican cause were not democratic forces.[20]

Roughly speaking, we could summarise the arguments of these different, connected 'anti-antifascist' narratives in four shared points:

- Opposing a 'scientific', 'objective' and 'rigorous' record of history to a 'militant' and partisan one (based on an 'antifascist paradigm');
- Equating antifascism to a form of totalitarianism because of its proximity with the communist ideology and movement;
- Equalising fascist and antifascist violence;
- Enhancing the so-called 'grey zone' between the opposed camps, suggesting that the only valuable attitude consisted in rejecting both fascism and antifascism.

*

The first argument, 'scientific' versus 'combat' history, exhumes the old myth of a 'value-neutral' scholarship.[21] It supposes a scholar disconnected from the society in which he lives, deprived of any subjectivity, indifferent to collective memory, and able to find, via archives, the peace that is indispensable for escaping the tumults and quarrels of the surrounding world. Usually, the proponents of such an argument find a favourable echo in the media, especially conservative newspapers and magazines.

Of course, there has been an antifascist historiography in the past. Fascism, National Socialism and Francoism had their official historiographies; exiled historians could only be antifascist. Many of them participated in the Resistance movements of their own countries. Such experiences finished several decades ago but their legacies remained and shaped a new generation of scholars. Today, the time has come for 'critical' history writing. A critical historian is neither a defence counsel nor a public prosecutor. He certainly would not deny the existence of the Gulag – a recognition that implicitly deserves a moral and political condemnation of Stalinism – and he would try to elucidate its origins, its purposes and functioning. He would try to contextualise, compare, and put the Gulag into a diachronic perspective. He would investigate the roots of Stalinism in Russian absolutism, or the consequences of both the Great War and the Civil War on Soviet society in terms of brutalisation and adaptation to violence. An 'anti-antifascist' historian, for his part, does not need this thorough investigation. For him, history contains no mysteries and he already knows the answer: the Gulag existed because the USSR was totalitarian and the Russian Civil War took place because it corresponded to the dogmas of Bolshevik ideology. This is the core of the USSR histories written by a historian such as Martin Malia for whom, 'in the world created by October, we were never dealing with a *society in the first place*; rather, we were always dealing with an ideocratic *regime*'.[22]

A critical historian would not deny the murderous experience of the Foibe, the mountains of Trieste at the border between Italy and Yugoslavia, where Tito's partisans killed several thousand Italian collaborationists. He would try to contextualise such a tragic event, inscribing it into the history of conflictive relations and fluctuant frontiers between Italy and Yugoslavia, and would take into account the violence of the fascist occupation of the Balkans as well as the brutality of the anti-partisan warfare fought by the Axis forces. For an 'anti-antifascist' historian, on the contrary, the only possible explanation of this tragedy is Communist totalitarianism.[23] It is a universal hermeneutic key already tested in multiple realms: in the late 1970s, a champion of liberal historiography like François Furet wrote a pamphlet against the 'Jacobin–Leninist vulgate' of the French Revolution which came to the general conclusion that 'Today the Gulag is leading to a rethinking of the Terror precisely because the two undertakings are seen as identical'.[24] In other words, 'value-neutral' history means anti-Communist history.

*

There is a simple syllogism that inspires 'anti-antifascist' historiography. It could be formulated in the following way: antifascism=communism and communism=totalitarianism; consequently, antifascism=totalitarianism. It is obvious that such an interpretation completely delegitimises antifascism, compelling any decent person to distance himself from antifascists as well as from their accomplices and supporters (*'fiancheggiatori'*). According to Renzo De Felice, the Italian Partito d'Azione – representative of liberal socialism and inheritor of the Giustizia e Libertà movement – played a vicious role in the Resistance insofar as it allowed 'the communist wine to achieve a democratic designation of origin'.[25] François Furet defines antifascism as a trick with which Bolshevism acquired a 'democratic blazon'. During the Great Terror, he writes, 'Bolshevism reinvented itself as a freedom by default' (its purely negative connotation).[26] Going further, he suggests the idea of a Communist origin of antifascism: a tactic invented by the Communist International in 1935, a derived product.

Unfortunately, such 'value-neutral' interpretation does not pay close attention to some disturbing historical facts: in Italy, it was Benedetto Croce, a liberal philosopher, who launched the first 'antifascist Manifesto' in 1925; in 1930, it was a non-partisan left weekly, *Die Weltbühne*, directed by Karl von Ossietzky, that claimed the antifascist union of both the SPD and KPD against the rise of National Socialism (at that moment the German Communists considered social-democracy as their enemy, qualifying it as 'social-fascist'); in 1934, it was not the French Communist Party but a group of left intellectuals who inspired a powerful antifascist campaign after the fascist riots of 6 February, culminating two years later with the Popular Front. Both the Section française de l'Internationale ouvrière (SFIO) and the Communist Party were compelled to join a huge, spontaneous movement. Furet's interpretation also neglects the variety of antifascism, an intellectual and political movement that included different anti-Stalinist currents, from anarchism and Trotskyism to social democracy and liberalism. In general, these interpretations tend to avoid any commentaries on the fact that, in 1941, the Allied forces created a united front with the USSR against the Axis. This simple fact powerfully legitimised antifascism.

Historicising antifascism implies the exploration of its internal contradictions and ambiguities. In the 1930s, antifascism was one of the most important currents of European culture, and by the end of the Second World War it had become a shared *ethos* for the democratic regimes that were emerging from the defeat of the Third Reich. How can one explain why so many intellectuals for whom antifascism had been a moral and political commitment refused to criticise Stalinism, to denounce the farce of the Moscow trials, the forced collectivisation of agriculture, and the concentration camps? Why were the intellectuals who criticised Stalinism within the antifascist movement – from Arthur Koestler to Victor Serge, from André Gide to Manès Sperber, and from Willi Münzenberg to George Orwell and Gaetano Salvemini – not heard or quickly forgotten? The syndrome of the 'besieged city' suggested by Upton Sinclair – one cannot contest the government of a city under siege without becoming the fifth column of the besiegers[27] – certainly played a significant role, but it does not justify the blindness of so great a number of gifted and, in other circumstances, independent minds.

Similar considerations could be extended to the attitude of antifascism with respect to the Holocaust. With very rare exceptions, antifascism viewed Nazi anti-Semitism as radical, demagogical propaganda rather than politics of extermination. This revealed a global incomprehension of the ideological roots of National Socialism as well as a deleterious indifference to the language and practices of an old European culture of discrimination and stigmatisation of the Jews. Roughly speaking, antifascist intellectuals were unable to grasp the 'dialectics of Enlightenment' subjacent to fascism; they viewed fascism as a kind of collapse of civilisation, as a throwback of civilisation to barbarism rather than a genuine product of modernity itself.[28] For them, fascism meant a radical form of anti-Enlightenment, not a form of *reactionary modernism*: a singular symbiosis of conservatism and authoritarianism with the achievements of modern instrumental rationalism.[29] The mixture of mythology and technology at the core of National Socialism was difficult to see for a movement completely pervaded by the idea of progress.[30] Nevertheless, the limits and ambiguities of antifascism cannot be reduced to a form of totalitarianism, as a symmetric version of fascism.

*

A supposedly 'value-neutral' scholarship leads 'revisionist' historians to equalise fascist and antifascist violence. Both of them were totalitarian and we should reject them, avoiding immoral distinctions. This is the thesis of 'equalviolence' (*equivolencia*) according to the sarcastic definition forged by Spanish historian Ricardo Robledo.[31]

Such a statement is not new, even if 'revisionist' historians permanently reformulate it. Its origins go back to the end of the Second World War, when several victims of the anti-Nazi purges claimed such an argument as a defence strategy. In 1948, Martin Heidegger wrote two letters to his former disciple Herbert Marcuse, presently exiled in the United States, where he compared the expulsion of the Germans from Eastern Prussia carried out by the Allied forces to the Nazi extermination of the Jews. Marcuse decided to interrupt his correspondence, explaining that such a statement made any further dialogue impossible:

> You write that everything I say about the extermination of the Jews applies just as much to the Allies, if instead of 'Jews' one were to insert 'East Germans'. With this sentence, don't you stand outside of the dimension in which a conversation between men is even possible – outside of *Logos*? For only outside of the dimension of logic is it possible to explain, to relativise [*auszugleichen*], to 'comprehend' a crime by saying that others would have done the same thing. Even further: how is it possible to equate the torture, the maiming and the annihilation of millions of men with the forcible relocation of population groups who suffered none of these outrages (apart perhaps from several exceptional instances)?[32]

At the same moment, Carl Schmitt complained that the public debates on the crimes of the Third Reich completely overshadowed the 'genocide' of civil servants perpetrated by the Allied forces inside the administration of occupied Germany.[33]

The tune did not change when, four decades later, the *Historikerstreit* broke out in the Federal Republic of Germany. Nolte explained that the Bolshevik, 'Asiatic' deed preceded the Nazi 'racial murder' as its logic and factual *prius*. It was the 'class murder' of the Bolsheviks that caused the 'racial' ones of the Nazis.[34] Both were regrettable, but the first one was the original sin. According to the director of the *Frankfurter Allgemeine Zeitung*, the journalist and historian Joachim Fest, there was no difference between Nazi and Communist violence, with the exception of the technical procedure of gassing: on the one hand, a 'racial' extermination, and on the other, a 'class' extermination.[35]

In Italy, Renzo De Felice had cleared the field in 1987 by suggesting that Italian fascism 'had stood outside of the shadow of the Holocaust'.[36] In the following years, his disciples concluded that the Resistance had been as intolerant and violent as fascism. In Spain, highlighting the symmetry between Franco and Republican violence is commonplace of 'revisionist' historians. Their campaign contagiously affected eminent historians such as Santos Juliá, who ended up separating the Republican cause from its Communist, Socialist, anarchist and Trotskyist defenders.[37] Nevertheless, he did not explain who, in the Spain of 1936, could defend the Republic except Communist, Socialist, anarchist and Trotskyist forces: perhaps José Ortega y Gasset? The same question must be asked for Italy in 1943–45: was a Resistance movement possible without the Communist Party? Which forces could have built a democratic society: perhaps Count Sforza? The courage and heroism of Claus von Stauffenberg is unquestionable, but the democratic character of the opposition to Hitler of July 1944 remains highly dubious. The military elite reacted neither to the demolition of Weimar democracy in 1933 nor to the promulgation of the Nuremberg laws two years later; they had defended the idea of *Grossdeutschland* and supported Hitler's war until the defeat at Stalingrad. Many of its members dreamed of an authoritarian Germany without Hitler.[38] Were they representatives of a democratic Resistance against 'totalitarian' antifascism? A positive answer would be very hazardous: some of them probably were; the entire dissidence certainly not. If Communism played such an important role in the Resistance movements, including in Germany, it is precisely because liberalism and conservatism had been unable to stop the rise of fascism in the previous years and did not appear trustworthy. The experiences of Italy in 1922 and Germany in 1933, where liberal elites had favoured the seizure of power by Mussolini and Hitler, made them unreliable, and explained the strength of Communist resistance, reinforced by the aura of the Red Army victories. Critically historicised, liberalism does not appear innocent. Led to logical conclusions, the idea of 'equalviolence' should not exclude liberalism itself. The Allied forces carried out air warfare against the Third Reich as a planned destruction of German civil society, and their systematic bombings of German cities resulted in six hundred thousand dead and several million civilian refugees.[39] The horror of Hiroshima and Nagasaki was not the result of a totalitarian ideology; it was planned by Roosevelt and ordered by Truman, not Stalin.

But the thesis of 'equalviolence' broke a taboo: if antifascism – the political base of postwar democracies in continental Europe – is proved to be the equivalent of fascism, no one should be ashamed of having been a fascist. It is with virile pride that in 2000, Italian historian Roberto Vivarelli revealed his own fascist past: '[W]hen somebody asks me if I am "repentant" for having fought as a militiaman of the Salò Republic, I will answer that I am not; I am glad for it, even if today I recognise that its cause was morally and historically unjust; … I accomplished my duty and that is enough'.[40]

The politics of memory carried out in the last three decades in many European countries are a faithful mirror of this significant change: the common visit of Helmut Kohl and Ronald Reagan in 1985 to the military cemetery of Bitburg, where both American soldiers and some members of the SS are buried; the inauguration of the Neue Wache in Berlin in 1993, a memorial devoted to *all* the dead of the Second World War, without any distinction of their camp or commitment; the speeches of many Italian statesmen who, after remembering the Italian Jewish victims of the Holocaust, paid tribute to the 'Salò boys' (*ragazzi di Salò*) who fought with Mussolini; a demonstration in Madrid in 2000 in which old Republican combatants marched arm-in-arm with several members of División Azul, the troop of soldiers sent to Russia by Franco in order to fight with the German armies.[41]

*

In most cases, 'anti-antifascist' historiography adopts a supposedly neutral, moderate and irenic attitude that could be defined as an apology of the 'grey zone', borrowing the concept from Primo Levi's *The Drowned and the Saved*.[42] In Levi's essay, the 'grey zone' designated the ambiguous, undefined and floating area between the executors and their victims in the extermination camps. Extending, and thus changing, this concept would describe the bystanders as the indistinct mass of people who, in the middle of a civil war, did not choose their camp, and were swinging between two opposed poles. Some scholars suggested apprehending such a passive, hesitant, frightened, sometimes tormented and cowardly attitude with a metaphor borrowed from another Italian writer: the temptation of the 'house on the hill'.[43] In Spain, 'anti-antifascist' historians claim their will to preserve the 'spirit of the Transition', criticising all the attempts – first of all with the 'law of historical memory' (2007) – to call into question the benefits of an amnesic transition to democracy grounded on a double amnesty: the exiled Republicans on the one hand, and Francoist crimes on the other.

Behind such attitudes are not only apologetic tendencies but a supposedly post-totalitarian wisdom as well that transforms humanitarianism from a practice of rescuing victims into a prism for interpreting the past. In this way, democracy becomes an abstract, disincarnated, timeless value. This is the approach that a sharp, critical mind such as Tzvetan Todorov suggested some years ago in an essay on the French Resistance.[44] Stigmatising both the Vichy militiamen (fascists) and the fanatic partisans (antifascists), he highlighted the virtues of the civilians who, equidistant from both camps, tried to mediate between them in order to avoid massacres. This means that the only legitimate resistance was the civil one, the resistance of rescuers, not of combatants. Historically understood, nevertheless, the civilians' resistance was deeply connected with both the political and military Resistance. Their different practices and methods shared mostly the same values and pursued the same objectives. Claudio Pavone, a historian who carefully investigated the 'morality' of antifascism in a seminal book, distinguished three correlated dimensions of the Resistance: a national liberation movement against the Nazi occupation, a class struggle for social emancipation, and a civil war against collaborationism. These different dimensions coexisted, and it is precisely through their connection that the Resistance expressed its 'morality'.[45]

It is dubious that the only valuable actors of a century of violence, wars, totalitarianism and genocides were rescuers, doctors, nurses and stretcher-bearers. The twentieth century cannot be reduced to a gigantic humanitarian catastrophe; such a hermeneutic is extremely simplistic and limited. Sergio Luzzatto asks rhetorically, '[S]ince the civilian victim is recognised as the authentic hero of the twentieth century – a sacrificial lamb of opposed murderous ideologies – why should we distinguish between them?'[46] The past century was an age of conflicts in which millions of people fought for ideological and political causes. Antifascism was one of them. Once de-historicised, democracies themselves become amnesic and fragile. It is useful to be aware of their origins and history, to know how they came about and how they were built, in order to understand their ambiguities and their limits. It is dangerous to cut them from their roots and oppose them to the historical experiences through which they have been engendered. This is why, in the countries of continental Europe that experienced fascism, we do not need 'anti-antifascist' democracies.

Notes

1. The pieces of this controversy are gathered in H. Tudor and J.-M. Tudor (eds), *Marxism and Social Democracy: The Revisionist Debate 1896–1898*, New York, 1988.
2. S. Fitzpatrick, 'Revisionism in Retrospect: A Personal View', *Slavic Review* 67(3) (2008), 704.
3. Cf. M. Malia, *The Soviet Tragedy: The History of Socialism in Russia, 1917–1991*, New York, 1994; R. Pipes, *The Russian Revolution*, New York, 1990.
4. Cf. A. Applebaum, *Gulag: A History*, New York, 2003; R. Conquest, *The Great Terror: Stalin's Purge of the Thirties*, New York, 1968.
5. Cf. A. Greilsammer, *La nouvelle histoire d'Israël: essai sur une identité nationale*, Paris, 1998.

6. F. Furet and E. Nolte, *Fascism and Communism*, Lincoln, 2004, 51; R. De Felice, *Rosso e Nero*, Milan, 1995, 17.

7. J. Habermas, 'Ein Art Schadensabwicklung: Die apologetischen Tendenzen in der deutschen Zeitgeschichtsschreibung', *Historikerstreit: Die Dokumentation der Kontroverse um die Einzigartigkeit der nationalsozialistischen Judenvernichtung*, Munich, 1986, 62–75 [English translation in *Forever in the Shadow of Hitler: Original Documents of the Historikerstreit, the Controversy Concerning the Singularity of the Holocaust*, ed. J. Knowlton, Atlantic Highlands, NJ, 1993, 34–44].

8. J. Habermas, 'Vom öffentlichen Gebrauch der Geschichte', *Historikerstreit*, 243–55.

9. See the interviews with De Felice in J. Jacobelli (ed.), *Il fascismo e gli storici oggi*, Rome and Bari, 1988, 3–11.

10. Cf. E. Gentile, *Fascismo: storia e interpretazione*, Rome and Bari, 2002.

11. De Felice, *Rosso e Nero*, 55. On 8 September 1943 as 'the death of the fatherland', cf. E. Galli della Loggia, *La morte della patria: la crisi dell'idea di nazione tra Resistenza, antifascismo e Repubblica*, Rome and Bari, 1996.

12. Cf. S. Luzzatto, *Partigia: una storia della Resistenza*, Milan, 2013.

13. Cf. A. Grunenberg, *Antifaschismus: Ein deutscher Mythos*, Reinbek, 1993. For a historical assessment outside such propaganda approaches, cf. D. Diner, 'Antifascistische Weltanschauung: ein Nachruf', *Kreislaufe*, Berlin, 1996. On the shift of West German historiography from antifascism to the Holocaust, see N. Berg, *Der Holocaust und die westdeuschen Historiker: Erforschung und Erinnerung*, Göttingen, 2003, 379–83.

14. Cf. R. Robin, *Berlin chantiers: essai sur les passés fragiles*, Paris, 2001; S. Combe and R. Robin (eds), *Berlin: L'effacement des traces*, Paris, 2009.

15. F. Furet, *The Passing of an Illusion: The Idea of Communism in the Twentieth Century*, Chicago, 1999, chapter 8.

16. Cf. his introduction in S. Courtois (ed.), *The Black Book of Communism: Crimes, Terror, Repression*, Cambridge, MA, 1999.

17. B. Bruneteau, 'Interpréter le totalitarisme dans les années 1930', in Philippe de Lara (ed.), *Naissances du totalitarisme*, Paris, 2011, 244, 251.

18. P. Moa, *Los Mitos de la Guerra Civil*, Madrid, 2003.

19. S.G. Payne, *The Collapse of the Spanish Republic, 1933–1936: Origins of the Civil War*, New Haven, CT, 2006. See also his highly positive appreciation of Pío Moa's 'Mitos y tópicos de la Guerra Civil', *Revista de Libros* 79/80 (2003), 3–5. On the Moa debate, cf. A. Reig Tapia, *Anti Moa*, Madrid, 2006.

20. See F. del Rey (ed.), *Palabras como puños: La intransigencia política en la segunda República española*, Madrid, 2011; M. Alvarez Tardío and F. del Rey Reguillo (eds), *El Laberinto republicano: La democracia española y sus enemigos 1931–1936*, Barcelona, 2012 [English edition *The Spanish Second Republic Revisited: From Democratic Hopes to Civil War (1931–1936)*, Brighton, Sussex, 2012]; G. Ranzato, *La Grande paura del 1936: come la Spagna precipitò nella Guerra civile*, Rome and Bari, 2011. On this Spanish 'Noltism', see E. González Calleja, 'La historiografía sobre la violencia política en la Segunda República española: una reconsideración', *Hispania Nova: Revista*

de historia contemporánea 11 (2013) http://hispanianova.rediris.es; and I. Saz Campos, 'Va de Revisionismo', *Historia del Presente* 17 (2011), 161–64.

21. Cf. the criticism of 'combat history' (*historia de combate*) in F. del Rey, 'Revisionismos y anatemas: A vueltas con la II República', *Historia Social* 72 (2012), 155–72.

22. Malia, *The Soviet Tragedy*, 8 (emphasis in original).

23. For a historical reassessment of this event, cf. J. Pirievec and G. Bajc, *Foibe: una storia d'Italia*, Turin, 2009.

24. F. Furet, *Interpreting the French Revolution*, New York, 1981, 12.

25. De Felice, *Rosso e Nero*, 69.

26. Furet, *Passing of an Illusion*, 224.

27. Upton Sinclair, *Terror in Russia? Two Views*, New York, 1938, 57. Cf. M. Flores, *L'immagine dell'URSS: l'Occidente e la Russia di Stalin 1927–1956*, Milan, 1990, 279.

28. Cf. M. Horkheimer and T.W. Adorno, *Dialectic of Enlightenment*, Stanford, CA, 2007.

29. J. Herf, *Reactionary Modernism: Technology, Culture and Politics in Weimar and the Third Reich*, New York, 1986.

30. Cf. J.D. Wilkinson, *The Intellectual Resistance in Europe*, Cambridge, MA, 1981.

31. R. Robledo, 'Sobre la equiviolencia: puntualizaciones a una réplica', *Historia agraria* 54 (2011), 244–46.

32. See 'Heidegger and Marcuse: A Dialogue in Letters', in H. Marcuse, *Technology, War and Fascism*, London, 1998, 261–67, quotation p. 267.

33. C. Schmitt, *Glossarium: Aufzeichnungen der Jahre 1947–1951*, Berlin, 1991, 282.

34. E. Nolte, 'Vergangenheit, die nicht vergehen will', *Historikerstreit*, 45. On the *Historikerstreit*, cf. R. Evans, *In Hitler's Shadow: West German Historians and the Attempt to Escape from the Nazi Past*, New York, 1989.

35. J. Fest, 'Die geschuldete Erinnerung', *Historikerstreit*, 103.

36. Interview with R. De Felice, in Jacobelli, *Il fascismo e gli storici oggi*, 6. On De Felice, see G. Santomassimo, 'Il ruolo di Renzo De Felice', in E. Collotti (ed.), *Fascismo e antifascismo: Rimozioni, revisioni, negazioni*, Rome and Bari, 2000, 415–29.

37. See Santos Juliá, 'Duelo por la República española', *El País*, 25 June 2010, as well as the reply by J. Fontana, 'Julio de 1936', *Público*, 29 June 2010.

38. See I. Kershaw, *The Nazi Dictatorship: Problems and Perspectives of Interpretation*, New York, 2000, chapter 8 ('Resistance without the People?').

39. See J. Friedrich, *The Fire: The Bombing of Germany, 1940–1945*, New York, 2006.

40. R. Vivarelli, *La fine di una stagione: Memoria 1943–1945*, Bologna, 2000, 23.

41. On Bitburg, see G.H. Hartman, *Bitburg in Moral and Political Perspective*, Bloomington, IN, 1986; on the Neue Wache, see P. Reichel, *Politik mit Erinnerung: Gedächtnisorte im Streit um die Nationalsozialistische Vergangenheit*, Munich, 1995, 231–46; on the speeches of Italian statesmen, see F. Focardi, *La guerra della memoria: La Resistenza nel dibattito politico italiano dal 1945 ad oggi*, Rome and Bari, 2005.

42. Primo Levi, *The Drowned and the Saved*, New York, 1988. On the extension of the concept of 'grey zone' to the civil war, see De Felice, *Rosso e Nero*, 55–66.
43. Cf. R. Liucci, *La tentazione della Casa in collina: Il disimpegno degli intellettuali nella guerra civile italiana 1943–1945*, Milan, 1999, which refers to C. Pavese, *The House on the Hill*, New York, 1961.
44. T. Todorov, *A French Tragedy: Scenes of Civil War, Summer 1944*, Hanover, NJ, 1996.
45. C. Pavone, *A Civil War: A History of Italian Resistance*, London and New York, 2013.
46. S. Luzzatto, *La crisi dell'antifascismo*, Turin, 2004, 44.

References

Alvarez Tardío, M., and F. del Rey Reguillo (eds). *El Laberinto republicano: La democracia española y sus enemigos 1931–1936*. Barcelona, 2012 [English edition *The Spanish Second Republic Revisited: From Democratic Hopes to Civil War (1931–1936)*. Brighton, Sussex, 2012].

Applebaum, A. *Gulag: A History*. New York, 2003.

Berg, N. *Der Holocaust und die westdeuschen Historiker: Erforschung und Erinnerung*. Göttingen, 2003.

Bruneteau, B. 'Interpréter le totalitarisme dans les années 1930', in P. de Lara (ed.), *Naissances du totalitarisme*. Paris, 2011.

Combe, S., and R. Robin (eds). *Berlin: L'effacement des traces*. Paris, 2009.

Conquest, R. *The Great Terror: Stalin's Purge of the Thirties*. New York, 1968.

Courtois, S. (ed). *The Black Book of Communism: Crimes, Terror, Repression*. Cambridge, MA, 1999.

De Felice, R. *Rosso e Nero*. Milan, 1995.

Diner, D. 'Antifascistische Weltanschauung: ein Nachruf', *Kreislaufe*. Berlin, 1996.

Evans, R. *In Hitler's Shadow: West German Historians and the Attempt to Escape from the Nazi Past*. New York, 1989.

Fest, J. 'Die geschuldete Erinnerung', *Historikerstreit: Die Dokumentation der Kontroverse um die Einzigartigkeit der nationalsozialistischen Judenvernichtung*. Munich, 1986.

Fitzpatrick, S. 'Revisionism in Retrospect: A Personal View'. *Slavic Review* 67(3) (2008).

Flores, M. *L'immagine dell'URSS: l'Occidente e la Russia di Stalin 1927–1956*. Milan, 1990.

Focardi, F. *La guerra della memoria: La Resistenza nel dibattito politico italiano dal 1945 ad oggi*. Rome and Bari, 2005.

Friedrich, J. *The Fire: The Bombing of Germany, 1940–1945*. New York, 2006.

Furet, F. *Interpreting the French Revolution*. New York, 1981.

———. *The Passing of an Illusion: The Idea of Communism in the Twentieth Century*. Chicago, 1999.

Furet, F., and E. Nolte. *Fascism and Communism*. Lincoln, 2004.

Galli della Loggia, E. *La morte della patria: la crisi dell'idea di nazione tra Resistenza, antifascismo e Repubblica*. Rome and Bari, 1996.

Gentile, E. *Fascismo: storia e interpretazione*. Rome and Bari, 2002.

González Calleja, E. 'La historiografía sobre la violencia política en la Segunda República española: una reconsideración'. *Hispania Nova: Revista de historia contemporánea* 11 (2013), 404–36.

Greilsammer, A. *La nouvelle histoire d'Israël: essai sur une identité nationale*. Paris, 1998.

Grunenberg, A. *Antifaschismus: Ein deutscher Mythos*. Reinbek, 1993.

Habermas, J. 'Ein Art Schadensabwicklung: Die apologetischen Tendenzen in der deutschen Zeitgeschichtsschreibung'. *Historikerstreit: Die Dokumentation der Kontroverse um die Einzigartigkeit der nationalsozialistischen Judenvernichtung*. Munich, 1986. [English translation in *Forever in the Shadow of Hitler: Original Documents of the Historikerstreit, the Controversy Concerning the Singularity of the Holocaust*, ed. James Knowlton. Atlantic Highlands, NJ, 1993].

———. 'Vom öffentlichen Gebrauch der Geschichte'. *Historikerstreit, Die Dokumentation der Kontroverse um die Einzigartigkeit der nationalsozialistischen Judenvernichtung*. Munich, 1986.

Hartman, G.H. *Bitburg in Moral and Political Perspective*. Bloomington, IN, 1986.

Herf, J. *Reactionary Modernism: Technology, Culture and Politics in Weimar and the Third Reich*. New York, 1986.

Horkheimer, M., and T.W. Adorno. *Dialectic of Enlightenment*. Stanford, CA, 2007.

Jacobelli, J. (ed.). *Il fascismo e gli storici oggi*. Rome and Bari, 1988.

Kershaw, I. *The Nazi Dictatorship: Problems and Perspectives of Interpretation*. New York, 2000.

Levi, P. *The Drowned and the Saved*. New York, 1988.

Liucci, R. *La tentazione della Casa in collina: Il disimpegno degli intellettuali nella guerra civile italiana 1943–1945*. Milan, 1999.

Luzzatto, S. *La crisi dell'antifascismo*. Turin, 2004.

———. *Partigia: una storia della Resistenza*. Milan, 2013.

Malia, M. *The Soviet Tragedy: The History of Socialism in Russia, 1917–1991*. New York, 1994.

Marcuse, H. *Technology, War and Fascism*. London, 1998.

Moa, P. *Los Mitos de la Guerra Civil*. Madrid, 2003.

Nolte, E. 'Vergangenheit, die nicht vergehen will'. *Historikerstreit*, 45.

Pavese, C. *The House on the Hill*. New York, 1961.

Pavone, C. *A Civil War: A History of Italian Resistance*. London and New York, 2013.

Payne, S.G. *The Collapse of the Spanish Republic, 1933–1936: Origins of the Civil War*. New Haven, CT, 2006.

Pipes, R. *The Russian Revolution*. New York, 1990.

Pirievec, J., and G. Bajc. *Foibe: una storia d'Italia*. Turin, 2009.

Ranzato, G. *La Grande paura del 1936: come la Spagna precipitò nella Guerra civile*. Rome and Bari, 2011.

Reichel, P. *Politik mit Erinnerung: Gedächtnisorte im Streit um die Nationalsozialistische Vergangenheit*. Munich, 1995.

Reig Tapia, A. *Anti Moa*. Madrid, 2006.

Rey, F. del (ed.). *Palabras como puños: La intransigencia política en la segunda República española*. Madrid, 2011.

———. 'Revisionismos y anatemas: A vueltas con la II República'. *Historia Social* 72 (2012), 155–72.

Robin, R. *Berlin chantiers: essai sur les passés fragiles*. Paris, 2001.

Robledo, R. 'Sobre la equiviolencia: puntualizaciones a una réplica'. *Historia agraria* 54 (2011).

Santomassimo, G. 'Il ruolo di Renzo De Felice', in E. Collotti (ed.), *Fascismo e antifascismo: Rimozioni, revisioni, negazioni*. Rome and Bari, 2000.

Saz Campos, I. 'Va de Revisionismo'. *Historia del Presente* 17 (2011), 161–64.

Schmitt, C. *Glossarium: Aufzeichnungen der Jahre 1947–1951*. Berlin, 1991.

Sinclair, U. *Terror in Russia? Two Views*. New York, 1938.

Todorov, T. *A French Tragedy: Scenes of Civil War, Summer 1944*. Hanover, NJ, 1996.

Tudor, H., and J.-M. Tudor (eds). *Marxism and Social Democracy: The Revisionist Debate 1896–1898*. New York, 1988.

Vivarelli, R. *La fine di una stagione: Memoria 1943–1945*. Bologna, 2000.

Wilkinson, J.D. *The Intellectual Resistance in Europe*. Cambridge, MA, 1981.

Enzo Traverso was born in Italy, studied history at the University of Genoa and received his Ph.D. from the École des Hautes Etudes en Sciences Sociales (EHESS) of Paris in 1989. He taught political science in France for many years and was visiting professor in many European and Latin American countries. Since 2013, he is Susan and Barton Winokur professor in the Humanities at Cornell University. His publications, translated into different languages, include a dozen authored and other edited books, among which are *The Jews and Germany* (1995), *Understanding the Nazi Genocide* (1999), *The Origins of Nazi Violence* (2003), *The European Civil War 1914–1945* (2016), and *The End of Jewish Modernity* (forthcoming 2016), whose Italian edition won the Premio Pozzale in 2014.

Index